# America since World War II

## Warren F. Kimball, Editor

# Decade of Disillusionment

# Decade of Disillusionment

## THE KENNEDY-JOHNSON YEARS

## Jim F. Heath

INDIANA UNIVERSITY PRESS

Bloomington & London

FIRST MIDLAND BOOK EDITION 1976

Published in Canada by Fitzhenry & Whiteside Limited,
Don Mills, Ontario

Manufactured in the United States of America


Library of Congress Cataloging in Publication Data
Heath, Jim F
Decade of disillusionment.
(America since World War II)
Bibliography
Includes index.
1. United States—History—1961-1963.  2. United
States—History—1963-1969.  I. Title.
E839.H42    1975    973.922    74-18871
ISBN 0-253-31670-7 cl    ISBN 0-253-20201-9 pa
3  4  5  6  80  79  78  77

*For Nancy and Ann*

# Contents

# Foreword

"How come we never get past World War II?" Teachers of United States history must hear that refrain a hundred times a year, and in all too many cases the complaint is valid. Having lived through the 1950s and 60s, many of us find it hard to think of those years as textbook-type history, and we have often failed to take the time to sit back and make the historical judgments that must precede any attempt to teach about those years. An even greater problem is posed by the scarcity of solid, fully researched syntheses dealing with the more immediate past. That gap is precisely what the series America since World War II is designed to fill.

Some will quarrel with the decision to construct the series along the traditional lines of presidential administrations. Granted, such an organization does tend to disguise the broader social, political, and economic trends which developed and/or continued after 1945 without regard for what Winston Churchill called America's "quadrennial madness." Yet, in each volume, the authors have consciously examined such trends and, when read as a whole, the series provides an overview of the entire postwar period. Periodization is not only a useful teaching device, but has a validity all its own. As will quickly become clear to the reader, each of these administrations possessed a personality that, while reflecting the broader ideals and attitudes of the American nation, nonetheless remained unique and identifiable. Nor have the authors merely summarized the political history of the period. Rather, each has carefully examined the cultural, social, and economic history which make an era much more than just dates and names.

The series provides, in relatively brief and readable fashion, a synthesis for use by teachers and students studying American history since the Second World War. In keeping with that purpose, the decision was made to dispense with all but a few necessary informational footnotes. Much more than a mere survey, each volume is a scholarly interpretation based on extensive research and thought. The extensive bibliographical essays, which are useful contributions by themselves, give an indication of the authoritative scholarship that underpins each book.

o     o     o     o     o

The Kennedy-Johnson years initially appeared dominated by personalities rather than events. The word *charisma* seems to have been invented for John F. Kennedy, and *ebullient* is the only way to begin any list of adjectives describing Lyndon B. Johnson. News reporters were captivated by Kennedy and fascinated by Johnson, with vastly different results in each case. But the surface image of a Kennedy-Johnson era has steadily given way to a more event-oriented picture of American history in the 1960s.

Jim F. Heath's interpretative history of those years strikes a balance between person- and event-centered history. The decision to treat the Kennedy and Johnson administrations in a single, unified book stemmed from the belief that the years between 1960 and 1969 possess a significant degree of internal unity. The war in Vietnam permeated both foreign and domestic policy throughout the period, and related events such as the economic boom and bust as well as unrelated developments such as the civil rights program spanned both administrations. Some people brought to the seats of power during John Kennedy's Presidency—McGeorge Bundy, Walt W. Rostow, Robert Kennedy, and a host of senators and representatives—continued to wield great influence during Lyndon Johnson's years in office, although the Johnson administration had its own clearly identifiable style. It was a decade made remarkable by the precipitous rise and fall of an optimistic belief in the ability of the American government to solve our national problems; a rise and fall illustrated by the economy, by the attitude of young people, and by the Vietnam war. What began as a celebration of youth, life, and optimism with the New Frontier in 1960 steadily deteriorated into gloom, pessimism, and frustration. The nation not only killed its heroes—John F. Kennedy, Martin Luther King, Jr., Robert Kennedy, and unnamed thousands in Vietnam—but also destroyed in race riots large portions of major American cities. Even the good life brought to the majority by the unprecedented economic boom of the early sixties had become a casualty by 1969. The Decade of the New Frontier and the Great Society had become the Decade of Disillusionment—and Death.

Heath has gathered all these themes together in a lucid, thoughtful, and provocative study. He has struck a balance between an examination of decisions and of decision makers. The events and the leaders of the sixties affected each other, and this book demonstrates and explains that interaction. Although there are moments of excitement and success, an overarching sense of sadness—almost tragedy—dominates the period. It is those moments and that feeling that the author has recreated and brought together.

Warren F. Kimball

Rutgers University
Newark College

# *Preface*

In view of the immense quantity of records still closed to researchers and the limited perspective of time, it is perhaps presumptuous to attempt an historical evaluation of the Kennedy-Johnson years. Yet, it is a safe bet that a great many more people are interested now in the happenings of the 1960s and the presidential leadership of John F. Kennedy and Lyndon B. Johnson than will be interested in a hundred years. At any rate, all conclusions, no matter how well researched, are always tentative, for the very simple reason that—as the distinguished historian Frederick Jackson Turner once explained —"each age writes the history of the past anew with reference to the conditions uppermost in its own time." It is hoped that this study will help to meet the needs of readers in the seventies about their immediate past.

Many people helped to make this book possible. The searching criticisms offered by those who took time from their own busy schedules to read and comment on the manuscript contributed heavily to improving its quality. The faults that remain are mine alone. Professor Warren F. Kimball of Rutgers University–Newark, the general editor of the series in which this work appears, was a constant source of encouragement as well as penetrating and provocative criticism. Barton J. Bernstein of Stanford University has for many years been an indispensable aide in my efforts both to understand and to write history, and he again provided valuable assistance, as did John Gallman, editorial director of Indiana University Press. Two of my colleagues in the History Department at Portland State University, Jesse L. Gilmore and Michael Passi, contributed important substantive and stylistic suggestions. I benefited greatly from many extended conversations about the sixties with Marvin J. Price, a perceptive political scientist. Judith A. Letcher helped me to clarify many passages that obscured rather than illuminated. During recent years, I have periodically taught a seminar called "The U.S. in the 1960's" at Portland State, and I owe much to the keen observations of students too numerous to name individually.

Research at the Kennedy and Johnson presidential libraries gave me a chance to scratch at least the surface of the voluminous collections of papers at those institutions, and a generous grant from the American Council of Learned Societies made it possible for me to travel to the libraries. Once there, efficient and knowledgeable archivists facilitated my research. Sylvie Turner, Jo August, and William Moss at the Kennedy library and Claudia Anderson at the Johnson library were especially helpful. The onerous task of typing successive drafts of the manuscript was handled largely by my daughter Nancy, but my thanks also go to Barbara Madigan, Anita Swartout, and Barbara Rossman.

A final note of appreciation goes to my daughters, Nancy and Ann, to whom the book is dedicated. For me, they make everything worthwhile.

Jim F. Heath

Portland State University

# Decade of Disillusionment

# I

## *Introduction*

As THE nineteen fifties drew to a close, optimistic Americans found little to suggest that the approaching decade would evolve into such a disaster. According to the 1960 census, the United States contained almost 180 million people, and, thanks to the economic boom that began during World War II and continued after the end of the conflict, most of them were more affluent than ever before. During the fifties, the total population grew faster than during any decade in half a century. The great bulk of the increase resulted from a soaring birthrate, although it had begun to decline in 1958. Because of restrictive immigration laws, the percentage of foreign born dwindled to but 5 percent, the lowest in America's history. Over 11 percent, however, were nonwhite, a proportion that was steadily rising. There were both more young and more old people. Medical advances lengthened the life span enough to offset the baby boom and keep the median age at 29.5, a fraction higher than in 1940. The gap in life expectancy between females and males widened dramatically, so that by 1960 the ratio of men to women was 100:97.

Americans had been moving west for over three hundred years, and in the fifties the trend continued. The sun states of the Southwest—California, Nevada, and Arizona—along with equally sunny Florida were the big gainers. Equally significant was the massive exodus from the farm to the city. Total urban population spurted by almost 30 percent between 1950 and 1960. Yet 60 of the 212 cities of 50,000 or more actually lost population. Huge numbers of middle-class Americans fled to the burgeoning suburbs—planned communities of small single-family homes, garden-type apartments, and convenient shopping centers—which ringed the congested center cities. The urban fringe grew an amazing 85 percent. As a result, the center cities became largely the homes of the wealthy in their high-rise apartments and the poor, including increasing numbers of blacks, in their decaying ghettos. Suburbia, however, was no longer so exclusively the domain of white-collar Americans. Substantial gains in wages enabled skilled blue-collar workers to join both the middle class and the flight from the cities. Accountant and carpenter increasingly lived side by side.

Per capita personal income was the highest in history, and although inflation had reduced the real gain by almost half, the increase from $1,501 in 1950 to $2,219 in 1960 was still an impressive measure of American prosperity. The distribution of total income remained roughly the same. Even compared to what it had been in 1929, before the Great Depression, the change was far from revolutionary. The share of the very wealthiest had declined modestly, to the benefit of the middle-income groups. But the percentage received by the poorest citizens was not much different. Millions—the exact number was a subject of sharp dispute—still lived in poverty or deprivation. Largely out of sight, either in rural surroundings or in urban ghettos often separated from the more affluent areas by the steel and concrete freeways which dissected major cities, the impoverished were generally ignored by the comfortable majority.

For those with jobs and rising incomes, life, judged by material possessions, was better than ever. Sixty-two percent of all families owned their own homes. Over five times as much life insurance was in force as before World War II. Shorter work weeks and longer vacations provided more time for leisure and spawned a booming recreation industry. By the end of the fifties almost seven million motorboats competed for space on the nation's waterways. Mechanical and electrical implements cut the time and the energy required to open cans, brush teeth, or mow lawns. Prepared foods, more expensive but also more convenient, enabled people to prepare full meals in a matter of minutes.

The standard measurement of economic growth, the gross national product, climbed to another record high, $503 billion, in 1960, continuing the trend that had been under way since the late thirties. The federal budget followed a similar upward spiral. Cold war tension inspired defense expenditures, which consumed over half of the 1960 budget, an amount equal to almost 10 percent of the gross national product. Interest costs on the $286 billion national debt and expenses for veterans services took additional sizable chunks of federal spending. The balance went for a wide variety of items, including subsidies for farmers and salaries for the record 2.4 million civilian federal employees.

Major corporations dominated American business, and self-employed individuals, long rhetorically celebrated as the "backbone" of America, continued to dwindle in number. A relative handful of large companies generated the bulk of activity in key industries. Although perhaps five times as many people owned stocks as in 1940, very few stockholders had much knowledge of or control over the operations of the huge organizations. Few people tried to argue that the American economy was a "pure free enterprise" system (if, indeed, it ever was). A "mixed" economy existed, in which business shared power and control with government and labor, and, to a much lesser extent, consumers.

Organized labor remained reasonably healthy, despite unfavorable legislation passed since the end of World War II. Serious worry persisted, however, because union membership, as a percentage of all nonagricultural workers, had slowly declined during the second half of the fifties. Perceptive labor leaders knew that to grow the unions had no choice but to change their tactics and aggressively recruit white-collar employees, such as teachers and clerks, who had previously been ignored, but many unions seemed to lack the drive and the spirit needed to make such a push. Automation still troubled some workers, but it was less feared than a decade before. For the most part, labor union members were quiet and contented because they, like most businessmen, had prospered handsomely during the past two decades.

Americans were better educated and better informed, albeit often superficially, than at any time in their history. The average adult was a high school graduate. Two of every five persons in the 18-to-21 age group attended college, but television had become an educational vehicle for an infinitely larger number. Although frequently castigated for its mundane and unimaginative programming, the visual medium's impact on America was, nevertheless, immense.

By filtering down ideas and attitudes previously confined to a small, educated segment of the population, it had increased political awareness and helped to produce a cultural revolution.

The "cultural explosion" quadrupled the number of local art museums, compared to the thirties, and virtually no city of 50,000 or more lacked a symphony orchestra. The paperback era in books, which had begun in 1939, enabled publishers to flood the market with almost 300 million copies per year by 1960. Despite these and other impressive indications of a cultural renaissance, young composers still found it extremely difficult to get their works performed, and many good-sized towns remained without a single legitimate bookstore. Skeptics warned that culture was becoming corrupted and commercialized and ridiculed the culture seekers as actually more interested in status.

Most Americans still professed a desire for personal achievement, but their actions often suggested that they were satisfied with mediocrity. The impulse to conform was unquestionably strong and pervasive. Being "well rounded" earned high marks of social approval even though it connoted a quality of noncontroversial blandness and a lack of special distinction in any facet of one's life. Since religious affiliation has traditionally been an important help in "getting ahead" in the United States, church membership, not surprisingly, increased sharply during the fifties. Many religious leaders, however, suspected that the surge was more quantitative than qualitative and frankly declared that although America was physically richer, it was spiritually poorer. Certainly, hypocrisy abounded. Americans talked about honesty, but many cheated on taxes and engaged in shady business practices while preaching ethical behavior. Even more incongruously, most lauded egalitarianism but passively accepted racism.

The relatively tranquil pace of the fifties and the good life enjoyed by the majority of Americans only partly concealed the anxieties that throbbed under the surface. Man's ability to expand the frontiers of knowledge to previously unfathomable limits had accentuated both his hopes and his frustrations. Science and technology had improved the prospects for a longer and richer personal existence. But they had also provided the means to end all human life in a matter of seconds or hours. A belief that traditional values should be preserved and that an individual could still determine his destiny clashed with the disturbing reality that change was occurring at an accelerating rate and that all aspects of life were increasingly dangerous, complex, and difficult to control.

Yet, on balance, Americans in 1960 remained basically optimistic. Writing in 1906, H. G. Wells had characterized the national temper as a "sort of optimistic fatalism." Despite anxieties, a similar mood persisted over a half century later. What worried many observers at the time, however, was the fear that Americans had become so comfortable and complacent that they had lost any real sense of national purpose. Describing the climate of the late fifties, historian Eric Goldman called the years probably "the dullest and dreariest in all our history" and declared that "we've grown unbelievably prosperous and we maunder along in a stupor of fat . . . ." A New York newspaper editorialist savagely characterized the decade as the "age of the slob."

Critics blamed Dwight Eisenhower for what they considered a loss of political idealism. Completing his second term in the White House, the President basked in seemingly unshakable popularity. Elected to lead a Republican crusade to purge Washington of corruption and disloyalty and to halt the progress of creeping socialism, Eisenhower had instead opted for a safe position in the middle of the political mainstream. He declined to launch any major campaign to reverse the social welfare programs begun during Franklin D. Roosevelt's New Deal and expanded by Harry S. Truman's Fair Deal. The federal government continued to function as a "broker," distributing money and privileges unequally among different interest groups according to their political and economic power. Unions and big business, because they had the means to exert pressure, obtained favorable legislation and executive decisions much more frequently and with considerably larger benefits than did unorganized workers, small business, minority groups, and consumers.

Despite the inequities, so many Americans supported the efficacy of New Deal–Fair Deal liberalism by the 1950s that alternatives attracted little serious attention. Although hard-core right-wingers thundered righteously against socialist trends, the mainstream of conservatism accepted substantially, if grudgingly, the likes of Social Security, federal guarantees of home loans, and agricultural subsidies. Spokesmen for the left side of the political spectrum were even more apathetic. Sociologist Daniel Bell struck a popular note when he declared that ideology—of the radical variety—was dead in America. Two reasons, he explained, accounted for its demise: the general disillusionment over the excesses of Stalinism in the Soviet Union, a country once envisioned as the model for collectivist Utopias, and the transformation of nineteenth-century predatory capitalism in the United States into the limited welfare state of the twentieth century. Although continued improvement and expansion of New Deal–type measures would be required, the pressure for a radical alternative no longer existed.

A similar consensus existed about foreign affairs. Since the end of World War II, the United States, commanding overwhelming military and economic strength, had exploited opportunities to expand its influence abroad much as other dominant world powers had done in the past. To rally public support for an activist foreign policy, leaders in both political parties had repeatedly pointed to the danger of monolithic world Communism, a fear that the great bulk of Americans accepted as valid. Under Truman the United States followed a strategy of containing the spread of Communism by using the least amount of force necessary. Some Republican spokesmen argued vehemently for a more aggressive policy. But despite much bellicose rhetoric early in the Eisenhower administration about rolling back the Iron Curtain and freeing people held captive by the Communist powers, the President, in effect—and with the strong support of the American people—substantially endorsed the containment policy, while carefully avoiding involving the United States in any new foreign wars.

His politics of moderation and continuation were explicitly designed not to rock the boat. Although Eisenhower delighted in delivering little moral lectures filled with dynamic platitudes about America's "nobler purposes," he refused to issue a plea for broad new social programs. Frankly, the average citizen evidenced little interest in receiving such a summons. The previous two decades had been frenetic. The thesis of Arthur M. Schlesinger, Sr. that in the United States reform and conservative reaction occur in an alternating pattern roughly every twenty years seemed to be borne out by the public's apathy during the late fifties. Indeed, the only crusade that attracted wide support was one against crusades. Professor Karl Shapiro bitterly wrote that "the vague but comforting symbol of Eisenhower has seeped into the vacuum of this generation's mind." James Reston of the *New York Times* lamented that "in a time when brain power is more important than fire power," Eisenhower had drifted apart from intellectual opinion, "filled up his social hours with bantering locker-room cronies, and denied himself the mental stimulus that is always available to any President."

Alienated by the President's failure to mobilize public sentiment and by his indifference to their talents, liberal intellectuals in particular looked with anticipation to the prospects of electing a chief executive who would put the country's vast intellectual, technological, moral, and physical resources to full and energetic use. Confident of their abilities almost to a point of arrogance, they hoped to play a major role in shaping America's destiny in the sixties.

Eisenhower's passive leadership contrasted sharply with the conception of the Presidency shared by John F. Kennedy and Lyndon B. Johnson, who believed that most of the progress in American history, in both foreign and domestic affairs, had been initiated by Presidents. During the previous thirty years especially, Congress had steadily relaxed its grip on national policy, sometimes to the point of irresponsibility. Modest efforts to reform the creaky machinery of both houses had failed to revitalize congressional leadership. State and local governments had similarly diminished in importance. Americans looked primarily to the White House for direction. As a result, something approaching an imperial Presidency had developed, a fact Kennedy and Johnson sensed quite clearly.

Although each man relished the opportunity to exercise the power at the chief executive's disposal, neither wanted to change drastically either the American social-economic system or the basic pattern of the country's foreign policy. They fully understood and respected the strong degree of agreement that existed among the great majority of the population that the American way, though not perfect, was the best way.

The absence of violent revolutions in America since its independence from Great Britain tends to obscure the wide variety of bitter conflicts that have punctuated the nation's history. Yet, although frequently prodded and accelerated by dissent, except for the Civil War, change has been essentially evolutionary. Effective political leaders have functioned within a shifting but viable mainstream of public mood and thought, accepting the principle that to be successful, democratic government in a two-party system requires a good deal of compromise. Compromise demands a considerable degree of consensus, and consensus works against wrenching change. Third-party candidates or nominees of the two major parties who have wandered outside the admittedly hazy limits of broad agreement have not won elections. The crucial fact has been that although not all Americans are middle class, both the Democrats and the Republicans reflect a basic middle-class consensus. Consequently, their policies and those of their nominees have consistently been quite similar. The transition from one presidential administration to another, even when the incoming chief executive is from the opposing party, has never produced a radical shift in national policy.

Nevertheless, different Presidents, even while operating within the boundaries of the general consensus, do differ, often dramatically, in such critical matters as instinct and style. Instinct implies ideological inclination, the direction a person tends to lean when confronted with a sensitive decision. Kennedy and Johnson, for example, favored a more aggressive federal role in racial integration and eradication of poverty than did Eisenhower. Instinct also guides a chief executive's selection of personal advisers and administration officials, those who have the greatest opportunity to influence his thinking and actions. Although it is also often necessary for a President to attempt to balance the interests of conflicting factions within his party when making appointments, his natural tendency is to choose individuals, whenever possible, with viewpoints and styles congenial to his own.

Style involves looks, charm, mannerisms, rhetorical eloquence, personality, and countless other intangibles relating to the impression that one person makes on others. It is about as easy to define as sex appeal. During the sixties, political campaigns were more than ever before influenced by the Madison Avenue mentality of trying to "merchandise" candidates in a way calculated to draw an irrational response from voters, but style has long been recognized as an important factor in winning elections. Critics accused Franklin Roosevelt of presenting a program with little substance in 1932. But by projecting an air of confidence and optimism to a public sadly in need of such qualities, Roosevelt not only contributed heavily to his solid margin of victory over the gloomy and pessimistic Herbert Hoover but also helped to set a new mood for politics in the thirties.

Although voters may indeed be influenced by irrational considerations, they nevertheless choose the candidate who they believe best suits their mood at the moment. The winner both reflects and is in a position to influence national attitudes. If he uses his office skillfully, he may convince his fellow citizens to follow him in mildly new directions. His style is critical to his success in doing so, for despite the great authority and prestige that a President enjoys, he is rarely free to act completely as he pleases. He must contend with strong and shifting public moods, compelling traditions that stifle swift and sharp change, powerful interest groups seeking advantages, federal legislators elected from their own constituencies, state governments that jealously guard against federal encroachment of their authority, previously appointed officials in critical judiciary and regulatory positions, and a massive bureaucracy of career civil servants capable of obstructing policies with which they disagree. A chief executive's success and his ultimate power thus depend heavily on his ability to persuade and to educate. "Where he leads," Theodore White accurately observed, "his party, his instruments, above all his reluctant people must be persuaded to follow. . . . This art of persuasion is politics—yet entirely different from the kind of politics that brings a man to the White House."

Presidents leave an indelible personal stamp on the years in which they occupy the White House. That is especially true of very strong chief executives and those whose tenure is marked by major disasters or scandals. Administrations, like other organizations, reflect the imprint of the top man. Whether an administration is witty or sober, socially chic or bland, open or relatively closed, depends largely on the chief executive. With few exceptions, the President, not Congress, receives the most credit for legislation passed, just as he is either praised or damned for accomplishments or failures in foreign policy. Perhaps unwisely, American history is subdivided and identified primarily according to presidential administrations. Periods are referred to as the Jackson years, the Harding era, or the age of Roosevelt. Thus, one of the most important, though unwritten, powers of the President is his ability to give definition to a period of history.

In Eisenhower's case, his approach to the Presidency had been to preserve the status quo. Kennedy and Johnson, however, sought to prod the United States into action to complete the unfinished social challenges at home and to reassert the nation's leadership as the moral champion of the free world. Binding them together was their firm conviction that New Deal–style liberalism and cold war containment were the correct policies for the United States in the sixties—if they were but energetically and intelligently applied. Despite vast differences in their backgrounds and personal styles, their views of the Presidency and their basic objectives were remarkably similar.

By nature, both were activists. Neither desired merely to reign; rather they intended to rule energetically. Simply to hold the line, as Eisenhower had done, or to be a caretaker of government, appealed not at all. Each had ambitious goals. Kennedy promised a New Frontier—new challenges and opportunities to revitalize the nation's sense of destiny. Johnson envisioned a Great Society, the fulfillment of the American dream of prosperity and equality for all. Their slogans and much of their thinking reflected how heavily they had been influenced by Roosevelt's New Deal and Truman's Fair Deal.

Similarly, their views on foreign policy placed them squarely in the camp of the cold warriors. As legislators during the forties and fifties, Kennedy and Johnson had generally supported and sometimes helped to formulate the specific strategies that shaped containment. Significantly, the great bulk of the American public so overwhelmingly accepted the containment of Communism that in 1960 no presidential candidate openly critical of the policy could have been elected. But it is probably also true that neither Kennedy nor Johnson realized the extent to which their own experiences and the anti-Communist mood in postwar America had straitjacketed their thinking about foreign affairs.

It was precisely the blandness of Eisenhower and his seeming lack of leadership that made it possible for Kennedy to run and win in 1960 as a bold and charismatic leader who would "move America forward." Impressed by his personal charm and his undeniable intelligence, Americans responded warmly to the youthful Kennedy's clarion call to action. He stimulated an aura of excitement and enthusiasm and helped to restore a sense of national purpose. A patrician himself, trained in the tradition of noblesse oblige, he inspired others to commit themselves to helping the less fortunate. But judged by his tangible accomplishments, though his promise seemed great, he actually achieved relatively little at home, and in some cases his foreign policy decisions pushed the world to the brink of nuclear conflict. John Foster Dulles, Eisenhower's strong-willed Secretary of State, had proudly boasted of engaging in "brinkmanship." Kennedy was too shrewd to advertise his actions by such a provocative term, but preoccupied with appearances and determined not to seem reluctant to stand firm against the Communist powers, he willingly risked global war.

Kennedy's assassination made him, at least for a time, a martyr-hero and enlarged his meager accomplishments well beyond reality. More important, the tragedy of his death made it possible for Johnson, who was even more of an activist by nature than Kennedy, to enlist a shocked Congress and public in a crusade to pass legislation that Kennedy had proposed but had been unable to deliver. When the Republican party succumbed to the efforts of conservatives to nominate someone for President in 1964 who would provide "a choice not an echo," Johnson gained an even greater opportunity to enlarge his presidential power. Casting himself as a candidate pursuing progressive goals at home and peace with honor abroad, Johnson easily preempted the political mainstream and won a landslide victory that also swept large numbers of friendly Democrats into Congress. The torrent of legislation that followed was awesome. A master of domestic politics with a deserved reputation as a wheeler-dealer, LBJ skillfully blended pressure with rewards to obtain his goals. Unfortunately, he seemed to think that world politics could be managed in much the same way. As he was to learn, especially in Vietnam, they could not.

Faced with a Communist-backed revolution in Vietnam, Johnson, like Kennedy, followed the same limited-war strategy that had been used a decade earlier in Korea—providing enough American manpower and materials to keep the Communist forces from winning but stopping well short of giving the American military a free hand to win the conflict. But there was a crucial difference in the two wars. The Korean engagement lasted only three years. As the struggle in Vietnam dragged on year after year and the United States' involvement increased, the patience of the American people began to wear thin. Kennedy, and especially Johnson, badly overestimated the willingness of the public to sustain a containment action that cost heavily in lives and resources but showed no sign of ending. Although during the Kennedy administration criticism of the war was limited almost exclusively to the methods being used, not to the American effort to stop the Communists from taking over South Vietnam, serious domestic opposition to American participation increased rapidly when Johnson began a massive buildup of American ground troops in 1965. Significantly, the size and intensity of the war protests paralleled almost exactly rising draft calls.

Huge numbers of Americans—especially among the young who had to fight the war—rebelled not only against American policy in Vietnam but against existing cultural patterns and the nation's social and economic system as well. At the same time, black citizens, frustrated by over a century of unfulfilled promises of equality, drastically intensified their own revolution. Ironically, Kennedy and Johnson did more to end racial injustice than did any previous President, but their efforts were too little and too late to calm black anger, and the escalation of the American participation in Vietnam— as it did in so many areas during the sixties—drained resources and energy away from programs to aid blacks. By rioting and burning cities they made violence as much a characteristic of the decade at home as it was in Vietnam.

As a result, after eight years of Democratic leadership under Kennedy and Johnson, the United States was being rocked by more dissension, tumult, and violence than at any time since the Civil War. Many of the accepted dogmas of American life were seriously questioned: the social and economic system, cultural values, the merit of technological expertise, New Deal–style liberalism, big government, and the whole concept of presidential power.

The sixties had begun optimistically, with Americans full of hope and expectation. New leaders confidently stood ready in 1960 to lead the nation, and indeed the world, to new plateaus of achievement. Tragically, something went wrong. Instead of finding its Utopia, America became a country struggling desperately to escape its Armageddon.

# II

## *The Torch Is Passed*

AS THE Eisenhower administration drew to a close, the torch of leadership, as John F. Kennedy later observed, passed to a new generation of Americans. The key figures guiding the United States during the sixties would be primarily younger men, born in the twentieth century and conditioned by their experiences during the depression of the 1930s, the Second World War, and the cold war. Three of those who actively sought to succeed Eisenhower in 1960—Kennedy, Johnson, and Richard M. Nixon—would serve as President during the chaotic decade. Each would be both a major contributor to and a principal victim of the centrifugal forces at work in the country.

Historically, the incumbent party has usually retained power when the nation was prosperous and at peace, as the United States was in 1960. But Eisenhower's success at the polls had largely been a personal, not a Republican party, triumph. Even with Ike, the GOP had controlled Congress for only his first two years in office. Voters tended to regard Eisenhower as above partisan politics. Although immensely popular himself, he was never able to transfer his appeal to his party or to Republican candidates generally. Nor was he able to heal the bitter split between GOP liberals and moderates on the one hand and dyed-in-the-wool conservatives on the other. As a result, the Republicans lost seats in 1954, 1956, and 1958, a demise of strength that was paralleled on the state level. After the 1958 elections the party held only fourteen governorships and the majority in but seven state legislatures. Almost certainly Eisenhower could have been reelected with ease had he wished to run and been eligible to do so in 1960. But the Twenty-second Amendment, ratified in 1951, blocked any possibility for a third term, making the Republicans' prospects for victory far from sanguine.

There was little mystery about who their standard bearer would be. Vice President Nixon had used his position under Ike to build a solid base of political support and clearly held the inside track for the nomination. As a former representative and senator from California, Nixon had established an early reputation as an anti-Communist crusader, particularly for his activities on the House Un-American Activities Committee. His selection as Eisenhower's running mate had balanced the ticket in a number of useful ways. Nixon's youth, West Coast base, solid party credentials, and acceptability with the conservative factions of the GOP contrasted nicely with Ike's advanced age, his ties with the eastern Establishment, his belated Republican affiliation, and his vigorous internationalism.

As Vice President, Nixon served loyally as his chief's principal liaison with party conservatives. He also campaigned tirelessly for Republican candidates in local, state, and national races. Although critics tabbed him the administration's hatchet man, he earned the gratitude of countless party members. Nixon collected numerous political "IOUs" that he could call in as the situation demanded, both in 1960 and later.

In 1960, although Nixon had been in public office for more than a dozen years, to all but family and a handful of intimate friends, he was something of an enigma. By nature he was not an expansive individual, neither gregarious or garrulous in the Hubert Humphrey–Lyndon Johnson mold nor a man of blunt-spoken charm like Barry Goldwater. An intensely private person, his style was sober, not flashy. Enemies noted his lack of charisma and characterized him as "graceless."

His parents had struggled to make a living. If not actually in poverty, they were, nevertheless, impoverished. Nixon attended public schools and a good but not distinguished small private college—Whittier—in his hometown before matriculating at Duke University to take a law degree. After graduation, he worked briefly for the new Office of Price Administration, then served as a naval officer during World War II. When the conflict ended, he practiced law for a brief time in his native southern California before answering an appeal for Republican candidates to run for Congress in his district. Elected in 1946 and reelected two years later, he moved up to the Senate in 1950 after a bitter campaign in which he painted his opponent, Helen Gahagan Douglas, as a Communist sympathizer. In 1952, still only 39, he became Vice President. His political rise was meteoric, a Horatio Alger success story in the hallowed American tradition.

He should have been a hero to those Americans who value self-made men who with self-help pull themselves from obscurity to fame. To a degree he did appeal to the so-called common man. But just as Nixon lacked those qualities that marked persons born into the elite class, so he revealed publicly little of the warm personality, the homespun philosophizing, or the folksy common sense that characterized Eisenhower, Lincoln, and Truman, other men from humble backgrounds who captured the nation's biggest political prize.

Although Nixon could and did attempt to practice all these traits at times and although he demagogued on occasion, his style was his own, and it did not fit the textbook model for successful politicians. He may well have liked people, but he preferred to like them at a distance. He was quite clearly a shrewd man, but he did not mix well with or appeal to most intellectuals. Among close friends he could be affable, but in large groups his attempts at warmth seemed forced, and he seldom kindled the sparks of enthusiasm that some public figures do easily and naturally. His looks were no asset. If he was not an ugly man, neither was he handsome, and he did not have the type of face that can be called "interesting." He was, in a word, an unexciting individual, capable, but not likely to win love from the masses and forced to struggle unceasingly even to win respect.

Nixon's public image and his personal traits paralleled in many respects those of Senator Robert A. Taft, the conservative Republican stalwart of the forties and early fifties. Although there were sharp differences between the two men—Nixon was more flexible in his political views than Taft, was emphatically more of an internationalist, and lacked the Ohioan's ease with himself—the similarities were striking. Like Taft, Nixon was—to use the words of Taft's perceptive biographer, James T. Patterson—"often impatient, testy, coldly partisan, hyperbolic." Both men prided themselves on being well prepared, laboring for hours, usually in private, to master a difficult subject. Driven by a sense of duty and ambition that gave little rest, each man demanded excellence of himself.

Taft and Nixon attracted strong support from many of the same people. Republicans who liked Taft's cool, sometimes cold, rational approach could appreciate Nixon. Admittedly, it is difficult to imagine Taft acting as Nixon did in his 1952 "Checkers" television speech, when he emotionally, at times tearfully, defended himself against charges of unethically using funds collected by friends to defray his expenses as a senator. But this incident was equally out of character for Mr. Nixon. He was forced to reveal his emotions far more than he preferred. Even if the performance was, as critics accused, simply a clever public relations gimmick, it could not have been easy for so private a person.

In other public appearances Nixon's style was distinctly different. His statements were carefully worded to show his grasp of a given situation, especially his tough-minded understanding of national and world problems. They stressed his experience and know-how and were often stridently partisan. Nixon was more a debater than an orator, and his speeches lacked both wit and eloquence. They were, as he seemed to be, sober and severe, and they appealed to listeners who were themselves stolid and serious, who shunned the demagogue, and who felt uncomfortable with the intellectual and jet-set elites.

Unlike Taft, Nixon had never been identified as an isolationist. As a legislator, and particularly as Vice President, Nixon had advocated the United States' vigorously exercising its responsibilities as a world leader. His record against Communism, of both the domestic and the foreign variety, was unimpeachable. His cool reaction when spat upon and stoned while on a 1958 goodwill tour of South America earned the public's admiration, and his widely publicized kitchen debate with Premier Nikita Khrushchev in the American model home on display at the Moscow trade fair in 1959 raised the level of respect for him enormously.

By 1960 Nixon was so popular with party regulars that no serious contender dared challenge him in the primaries. Governor Nelson Rockefeller of New York badly wanted to run, but as he would also do in 1964 and 1968, he hesitated to commit himself to an all-out fight for the nomination. A frequent critic of Eisenhower's policies, which he regarded as characterized by too much drift and indecision, Rockefeller appealed to the more liberal elements within his own party and to independent voters. He was a marvelous campaigner, who obviously enjoyed baby-kissing, blintz-eating, and modeling Indian headdresses. Using his enormous wealth to assemble a talented advisory staff, the governor in late 1959 attempted to determine whether he should make a formal bid for the party's top prize. Rockefeller and his representatives were received cordially by Republican leaders and enthusiastically by many of the party's rank and file. But by the end of the year, it was clear that the GOP regulars—the state officials, fund donors, and probable convention delegates—were committed overwhelmingly to Nixon. As a result, the handsome New Yorker cancelled plans for entering any state primaries. Technically he was not a candidate, though the Nixon organization correctly recognized that Rockefeller remained distinctly available in case the front runner should stumble.

For Nixon, Rockefeller's withdrawal was a mixed blessing. It meant that the Vice President could avoid the party-splitting dangers inherent in hard-fought primary contests. He could also play the statesman role for several more months before engaging in bald partisan politics. But he lost the valuable opportunities provided by primary battles for wide exposure through the national media, for testing and tuning his campaign organization, and for reinforcing his image as a winner.

For Nixon's opponent, John F. Kennedy, the road to the Democratic nomination was enormously more difficult. He had come within an eyelash of being his party's vice-presidential nominee in 1956, and in the years that followed he had clearly established himself as a party celebrity. But he was young—forty-three—and he was Catholic. If these factors were not enough, he also suffered the disadvantage of being a senator. And the last time that the Democrats had nominated a member of the upper house was in 1860, exactly a century before. It is not surprising that many professional politicians discounted his chances of obtaining the party's top position until his selection had become virtually a reality.

Despite his handicaps, Kennedy possessed certain advantages that would make him a winner. For one thing he was undeniably handsome, and he had a distinctive knack for communicating with the public. His intelligence was obvious, and just as he attracted women supporters without alienating male voters, so his mental abilities aroused the enthusiasm of intellectuals without driving away persons with average or less intelligence. Kennedy and his kin were also rich, no small factor considering the high costs of campaigning. His glamorous family added an additional dimension to his appeal.

His parents, Joseph P. and Rose Fitzgerald Kennedy, were the children of colorful Boston politicians. John and his brothers and sisters enjoyed the advantages of wealth, for Joseph Kennedy had done exceedingly well in his business investments. They also suffered the twin disadvantages of being Irish and Catholic in a high society still dominated by old, established, Protestant, Anglo-Saxon families. As Kennedy grew richer, his frustration at failing to be accepted as a social equal by the Boston Brahmins prompted him to live elsewhere. The family divided its time between homes in New York, Florida, and Hyannis Port, Massachusetts. Even after he attained a measure of fame as a shrewd businessman and as chairman of the Securities Exchange Commission and later ambassador to England under Franklin Roosevelt, the stigma of being Irish continued to plague him. "I was born here," he complained. "My children were born here. What the hell do I have to do to be an American?" His desire to be recognized as a success for the sake of identification drove him throughout his life. So did his desire to provide some functional service to America as a means of establishing his right to "belong." He drilled the qualities of striving to excel and of service into his children with compelling intensity.

The spectacular rise to political prominence by John, Robert, and Edward Kennedy in the 1960s made the family a source of national fascination. Hostile critics savagely attacked the Kennedys for, among other things, fostering aggressive competitiveness, personal omnipotence, and a drive for dominance and power. In many cases, however, the criticism reflected a frustration with America generally and an attempt to find scapegoats for the traumas of the decade. Even admirers of the family conceded that Joseph P. Kennedy had attempted to shape his children to achieve the ambitious purposes he conceived for the family as a whole. But most Americans approved of the Kennedys. Many probably saw in the family what they would like themselves or their children to be: attractive, intelligent, personable, rich, and successful. The Kennedys had their warts and, even before the sixties, their share of bitter disappointments—the death of the eldest son, Joseph, Jr., during World War II; the loss of a sister, Kathleen, in a plane crash; and the mental retardation of the first daughter, Rosemary—but they were a family to be envied according to the standards of most Americans.

Friends of the Kennedys marvelled at their zest for life and the remarkable closeness of the family. Whether at their large compound at Hyannis Port or at their winter retreat at Palm Beach, Florida, when the fun-loving clan gathered, frivolity mixed easily with serious political discussion. On most occasions, a touch football game followed breakfast, with able-bodied members of the family, both male and female, as well as guests expected to participate. Swimming or sailing often occupied the afternoons. At dinner, Joe Kennedy presided in an impressive fashion, reminiscing about past experiences, sometimes chiding a family member for extravagant spending, or speculating about current events. Although he had numerous intimate political contacts, the patriarch seldom tried to impose his views on his sons once they became officeholders. He readily acknowledged that they were closer to the political scene. At times he disagreed with their positions and decisions, but he never wavered in his uncompromising support for their actions.

Young John—or Jack as he was known before the dignity of the Presidency caused him to shun the nickname—enjoyed the kind of education and experiences that his affluent parents could afford to give. He attended quality private schools, including the prestigious Choate, and graduated from Harvard in 1940. In the summer between prep school and college, he attended the London School of Economics because his father wanted him to study under the famous socialist professor Harold J. Laski and to come in contact with the remarkably wide cross section of students who went to school there. Unfortunately, Kennedy became ill with jaundice and went to few classes.

He was not a particularly outstanding student either at Choate or during his first two years at Harvard. Nor was he aroused by the depression to join in the burgeoning student enthusiasm for politics.

His main loves were sports and socializing, and he engaged in those pursuits with a relish.

As Kennedy started his third year at Harvard the world stood on the brink of war. Since his father had been appointed ambassador to Great Britain in 1937, he convinced university authorities to allow him to take a semester to tour Europe. His trip sparked an interest in foreign affairs that he never lost, and he transferred his enthusiasm to his college work on his return. Majoring in political science, he improved his grades substantially, and his senior thesis, "Appeasement at Munich," won him graduation *cum laude*. After considerable rewriting and polishing and with help from friends of his father, Kennedy succeeded in publishing his thesis as *Why England Slept*. Surprisingly, it became a best seller.

After trying Stanford University's Graduate School of Business for a few months, Kennedy toured South America. He then tried to enlist in the Army, but did not pass the physical examination because of a back injury he had suffered playing football. He spent five months doing strengthening exercises and finally enlisted in the Navy three months before Pearl Harbor. His experiences as commander of a PT boat in the South Pacific, later described in detail by Robert Donovan in *PT Boat 109*, made him a war hero but also damaged his health.

Casting about for something to do after his discharge from the service in 1945, he worked briefly as a reporter, covering the founding meeting of the United Nations, and toyed briefly with the idea of becoming a teacher. Neither law nor business appealed to him. On the other hand public service and the sense of noblesse oblige had been ingrained in all the Kennedy children by their parents. Joe, Jr., had been programmed by his father to enter politics, and it seems likely that the patriarch had hoped that his eldest son would "go all the way" to the White House.

In retrospect there should have been little surprise that Jack would assume the mantle of his dead brother. How much influence his father had on his decision to run for public office is the subject of many colorful stories, although Jack himself later told newsman Walter Cronkite that he did not feel obligated to fill Joe's shoes. He added, however, that he certainly would not have gone into politics had Joe lived. (Cynics, remembering the activities of brothers Robert and Ted while John was President may question this sentiment.) His long-time associates, Kenneth O'Donnell and David Powers, point to Kennedy's experience as a reporter at the United Nations and Potsdam conferences as critical to his decision. He was a young man with an enviable education, well traveled, with enough money from a family trust fund to live in comfort, and blessed with keen intelligence. Politics was a natural choice for a career.

John Kennedy did not start at the bottom when he entered public life. Instead he ran for and won election to the House of Representatives from Boston. His family's prestige, influence, and wealth were unquestionably important to his victory. Skinny, even younger looking than his twenty-nine years, and still rather shy, Kennedy did not seem to opponents at first to be a formidable foe. But as they quickly found out, he impressed voters favorably. He possessed enormous energy, a willingness to work hard, and a knack for enthusing volunteer campaign workers. In addition, he also managed effectively the first-class organization his political connections helped him to build.

Kennedy struck most of his fellow members in the House as a very pleasant and not overly zealous young man who did not care to get chummy with most of his colleagues. His habit of changing into old clothes and dashing from his office to play touch football or softball underlined his youth and vigor. In character with his background, he took a rather conservative stance on many issues. Although he voted with northern Democrats most of the time, he was not firmly identified with the liberal wing of the party. He garnered considerable publicity as a champion of veterans' causes for his criticism of the American Legion's opposition to low-cost housing and created a mild furor by attacking Truman and the State Department for the loss of China. But such occasions were exceptions. Generally he maintained a low profile, only rarely attracting attention.

He showed considerable shrewdness in taking care of the needs and problems of his constituents. This skill paid off handsomely in 1952, when he surprised the experts by defeating the popular Republican incumbent, Henry Cabot Lodge, for the Senate, despite Eisenhower's landslide victory for the Presidency. Kennedy was glad to leave the House, where his restless nature made him too impatient to relish the long apprenticeship necessary to attain a position of influence. The upper chamber offered him a more significant base for his ambitions by exposing him to the spotlight far more frequently.

During his years as a senator, Kennedy found both joy and sorrow. A recurrence of back trouble almost cost him his life in 1954, and he narrowly lost in his bid to become the Democrats' vice-presidential nominee in 1956. But he also acquired a beautiful and cultured wife, Jacqueline Bouvier; a Pulitzer prize for his book *Profiles in Courage*; and a national reputation and following. Foreign policy, as his close confidante Theodore Sorensen noted, held his attention far more than domestic issues. Nevertheless, his handling of Massachusetts affairs continued to be nearly flawless, so that when he ran for reelection in 1958, needing an overwhelming margin to reinforce his chances for the presidential nomination two years hence, he won by almost 900,000 votes.

Among his fellow senators, Kennedy was well liked but not particularly influential or sought-after. He was not, as was often said, a member of the Senate "club," the inside power brokers who actually run the upper house. That was his choice; he eschewed after-session conversation over a tumbler of bourbon and seemed indifferent to the easy conviviality among colleagues that so many senators found rewarding. Kennedy made a mark for himself with his work on the Labor and Public Welfare Committee and gained notice for his periodic intelligent statements on foreign policy, but he was anything but a nose-to-the-grindstone legislator. By 1958 he was receiving hundreds of speaking invitations each year. Eager to obtain as much public exposure as possible, he accepted many and was frequently absent from the Senate.

In part because of political expediency, Kennedy moved closer during the late fifties to the positions of liberal senators, firmly supporting them on welfare issues, civil rights, and civil liberties. He worked diligently in 1959, for example, to secure repeal of the Federal Defense Education Act clause requiring students to sign a disclaimer of disloyalty if they wanted loans for college. Yet even some of his closest friends and admirers believed that he did so mainly in an attempt to remove the taint of his earlier conduct regarding Joe McCarthy, the controversial anti-Communist crusader. It became, as Kennedy's pre-Presidency biographer, James MacGregor Burns, put it, "The Issue That Would Not Die."

In 1954, when the Senate was considering whether to censure the demagogic senator from Wisconsin, Kennedy lay in the hospital recovering from the back surgery that almost killed him. He offered no clue about how he would vote if he were present, but his previous actions regarding McCarthy, a friend of his father's, had been mixed. He had voted both for and against funds for McCarthy's investigative activities and had taken no public stand. However, at one private gathering, Kennedy had defended his fellow senator. After McCarthy's condemnation, Kennedy at first evaded questions on the subject but ultimately indicated his approval of the action. Some practical politicians, noting the high percentage of Catholics in Massachusetts and the popularity of McCarthy among Catholics, argued that it made good sense for Kennedy to straddle the fence on such an emotion-laden issue. Burns, noting that many Catholics also opposed McCarthyism, described Kennedy's stance more logically: "He was shaping his liberalism by fits and starts, out of his experience with concrete problems." He also underestimated the intensity of feeling among Democratic liberals on the subject. As Kennedy once ruefully explained, "Some people have their liberalism 'made' by the time they reach their late 20's. I didn't. I was caught in cross currents and eddies. It was only later that I got into the stream of things."

By 1960 Kennedy's political posture essentially coincided with the consensus liberal position: the rhetoric of egalitarianism; a positive role for government, particularly against business excesses; the achievement of civil rights through federal action; and international cooperation and activism in foreign affairs. But the faith he consistently displayed in established, traditional institutions—the family, organized religion, the Constitution—and his own sense of noblesse oblige, also marked him as a man with strong conservative convictions. He prided himself on his friendly relations with southern conservatives and even with the darling of right-wing America, Senator Barry Goldwater of Arizona. On the other hand, his efforts on behalf of organized labor made him acceptable to AFL-CIO President George Meany and the trade union movement.

Many liberals continued to question his emotional commitment to their cause and wondered if he were capable of providing the moral leadership they believed necessary for high office. Intellectually, neither liberals nor conservatives challenged Kennedy's abilities. A speed-reader long before the Evelyn Wood System became fashionable, his voracious reading habits attracted wide attention and considerable envy. His fascination with learning, his insatiable curiosity, and his knack for grasping complexities appealed to many intellectuals. Personally, Kennedy was an intellectual, but, as Burns explained, "of a very special type . . . more analytical than creative, more curious and penetrating than wide-ranging or philosophically speculative, more skeptical than confident, more catalytic than original or imaginative." Shunning doctrinaire rhetoric and dogmatism, Kennedy felt uneasy with slogans and stereotypes. He preferred to use ideas to solve problems, not as a means of impressing others or as a way to pass time. He began to court academics and "eggheads" during 1958, not because they represented political power—they were much too resented for that—but because he liked brilliant people. He never patronized them; nor did he tell them that they were essential. But he respected and enjoyed the company of practical intellectuals.

Kennedy's brilliance, however, was less important in his appeal as a politician than his ability to convey compassion and understanding. T. S. Eliot once wrote that "intellectual ability without the more human attributes is admirable only in the same way as the brilliant chess prodigy." Kennedy's humaneness was as important to his success in politics as his celebrated charm, good looks, and glamour. Yet, he was not simply a "bleeding-heart" idealist. Self-possessed and cool, he once remarked, "I'm not the tragic lover type." But although skeptical by nature and inclined towards a personal fatalism, he was deeply sensitive to the afflictions and deprivations of people to whom life had not offered the enjoyments he had known.

Kennedy was enormously ambitious, and by 1959 it was clear that he was aiming for higher office than the Senate. He savored the thought of having and using power, although he realized that politically it was not wise to admit such a desire. Sorensen later recalled that in 1960 Kennedy was "slightly annoyed by all the newspaper fuss . . . over the fact that he enjoyed reading Dick [Richard E.] Neustadt's *Presidential Power*, with its emphasis 'on personal power and politics; what it is, how to get it, how to keep it, how to use it.' " But in various statements, such as his speech to the National Press Club marking the opening of his bid to win the Democratic nomination, Kennedy emphasized that the next chief executive "must be prepared to exercise the fullest powers of that office—all that are specified and some that are not. . . ." He quoted with approval Woodrow Wilson's statement that "the president is at liberty, both in law and conscience, to be as big a man as he can," and declared his belief that the President must risk conflict with Congress to enact the domestic policies that he initiates, and alone must make the major decisions in foreign policy. He frankly accepted the fact "that to be a big man in the White House inevitably brings cries of a dictatorship."

He was arguing frankly and boldly for a view of presidential leadership very different from that exercised by Eisenhower. Kennedy recognized that power went with the nation's highest office; it was there to employ to get things done. He intended to use it and saw no need to feel guilty about doing so. Yet, as the thoughtful Washington correspondent David Broder later observed, Kennedy "understood that the exercise of power was legitimate only when those he sought to lead understood and approved the purpose for which it was used . . . he accepted that the public judgment, rendered through the political process, would ultimately control his use of presidential power."

Once Kennedy decided to go for the White House in 1960, he went all out to become his party's standard bearer. With contributions from members of his family, he acquired a forty-passenger jet aircraft to use on his endless jaunts around the country. The polls placed him at the top, though narrowly, of the potential Democratic contenders, and during the last part of 1959 he accelerated his public appearances. Very early in his political career Kennedy had decided not to rely on the Democratic machine in Massachusetts to keep him in office but to depend primarily on his own independent organization. As a result, when he began his drive for the Presidency, an experienced, devoted, and tested core of workers—family, old school and Navy chums, his Washington and state staffs—provided the man- and woman-power, while the Kennedy fortune eased initial worries about money.

The senator's younger brother, Robert, directed the campaign staff with remarkable skill. At age twenty-six he had assumed command of Jack's bid for Lodge's seat in 1952, cleared up the confusion that existed before he took over, and made the Kennedy organization a potent force. O'Donnell and Powers believed that without Bobby's efforts Jack would not have won in 1952. The key to the younger Kennedy's success was twofold: he had unquestioned administrative ability, and he clearly possessed his brother's complete trust and confidence. At times he could be abrasive, but he had the will to act decisively. And when he bruised feelings to get things done, Jack, having been spared the need to do so, could smooth ruffled feathers and hold the support of those who felt abused.

Lawrence O'Brien, a superb outside man for dealings with the professional party people, and Kenneth O'Donnell, taciturn and dour but marvelous at handling the multitude of inside details connected with policy, scheduling, and paper work, functioned in 1960 as they had in earlier Kennedy campaigns. Meanwhile, the large Kennedy family, with the exception of father Joseph, worked wholeheartedly. Their efforts were important, for example, in the tea-party routine that Kennedy had used effectively in campaigns since 1946. His supporters hosted small gatherings of neighbors, thus allowing brief personal contact between the candidate and the voters. Gradually this activity expanded with members of his family as his surrogates. Mr. or Mrs. Jones might not be able to boast that they had talked personally with the candidate, but they could claim to have chatted with mother Rose or sister Eunice.

Joseph P. Kennedy sat out the 1960 campaign, afraid that his conservative image would damage John's chances. Not until after the election did he make a public appearance with his son. But he helped in other ways. As O'Donnell and Powers recalled, "If Jack had known about some of the telephone calls his father made on his behalf to Tammany-type bosses . . . Jack's hair would have turned white."

By early January 1960 when Kennedy formally announced his candidacy, the field of other serious Democratic hopefuls had dwindled to three other senators—Hubert Humphrey, Lyndon Johnson, and Stuart Symington—plus two-time nominee Adlai Stevenson. Only Humphrey, whose long association with civil rights, labor, and the ultraliberal Americans for Democratic Action caused many Democrats to regard him as something of a radical, tried—like Kennedy—to win the nomination by running in the primaries. The rest preferred to concentrate on wooing delegates in states that used the convention method. Kennedy believed that because of the disadvantages of his youth and his religion, the only sure way to convince the party that he could win the Presidency was to win in the primaries.

Three state contests were especially critical: New Hampshire in March, Wisconsin in April, and West Virginia in May. Kennedy triumphed handily in the first, as Humphrey, recognizing his foe's formidable advantages as a native New Englander, sat the contest out. Wisconsin figured to favor Humphrey, since he came from adjoining Minnesota. But Kennedy and his smoothly functioning organization managed to carry the state by roughly a 4-3 margin, a victory definitely helpful to his hopes but far from decisive.

Analyses of the Wisconsin vote indicated that Catholics and Protestants divided heavily along religious lines when marking their ballots. That made the West Virginia contest even more crucial, because the state was 95 percent Protestant. The myth that a Catholic could not be elected President had been pervasive ever since Al Smith lost to Herbert Hoover in 1928. Believers viewed West Virginia as the spot where the Kennedy victory train would be derailed, and polls taken as late as two weeks before the voting there confirmed this opinion. When the tireless Kennedy organizer for the state, Bob McDonough, arranged for Bobby Kennedy to meet with key workers, the candidate's brother found the religious issue paramount. When he asked, "What are our problems?" he received the blunt reply, "There's only one problem. He's a Catholic. That's our God-damned problem."

John Kennedy had hoped to ignore the Catholic issue. It was political dynamite; to discuss it openly simply focused attention. But in West Virginia, he had no choice. In roadside comments, major speeches, and television appearances, including one with Humphrey, he sharply challenged the idea that he was a captive of the Pope or that a person's faith was a valid criterion for being chief executive. He campaigned at his fighting best, more confident and determined than his staff. His anger flared when it became apparent that his opponents who had elected not to follow the primary route, especially Johnson, were urging West Virginians to back Humphrey in order to stop Kennedy.

To the surprise of skeptics, Kennedy's vigorous efforts turned the tide. He captured an impressive 61 percent of the vote, convincing Humphrey to withdraw as an active contender. The Massachusetts senator's ample financing, which provoked unsubstantiated charges of vote buying, was undoubtedly vital to his success. His adversary scrambled for funds continuously, while Kennedy always had money available for a last-minute television broadcast or other needs.

Kennedy won other primaries easily and chose to stay out of some because of bargains struck with favorite sons. He also did reasonably well at state conventions, the prime targets of his challengers. By the time the nominating process began in Los Angeles, he had enough votes to win, though most of the news media placed his delegate strength somewhat lower. A so-called debate between Kennedy and Senate Majority Leader Johnson highlighted the last-ditch jockeying for votes. The two appeared before the delegations from each other's home state. The Texan, obviously behind in the race for the nomination, jabbed sharply at the front runner. Kennedy's witty, yet sensible, comments won him points even with those favoring Johnson.

Especially unnerving to the Kennedy forces was the surge of grass-roots popularity for Stevenson. Thousands of exuberant people of all ages and appearance ringed the convention hall, their chants, "We Want Stevenson!" easily audible inside. The arrival of the former presidential candidate on the floor touched off a massive and emotional demonstration. Stevenson did not really hunger for a third try at the White House and had not campaigned, though he would have been pleased had he been nominated. He delayed making a full commitment, and when at last he appeared willing to give the marching orders to his eager supporters, he found that he lacked a key element—the backing of his home-state delegation from Illinois.

A variety of forces, nevertheless, coalesced behind a short-lived Stevenson boomlet. Old friends and true believers from his previous campaigns were the most prominent, but others joined in hoping to use Stevenson to stop Kennedy. Many of the party stalwarts backing the urbane man from Illinois regarded Kennedy as excessively

ruthless and flatly questioned his liberal credentials. Eleanor Roosevelt, still a power among Democrats, and others had never forgiven
the young senator for his ambivalence towards Joe McCarthy.

The Stevenson threat slowed the momentum for Kennedy's
nomination but briefly. A final roadblock—the adoption of the
platform—fell easily when the convention rejected by voice vote a
minority report signed by most of the southern committee members.
Since both Kennedy and the southern favorite, Johnson, endorsed
the platform, the southern delegates, despite their objection to the
civil rights plank, did not seriously consider walking out as they had
done in 1948. Once the voting began, Kennedy confirmed the
estimates of his staff by steamrollering to victory on the first ballot.
His triumph was highly sectional. The Northeast and Middle West
gave him over three-fourths of their votes, the West over half, and
the South almost none.

Kennedy's choice of Johnson as his running mate provided the
biggest surprise at the convention and provoked the hottest behind-
the-scenes controversy. Kennedy's staff routinely listed LBJ as a
potential vice-presidential possibility on all lists of contenders, even
though few believed that he would consider giving up the power he
so obviously enjoyed and wielded so effectively as Senate majority
leader. Much less than his associates, Kennedy failed to get too upset
by the inevitable friction that developed between the Democratic
hopefuls during the preconvention sparring. He accepted as part of
the political game charges by some of Johnson's supporters that the
Massachusetts senator was very sick, would likely not live four years,
and was kept alive on pills, although a few individuals were blatant
enough in the rumor mongering to arouse his ire. Essentially,
Kennedy respected Johnson for his work in the Senate. But he
regarded LBJ's staff as not too bright and believed that Johnson's
campaign strategy of running for President on the basis of being
majority leader was wrong and would not impress the grass roots.

Before his own nomination, JFK could not dare allow word to
get around that Johnson was a possible choice. It would have
seriously weakened the support of liberals who were leery of
Kennedy's commitment to their cause anyway. But he registered no
shock when urged by newspaper friends Philip Graham, publisher of

the *Washington Post*, and columnist Joseph Alsop to tap Johnson for Vice President.

After his first-ballot victory, Kennedy had less than twenty-four hours to pick a running mate, secure his consent, convince key party officials, and prepare his acceptance speech. It was a hectic and confusing period. Among his own staff, opposition to Johnson was blunt and heated. And for liberals like Joe Rauh of the Americans for Democratic Action and labor leader Walter Reuther, the Texan was a conservative anathema. Johnson faced similar problems with his own advisers, who maintained that he would be selling out if he accepted Kennedy's offer.

For a brief time it appeared that the liberals might fight Johnson's selection on the convention floor. Historian Arthur Schlesinger, Jr., an adviser to Kennedy, described their feelings: "The choice of Johnson was regarded as a betrayal. It seemed to confirm the campaign stereotypes of the Kennedys as power-hungry and ruthless." Fortunately for the Democrats, open revolt was headed off. Persuasive liberals like Schlesinger and John Kenneth Galbraith helped cool the agitation, while Johnson made his peace with the dissidents by giving strong assurances that he would fully support the convention's civil rights plank.

Accounts as to why Kennedy chose Johnson vary in detail and emphasis. Sorensen stressed the admiration his chief had for LBJ and the fact that Johnson simply had the most qualifications for the post. Schlesinger noted that Kennedy hoped the selection would unite the party and please the older professionals who resented the "angry young men." O'Donnell, who objected strenuously when he heard that Johnson was to be named, claimed that Kennedy angrily declared that "the Vice-Presidency doesn't mean anything" because "I'm not going to die in office." But, he added, "If we win, it will be by a small margin and I won't be able to live with Lyndon Johnson as the leader of a small majority of the Senate." Along with Theodore H. White in his splendid *The Making of the President 1960*, all agree that since Kennedy's main strength lay in the North and Northeast, his desire for someone capable of bolstering the ticket in the South and Southwest received high priority in the decision. Johnson, in his memoirs, concurred, pointing to Kennedy's stress on the sectional issue when he proffered the nomination. Bobby Kennedy preferred border-state Senator Stuart Symington of Missouri, who was Truman's choice for the top slot on the ticket. But JFK knew that the ebullient and persuasive Johnson would be a much stronger campaigner. In addition, with Congress still in session, he would be immensely valuable as majority leader in guaranteeing that nothing embarrassing for Kennedy occurred before the legislators finally adjourned. Bobby swung quickly behind his brother's choice, causing David Powers to quip, "Even if Jack wanted to give the Vice-Presidency to Eleanor Roosevelt, Bobby probably would have said all right." The full story of why Kennedy chose Johnson will never be known. Only JFK knew, and he never told. When asked later, he merely smiled and answered enigmatically.

Johnson's strongest supporters were surprised by his decision to accept Kennedy's offer. They found it difficult to believe that he would be willing to surrender the power he wielded as Senate majority leader for a job that Franklin Roosevelt's Vice President, John Nance Garner, had once described as "not worth a pitcher of warm spit." Johnson, however, shrewdly recognized that much of the prestige he enjoyed as majority leader was because a Republican, Eisenhower, occupied the White House. If Kennedy won, he, not the Senate leader of the party would speak for the Democrats. Thanks to a convenient act passed by the friendly Texas legislature, it was possible for LBJ to run simultaneously for President (or Vice President) and for another term in the Senate. It was the best of both possible worlds. Even if Nixon triumphed, Johnson was almost certain to return to the upper chamber.

Added to this factor were two important personal considerations. Both Johnson's close friend and fellow Texan, Speaker of the House Sam Rayburn, and his wife, Lady Bird, whose judgment he respected enormously, urged him to accept Kennedy's invitation to join the ticket. At first, Rayburn counseled Johnson not to run. Then, fearing that Nixon, whom he detested, might win otherwise, "Mr. Sam" quickly changed his mind. Mrs. Johnson regarded the Vice Presidency as a way for her husband to remain active in politics—the passion of his life—while at the same time relieving some of the intense and incessant pressure he experienced as majority leader. Since LBJ had suffered a severe heart attack in 1955, becoming Vice President could conceivably preserve his health and lengthen his life.

An additional factor also influenced Johnson's thinking: he still craved to be President. Keenly aware of the handicap of being a southerner, he hoped that being Vice President would help him gain recognition as a national leader.

The Kennedy-Johnson slate continued the long-established American political tradition of ticket balancing. The contrast in the backgrounds of the two men was striking. Despite almost thirty years' residence in the nation's capital, Johnson was solidly rooted in the unique blend of southern and western cultures that prevailed in central Texas, where he was born and raised and where he maintained his permanent home. His Texas was a land of poor soil, gentle hills, scrubby trees, struggling dirt farmers, and small ranchers—not throbbing oil wells or rolling cotton fields. To outsiders the area seemed barren and boring. But the people who lived there, like Johnson himself, were folksy, Protestant, and invariably friendly.

Although LBJ liked to refer to the hard times of his youth, his family, by the standards of Blanco County, was relatively prosperous. His father made and lost modest sums in real estate, agriculture, and insurance and also pursued an active career in politics, serving several terms in the Texas legislature. Like most southerners, he bitterly resented and often railed against the financial control exercised by the eastern money centers over the Texas economy. Lyndon Johnson came by his reputation as something of a political Populist quite naturally. He graduated from Johnson City High School at age fifteen, the valedictorian of a six-member class. At first he shunned college, but after working for a time with his hands, he decided, as he told his parents, that he was ready to try working with his brain. He enrolled at nearby Southwest Texas State Teachers College in San Marcos, and while attending classes he held part-time jobs, wrote for the school newspaper, and established a reputation as a debater. After graduation, he taught school for a year, obtaining the first-hand experience as an educator that he loved to refer to in his later years.

Teaching, however, was too restraining for Johnson's restless drive, and in 1931 his father called in a political debt to secure his son a job as an administrative assistant for a newly elected Texas congressman. From that point on Washington was the center of Johnson's universe. He thrived on politics, quickly establishing himself as a "comer." In 1935, at age twenty-seven, he returned to Texas with the impressive title of director of the National Youth Administration in the state and a newly acquired political ally, his wife. The year before he had been married to the gracious and keenly intelligent Claudia Taylor, nicknamed Lady Bird. She subsequently inherited a modest sum of money upon the death of her parents, which she invested largely in radio and television stations and land. Within a few years, the Johnsons were independently wealthy, a position critics claimed was due less to their shrewdness than to their unethical use of political contacts.

In 1937 Johnson made his first venture into elective politics, winning easily in a ten-man field to fill a congressional vacancy in his home district. He did so by being the only candidate to support unequivocally the New Deal and Roosevelt's controversial Court-packing plan. Appreciative of such support, the President purposely sought to push the neophyte legislator's career. At the chief executive's request, LBJ received an appointment to the prestigious Naval Affairs Committee. The young Texan also established useful relationships with important New Dealers in both Congress and the executive branch which helped him obtain vast quantities of federal monies for his impoverished district. His efforts paid dividends with his constituents, and he ran unopposed for reelection in 1938 and 1940. Most of the time he loyally supported the administration, but when political necessity dictated otherwise, he opposed the President. Roosevelt understood why. By the late thirties, Texas was moving increasingly to the right politically. Eager to move to the Senate, Johnson, as a man from the hill country, had little in common with the powerful oil, cotton, and urban interests, who found much to dislike about the later New Deal. He consequently voted against some of FDR's domestic proposals but became increasingly outspoken in supporting the chief executive's calls for bolstering the armed services, a safe issue that was popular with both liberals and conservatives in Texas.

In 1941, LBJ made his bid for the upper chamber, losing narrowly to a colorful archconservative, W. Lee "Pappy" O'Daniel. But since the Senate race was to fill an off-year vacancy, Johnson's seat in the House was secure. He remained there for seven more years, except for seven months' active duty early in World War II as a lieutenant commander in the Navy. Cynics asked what special qualifications he possessed for such a high rank and questioned his receipt of a Silver Star after the reconnaissance plane he was flying in was shot at over New Guinea. The answer was simple: his seat on the Naval Affairs Committee. Regardless, his brief service "over there" made him a "military expert" on his return to Congress in late 1942.

Roosevelt's death in April 1945 hit Johnson hard but made it easier for him to follow the trend in his home state and move towards a more conservative posture, voting, for example, for the Taft-Hartley Act, which organized labor detested. His move to the right was instrumental in building support for his second try for the Senate, an attempt that succeeded in 1948 by the embarrassingly narrow margin of eighty-seven votes. Opponents sarcastically dubbed him "Landslide Lyndon" and charged that he had stolen the election. President Truman, despite LBJ's failure to support his administration on several key issues, much preferred Johnson to the more conservative Coke Stevenson, the losing candidate, and threw the full weight of his office behind LBJ's successful battle to preserve his victory in the courts. Truman clearly understood, then and later, that Johnson's voting pattern was designed to help him at home.

In only four years LBJ climbed from relative obscurity as a freshman senator to Democratic leader in the upper chamber. The brilliant and cunning Richard B. Russell, as close observers recognized, was the real force among Democrats in the Senate, but the courtly Georgian preferred to remain in the background while someone else suffered the drudgery and detail work of the titular position. Johnson knew that, but the opportunity for power was too great to turn down. And gradually, although Russell retained much of his influence, Johnson began to assert his own authority. In 1952 Eisenhower carried enough Republicans into office with him to give the GOP control of both houses of Congress. The wily Johnson, recognizing that the President was much too popular to attack head-on, emphasized the disparity between the moderate Eisenhower and the reactionary stance of many Republican legislators. He and the Democratic minority leader in the House, Sam Rayburn, stressed that the Democrats would be the "party of responsibility" helping the President against the Republican Old Guard. When the

Democrats regained control of both chambers in 1954, Johnson was
in a position to exert strong influence over national policy.

His ability to tiptoe a narrow line between the conservative and
liberal elements in his party consistently amazed close observers. To
secure maneuvering room in his home state he diligently, and at
times ostentatiously, protected the booming oil and gas interests,
even though he had no particular love for the industry. Although few
oilmen ever became ardent Johnson supporters, his actions placated
them to an important degree and made it safer for him to move to a
more moderate position on civil rights. Until the mid-fifties, his
record in this area differed little from that of other Texas politicians.
But as majority leader, he refused to sign the Southern Manifesto
opposing the Supereme Court's 1954 decision against school segregation, and his leadership was vital in obtaining passage of the Civil
Rights Acts of 1957 and 1960. Being regarded as "sound" on oil also
enabled him to work for other liberal programs, such as public
housing, urban renewal, and foreign aid.

Johnson's reputation for leadership of the upper chamber did not
rest on his ability as a debater or public speaker. He seldom spoke
from the floor of the Senate and usually worried when he did that he
would be ineffective. His forte was the behind-the-scenes maneuver.
In planning, plotting, and pressuring to achieve his legislative goals
he had few peers in American political history. The "Johnson
Treatment" became a legend. As newspaper columnists Rowland
Evans and Robert Novak explained, it "could last ten minutes or four
hours," and it could take place anywhere—"whenever Johnson
might find a fellow Senator within his reach. Its tone could be
supplication, accusation, cajolery, exuberance, scorn, tears, complaint, the hint of threat. . . . It ran the gamut of human emotions.
. . . Interjections from the target were rare. Johnson anticipated
them before they could be spoken. . . ." Evans and Novak concluded, "The Treatment was an almost hypnotic experience and
rendered the target stunned and helpless." Johnson used the
"Treatment" with devastating effect to convince his colleagues to
reconcile differences enough to pass legislation. Constantly quoting
the biblical prophet Isaiah, "Come now, let us reason together," he
understood perfectly that compromise was the essence of politics. He
distrusted ideological purists who were unable or unwilling to

recognize that give-and-take is necessary to accomplish goals. To LBJ, America was a system that worked precisely because people and interest groups were willing to compromise. Consequently, one worked with adversaries; one did not abuse or ridicule them—at least not in public.

Virtually no one, Democrat or Republican, disputed Johnson's brilliance as a legislative leader. As Senator William Fulbright of Arkansas explained, "He made the Senate function better than anyone." But when LBJ began to show an interest in the Presidency, many of the very attributes that distinguished his work in Congress were used against him. Wheeling-and-dealing was fine for a legislator, critics charged, but it did not suggest the noble purposes of a chief executive. Many argued that Johnson's single-minded interest in politics was another drawback. He was accused of being "too much" or "only" a politician, the implication being that the person in the White House should be somewhat above politics. Liberal idealists condemned him for his willingness to compromise. Yet, as historian T. Harry Williams observed, "They did not similarly denounce northerners with civil rights records who also accepted compromises."

Most of all, Johnson's identification as a southerner and his own personal style crippled his bid for the White House. His attempt to represent himself as a westerner gained him few additional allies, and he enjoyed little success building national support. A big, coarse-looking man who delighted in being described as a "tall, tough Texan," his wit was earthy and his mannerisms gauche. Although shrewdly intelligent, he made no pretense of being an intellectual nor did he enjoy the company or the backing of the intellectual community. He knew that he needed the help of those who shaped or tried to shape opinions and tastes, but his overweening ego, vanity, and tendency to exaggerate often alienated their sensitivities. In addition, his fondness for sprinkling barnyard words throughout his conversation shocked some listeners and appalled others. Johnson was something of a Horatio Alger story himself, but his efforts to appeal to the "common people" directly were seriously hampered by his grating Texas accent. Although in small groups he could mesmerize listeners with his commanding presence and endless string of anecdotes and political fables, when he spoke to large gatherings or on radio and television he was dull, uninspiring, and—to some—flatly unpleasant. To those uninitiated in the mysteries of the Texas dialect, Johnson's twang could sometimes be baffling. Douglass Cater remembered Johnson telephoning to ask him to go to work as an aide: "I want you to come 'thank' for me,' said LBJ. Cater responded, "What's that? Thank?" To which Johnson replied, "Thank, T-h-i-n-k! Don't you know the word?"

Johnson's problems added up to his emphatic defeat by the well-oiled Kennedy machine at the Democratic convention and the offer to become JFK's running mate. He accepted knowing that if the Democrats won and he became Vice President, he would be like a duck out of water, the holder of an office with prestige but no real power. There was no question, however, that his willingness to run as the number-two man made the task facing the Republicans infinitely more difficult.

Assured of the GOP nomination, Richard Nixon worried about disagreements between his party's liberal and conservative wings that might rupture Republican harmony and undermine his chances for victory in November. Initial release of the platform planks provoked strong criticism from Nelson Rockefeller. Fearing a floor flight, Nixon hastened to New York to confer with the governor. Following a lengthy meeting, Rockefeller issued a magisterial fourteen-point statement—called by the press the "Compact of Fifth Avenue," after the governor's residence—to which the two men had agreed. As Theodore White described what happened next, "Two simultaneous explosions now occurred," one in Chicago where the GOP platform committee was assembled, the other in Rhode Island, where President Eisenhower was vacationing. To many on the committee and to the chief executive, Nixon had surrendered far too much. The statement reflected adversely on Ike's defense and diplomatic policies and endorsed Rockefeller's liberal views on economic policy, civil rights, and welfare programs. To conservative Republicans the compact offered proof that the eastern Establishment was continuing its two-decade-old practice of dictating the GOP's candidate and basic strategies. When Senator Barry Goldwater rejected the Nixon-Rockefeller bargain as "the Munich of the Republican Party," he received warm support. But Nixon had the power, and, by careful wording, his backers hammered out compromise planks on defense and civil rights acceptable to both the President and the New York governor. The rest of the convention was anticlimactic. Goldwater garnered a handful of votes, but Nixon captured the rest, chose Henry Cabot Lodge, Kennedy's victim in 1952, as his running mate, and prepared to battle the Democrats for the nation's highest office.

Kennedy's campaign organization may well have been the most efficient in American political history. Robert Kennedy was clearly in charge, second in command only to the candidate. Specialists added expertise in both operational and policy areas. Many, such as the so-called Irish Mafia—O'Donnell, O'Brien, Powers, Timothy Reardon, and Richard Donahue—were long-time Kennedy loyalists. So was Theodore C. Sorensen of his Senate staff, whom Kennedy once termed his "intellectual blood bank" and whom others viewed as virtually his alter ego. Sorensen, who was a gifted speech writer, and the equally talented Richard Goodwin wrote most of Kennedy's campaign addresses. They drew upon ideas generated by many, including a host of brilliant professors, largely from Harvard and Massachusetts Institute of Technology, especially historian Arthur Schlesinger, economists John Kenneth Galbraith and Seymour Harris, and law mentors Archibald Cox and Abram Chayes. A dedicated, if less publicized, cadre of subordinates handled such vital tasks as maintaining instant communications between the candidate in the field and advisers elsewhere, keeping the thick Nixopedia—a book containing every statement Nixon ever made—up to date, and doing advance work to ensure the optimum use of Kennedy's time when he arrived in a town. The Democrats were especially successful in cultivating the field representatives of the news media. As a result, Kennedy received much more favorable coverage, despite the fact that among newspapers that took an editorial stand on the election, four times as many backed Nixon as endorsed Kennedy.

Nixon's organization was only a notch below his opponent's in efficiency. Three men shared the major responsibilities: Senator Thruston Morton, chairman of the National Committee; campaign manager Leonard Hall, an experienced and very "savvy" political operator; and Robert Finch, a Los Angeles lawyer and close friend of the candidate. Like Kennedy, Nixon drew his ideas and speeches from a core of prominent advisers, and he had ample funds to finance a first-class campaign. But he unwisely tried to do too much himself. In the most grueling and physically demanding political struggle on record, he insisted on making all key decisions, frequently failing to consider carefully the counsel of his associates.

Kennedy capitalized heavily on his urbane good looks and charm. The campaign was the first national contest in which television was used extensively, and he employed it with great skill. In public Kennedy seemed natural and relaxed, projecting effortlessly what columnist James Reston would later term "grace under pressure." Nixon, the introvert, often appeared uncomfortable and ill at ease. He was also given to posturing. For example, following one of their television debates, the two candidates were chatting idly for several minutes, but when photographers started snapping pictures, Nixon began to shake his finger at Kennedy in a manner strikingly reminiscent of the countless photographs of Nixon as Vice President pointing at Khrushchev during their publicized confrontation in Moscow.

Both candidates drew huge crowds, but Kennedy's audiences were usually more animated, excited, and demonstrative. They seemed to regard the young senator as much a personality as a politician. Listeners loved his dry, often self-deprecating wit. "Someone was kind enough, though I don't know whether he meant it kindly," he told a crowd in New York City, "to say the other night that in my campaign in California I sounded like a Truman with a Harvard accent." Kennedy also needled his opponent deftly and with obvious pleasure: "Mr. Nixon in the last seven days has called me an economic ignoramus, a Pied Piper, and all the rest. I've just confined myself to calling him a Republican, but he says that is getting low." Certain of Kennedy's jibes became so well known that audiences waited in anticipation for him to begin his routine. A special favorite compared Eisenhower-Rockefeller-Lodge-Nixon to a circus elephant parade: "You have seen those elephants in the circus. They have their heads of ivory, thick skin, no vision, long memory, and when they move around the ring in the circus, they grab the tail of the elephant in front of them. Well, Dick grabbed that tail in 1952 and 1956, but in 1960, he is running, not the President." In contrast to Kennedy's rapier-like thrusts and infectious enthusiasm, Nixon seemed heavy-handed and wooden, a fact repeatedly noted by reporters.

Each of the nominees utilized a basic theme in speeches. Nixon stressed the experience he had gained as Vice President and his contributions to the incumbent administration. Kennedy hammered hard on the need "to move America forward." Repeatedly he declared, "Mr. Nixon says 'We never had it so good.' I say we can do better." To emphasize his point, Kennedy employed a crisis psychology: warning about the existence of a "missile gap" between the United States and the Soviet Union, pointing to the dangers of a Communist Cuba, and lamenting the condition of the nation's educational system.

Foreign policy, as all opinion polls clearly indicated, was a paramount concern among Americans. Several diplomatic embarrassments marred Eisenhower's last months in office and seemed likely to benefit Kennedy. The shooting down of a United States U-2 reconnaissance plane over the Soviet Union caused the scheduled summit conference between the President and Khrushchev to collapse, while student riots by radicals in Japan forced Eisenhower to cancel a planned visit. Closer to home, the growing power of Fidel Castro in Cuba entrenched a Communist regime only ninety miles from the American mainland.

As elected officials during the forties and fifties, Kennedy and Nixon had generally backed and sometimes helped to formulate the containment strategy. Not surprisingly, their views in 1960 placed them squarely in the camp of the cold warriors. The two candidates developed basically the same international scenario: the age was dangerous, and the United States was struggling for its very survival in its confrontation against monolithic Communism directed by the Soviet Union. Both men emphasized the importance of wooing the friendship of underdeveloped nations, but neither showed a particularly sensitive ability to distinguish civil wars of liberation in Asian, African, and Latin American countries from Communist aggression. They agreed that it was imperative for America to maintain a strong military posture. Nixon, however, anxious not to appear to be repudiating Eisenhower's judgment in defense matters, insisted that the strength of the armed forces was adequate. Kennedy argued to the contrary, assailing the Republican administration not only for the alleged "missile gap" but also for the weakened condition of the nation's non-nuclear forces, which might be needed to fight a limited, "brushfire" engagement. Each put more stress on national security through weapons superiority than through negotiated arms reduction, despite the fact that any significant increase by either the United States or the Soviet Union inevitably sparked a reciprocal buildup by the other in order to ensure the prevailing balance of power.

Among domestic issues, the health of the economy became a significant factor by early autumn. Nixon boasted repeatedly about the record level of jobs, incomes, savings, and spending enjoyed by Americans under the Eisenhower team. Republican spokesmen rebuked talk of a recession and assured the public that the economy was undergoing a period of readjustment to be followed by a new upward surge. But since early spring, a succession of falling indicators had prompted uneasiness. Bad news in the weeks immediately preceding the election far outweighed the good, and business leaders exhibited a growing pessimism. Rumors that the Eisenhower administration was quietly making plans to stimulate the economy undercut the GOP's efforts to convince voters that all was well, and the fact of mounting unemployment played nicely into Kennedy's hands. At first, he mentioned recession only tangentially during campaign speeches, usually when stressing the need for economic growth generally or when talking in communities with large numbers of unemployed workers. Late in the campaign, however, he began to warn specifically that a recession was imminent unless the Democrats took command of the federal government.

Although neither party wanted it to be, Kennedy's religion persisted as a critical issue throughout the campaign. Pamphlets attacking Catholicism circulated widely. Some fundamentalist Protestant ministers used their pulpits to charge that Kennedy would be the "Pope's puppet," and other individuals who came into momentary contact with the Democratic nominee reviled him for daring to try to become the first Catholic President. In an attempt to defuse the explosive issue, JFK frequently used wit. Asked facetiously, "Do you think a Protestant can be elected President in 1960?" he replied, "If he's prepared to answer how he stands on the issue of the separation of church and state, I see no reason why we should discriminate against him." On another occasion, he commented, "Mr. Nixon, like the rest of us, has had his troubles in this campaign. At one point even the *Wall Street Journal* was criticizing his tactics. That is like the *Osservatore Romano* [the official Vatican newspaper] criticizing the Pope."

Most important, however, Kennedy, against the advice of most aides, decided to face the religious question head-on by speaking before the Houston Ministers Association, an audience openly skeptical about the propriety of having a Catholic in the White House. At his best in the tense situation, he forcefully affirmed his belief in an America, "where there is no Catholic vote, no anti-Catholic vote, no bloc voting of any kind . . . and where religious liberty is so indivisible that an act against one church is treated as an act against all." His remarks did not end bigotry or still the barrage of jokes (such as, "JFK will rename the Statue of Liberty, 'Our Lady of the Harbor' ") about his religion. How many votes his speech before the ministers changed is impossible to say, but the warm response he received from the clergymen gave him a valuable psychological boost and reinforced his support among previously doubtful southern leaders like Speaker of the House Sam Rayburn.

During the early part of the campaign, Nixon appeared to be solidly in front of his opponent. Shortly after the Republican convention adjourned, a Gallup poll reported Nixon leading 53–47, almost an exact flip-flop from the survey which showed Kennedy ahead just before the Democratic session opened. Possibly the change reflected the more recent heavy media exposure of the Republicans. At any rate, the Democrats began the campaign believing that they had to come from behind, a feeling that probably helped to unify the party and to intensify their eagerness to register voters. The GOP also mounted a registration drive, which, although determined, was somewhat less energetic than the one conducted by the Democrats.

Starting as a slight underdog, Kennedy slowly cut into the Nixon lead, finally surging ahead in the polls, then worrying that the momentum was shifting back the other way. Kennedy's concern was thoroughly justified. Of the more than 68 million votes cast, he won by only 118,574. His more comfortable edge in the electoral college, 303–219, rested on such thin popular margins in several large states that charges of fraud were made. A shift of a handful of votes in Illinois and Texas would have placed those states in the Republican column and made Nixon President. For a brief time Kennedy's victory seemed likely to be challenged in the courts. Nixon, however, declined to contest the disputed returns. He believed, as he explained in his memoirs, *Six Crises*, that such action—certain to take many months to complete—would create chaos in the federal government and damage America's reputation throughout the world. Unstated was the possibility that any investigation might disclose equal or worse examples of Republican vote stealing.

Post mortems of the election suggested that any one of several factors may have tipped the outcome towards Kennedy. Unquestionably he benefited from his showings in four televised debates with his opponent. One survey indicated that four million voters made up their minds on the basis of the debates, and three out of four decided for the winner. The first meeting was particularly critical. It attracted the largest number of viewers, over 70 million, and was Kennedy's best performance. Nixon's appearance alone hurt his chances. He was poorly made-up for the penetrating eye of the camera; having a heavy beard shadow and being underweight made him look gaunt and grim. In contrast, his opponent, highly photogenic and poised, sparkled. Kennedy shrewdly concentrated on the audience, while Nixon spoke primarily to his adversary, as if trying to score points in a debating match. By displaying a keen intelligence and a solid grasp of critical issues, JFK convincingly rebuffed charges that he was too young and inexperienced for the White House. He clearly won the first meeting, and although Nixon was much more impressive in the final three debates, fewer people were watching. Ironically, radio listeners, according to polls, thought Nixon sounded like a stronger candidate than Kennedy, but far more people saw their meetings than heard them. In retrospect it seems clear that the Vice President erred in providing his less-known competitor such a valuable forum. But Nixon feared giving the impression that he was reluctant to defend his or the Eisenhower administration's record, and he sensed that the majority of the public wanted a joint appearance.

Nixon also blundered badly in not using Eisenhower as a campaigner more extensively. An incident shortly after the Republican convention plagued the GOP nominee throughout the balance of the race. Asked by a newsman, "What major decisions of your Administration has the Vice-President participated in?" Ike flippantly replied, "If you give me a week, I might think of one." Apologizing to Nixon later, the chief executive explained that he was trying to be humorous. But his remark undercut the asset that Nixon stressed so heavily—his experience. It also reminded the candidate that on occasions as Vice President he had felt deliberately slighted by Eisenhower. In 1960 Nixon stubbornly insisted on running the campaign himself. Not long after his nomination one of his staff bluntly told Theodore H. White that all they wanted from the President was for him to keep things calm on the international front. Consequently, although there was no doubt that Eisenhower badly wanted his subordinate to win and was eager to help, Nixon hesitated to ask for his aid. Finally, in the last days before the election, the Vice President—trailing JFK, according to the polls—urged the immensely popular Ike to deliver several speeches on his behalf. The few appearances by the President were enormously valuable. They sparked a last-minute upsurge in pro-Nixon attitudes, which the Democratic candidate correctly sensed.

Kennedy helped his chances of victory significantly by his adroit handling of an opportunity to offset the negative attitude caused by his religion among the predominantly Protestant Negro population. A Georgia court had sentenced civil rights leader Martin Luther King, Jr., to the penitentiary for sitting-in at an Atlanta department store in protest against the firm's segregation practices. His friends and family feared for his safety. Neither the federal government nor Richard Nixon said anything. But Kennedy acted. At the suggestion of Harris Wofford, a talented Notre Dame law professor who headed his Civil Rights Section during the campaign, JFK telephoned Mrs. King, then six months pregnant, to express concern. Bobby Kennedy followed up with a telephone plea to the Georgia judge in charge of the case, and shortly afterwards King was released unharmed. Word of the Kennedys' actions, aided by millions of pamphlets their staff had printed, spread quickly throughout the black community. King's father, a Baptist minister, announced his intention to switch his support from Nixon to Kennedy because of the Democrat's kind gesture. The payoff for Kennedy came in the heavy Negro vote he received, particularly in the crucial big states like Michigan and Illinois, which he carried by small margins.

Numerous other factors aided Kennedy or hurt Nixon, and any one of them could have been decisive. To at least some degree, rising unemployment helped the Democratic nominee, especially in the large and critical industrial states, since those out of work tended to blame the incumbent party. Nixon lost valuable time when a knee injury early in the campaign caused him to be hospitalized. His decision to keep his promise to campaign in all fifty states meant that he foolishly flew to far-off and sparsely populated Alaska late in the race when he could have better used his energy, as his opponent did, working in states with large numbers of electoral votes. Lyndon Johnson's sometimes corny but usually effective brand of "down home" politicking produced results in the South and enabled Kennedy to carry Johnson's native state of Texas. Johnson was always ready to speak and shake hands, and like the two principals, he pushed himself unmercifully throughout the fall. In contrast, his Republican counterpart, Henry Cabot Lodge, campaigned in a leisurely fashion. Although handsome and articulate, he was no human dynamo like Johnson.

JFK's victory ended the myth that no Catholic could be elected to the White House, and his diligent efforts as President to avoid any hint of special favor for his church caused most Americans to forget the deep animosity his Catholicism engendered during the 1960 campaign. More than any other issue peculiar to the election, however, the impact of the religious controversy remained the most difficult to evaluate precisely. Opinion polls attempted to provide answers with surveys that obtained the religious faith and candidate preference of individual voters. But whether those polled voted as they did *because of* religion remained a mystery. Some Protestants, for example, may have supported Kennedy to prove to themselves or to others that they were not prejudiced. Others may have ignored the religious aspect altogether. Even if one discounts such imponderables, the polls still provide a most ambiguous basis for analyzing the influence of religion in the Kennedy-Nixon race. Approximately the same proportion of Protestants (38 percent) voted Democratic in 1960 as in 1956 (37 percent). Since in the earlier contest the popular Eisenhower was the Republican candidate, it seems reasonable to say that in 1960 many Protestants refused to vote for a Catholic for President. Roman Catholics, however, voted much more heavily for Kennedy (78 percent) than they had for Democrat Stevenson (51 percent) four years before. Based on these findings, the distinguished political scientist V. O. Key, Jr. concluded that "probably the best guess is that Kennedy won in spite of rather than because he was a Catholic." But it is equally arguable that although Protestant voters outnumbered Catholic, Kennedy's preponderant support from those of his own faith enabled him to squeak through. Especially in the electoral college, his religion helped, because of the large concentration of white ethnic-Catholic citizens in the populous northern industrial centers. It is conceivable that a Protestant Democrat, even a Protestant Kennedy, might not have done as well.

In sum, no single factor decided the 1960 election. Instead, a combination of many and a measure of good luck as well made John F. Kennedy President. He could not easily forget the closeness of his victory or the fact that he ran substantially behind the percentage of total votes cast nationally for Democratic congressional candidates, even if the southern states, where few Republicans bothered to campaign for Congress, were disregarded. He actually won fewer states than Nixon, but he carried the South and the populous urban North, the same combination that had for so long formed the foundation of Democratic strength.

Southerners, however, particularly those living in the burgeoning, economically prosperous cities, were clearly finding the Republican party more appealing than ever before. Although Nixon triumphed only in Florida and Virginia in the Deep South, he captured Kentucky and Tennessee among the border states and ran extremely well throughout Dixie. Furthermore, Democratic electors from Alabama, who were unpledged, and from Mississippi, who were uninstructed, indicated the disenchantment with the President-elect in their states by casting their electoral votes for Senator Harry F. Byrd, a conservative Virginia Democrat. The time for a two-party South had arrived.

Southerners increasingly blamed liberal northern Democrats for the upsurge of racial tension, a sentiment not likely to be ignored by southern Democrats in Congress. Their votes, combined with the minority Republicans, who gained two Senate and twenty-two House seats in the election, meant trouble for any far-reaching civil rights or social welfare legislation proposed by JFK. The blunt fact was that the voters had not handed him a mandate for drastic change. But it was also true that Kennedy, despite his general promise "to move America forward," had staked out no particularly adventurous specific programs during the campaign. Although his administration seemed certain to be more active than Eisenhower's, whether activity would be equated with accomplishment remained to be seen.

# III

*Opening the*
*New Frontier*

DURING the period between his election and his inauguration, Kennedy mixed rest and relaxation with planning for his administration. In late November, he made it a point to confer with Nixon, a meeting which helped to soothe, at least modestly, passions that their hard-fought contest had aroused. JFK's main purpose in seeing his opponent—to discuss the possibility of appointing Republicans to office, particularly to posts abroad—reflected the impact of the narrowness of his victory.

Whatever possibility remained of a Republican challenge to the final election returns ended in early December when President Eisenhower invited Kennedy to call at the White House, thus confirming the legitimacy of the succession. Their talk, which each reported as congenial, focused on the smooth transfer of government responsibilities. To coordinate relations with the Eisenhower administration, Kennedy relied on Clark M. Clifford, former special counsel to President Truman and later Secretary of Defense under Lyndon Johnson. Since August, Clifford had been working for JFK to determine the priority decisions that would be required of the President-elect, what positions would have to filled immediately, and how to establish relations with the outgoing administration. Eisenhower designated an assistant, Major General Wilton B. Persons, to serve as his liaison in the "transfer" of power. Ike disliked the term *transition,* because it suggested a gradual change, something he rejected. He made it perfectly clear to Kennedy that he intended to retain full authority and responsibility until the end of his term, but he encouraged members of his administration to cooperate fully with their incoming counterparts, insisting only that they clear their actions with Persons.

In the opinion of Laurin L. Henry, who studied the transfer for the Brookings Institution, there was a substantial improvement in 1960 over 1952; "the Kennedy administration leaders seemed to have a better grasp of the problems facing them and clearer ideas about the courses they wished to pursue than any recent previous set of new appointees." Henry might have added that many of the Kennedyites were also supremely confident, indeed cocky, about their abilities. Myer Feldman and Theodore Sorensen became even more so after they met with members of Eisenhower's White House staff and concluded that Ike's people were "not too sharp."

Planning a program for the new administration was facilitated by a Kennedy innovation, the extensive use of preinaugural task forces. Shortly after his nomination, JFK confidently commissioned a number of advisory committees to prepare reports for delivery before he took office. To an extent the naming of committees manned by prestigious Democrats served as a valuable publicity device for political purposes, but it was also a useful way to flatter the egos of party dignitaries like Adlai Stevenson and Averell Harriman and draw them actively into the campaign. After Kennedy's victory, the work of the groups assumed a new importance, both for ideas and, in a few cases, to launch trial balloons on controversial issues.

The President-elect added new task forces after the election. Altogether more than two dozen groups labored on such subjects as foreign economic policy, education, space programs, education, and the balance-of-payments problem. Most were composed of four or five experts, mainly with academic or government backgrounds, though a few committees were much larger. In order to underline his concern, Kennedy deliberately publicized the study of depressed areas being made by a group directed by Senator Paul Douglas of Illinois, but most of the task forces operated with little or no public notice.

The bulk of the committees delivered their reports in late December or early January, and about half were released, either in part or in whole, to the news media. The report on depressed areas by the Douglas group and the recommendations on the state of the economy by the task force headed by the talented economist Paul Samuelson directly influenced Kennedy's early legislative proposals. Others, such as the study of international affairs directed by Senator Henry Jackson, appeared to have little impact on the President-elect's thinking. Senator Stuart Symington's report on the Department of Defense proposed such a drastic reorganization of the military that it was deemed too controversial for serious consideration. Surprisingly, despite the growing activism and unrest in the black community, no group of experts was asked to make a comprehensive inquiry into civil rights. Some of the task forces were undoubtedly intended mainly for window dressing, but all contributed valuable information for future use and, significantly, also provided Kennedy with an opportunity to size up the ability of individuals working on them.

Clearly the most important of Kennedy's preinaugural tasks was the selection of individuals to staff his administration. It was not an easy chore. As JFK told Sorensen, "This is the one part of the job I had hoped would be fun, but these are the decisions that could make or break us." Hundreds of key positions, high and low, had to be filled. His capable brother-in-law, Sargent Shriver, and the ubiquitous Lawrence O'Brien, aided by Ralph Dungan, Harris Wofford, Richard Donahue, and Adam Yarmolinsky, directed the talent hunt, systematically compiling and screening the names of possibilities. The final decision on all appointments was Kennedy's, but he focused most of his attention on the thirty to fifty top jobs to be held by those slated to work most closely with him.

Several factors dictated Kennedy's choices. One was his desire to satisfy the disparate wings of his own party. Fortunately, he was not bound by any special commitments or political debts incurred to obtain the nomination. Although aligned mainly with liberals during recent years, JFK recognized the need to woo the support of conservative Democrats. Without it, the long-standing coalition of southern Democrats and Republicans could easily block his legislative programs. Even among liberals, there were substantially different schools of thought, especially on foreign policy.

Ever mindful that the closeness of his victory implied no overwhelming call from the voters to change radically the policies of the Eisenhower administration, Kennedy deliberately sought to appoint individuals who would not unduly agitate conservatives or moderates. Most businessmen regarded some of his supporters as distinct threats to the free enterprise system. For example, the thought of economist John Kenneth Galbraith as Secretary of the Treasury or Michigan Governor G. Mennen Williams at the head of the Department of Health, Education, and Welfare (HEW) caused most Republicans and a sizable number of Democrats to shudder, making it highly unlikely that such outspoken liberals could receive Senate confirmation. Kennedy shrewdly blunted such worries by dispatching Galbraith to India as ambassador and naming Williams Assistant Secretary of State for Africa. Equally reassuring was JFK's announcement immediately after his election that he intended to continue the veteran stalwarts J. Edgar Hoover and Allen Dulles as directors of the Federal Bureau of Investigation (FBI) and the Central Intelligence Agency (CIA), respectively.

Political considerations aside, the incoming President strongly preferred to surround himself with sensible, practical individuals who shared his own realistic approach to solving problems. Desiring a "ministry of talents," he turned naturally to those who possessed the attributes he admired most: intellectual brilliance combined with a hard-nosed "can-do" attitude. There were exceptions. Kennedy installed an old friend, Paul B. "Red" Fay as Under Secretary of the Navy simply because he found Fay amusing, enjoyed his company, and wanted him nearby. But his basic approach to government reflected a strong inclination for placing the nation's leadership in the hands of a cultured elite trained in institutions directed and managed by men of their own class and ready to accept the responsibility of serving as trustees for the country.

Although the Kennedys had never been received into the upper echelons of American society, they nevertheless knew many of the individuals who consistently seemed to exert extensive, if not comprehensive, influence on national policies. Commonly referred to as the "Establishment," estimates varied widely as to the precise extent of its power and even its membership. Most observers agreed that the Establishment centered on the East Coast, with New York City as its headquarters, and that it included both Democrats and Republicans. Uniting them was not conspiratorial intent but a loose community of experience and interest: attendance at Ivy League prep schools and colleges, ties with Wall Street and international finance, and family and social relationships. Most shunned publicity, recognizing that it was more important to be known within the inner group than to be a national celebrity. Although flexible and nonmonolithic in membership and ideology, the Establishment endeavored to have both parties nominate presidential candidates who were in agreement with certain general policies, including modestly liberal domestic programs, foreign aid, and active international cooperation.

Not surprisingly, Kennedy looked to members of this group both for advice and for individuals to serve in his administration. In early December he had a particularly significant and revealing meeting with Robert A. Lovett. Lovett was the son of a lawyer for the Union Pacific Railroad (owned by Averell Harriman's father); he was educated in the East, was connected by marriage with a senior partner of a prominent New York banking firm, and became a power himself in the financial world as a member of Brown Bros., Harriman & Co. He worked for a time in London, gaining experience in both international banking and foreign affairs. Later he served as a top civilian official during World War II, ably assisting Secretary of War Henry Stimson and Army Chief of Staff George C. Marshall. In Washington he strengthened his ties with other New York banking and legal dignitaries who figured prominently in the national security program. After the conflict ended, Lovett became one of the architects of America's cold war policies, moving to the State Department as Under Secretary in 1947 and becoming Secretary of Defense in 1950. Witty and graceful, he was a continuing link in a chain of earlier patricians with impeccable credentials, like Elihu Root, John Foster Dulles, and Stimson, who, without holding elective office, wielded enormous influence. Whether they were in or out of government mattered little, for they were never far from the center of power.

For Kennedy, Lovett was a man to consult and, he hoped, even to bring into his administration. His age and experience would be a useful contrast to Kennedy's youth, while Lovett's prestige among the Establishment would be invaluable in easing any apprehension that the President-elect might engage in ideological adventurism. But no, the older man was not well; his doctors would never consent to his active service in a major governmental position. So when Kennedy offered him his choice of Secretary of State, Defense, or the Treasury, Lovett refused, though he agreed to serve as an administration consultant. He was happy also to make suggestions for those vital posts, and JFK listened with keen interest. Kennedy's field of expertise was politics, and, as he told Dean Acheson, former Secretary of State under Truman and another member of the Establishment sought out for advice, he had spent so much time in the last few years getting to know people who could help him *become* President that he found he knew very few people who could help him *be* President. Lovett, on the other hand, knew the individuals who could make government work efficiently. How much Kennedy respected his judgment was evidenced by the fact that the three key cabinet posts—State, Defense, and Treasury—were filled by men Lovett either suggested or endorsed.

The selection of the Secretary of State aptly illustrated both the diversity of opinion among Democrats and Kennedy's conception of his role as chief executive. Adlai Stevenson wanted the post badly and enjoyed strong backing from many liberals who believed that he would be receptive to fresh ideas about foreign policy. Hard-liners like Acheson, however, regarded Stevenson as not tough enough for the job. To their relief, Kennedy adamantly refused to appoint the former presidential candidate to head the State Department. As his comments to Lovett and others clearly suggested, the President-elect intended to make foreign policy himself. Stevenson, because of his prominence, would almost certainly have demanded more independence than Kennedy was willing to give. JFK contended, perhaps in part as a rationalization, that Stevenson had taken so many controversial positions that he would have difficulty dealing with Congress. Privately, Kennedy maintained that Stevenson was indecisive.

Once Lovett turned down the post, Kennedy leaned strongly towards Senator J. William Fulbright of Arkansas, to the dismay of rigid cold warriors. As chairman of the Senate Foreign Relations Committee, Fulbright enjoyed a reputation as an innovative thinker and a penetrating critic of cold-war shibboleths. But he also had a segregationist voting record, and Kennedy reluctantly decided against Fulbright's appointment because as a southerner he would be a liability in relations with the emerging African nations that Kennedy intended to court.

The name of Dean Rusk appeared repeatedly, though not as a first choice, on numerous lists of possibilities to head State. He received a strong recommendation from Acheson, a judgment enthusiastically affirmed by Lovett. Although a southerner, Rusk had long been on record as actively opposing racial discrimination. A Rhodes scholar, he had served in military intelligence during World War II, then moved to the State Department, where he quickly became known as an excellent staff man and a dedicated team player. In 1950, with the Truman administration under stinging attack because of its China policy, the tall quiet man courageously volunteered to step down from Deputy Under Secretary to head the department's hot seat, the Bureau of Far Eastern Affairs. His work was first-rate, and it did not go unrecognized or unrewarded. In 1951 he was chosen to head the Rockefeller Foundation. When JFK met him for the first time, in December 1960, he impressed the President-elect with his warm, genial manners and his breadth of knowledge, particularly about Asia. Since Kennedy intended to make foreign policy himself, Rusk's reputation for loyalty and for shunning the spotlight appealed to him. Stevenson also liked Rusk and promptly agreed to accept the post as ambassador to the United Nations that Kennedy urged upon him.

Secretary of Defense Robert S. McNamara was no better known to the general public than Rusk. A statistical control expert with a Harvard MBA, he joined a unique group of former Army officers—dubbed the "whiz kids"—who had worked to modernize military logistics during World War II in selling themselves as a package to help Henry Ford II reorganize the antiquated Ford Motor Company. McNamara's career at Ford was meteoric. A little over a month before Kennedy asked him to join his administration, he had become president of the firm.

He was a very untypical auto executive. Shunning the normal social circles, he lived quietly and unostentatiously in Ann Arbor, Michigan, a ninety-minute drive from his office but a university town with a stimulating atmosphere which he thoroughly enjoyed. His ascetic looks, accentuated by rimless glasses and slicked-down hair, matched his disciplined personal behavior. He seemingly planned every minute of his day, and his tastes ranged far afield from business subjects to literature and philosophy. He enjoyed art, read widely, and never stopped trying to learn. His analytical mind was most at home with "facts," and he amazed associates with his ability to store and recall enormous quantities of information, which he used to make incisive decisions. Although he was hard-driving to a fault, labor leaders and public officials he dealt with regarded him as intelligent, fair-minded, and honest. He was, as newsman Elie Abel described him, "the thinking man's business executive," an apparently superb choice to manage the far-flung military establishment.

Unlike Rusk and McNamara, Secretary of the Treasury C. Douglas Dillon had not voted for Kennedy. As Under Secretary of State in the Eisenhower administration, his loyalty had logically gone to Nixon. But he and the President-elect were old acquaintances and appreciated each other's talents. Very wealthy and very prominent socially, he had become chairman of his father's investment banking firm—Dillon, Read—at age thirty-seven. Like Kennedy, he wanted more out of life than money, and after becoming active in Republican affairs in the late 1940s, he moved rapidly into public office. Named ambassador to France in 1953, he proved to be a sophisticated and capable diplomat. His Republican banker background made him a masterful choice to reassure conservatives of Kennedy's fiscal soundness. Significantly, Dillon agreed with Kennedy that the rate of economic growth under Eisenhower was too low, and while basically an economic moderate, he was also willing to experiment when orthodox methods failed to work.

The only seriously controversial cabinet appointment was Robert Kennedy as Attorney-General. Although he enjoyed a good reputation for his work as counsel for several Senate committees, his legal background was so obviously limited that JFK could do little more than use his dry wit to defend his choice against Republican criticism: "I see nothing wrong with giving Robert some legal experience before he goes out to practice law." The younger Kennedy, whose dogged determination impressed admirers but convinced enemies that he was a dangerous zealot, accepted the position reluctantly, fully appreciating the furor his appointment was bound to create. The choice actually made a good deal of sense.

Bobby was JFK's closest adviser; it was obvious that he would want to continue to rely on his brother for counsel. The Justice Department, particularly in view of rising tensions in civil rights, promised to be the scene of lots of action. Who better to be Attorney-General than the person JFK trusted the most? On the other hand, it was also true that those hostile to the Negro revolution could not say, "President Kennedy is all right; it is that Attorney General of his who's causing the trouble." Instead they would blame the Kennedys collectively.

A bonus consideration was that Bobby could play the role that Louis Howe handled so well for Franklin Roosevelt—being willing and able to tell the chief executive quite literally "to go to hell" when he believed him to be wrong. As former Johnson aide George Reedy tartly observed, Presidents operate in an "environment of deference approaching sycophancy," which normally protects them from refreshing candor. Far better than anyone else, Bobby could be and was blunt and critical with his brother.

Although the selection of the cabinet attracted the greatest attention, many of the less-publicized appointees would actually deal much more closely with the chief executive than would the department heads, and Kennedy felt less constrained in making their selections. The emphasis was clearly on practical intelligence and professional expertise. Budget Director David E. Bell; Chairman of the Council of Economic Advisers Walter W. Heller; Special Assistant for National Security Affairs McGeorge Bundy and his deputy, Walt W. Rostow; and Special Assistant for Science and Technology Jerome Wiesner came from the academic world, primarily the northeastern elitist schools. All but Heller were old acquaintances of Kennedy's, and all enjoyed distinguished reputations among their peers. Without exception they were dispassionate dissectors of ideas, energetic men who expressed their views forcefully and were used to having their carefully honed opinions listened to. Bell and Bundy were also exceptionally able administrators.

Kennedy drew heavily upon longtime associates for his personal staff. Friendly journalists, dazzled by the President's brilliance and glamor, often attributed similar qualities to his close associates, but David Powers realistically placed his colleagues in perspective when he explained after Kennedy's death, "He made everybody around him look ten feet tall. Now he's gone and they're shrinking." Despite a carefully cultivated reputation for being a happy band of brothers, the staff was not free from petty jealousy, rivalry, and friction. They were united, however, in their intense loyalty to JFK and—above all—in their compelling desire to make the President and his administration always look good. Although hard-working and disciplined, they were neither idealists nor reformers. Instead, they were essentially political pragmatists who could and did act quite ruthlessly when necessary.

Boyish-looking Theodore Sorensen was clearly the strongest of the White House aides on domestic issues, a position paralleled by Bundy on foreign affairs. Sorensen was born and educated in Nebraska, had worked for Kennedy since 1953, and was only thirty-two when Kennedy became President. He had so closely merged his philosophy with JFK's that it was almost impossible to know whether he was stating his own views or Kennedy's. One of his indispensable qualities was his ability to obtain and master material for speeches at a fantastic rate of speed and to express JFK's ideas and personal style so well that they required only minor editing by the speaker himself. To some, he had an oppressive personality. Sharp, brusque, and occasionally impolite, he had little use for idle chit-chat. Although he had a keen wit, especially with the written word, he was not a warm human being. But as a speech writer and clarifier of ideas, he was invaluable to the President.

Kenneth O'Donnell handled appointments and, although considerably less dictatorial than Sherman Adams had been about who saw Eisenhower, guarded access to the President tenaciously. Lawrence O'Brien transferred his political savvy to directing the administration's congressional liaison and had a heavy say on patronage. Myer Feldman, Ralph Dungan, and Timothy Reardon, like Sorensen veterans of Kennedy's senatorial staff, were able and experienced hands who became trusted White House aides. Pierre Salinger, the cigar-smoking former newspaperman with the knack for keeping reporters reasonably happy, proved his mettle as press secretary during the campaign and held the same position in the new administration.

Organizationally, there were clear areas of responsibility which the staff respected, but which the President often blurred, frequently making assignments in an ad hoc manner. For example, Arthur Schlesinger, Jr., the brilliant Harvard historian who served as a "sort of roving reporter and troubleshooter," happened to be in the chief executive's office when Latin American and United Nations issues came up. Kennedy asked him to investigate, although it had been commonly assumed that Schlesinger would focus on domestic affairs. Actually the President leaned towards rational men with a breadth of interests rather than specialists, an inclination greatly strengthened by his disillusionment with the "experts" who planned the Bay of Pigs fiasco in April 1961.

A particularly significant feature of the way the Kennedy administration worked was the existence of a communications network composed primarily of people who had had links with each other and JFK before they got to Washington. Positioned in the various departments and agencies, they now had direct ties with each other and the President. When the interests of several departments or agencies overlapped, the "Kennedy people" in each usually worked together compatibly to resolve differences. In a negative sense, however, the "old-school tie" connections made it more difficult for outsiders to bring dissident views to the attention of their superiors or the chief executive.

The "Kennedy network" did little to relieve the anxieties of some cabinet members who felt that they were being excluded from the inner circles of the administration. Unlike Eisenhower, JFK placed little emphasis on cabinet meetings. He disliked meetings generally and saw little use for the Postmaster General to sit through a briefing on Laos. This policy saved the time of all concerned, but, as Schlesinger noted, it meant that the President "did not use the cabinet as effectively as he might have either to mobilize the government or to advance public understanding of administration policies." Kennedy much preferred to deal with the department heads individually. Because they held the most critical positions, he conferred with McNamara, Rusk, Dillon, and his brother Robert frequently. The other cabinet members he saw much less. Secretary of Commerce Luther Hodges and Postmaster General J. Edward Day, in particular, resented the difficulty they had getting to see the chief executive. But as O'Donnell later explained, those who called the most often had the least to say. He knew whom Kennedy wanted to see and acted accordingly.

Almost without exception, the Kennedy team reflected JFK's penchant for moderation. Extremists were ignored in favor of practical realists and individuals of demonstrated ability and intellect. Most were close to the President's own age. No fewer than fifteen Rhodes scholars joined the administration, and it was said that his appointees had written more books than he could read in a four-year term, even at his celebrated rapid rate. Their glittering brilliance so impressed Lyndon Johnson that after the first cabinet meeting he rushed back to tell his old friend, Speaker Sam Rayburn, how smart they were. "Well Lyndon, you might be right and they may be every bit as intelligent as you say," the cagey Rayburn replied, "but I'd feel a whole lot better about them if just one of them had run for sheriff once."

As 1961 began and the Eisenhower administration came to a close, an air of excitement gripped the incoming President and his appointees. They waited eagerly for a chance to take charge—to apply their rational intellect, their "know-how," their sophisticated tools to the challenges of national leadership. They exuded confidence in their ability to solve problems, right wrongs, and make the world a better and safer place to live. Their attitude was infectious. Particularly after the drabness of the Eisenhower administration, the Kennedy people—chic, brainy, cultured—seemed radiant and glamorous. Not only Washington but the entire nation sensed the exuberance manifested by the New Frontiersmen. The term, the "New Frontier," used by Kennedy in his acceptance speech in July, had stuck; it aptly symbolized the theme of "moving America forward," efficiently, of course, beyond the old horizons and onto new and uncharted paths of greatness.

Left unanswered was whether the "best and brightest," as David Halberstam would later dub them, really knew what their goals were, or, more precisely, what the accomplishment or the failure to achieve their goals might mean. Action brings reaction, and political programs are two-edged swords: solving one problem often creates or reveals another; sometimes moving slowly or simply doing nothing may be wiser than doing something. And at times, "results" may be illusions.

The Kennedy forces gave little pause to such doubts. Their theme was movement and the watchword was "go." The "can-do" people had taken over. Walt Rostow's wife, Elspeth, incisively summed up their attitude a few months later. When her husband came home at three in the morning, bone-tired but still exhilarated after working countless hours during the Bay of Pigs crisis, she told him: "I've not seen you for years more cheerful or effective. You're an odd lot. You're not politicians or intellectuals. You're the junior officers of the Second World War come to responsibility."

Their self-righteous self-confidence would later be seriously and properly challenged. Indeed, by the early 1970s the word *hubris*, meaning "wanton arrogance," had become almost as commonly used as "New Frontiersmen" to characterize many of the people who came to power with Kennedy. Still, the Kennedy attitude reflected the American mood of optimism in the early 1960s. Republicans had smugly stressed how well off the public was during the campaign. Kennedy had not denied the fact; rather he argued that "we can do better." Even social scientists, who by training and inclination are normally sharp critics of the status quo, seemed reasonably satisfied: the system needed not a major overhaul but refinements and modifications; they would be made when intelligent men and women willing to act again managed the federal government.

For millions of Americans, even for many who voted for Nixon, the inauguration of the youthful and handsome John Kennedy would forever remain the springtime of their lives. He inspired them in a much more emotional way than had Eisenhower. They revered Ike as they might a beloved grandfather, but they wanted to touch Kennedy, as if hoping that some of his glamour might rub off on them. His Secret Service guards had to wear cheap suits because of the damage done to their clothes by the crowds who crushed in whenever the President appeared in public.

Even an exceedingly heavy snow storm failed to dampen the festival atmosphere of his inauguration. To romantics, the snow, sparkling and white, seemed to symbolize the fresh, vibrant qualities Kennedy brought to the capital. The aged Robert Frost, reading his poetry at the swearing-in ceremony, signified the emphasis on culture that would be so distinctive a part of the Kennedy administration. The new President's inaugural address, brief but eloquent, called attention to his own youthfulness and that of most of his associates. "Let the word go forth from this time and place, to friend and foe alike, that the torch has been passed to a new generation of Americans—born in this century, tempered by war, disciplined by a hard and bitter peace, proud of our ancient heritage. . . ." In his most memorable phrase, he called upon his listeners for commitment: "And so, my fellow Americans: ask not what your country can do for you—ask what you can do for your country."

Reasoning that domestic issues were partisan and divisive, he virtually ignored them. Instead, he chose to emphasize foreign policy with words on which Democrats and Republicans alike could agree: "Let every nation know, whether it wishes us well or ill, that we shall pay any price, bear any burden, meet any hardship, support any friend, oppose any foe to assure the survival and success of liberty." At the time, his speech received high praise. But years later, after the frustrating American involvement in Vietnam, many critics savagely attacked his remarks. English journalist Henry Fairlie indignantly wrote in 1973, "By what right does the leader of any free people commit them 'to pay *any* price, bear *any* burden, meet *any* hardship,' when their country is not even at war, and not directly threatened?" Fairlie clearly understood, but rejected, the cold war as justifying the theme of the President's address. Yet the cold war consensus was so strong and popular in America that no one could dare attack or ignore it without seriously endangering his ability to lead. Kennedy recognized that he would have the opportunity as President to reappraise and reevaluate the wisdom of America's cold war policies, and, if he found them wanting, to educate and orient his countrymen in other directions. But as a political realist, he elected to launch the New Frontier by riding safely with the prevailing tide of opinion—an opinion he basically shared.

From its beginning the administration pledge "to move America forward" conveyed a sense of urgency and motion. The staff polished up the State of the Union message, delivered ten days after the inauguration, and continued working feverishly to hammer the task force recommendations and agency requests into specific measures to present to Congress. Kennedy clearly recognized that his hopes for legislative success depended on the cooperation of the Democratic congressional leadership. The situation in the Senate looked favorable. Mike Mansfield of Montana, Johnson's successor as majority leader, and Hubert Humphrey, the new party whip, could be counted on to back the President. But the House was a different story, and the battle that developed there became Kennedy's first major crisis, threatening to cripple the new administration before it could really get under way.

At issue was the power of the twelve-man House Rules Committee to decide which bills of the thousands introduced each session would go to the House floor for a vote. A coalition of Republicans and southern Democrats led by Chairman Howard W. Smith, a crusty but crafty seventy-eight-year-old conservative Democrat from Virginia, perennially bottled up liberal legislative proposals. Speaker Sam Rayburn of Texas, loyal party man that he was, decided to back the new administration. A respected veteran of almost half a century in the lower chamber, Rayburn reluctantly proposed—Kennedy dared not dictate to the forceful "Mr. Sam"—to "pack" the Rules Committee by adding three members, two of whom were deemed loyal to the party leadership. If the House agreed to this maneuver, the conservative stranglehold would be broken.

It was a vote Kennedy *had* to win. A loss on such a key issue at the outset of his administration would severely, perhaps even permanently, undermine his relations with Congress and critically weaken his image as a sure-handed, confident leader. The President and his supporters put intense pressure on the representatives to back Rayburn. Conservative lobbyists, such as the American Medical Association (which feared JFK's health care plan), pressed with equal fervor to defeat the proposal. By a mere five votes, 217–212, the liberal Democrats won, theoretically clearing the way for enactment of the New Frontier's legislative program.

Having focused almost exclusively on foreign concerns in his inaugural speech, Kennedy reversed the emphasis during the next few weeks. Although the Eisenhower administration had disputed the existence of a recession during the campaign, by late 1960 most businessmen and economists agreed that the economy was slumping dangerously. Paul Samuelson's task force report, delivered to JFK early in January, flatly declared that America was in the midst of its

fourth postwar recession. The same month, the rate of unemployment soared to 7.7 percent (6.6 percent seasonally adjusted).
Kennedy, much like Eisenhower, accepted the prevailing view that
America had basically solved its most critical domestic problems, and
regarded foreign policy as the area where he could make his greatest
contribution. But he also recognized that the recession, if it persisted
and worsened, could seriously affect his leadership in foreign affairs.
The situation at home demanded an immediate response.

Consequently, in his State of the Union address, delivered the
day before the final vote on enlarging the Rules Committee, the
President warned that the American economy was in trouble and
promised to submit remedial legislation. Three days later, in his
special message on economic recovery and growth, he proposed
more than a dozen specific measures, including an increase in the
minimum wage and an expanded definition of those covered, an
extension of temporary unemployment insurance benefits, aid to
dependent children of the unemployed, a program to aid chronically
distressed areas, and improvements in Social Security benefits. At the
same time he announced executive actions taken to lower interest
rates in order to stimulate housing and community development,
attack the nation's international balance-of-payments problems,
accelerate the distribution of surplus foods to the needy, and speed
up federal procurement and construction as a means of stimulating
employment. Within the next few weeks the administration added
still more requests to the growing backlog of congressional business
with bills concerning the balance-of-payments dilemma, health care
for the aged, grants for school construction and teachers' salaries, a
comprehensive housing program, a general farm bill, and increased
highway construction.

It was an ambitious liberal program, calculated to convey the
sense of a vigorously active administration committed to reversing
the downward trend in the business cycle. In reality most of the
President's requests were of a stop-gap variety, not bold new
approaches to solve the sluggish rate of economic growth that had
plagued America during the fifties. Conscious of his campaign
pledges of fiscal responsibility, he initially demanded that the
recession be fought within the bounds of a balanced budget. To the
relief of his Council of Economic Advisers he did leave some

loopholes permitting essential deficit spending. To dramatize the need for immediate action, in early February Kennedy dispatched Labor Secretary Arthur Goldberg on a politically useful tour of depressed areas in the Middle West and briefed Democratic congressional leaders on the health of the economy. Goldberg urged prompt action to forestall a "real depression," while House Speaker Sam Rayburn referred to the situation as "the most serious since the 1930's."

Congress, however, refused to be rushed into enacting the administration's proposals. The economy, basically, was sound, and before any of the President's requests became law, the recession ended. Judged by statistical indexes the slump reached its low point in February, and a gradual upturn began the following month. By mid-March a Gallup poll reported that 73 percent of the public were not noticeably affected by the recession.

Pleased to see the economy improve, Kennedy still recognized the need for more positive long-range solutions to flatten the up-and-down rhythm of the business cycle. He encouraged Walter W. Heller, his thoughtful and articulate chairman of the Council of Economic Advisers, to "use the White House as a pulpit for public education in economics," an assignment the lanky Minnesotan accepted with relish. Heller argued that to reduce unemployment to an acceptable level of around 4 percent, it was essential to accelerate economic growth. Cabinet officials and the Federal Reserve Board maintained that technological developments in industry were the primary cause of unemployment. Combatting that problem required better schools, vocational training, and area redevelopment. Heller disagreed, contending that while such programs would help, they alone could not eliminate hard-core unemployment. In his view, insufficient aggregate demand was the chief culprit, because "fiscal drag"—high tax levels draining purchasing power—caused business to stop short of expanding enough to provide the necessary jobs. His recommendation was simple: cut taxes and stimulate expansion.

His argument impressed but did not convince Kennedy in 1961. The President had declared in his economic message that if the measures he proposed failed to put America on the road to full recovery, he would submit additional requests. Most observers assumed that this remark was an unmistakable reference to the second line of attack recommended by the Samuelson task force on the economy—a temporary tax cut coupled with a massive federal spending program. But once recovery began, JFK quickly discounted the idea because of his sensitivity to charges of fiscal irresponsibility. In March, reviewing the budget situation in detail, he specifically criticized the Eisenhower budget for overestimating revenue and underestimating expenditures. These miscalculations, he explained, when added to the essential antirecession spending entailed in the measures he had proposed, would result in a federal deficit. Ill prepared himself by emotional attitude and background to accept a deliberately unbalanced budget, the President was also absolutely certain that Congress would neither pass a tax cut nor vote funds for additional domestic projects.

However, in midsummer, when a confrontation with the Soviets over Berlin threatened, the President willingly asked the legislators for an additional three billion dollars in defense appropriations. The cold war–conscious legislators quickly agreed. Spending for national security, with its remarkable sanctity from attack by pressure groups, thus took the place of massive public works in stimulating the economy, just as it had under Roosevelt, Truman, and Eisenhower. To the dismay of his economic advisers, the chief executive toyed briefly with the idea (pushed by his brother Robert, among others) of raising income taxes, both as a means of paying for the extra military costs and of emphasizing to the American public the seriousness of the international situation. Energetic appeals by Sorensen, Heller, and Samuelson, however, confirmed his judgment that such an act, even if Congress agreed—which was very doubtful—would badly cripple the momentum of recovery.

The Council of Economic Advisers recognized that with the waning of the recession it would be even more difficult to convince Kennedy of the need to cut taxes. On one occasion during the weeks when the signs of recovery were becoming more certain, Sorensen, seeing the CEA in a solemn huddle, called out, "There they are, contemplating the dangers of an upturn." Kennedy lacked extensive formal training in economics, but he was highly intelligent, well educated, and receptive to new ideas. He also appreciated and respected the abilities of Keynesian economists, such as Heller, Samuelson, Carl Kaysen, Seymour Harris, and James Tobin. Under their tutelage Kennedy's instinctive conservatism gradually evolved into a cautious liberalism. But his conversion did not come overnight. He was still hesitant in 1962 to commit himself fully to the so-called "new economics," and it was not until 1963 that he began to use aggressively the government's fiscal (tax and budget) and monetary (money and credit) policies to stimulate growth, high employment, and stable prices.

Although the President's antirecession program actually contributed little to the end of the business slump in 1961, the New Frontiersmen and their admirers made much of the energetic efforts undertaken by the administration. The Kennedyites boasted freely about their own "First Hundred Days," evoking memories of the ambitious legislative program enacted at the beginning of Franklin Roosevelt's Presidency. Walt Rostow suggested that the President make a major speech as his first hundred days drew to a close, taking stock, citing things done, and stressing that the pace and scale of activity needed to be expanded even more. Sorensen prepared a document comparing JFK and his three predecessors according to the number of proclamations, executive orders, messages to Congress, bills signed, communications to the Speaker and the Vice President, nominations, letters written, and press conferences held by each. In an administration that prided itself on activity, it was obviously important to measure movement.

By the end of June, seven of the major legislative programs (minimum-wage extension, supplemental unemployment compensation, aid to children of unemployed workers, area redevelopment, increased Social Security benefits, emergency relief for feed-grain farmers, and federal financing for home building and clearance) asked for by the President had become law. "It had been," Sorensen later wrote with pride, "161 days of action."

On the surface Kennedy's domestic record did look good, but congressional liberals were less enthusiastic than Sorensen. To many of them the President had failed to provide the magical kind of leadership that the 1960 campaign had promised. They pointed with displeasure to the administration's shoddy handling of the minimum wage bill. Despite some extremely distasteful examples—to liberals at least—of logrolling, the administration had been unable to turn out the votes to pass the bill without substantial compromises, and it had surrendered too much. The final act exempted more than

700,000 workers who would have been covered under the original version of the bill. Mainly employees of laundries and intrastate enterprises with small annual sales volumes, they were the lowest-paid workers, precisely those who needed help the most.

Even more frustrating to the liberals was Kennedy's inept guidance of his bill to provide federal aid to education. Admittedly, the issue on which the measure foundered was highly controversial—whether parochial schools should share in any government assistance. Obviously sensitive about any charges of favoritism towards the Catholic church, Kennedy at first adamantly refused even to consider aid to any but public schools. But then, in a televised press conference in early March, he hedged, saying that special-purpose loans to build classrooms, for example, might be a debatable question. Although he quickly added that special-purpose loans were a "separate issue" and should not be tied together with his general aid program, the damage was done. The hierarchy of the Catholic church, on record as ready to oppose any education bill that did not aid its schools, was given a little breathing room; while conservative, Protestant, race-conscious southern Democrats, lukewarm at best to any federal involvement in their local schools, found a new and powerful reason to be suspicious of the administration's proposal.

Although congressional debate on the bill dragged on until summer, prospects for its passage were nil after the confusion occasioned by the President's statement. Kennedy earned the gratitude of worried Protestants by holding firm to his position of no aid for Catholic schools in the general education bill, even though he agreed to a separate amendment to the National Defense Education Act (NDEA) providing for long-term, special-purpose loans to private and parochial institutions. Both died in the House Rules Committee, along with a third bill concerning higher education, when a New York Catholic Democrat, determined to uphold in principle the right of parochial schools to federal aid and convinced that the NDEA amendment would fail, voted with the conservatives.

Kennedy's handling of the education bill can only be characterized as clumsy. Liberal senators candidly admitted that he was "pretty timid." Attempting to woo southern support, Kennedy refused to buck the conservative establishment in Congress. His failure to throw the full weight of his office behind the Democratic leadership in their efforts to pass his program had a significant and far-reaching effect, especially on liberals. He had talked their language during the campaign, but he had not been able to deliver. As Tom Wicker, the knowledgeable *New York Times* reporter later wrote, "From March 8, 1961, when he yielded to pressure in his news conference on education, some members of Congress date the decline of Kennedy's ability to lead that body. . . ." He would still be struggling to reassert his command of Congress at the time of his death.

Caution also characterized the President's early attitude towards civil rights. As a representative and as a senator, Kennedy had quietly supported the extension of full equality to black Americans. But he was not identified with the white vanguard of the movement. Not surprisingly, civil rights leaders generally supported established liberals with proven track records like Hubert Humphrey before the Democratic nominating convention. Most regarded JFK as a man of goodwill and good intentions but without much knowledge or "feel" for civil rights. However, once Kennedy captured the nomination, he slowly began to pick up significant support in the black community. Negroes had not been happy with Eisenhower's indifferent stand on civil rights. With Nixon as the Republican standard-bearer they seemed sure to vote Democratic—if they voted. Once the Kennedy brothers made their timely gestures on behalf of the imprisoned Martin Luther King, Jr., black support developed into a powerful and highly important ground swell for the Democratic candidate.

Since Kennedy collected approximately 70 percent of the total Negro vote, and did even better in some key northern industrial cities, blacks could fairly claim that they were as responsible as any other group for electing him to the White House. Yet, ironically, the very closeness of the election that made their votes so important influenced JFK to move gingerly on civil rights. Worried about the conservative tint of the new Congress, he decided well before his inauguration that he would not ask any civil rights legislation during his first year.

When word of his intention leaked out, angry civil rights leaders met with the President-elect to argue against his decision. He listened politely but held to his position. When he promised to use executive orders extensively to eliminate discrimination in specific areas of federal responsibility, they urged him to issue a sweeping decree taking in the entire scope of the problem. Kennedy was skeptical of his authority to issue such a broad executive order but countered by suggesting they talk to Sorensen and prepare a detailed memorandum on the issue for his use.

In actuality, JFK used the executive order only once in the interest of equal rights during 1961, to establish the President's Commission on Equal Employment Opportunity (CEEO) under Vice President Johnson. The idea was by no means novel, since Eisenhower had employed a similar committee. The order made it mandatory that holders of government contracts end discrimination in employment; the ultimate penalty for firms that refused to cooperate was the requirement that government agencies refrain from doing business with them. Efforts to win voluntary compliance were relatively successful, but the CEEO functioned largely as a clearinghouse for persuasion, only rarely disciplining violators.

During the campaign, Kennedy had wisecracked that federally financed segregated housing could be ended "with the stroke of a pen" and that Eisenhower should issue the executive order doing so. After his blithe remark, JFK's own delay in signing such a decree was difficult to rationalize. He soon began to receive countless gifts of pens and bottles of ink, pointed reminders of his campaign comment. Although he appreciated the joke—at least at first—he refused to sign the promised order.

Sorensen explained that the President hesitated "until Congress acted on the nomination of Robert Weaver [a Negro] as head of the Housing and Home Financing Agency, then until Congress acted on his housing bill, of immense importance to Negro families in the low-and-middle-income brackets. Then he waited for a full-scale report on housing from the Civil Rights Commission and for a more carefully drafted Executive Order to be prepared by lawyers." By that time 1961 was over. In 1962 the President hoped to establish a Department of Urban Affairs and name Weaver as its Secretary. Although Weaver strongly urged that the housing order be issued even if it meant sacrificing his opportunity to be the first Negro cabinet member, Kennedy gambled on holding back on the decree until the legislators passed the bill creating the new department. To his disappointment, the measure was killed by southern Democrats and Republicans in the House Rules Committee. After a reasonable delay to avoid the appearance of acting in spite, the chief executive, late in November 1962, at last quietly issued the long-awaited order eliminating segregation in federally financed housing. Clarence Mitchell, the veteran head of the NAACP's Washington office, found Sorensen's excuses for the long delay neither very good nor legitimate. The key, Mitchell argued, was the tendency of the administration "to find out, first, which way the wind is blowing before acting."

Kennedy's appointment policy was more encouraging to black Americans. He named distinguished Negroes to high offices, including Weaver, Carl Rowen as ambassador to Finland, Thurgood Marshall as a United States Circuit Court judge, Andrew Hatcher as JFK's associate press secretary, and the first black district judges ever to serve in the continental United States. Also important were the whites selected to head critical posts under Robert Kennedy in the Justice Department—Byron White, Nicholas de B. Katzenbach, John Siegenthaler, John Doar, and especially Burke Marshall, the head of the Civil Rights Division. All were committed to equal rights and willing to back their beliefs with deeds. Doar would become a living legend for his bold behavior in the face of a hostile racist mob, and Siegenthaler was beaten severely attempting to protect a civil rights demonstrator. On the President's staff, Lee White and Harris Wofford, along with Sorensen and Myer Feldman, were consistent and vocal champions of the civil rights cause.

Unfortunately, not all the President's appointments were so sympathetic to Negroes. Some of the federal district judges he appointed in the South—J. Robert Elliott in Georgia and William Harold Cox in Mississippi, for example—were obviously biased in civil rights cases. Their selections clearly reflected the President's reluctance to offend the powerful southern politicians who supported their appointments. As Roy Wilkins of the NAACP complained, it was inevitable that here and there a hostile judge would slip through, but under JFK, there were simply too many. And since their tenure was for life, their selection sorely strained the patience of Negroes. Kennedy's "Southern strategy" prompted a white Alabaman who supported civil rights to complain to Marshall that Bull Connor, the notoriously racist police commissioner in Birmingham and also a Democratic national committeeman, was being given federal patronage to dispense: "So here we are, dealing with violence, segregation, complete defiance of the law and the very men who are doing it are the ones whom the Federal government rewards."

The Kennedy administration's preliminary actions convinced many Negro activists that it needed prodding. Naming Negroes to prestigious positions or demanding, as JFK did, to know why no black men were in the Coast Guard unit that marched in his inaugural parade were symbolically valuable gestures but not much help to the Negro masses. Consequently, when the Supreme Court ruled that restaurants in bus stations could not legally discriminate against interstate travelers, a group of "freedom riders" from the Congress of Racial Equality (CORE) decided to test the decision in the Deep South. Their journey exposed the New Frontier to its first serious racial confrontations. Mobs in Alabama burned a bus carrying some of the protesters, mauled several riders, and seized the Montgomery bus terminal. The President then decided that federal powers must be used and rushed hundreds of federal marshals to Alabama to restore order. The freedom riders left the state and continued on into Mississippi, where state authorities cleverly prevented violence by resorting to mass arrests to stop the rides.

The freedom riders' intent—to apply pressure on the administration—worked. Robert Kennedy persuaded the Interstate Commerce Commission to implement the Court's ruling by banning segregation in carriers and terminals. He secured voluntary desegregation for thirteen of the fifteen segregated airports and took legal action against the other two. The Justice Department also pushed its already energetic efforts to insure that Negroes were not denied an opportunity to register and vote in the South, filing a great many suits to prevent southern officials from declaring Negroes who fairly met the legal standards "unqualified." Such abuses were common throughout much of Dixie. Just how flagrant they often were was revealed in a letter from Burke Marshall to the Alabama Attorney General about the Justice Department's analysis of rejected applications for voter registration in Montgomery County. Between January 1, 1956 and October 17, 1960 more than 700 Negro applicants with a twelfth-grade education or higher, including 108 teachers, were rejected. Marshall noted that "Prior to our request to copy the records . . . practically no white applicants of similar educational backgrounds had been rejected."

By any reasonable standard of judgment, civil rights, in 1961, were simply not in the forefront of Kennedy's thinking. At the time, the chief executive was still somewhat insensitive to the needs of Negroes. As Victor Navasky explained in *Kennedy Justice*, "Robert Kennedy, who was ahead of his brother in these things, himself required a few years of on-the-job sensitivity training before he caught up with the NAACP. . . . From 1961 to 1963 Robert Kennedy had no civil rights program in the sense that he had an organized-crime program." For example, the involvement of the Federal Bureau of Investigation in the struggle for equal rights was nil. As one historian wryly noted, "SNCC's [Student Non-Violent Coordinating Committee] only contact with federal authority consisted of the FBI agents who stood by taking notes while local policemen beat up SNCC members."

Kennedy's early approach to civil rights was basically reactive, not creative. Believing that integration was inevitable, he wanted to encourage it but with the minimum disturbance of the country's social equilibrium. Thus the President, aside from refusing to ask for new legislation, hesitated even to use the full range of executive authority at his disposal to end inequality. The Defense Department, for instance, did not demand that National Guard units be integrated for fear that the crack southern units would withdraw from the Guard program, a result that would be detrimental to national security. Believing that he had no mandate from the voters for peremptory action, JFK reasoned that by pushing too aggressively and too fast he might destroy his chances of obtaining congressional support for his other domestic and, especially, his foreign goals.

Nothing happening on the domestic front when Kennedy took office, not even in civil rights, compared to the attention given to foreign affairs. "The prestige of foreign policy in 1961," John Kenneth Galbraith wrote, "was enormous. No one much cared about who was to run the Treasury. It mattered greatly who was to be the Secretary or Under Secretary or even an Assistant Secretary of State, although there were enough of the latter to form a small nation." Kennedy's inaugural address typified this attitude. Throughout the speech, which shrewdly blended a firm determination to defend the "free world" against adversaries with a pledge to help the poorer nations of the world to cast off their "chains of poverty," action stood out as the imperative. As the British writer Anthony Hartley noted, the New Frontiersmen wanted to solve problems, not merely cope with them. Their device was "when in doubt, do something," even though that inevitably meant more commitments. The concept of "attentive watching and patient waiting" held little or no appeal. By learning from the mistakes made in the previous fifteen years, they intended, as rational and intelligent men, to do things better.

Kennedy made no attempt to conceal his desire to "shake up" the tradition-laden State Department. Diplomats were good reporters and negotiators, but they were not facile at analyzing information and providing alternative courses of action. He described the department as "a bowl of jelly," and declared, "It's got all those people over there who are constantly smiling. I think we need to smile less and be tougher." Secretary of State Rusk acknowledged that changes needed to be made, but efforts to instill a new spirit and alertness in the diplomatic bureaucracy proceeded at a snail's pace. The impatient President grew ever more annoyed. At one point in mid-1961 it took the department six weeks to produce an answer to a Soviet memorandum, and, when it was finally completed, it contained no original thinking. Abram Chayes, one of the new men JFK brought to State, described it as "turgid and more Stalinist than the Soviets in style."

If giving State an instruction was, as the President once told Schlesinger, "like dropping it in the dead letter box," other bright minds in the administration were ready and willing to provide new ideas. Many of their concepts were sweepingly grandiose: an "Alliance for Progress" for Latin America, a "New Africa" policy, and later the "Grand Design" for Europe.

Latin America was a particular worry. Plagued by poverty and an exploding population, their history punctuated by repeated revolutions and coups, the Latins correctly regarded the "colossus of the north" as officially indifferent to their needs and unofficially exploitive of their resources. The Castro revolution in Cuba, ominously close to the American mainland, made the threat of Communism in the Western Hemisphere very real. If Castroism spread to the south, the containment policy, so successful in Europe, would be gravely crippled.

Only days before the New Frontier began, Eisenhower suspended diplomatic relations with the Havana regime. Kennedy wisely chose not to associate himself with a decision that he had no hand in making. He unveiled his own plan for Latin America in his inaugural speech—an Alliance for Progress. Unquestionably he felt a sense of urgency because of Cuba. In the next few months, his administration, building on an earlier task force report, worked out a detailed program for the Alliance. Revealed by Kennedy in March, it became the core of an agreement between the United States and the Latin American republics signed in August at Punta del Este. Kennedy pledged $20 billion of American aid during the next ten years. The other nations promised to invest $80 billion and, most critical of all, to initiate land, tax, and socioeconomic reforms. The 1960s were to be a decade of hope and growth for Latin America.

At the outset, administration spokesmen were excessively optimistic about what the Alliance for Progress could realistically expect to accomplish. But as the decade unfolded, both the rhetoric and the optimism sagged. Events, in the United States as well as abroad, seriously undermined the basic goals of the Alliance: simultaneous achievement of social equality, political stability, economic growth, constitutional democracy for the Latin American countries, and the strengthening of national security for the United States. Lack of enthusiasm for the program by American business, counted on for substantial private investments, hampered the prospects for success. So did the tangled and, at times, naive, bureaucratic framework charged with administering the Alliance. Also, few of the Latin American countries had governments that were fully responsive, and during Kennedy's short term as President, seven military coups added additional strains. Generally Kennedy followed a pragmatic pattern of nonrecognition and suspension of all aid programs if the new regime appeared opposed to the Alliance. But, as in Peru in 1962, if the new government attracted popular support, seemed sympathetic to the aims of the Alliance, and held a firm line against Communism, he was willing to work with it as best he could. Basically, he was concerned about any instability that provided Communists with an opportunity to take advantage. Thus he was consistently preoccupied with "what have we got to take its [the existing government's] place; how do we know it will be better?"

Kennedy's intentions towards the emerging nations and the poor countries were honorable. He wanted them to improve their social and economic conditions and to enjoy freedom. He wanted diplomats who were sympathetic to the democratic left, as he was, not those who favored the established elites. But at the same time, conditioned as he had been by the cold war, he tended to react whenever Communism threatened or appeared that it might threaten. At times it was hard for him to avoid overreacting.

Kennedy was remarkably attuned to the attitudes, problems, and concerns of the less-developed and newly independent lands and established a warm rapport with African leaders, including those who leaned towards socialism. On numerous occasions he affirmed his belief that foreign countries should pursue economic systems that best suited their peculiar needs. Unlike John Foster Dulles, he accepted completely the right of a nation to be neutral in the confrontation between the United States and the Soviet Union. On the other hand the Soviets had long wooed the unaligned countries, and he did not intend to drop out of the competition. William Atwood, one of JFK's bright and enthusiastic diplomatic appointments, who served as ambassador to Guinea, expressed this spirit when he wrote that he refused to accept a defeatist attitude that "Guinea was down the drain" because the Soviets got there first. He explained that if the New Frontier meant anything it was that the United States was not sitting back and giving up.

The Peace Corps typified Kennedy's concern for the problems of the less-fortunate nations. Contrary to popular myth, the idea for a group of dedicated American volunteers willing to serve at low pay in backward foreign lands as teachers, agricultural specialists, and the like was not original with JFK. Hubert Humphrey, Representative Henry Reuss of Wisconsin, and others could claim to have made statements that were antecedents of the concept. During the 1960 campaign, former Governor Fritz Hollings of South Carolina called Myer Feldman's attention to a speech by General James Gavin about Americans' volunteering to help others in the world. Gavin had no text of his remarks, but he did have his notes, which he sent to the Democratic speech writers. Kennedy began talking off-the-cuff about the idea in speeches. When it seemed to catch on with his listeners, it was given more importance and ultimately became one of the new administration's most exciting and innovative programs.

Created by executive order even before Congress authorized funds, the Peace Corps prompted attack from both conservatives and Communists, the former visualizing it as a wasteful haven for beatniks, the latter attacking it as a cover for espionage. The President and the Corps director, the hard-driving Sargent Shriver—Kennedy's brother-in-law and a talented business executive—promised that a nonpolitical posture would be maintained and that volunteers would be dispatched only to countries to which they had been invited.

More than any other of Kennedy's presidential programs the Peace Corps symbolized the high idealism and promise of the New Frontier on the one hand, and the disappointments of the administration's performance on the other. The concept of unselfishly helping others was unarguably noble, representing the very best in the Judeo-Christian tradition, but like the Kennedy administration itself, its glow faded as the decade wore on. Some host countries bluntly asked "Kennedy's children" to leave; isolated tales of blunders and incompetence marred the Corps' reputation. By the early 1970s a former member of the organization summed up the record as "at the most, a kind of experiment in international living." No one, he declared, pretended any longer that the Peace Corps had even the remotest connection to real social and economic development in the Third World.

In other ways the new President sought to use American wealth to do good in the world. He appointed George McGovern to head the sluggish Food for Peace program and vastly expanded the amount of surplus food shipped to hungry foreigners. He also attempted to streamline the nation's foreign aid efforts, creating a new Agency for International Development (AID) and, most important, shifting the emphasis from military to economic assistance.

But while extending the helping hand internationally, Kennedy also took steps to make the military—which, he realized, had participated actively in the formulation of foreign policy since World War II—leaner, tougher, and more responsive to diverse threats to national security. In this regard his choice of Robert McNamara as

Secretary of Defense proved to be more fortuitous than JFK could possibly have anticipated. An activist by nature and one who eagerly accepted ever greater responsibilities and challenges, the auto executive was a cost-efficiency expert perfectly suited for the task the President had in mind.

McNamara believed that previous Secretaries of Defense had essentially functioned as referees between the competing military services. Although such a role was less demanding personally and less risky politically, it was far different from the one he determined to play. "I'm here to originate and stimulate new ideas and programs," he once explained, "not just to referee arguments." His premise was active management at the top with power concentrated overwhelmingly in the Secretary.

To guarantee that his decisions were always "informed," he tried to implement a system that would consider alternative ways to satisfy military requirements, calculate the cost of each alternative, weigh the military effectiveness of each, and compare all alternatives in terms of cost and effectiveness. To make the system work, he surrounded himself with a cadre of key civilian subordinates, such as Charles Hitch and Alain Enthoven, who shared his philosophy and possessed the necessary expertise. McNamara disliked men in uniform reading off information or using elaborate flip-charts. Not long on tact or diplomacy, he preferred to ask his own questions, and he wanted unstereotyped answers. The new men he brought into the department enabled him to free himself, Robert J. Art explained, "from the secretary's usual dependence on the experience and knowledge of the military officer and career civil servant."

McNamara's candid, bare-facts approach to problems created a mild, but not permanently damaging, public relations rift with the White House. The alleged "missile gap" was one of the three or four prominent themes during the 1960 campaign, although, as Sorensen emphasized, it was primarily used as a symbol of the lack of vitality and vision in the Eisenhower administration. Psychologically, the Soviets' success in launching big space satellites in the late fifties—years before the United States was able to do so—hurt Ike's credibility on defense matters badly. Republican spokesmen conceded the Soviet lead in rockets capable of delivering nuclear warheads but, considering American ability to retaliate by both manned bombers and missiles, heatedly denied any "deterrence gap," which in reality was the critical factor. Long before JFK raised the issue, a heated debate had been under way, in both Congress and the media.

In his State of the Union address Kennedy announced that McNamara would appraise the entire missile program. In early February the Secretary of Defense told newsmen present at an off-the-record briefing that there was no gap. After the story appeared in the *New York Times,* the press queried Kennedy, who replied that it was still premature to say, since the Defense Department's report was not completed. McNamara, after a White House complaint, hurriedly hedged on his earlier statement. Until Autumn the matter remained publicly unsettled, but on October 11, 1961 the President declared at a press conference that the United States possessed ample strength to meet its commitments. The confusion occurred because of sharply contrasting analyses of Soviet missile strength by different American intelligence organizations. As Kennedy quickly found, he could take his pick of high, medium, or low estimates. He reacted by creating, in October, a Defense Intelligence Agency, under the control of the Secretary of Defense, which combined all military services strategic intelligence estimates.

Long before the furor over the "missile gap" waned, JFK and especially Robert Kennedy were pushing hard for a new dimension to the military's arsenal—counter-insurgency units, trained and equipped to fight guerrilla wars effectively. Rejecting the Eisenhower-Dulles doctrine of "massive retaliation" as a singular policy for national defense, they advanced the arguments of critics like General Maxwell Taylor and Henry Kissinger, who warned against depending solely on nuclear deterrence to the virtual exclusion of modern forces capable of fighting small, "brushfire wars." Khrushchev's speech in early January 1961 pledging Soviet support for wars of national liberation, like those in Algeria and Vietnam, greatly impressed the Kennedys.

At first, McNamara was cool towards the concept. The Marines and then the Army, however, jumped on the bandwagon. But the real stimulation came from the White House. Robert Kennedy attended practically every meeting of the interdepartmental Counter-Insurgency Group and took upon himself the role of prime mover. Significantly, as the counter-insurgency program got under way, it was not restricted to American personnel. The Southern Area Command in Panama trained friendly "effectives" of some Latin American nations in ways to stifle internal revolts.

In principle it is difficult to fault the Kennedy brothers' thesis that the military should be prepared to provide a more "flexible response"—alternatives other than unlimited nuclear combat—for national security. Yet, however sensible their intentions, the results were less than reassuring. Adam Yarmolinsky, one of the brilliant young experts who worked for McNamara, was one of those who later expressed misgivings. Yarmolinsky worried that having more military options might induce chief executives to ignore diplomatic or political possibilities. Looking at the 1960s, he noted that "theories of limited war and programs to widen the President's range of choice made military solutions to our problems more available and even more attractive. Without question, they contributed to the size of the defense budget and to the deepening involvement in Vietnam."

Although there were innumerable trouble spots around the globe, the new administration faced no imminent international crises when it took office. As Eisenhower warned Kennedy the day before the inaugural ceremony, the most likely candidate to disrupt the relative tranquility was Laos. Originally part of Indochina, that quaint land had been declared officially "neutral" by the Geneva Accords of 1954, but neither the United States nor the Soviet Union paid much attention. Each funneled military supplies and advisers to friendly forces inside the country. By early 1961 the Communists seemed to be winning. Ike bluntly told JFK, "You might have to go in there and fight it out." Laos was a "mess" of classic proportions, a chaos worsened by the lack of coordination between the State, Defense, and CIA operatives in the field. Even inside these organizations, there was no unified opinion as to what course of action the United States should take. Activists in the CIA, for example, thought Laos was a great place to have a war, and indeed they did run a small war with their Meo tribesmen allies. Admiral Arleigh Burke, chairman of the Joint Chiefs of Staff, argued the domino theory about Laos, urging JFK to make a stand there. So did other military leaders and some State Department officials.

During his first two months in office, Kennedy invested much of his time in trying to find a solution to the Laos imbroglio. As the crisis worsened, he agreed in late March that troops should be prepared for possible commitment and secured reluctant British support for limited intervention if necessary. The State Department wanted just this type of modest effort, but according to Roger Hilsman, director at the time of State's Bureau of Intelligence and Research, "the Pentagon insisted on all-out force or none . . . the Joint Chiefs' position in general was to oppose any intervention at all . . . unless they were given advance approval for the use of nuclear weapons if, in the judgment of the Joint Chiefs themselves, nuclear weapons should prove necessary—a condition which no President could ever accept."

Kennedy refused to take an either-or position. He concluded that Laos was not the place for a heavy American involvement. The uncommitted nations of the world, marshaled by Indian leader Nehru, pressured for negotiation. When the Soviets signaled their willingness, Kennedy gladly accepted, in spite of stinging criticism at home from some newspapermen, like Joseph Alsop, and numerous Republican spokesmen. Neutralization of Laos seemed to the President the best of the available options. The Laos talks began in Geneva during May, but though a cease-fire was technically in effect, fighting continued to rage in that troubled country, causing skepticism in Washington that the Communists really wanted a settlement.

As the Laos situation was becoming tenser in late April, Kennedy suffered his most publicized diplomatic debacle—the Bay of Pigs affair. It involved an attempt by 1,500 Cuban exiles, trained for months by the CIA, to invade their homeland and instigate an uprising against Fidel Castro. It was a disaster. The invaders were either killed or captured, and the prestige and integrity of the United States and the Kennedy administration were painfully damaged.

The story behind the attack was—and is—tangled and controversial. Planning for the operation began during the Eisenhower administration. During the 1960 campaign, Nixon, believing that CIA Director Allen Dulles had briefed Kennedy on the plan, angrily resented his opponent's call for American intervention in Cuba. In order not to expose what was under way, the Republican candidate ridiculed Kennedy's proposal as unwise and irresponsible. CIA official Richard Bissell, however, expressed his belief that JFK did not know about the covert operation until he and Dulles informed him about it after Thanksgiving.°

Once in office, Kennedy had to decide whether planning for the invasion should continue. On being told that the Joint Chiefs of Staff had not evaluated the CIA-directed adventure, he ordered them to do so. To the CIA's dismay, the Joint Chiefs did not emphasize the need for strong air support, and the President and Rusk opposed air strikes by American "volunteers" because they would cause adverse world opinion. Their feelings underscored perhaps the key weakness in the whole affair: those involved failed to realize that the United States would be blamed anyway and that few individuals or nations would conceivably believe that the Cubans and not the United States initiated the attack.

Support for the landing within the administration was over-whelming, although the degree of enthusiasm varied. At a meeting of key national security officials in early April opinions were canvassed and each had a chance to vote. Only Senator J. William Fulbright voiced firm opposition, and the verdict was, in the words of one of the meeting's participants, "let her rip." But it would be done without the type of air cover that many of those involved in the operation believed was essential for success.

The impact of the disaster that resulted was enormous. Kennedy, his confidence rattled, insisted on taking full responsibility, manfully refusing to pass the buck, and saying privately that if America had a cabinet government, he would have resigned. Why the administration decided to launch the assault is a riddle with many possible answers. Some officials saw it as probably the last chance to oust Castro. Too many advisers tried to influence the decision; they could not discuss in depth because of their numbers and, because the Kennedy team was so new, people really had not had time to work together. Robert Lovett, who served as a consultant to JFK on many issues, believed that the President was simply not served well by his

---

° Nixon, however, believed that the CIA had briefed Kennedy about the Cuban invasion plan during the election campaign. As revealed in one of the Watergate tapes, Nixon told aide H. R. Haldeman that CIA officials had deliberately lied to protect Kennedy once the Democrat had been elected President. Nixon used the incident to justify telling Haldeman to order the CIA to cooperate in covering up the break-in of Democratic party headquarters in 1972 by agents of the committee to reelect Nixon.

advisers. There was also considerable apprehension that if the new administration cancelled a plan approved by Eisenhower to free Cuba, the news would be leaked and it would stimulate politically damaging charges that Kennedy was weak on Communism. Another plausible explanation was sheer bureaucratic momentum. Ironically, as Sorensen noted, if the venture had succeeded, it would have been hailed by most Americans as a great move, even if they admitted that it was the wrong way to get things right in Cuba.

The Bay of Pigs, said Acheson, who was in Europe at the time, "shattered the Europeans" as "a completely unthought out, irresponsible thing to do. They had tremendously high expectations of the new administration, and . . . they just fell miles down with a crash." Kennedy recognized the damage he had suffered. He also felt a strong sense of guilt about the imprisoned Cuban invasion brigade and would later strongly endorse successful efforts to ransom them.° But he also learned something from the unfortunate affair. On two occasions he told Sorensen that had the Bay of Pigs not occurred the United States would have gotten involved in a much worse situation in Laos. His judgment to keep large numbers of American troops out of that country was strongly influenced by the Cuban disaster. When the Administration, so full of élan and excitement, fell flat on its face in Cuba, it also destroyed some of the youthful and adventurous spirit that pervaded the early days of the New Frontier. It would take a major triumph to rekindle the early enthusiasm, and that would not come for another eighteen months, when another Cuban crisis provided Kennedy with what he saw as his greatest foreign policy success.

One of the side effects for Kennedy of the Laos and Bay of Pigs confrontations, particularly the former, was his decreased confidence in the members of the Joint Chiefs of Staff he inherited from Eisenhower. Their views on Laos, involving the heavy commitment of troops and massive bombing forays, struck him as exaggerated.

---

° In late December 1962 almost 1,200 men captured during the Bay of Pigs invasion were freed by Castro in return for $50 million worth of food and drugs, donated by American businesses, plus almost $3 million in cash, contributed by private individuals. Officially, the President was uninvolved in the negotiations to ransom the prisoners, but it was well known that he backed the effort, particularly since Robert Kennedy headed the drive to obtain the necessary donations.

The Joint Chiefs in turn thought the President abused channels of communication. They recognized McNamara's brilliance but regarded him as naive about the Washington ways of life. In fact, neither Kennedy nor McNamara especially appreciated the typical high-ranking military officer or the military-promotion and career-management system. The President was youth-conscious and thought many of the top brass were too old. By early spring he had determined to speed up the retirement date of Admiral Arleigh Burke, chairman of the Joint Chiefs, and replace him with General Maxwell Taylor, who had left active duty in despair with the "massive retaliation" dogma of the Eisenhower administration, but who impressed Kennedy with his well-rounded intelligence. He also replaced the other members of the Joint Chiefs, except for David Shoup of the Marines, a man he admired. Ironically, the President agreed to make hard-bitten Curtis LeMay, a legend as commander of the Strategic Air Command, Air Force Chief of Staff. Roswell Gilpatric, McNamara's number-two man at Defense, related that every time Kennedy saw LeMay, who was notorious for his outrageous proposals, the chief executive ended up in something of a fit. But he kept the unreconstructable LeMay on because the alternatives of having the superhawkish general out of the administration were worse than having him in.

Although Kennedy was generous in many ways to the CIA—he refused to put the blame on the agency even though it had directed the Bay of Pigs operation—after that disaster he was determined to shake up the organization and monitor its activities more closely. Unquestionably the debacle undermined his confidence in the agency's decision-making process. Until the Cuban missile crisis of October 1962, the CIA had permission to put agents into Cuba for the purpose of disrupting the Castro regime, but the so-called Mongoose Committee, chaired by McGeorge Bundy, carefully audited American intelligence and paramilitary activities and kept the President informed of what was going on. Kennedy also accepted the voluntary retirement of Allen Dulles as head of the CIA, replacing him with businessman John McCone. McCone, who had served other administrations in various capacities, did an outstanding job of rebuilding sagging morale among the agency's personnel. The President also placed all American personnel in foreign countries, including intelligence operatives, under the local ambassador. The CIA pled to be exempted, but Kennedy refused.

Intrigued, like most Presidents, by the lure of personal diplomacy, Kennedy from the start deliberated the wisdom of a personal meeting with Khrushchev. The Soviet premier sent Kennedy friendly messages at the time of his election and later upon his inauguration, and reinforced his cordiality by agreeing, in the President's first days in the White House, to release the survivors from the RB-47 reconnaissance place shot down over Russia some months before. Kennedy responded with kind words for improving Soviet-American relations and affirmed his intention not to resume the U-2 intelligence flights over the Soviet Union. Khrushchev made clear to American Ambassador Llewelyn Thompson that he would like to meet soon with the new President.

Neither Kennedy nor the men he relied on heavily for advice in dealing with the Soviets, notably Bundy, Rusk, Thompson and three former ambassadors to Moscow, Special Assistant to the Secretary of State on Soviet Affairs Charles Bohlen, Ambassador to Yugoslavia George Kennan, and Ambassador at Large Averell Harriman, favored a "summit" meeting as such. Detailed negotiations, in their view, should be conducted at a lower level. But they agreed that a face-to-face, informal meeting between the two heads of state could be valuable. Discussion with the Soviets on the matter continued throughout the spring of 1961, and in early June Kennedy flew to Vienna to confer with his Soviet counterpart.

Rumors to the contrary, the meeting was not a result of Kennedy's embarrassment over the Bay of Pigs, though the Cuban disaster must have influenced each man's mood. It may have helped to make Khrushchev more aggressive and Kennedy less confident. Certainly the mood at the Vienna conference was tense. Although superficially polite, Khrushchev made demands which, had he adhered to them, would have led to a major confrontation over Berlin. Kennedy asked Thompson, "Tommy, is it always like this?" It was "par for the course," the ambassador replied. Kennan, who read the verbatim transcript of the meeting, was disappointed, feeling that Kennedy was "strangely tongue-tied" and had failed to rebut the characteristic Communist exaggerations. Bohlen, who was there, believed that the President conducted himself well in the conversa-

tions but erred in assuming that Khrushchev's positions on issues
were fixed and in getting drawn into an ideological discussion with
his adversary. Kennedy did not lose his sense of humor or his nerve,
as his last words to the Soviet leader, "I see it's going to be a very
cold winter," showed.

Three specific issues dominated their talks: a nuclear test ban,
Laos, and Berlin. On the first two, no understanding was achieved,
although Kennedy did obtain a helpful commitment from Khrushchev to pursue a negotiated settlement in Laos. It was the Soviets'
seemingly irresolute stance on Berlin that most unnerved and upset
the President. Khrushchev adamantly demanded that by the end of
the year a treaty be signed recognizing the permanent existence of a
separate East and West Germany. If the United States and its allies
refused, the Soviets intended to sign one alone with East Germany.
The significance would be that all commitments stemming from
Germany's surrender at the end of World War II would be
terminated. Berlin, Khrushchev added, would become a "free city,"
but the responsibility for access routes—corridors—from Berlin to
West Germany would pass from the Soviets to the "sovereign" East
Germans. Before he left Vienna, Kennedy, in a depressed mood,
pointedly disclosed his dismay at the Soviet attitude to James Reston,
the influential correspondent for the *New York Times*. Reston's
subsequent story revealed the administration's grave concern; although that anxiety was not directly attributed to the President, it
was widely known to have come from him.

On his way to Vienna Kennedy had enjoyed a pleasant and
cordial meeting with de Gaulle in Paris. After the meeting he
stopped briefly in London to confer with Prime Minister Harold
Macmillan, then hurried home to give a televised report to the
American people. His speech was candid and sober. He pointedly
noted that Khrushchev had stressed, and that he had agreed, that not
*all* revolutions were fomented by Communists. But he also warned
that poverty and illiteracy and the absence of hope provided the
Communists with opportunities to exploit. The United States and the
free world, he declared, could not sit idly by; they must use their
resources and talents to foster conditions where freedom could
flourish.

Only briefly did the President refer to Berlin, but he was

preoccupied with that divided city. Nestled over one hundred miles inside East Germany, West Berlin was a persistent source of embarrassment to the Communists. West Berlin and West Germany were much more prosperous than East Germany; they attracted technicians and professionals living in the East; and West Berlin offered an easy escape hatch for East Germans who wanted to flee. West Berlin also provided an invaluable base for propaganda and espionage activities against the Communist-bloc countries.

Kennedy was less concerned about the tangible impact that acceding to Khrushchev's demands and recognizing East Germany would have on West Berlin than he was about the psychological repercussions. West Berlin was a show place for the Western democracies and the prime symbol of their determination to stand firm against Soviet threats. The United States and its allies had successfully frustrated previous Soviet attempts to force them out of West Berlin. They had mounted a massive airlift to supply the city in 1948–49, when the Russians closed ground transportation routes in and out of Berlin. If Khrushchev's bluster won him his way in 1961, the credibility of America's commitment to contain Communism would, in the President's view, be dangerously weakened—not only in Europe but throughout the entire world. Concerned by his loss of prestige because of the Bay of Pigs and worried that at Vienna Khrushchev might have underestimated his resolution to protect Western interests, Kennedy believed that he had no choice but to stand firm on Berlin. To do otherwise, he reasoned, would actually increase the danger of nuclear war by encouraging the Soviets to make new demands.

Exactly how to convince the Soviets not to make any precipitous moves over Berlin that might lead to war puzzled the President. Some of his more bellicose advisers, notably former Secretary of State Acheson, Kennedy's special consultant on Germany and Europe, recommended that the United States immediately mobilize its military forces and declare a national emergency. Such actions, the imperious elder statesman argued, would underline to the Russians and the American public the gravity of the situation. As cutting and irascible as ever, Acheson maintained that there was nothing to negotiate with the Soviets.

Kennedy sensed that Acheson's hard-line, unyielding approach would be an overresponse, but he too believed that Khrushchev had to be persuaded that the United States meant business. When Soviet Ambassador Menshikov reportedly stated that America was neither prepared nor ready to go to war over the divided city, the chief executive coolly assured a press conference that "we intend to honor our commitments." In a gloomy television address to the public in late July, he stunned listeners with his pessimistic analysis of the Berlin situation. The actions he announced at the same time gave bite to his rhetoric. He sharply increased draft calls, activated certain reserve and national guard units, and requested an additional $3.2 billion from Congress to pay for building up the armed forces. Even more unnerving, he raised the spectre of a nuclear holocaust by accelerating efforts to develop a viable Civil Defense program, with special emphasis on providing air raid shelters for use in the event of aerial attack. On the other hand, he refused to declare a national emergency, and he stressed his willingness to negotiate. Ironically, the news media greatly overplayed the militant part of his address, a fact which helped to escalate public alarm.

The Soviets' response was dramatic. On August 13 they erected a wall—first of barbed wire, later of more solid substance—between East and West Berlin, thus stopping free movement between the city's two halves. Kennedy refused to be stampeded into provocative action. After considerable debate, he did agree to send 1,500 American troops by road from West Germany to West Berlin and to dispatch Vice President Johnson to meet the troops upon their arrival as gestures of America's commitment to West Berlin. Khrushchev continued to make blustering statements for a time and ended the three-year Soviet-American moratorium on the testing of nuclear bombs. Kennedy countered in September by resuming underground tests and by trying—unsuccessfully—to reconvene the Geneva Disarmament Conference, which since 1958 had been intermittently attempting to secure an international agreement banning nuclear tests. Despite this renewed danger to the world's safety, no shooting war broke out over Berlin. In mid-October Khrushchev publicly abandoned his year-end deadline for signing a German treaty, and the impasse gradually faded away. The wall, however, did not.

Critics of the President have sharply disputed claims by his admirers that his handling of the Berlin crisis was deft. Jack D.

Schick, who made a detailed analysis of the episode, argued that "West Berlin by itself is not the same symbol—as was all Berlin—of a reunited Germany." By defending West Berlin but acquiescing to the erection of the wall sealing off East Berlin, the United States did not protect vital German and French interests; hence those two countries reasserted their traditional interests, to the detriment of the Atlantic Alliance. Richard J. Walton, on the other hand, attacked Kennedy for approaching the brink of war over Berlin, charging that "there would have been no crisis if Kennedy had done sooner [stress his willingness to negotiate] what he did later." Louise FitzSimons basically agreed, emphasizing the dangerous preoccupation of the New Frontiersmen with protecting "the personal prestige of the President, an enduring theme of the Kennedy administration. . . ."

In truth the President's reactions to international crises in 1961 were neither sure-handed nor particularly brilliant. His failure to stop the abortive Bay of Pigs assault was unfathomable; his handling of the Laos situation almost led to a major commitment of American troops, a move which, in his own words, "would be a hundred times worse" than the Cuban disaster; and hindsight suggests that he overresponded to the Berlin pinch, accepting Khrushchev's rhetoric at face value and, despite his administration's claims to the contrary, not pursuing diplomatic possibilities as energetically as he did military alternatives. Furthermore, the President's call for a vastly enlarged and ultimately discredited Civil Defense program, which he coupled with the Berlin buildup, generated a modest degree of panic and a large measure of confusion, provoking criticism for doing too little or too much. By fall it was, Sorensen informed his chief, "rapidly blossoming into our number one political headache."

Kennedy's policies strongly suggested his fear of losing his ability to lead effectively if he bent too far from the prevailing consensus against the Communist threat, a consensus he shared. The razor-thin margin of his election and the increasingly audible rumble from the political right underscored his apprehension. Being tough in foreign affairs was an effective technique for shutting off right-wing criticism, and, politically, he could afford to do so because the disorganized left and the independent liberals had no alternative but to support his administration. Yet, it is also true that the President held back from following the counsel of some of his more hard-line advisers that might have resulted in even more dangerous results: American air cover for the Cuban invasion, a full-scale ground war in Laos, and a forced military confrontation over Berlin.

Despite his professed desire to inject some fresh thinking into American foreign policy, Kennedy contributed little in the way of new ideas or approaches. During his learning year of 1961, he basically continued his predecessors' policy of doing what was necessary to maintain and protect America's foreign interests and commitments. He made some faulty judgments and risked exacerbating dangerously explosive situations, but he always stopped short of actions that would irreparably unbalance the fragile global status quo. In the revolution-torn Congo, for example, he judiciously followed the lead of the United Nations, resisting pressure from certain interest groups and some congressmen to pursue a more adventurous independent course.

The President also moved with caution on Vietnam, carefully probing for a better understanding of the murky situation. The roots of American concern with Indochina began during the depressing early months of World War II. Expansionist-minded Japan sent troops into the northern half of French Indochina in June 1940, the same month that France surrendered to Germany. Alarmed, the United States invoked stiff economic pressure against the Japanese, but Tokyo refused to withdraw and occupied the rest of the country in July 1941.

Once the war ended, the French returned to their colony. After a half-hearted effort to work out a compromise arrangement for self-government with native forces seeking independence, led by Ho Chi Minh, the French determined to use force to establish their dominance. At first the United States was preoccupied with building defenses against the Communist threat in Europe and showed only mild interest in the Indochina dispute. But in 1949 American concern with Europe and France's war in Indochina became intimately connected. The Truman administration anxiously urged the North Atlantic Treaty Organization (NATO) countries in western Europe to enlarge their military forces and to accept the rapid expansion of West Germany's industrial production in order to counter the threat of Soviet aggression. France refused, contending that because of the demands of the Indochina conflict it could not spend more for defense in Europe nor could it risk the danger of a stronger Germany, a country that had invaded France three times in less than a century. To woo French cooperation, on May 8, 1950 the United States announced its decision to send military aid to France for use in its colonial conflict. Truman assured the American public that the assistance was essential to stop the spread of Communism.

American emphasis in containing Communism gradually began to shift from Europe to Asia. Mao Tse-tung's victory in China and the Korean war unquestionably accentuated the fear, and the Indochina war evoked rhetorical descriptions as the southern part of a comprehensive Red Chinese–Soviet campaign to subdue all of the Far East. Despite more than a billion dollars of American aid, the French position grew increasingly grim in Indochina. Advancing the "domino theory," Eisenhower worried about what would happen in other Southeast Asian countries if Indochina fell to the Communists: "You have a row of dominoes set up. You knock over the first one, and what will happen to the last one is the certainty that it will go over very quickly." Yet, when the French requested direct American military intervention in March 1954 to save their embattled garrison at Dien Bien Phu, Eisenhower refused to commit United States forces to another Asian ground war.

Nevertheless, the United States slowly but surely became ever more deeply enmeshed in Southeast Asia. The humiliating French surrender at Dien Bien Phu on May 7, 1954 led to the Geneva Accords, which neutralized two of the three Indochina states—Laos and Cambodia—and temporarily partitioned Vietnam at the seventeenth parallel. Ho Chi Minh was to command in North Vietnam, while native forces who had supported the French were to govern the South until elections scheduled for 1956 determined a government for the reunified country. The United States participated in the Geneva conference only as an "observer" and did not sign the agreement, though it gave its tacit support. Almost immediately, however, the Eisenhower administration sought to bolster the viability of the new South Vietnamese regime of Premier Ngo Dinh Diem by negotiating the Southeast Asia Treaty Organization (SEATO), which guaranteed the security of Indochina. Shortly afterwards, American military advisers arrived to take over the training of the South Vietnamese army.

When the critical date for reunification elections approached in 1956, Diem, with United States backing, decreed that elections would not be held on the grounds that his country had not signed the Geneva Accords. From this point on Ho Chi Minh's supporters intensified their guerilla warfare in the South, murdering hundreds of Diem's local officials. The South Vietnamese ruler promised extensive social change, including badly needed land reform and an end to the blatantly corrupt practices of the bureaucracy. When he failed to keep his word, large numbers of embittered South Vietnamese joined the Viet Cong guerillas and their political arm, the National Liberation Front. Meanwhile, the Eisenhower administration gradually increased the flow of military advisers and equipment to Diem. By the end of the decade almost one thousand American military men were assisting the Saigon regime.

Despite such help, the Viet Cong continued, during early 1961, to extend its control over the Vietnamese countryside. Trying to determine if Eisenhower's policy could be salvaged, Kennedy read the incoming cables from the American mission there with great care and in April created an interagency task force to examine and refine previous recommendations for military and social reforms. He also appointed a new ambassador, Frederick Nolting, and in May sent Vice President Johnson to Saigon for a firsthand report. The visit was valuable to the Diem regime as a symbol of American support, but Johnson, unfortunately, got carried away, incongruously hailing Diem as the Winston Churchill of South Asia, a hyperbole of ludicrous proportions. Flattered, Diem promised to make vital changes in his operations in order to rally public support. But, as in the past, his pledge was hollow.

By September, the picture in Vietnam looked even grimmer as the Viet Cong continued to rack up victories in the field. With Johnson pushing for a heavier commitment of American troops, Kennedy ordered General Maxwell Taylor and Walt Rostow to visit Saigon and see 'if the situation could be stabilized. Their answer was strongly affirmative, but like the earlier task force report and Johnson's recommendation, they tended to focus overwhelmingly on the military aspects of the problem. They proposed to send in 6,000–8,000 men under the utterly dubious guise of being a "flood control unit." Kennedy flatly refused. He told Schlesinger, "The troops will march in; the bands will play; the crowds will cheer; and in four days everyone will have forgotten. Then we will be told we have to send more troops. It's like taking a drink. The effect wears off, and you have to take another." Perhaps remembering his embarrassment at the Bay of Pigs, the President cautiously chose a much less dramatic plan—a major increase in the number of American "advisers." It was hoped that they could put some steel into the efforts of the South Vietnamese to defend themselves and fill some of the void created by Diem's inept and uninspiring leadership. By early January 1962 more than 2,600 American military men were in South Vietnam. In addition Navy minesweepers patrolled the Vietnamese coast and Air Force planes flew surveillance and reconnaissance missions. In essence, Kennedy only continued Eisenhower's policy of doing the minimum to prevent a Communist victory. The President carefully avoided a specific open-ended commitment of support to Diem, but he never questioned the basic premises of his predecessor. Nor did he tie American military aid unequivocally to political and social reform in South Vietnam.

As 1961 ended, the United States remained at peace and the cold war consensus continued to hold. Still, Kennedy did not delude himself that he had been a smashing success diplomatically. When a reporter told him that he wanted to write a book about the President's first year in office, Kennedy responded by asking, "Who would want to read a book about disasters?"

# IV

## Ambivalence
### and Action

DURING 1961 and on into 1962, Kennedy often seemed indecisive and uncertain. His first two years constituted a period of intensive learning, and at times his actions reflected his lack of administrative and executive experience. Only gradually did he begin to feel comfortable with the awesome powers and responsibilities of the nation's highest office. Worried about his characterization as a "power-hungry young careerist" and about the narrowness of his election, he sought to win the nation's confidence by avoiding premature battles over partisan issues. By following the politics of consensus instead of the politics of conflict, JFK hoped to reassure the public that he was, as he honestly believed himself to be, a person who generally saw reason on both sides of complex issues. A moderate by temperament, he moved cautiously on controversial, emotional questions, prompting complaints that he cared more for "image" than substance.

All chief executives are image-conscious, but in Kennedy's case the concern often seemed excessive. His unusually warm rapport with most newsmen made the task of cultivating favorable publicity relatively easy. Even more important, his administration raised the skill of deliberate news management to a fine art. Allusions by friends and foes alike to the New Frontier as a modern-day Camelot—the legendary kingdom of King Arthur—added an aura of romance to the Kennedy image. As the veteran journalist I. F. Stone seriously wrote in 1963, "the atmosphere of Washington . . . is like that of a reigning monarch's court."

Nevertheless, the President frequently ignored protocol and stressed naturalness. His low-key wit was an invaluable ally. Sailing with Prime Minister Nehru of India, Kennedy pointed towards several huge mansions of an older era and quipped, "I wanted you to see how the average American family lives." He broke through the chilly reserve of Canadian Prime Minister Lester Pearson by summoning David Powers, renowned for his knowledge of baseball records, to test the Canadian's equally celebrated memory of diamond trivia. Kennedy listened silently while the two men bantered back and forth, then told Powers, "He'll do." From that point on the two national leaders got along famously. The President's dislike of stuffiness did not, however, extend to how his aides dressed for work. Button-down shirts were out, and he frowned on loud colors. As if to underline the serious nature of their roles as public servants, Kennedy men were expected to be neat and conservatively groomed.

Off duty, the New Frontiersmen played with the same hard-driving enthusiasm that they displayed in their jobs. The sports-loving President made physical-fitness activities a mark of social distinction. After reading a letter President Theodore Roosevelt had written in 1908 to the commander of the Marine Corps suggesting that Marine officers should periodically hike fifty miles to prove their fitness, Kennedy suggested that his aides do the same. (Press Secretary Pierre Salinger demurred, explaining to newsmen that while he might be plucky, he was not stupid.) At one point JFK asked his entire staff to lose five pounds each.

The Kennedy group—lavishly described by one dazzled writer as the "richest, prettiest, most interesting" young people in the country—generated a wave of excitement socially. The success of Washington events was measured by how many of the glamorous top-ranking New Frontiersmen attended. For the first time in many years the capital social scene was dominated by White House entertaining rather than by the parties given by such celebrated Washington hostesses as Perle Mesta and Gwen Cafritz, with the lively gatherings at Bobby Kennedy's Hickory Hill estate a close second in interest.

The President and his wife made the White House a showplace of refinement and elegance. Jacqueline Kennedy sought to preserve the historical greatness of the mansion by restoring many rooms to the way they had looked under various past chief executives. Performances by talented artists, such as cellist Pablo Casals, Shakespearean actor Ralph Richardson, and composer Igor Stravinsky, highlighted many state dinners. By honoring persons of creative achievement, the Kennedys endeavored to call national and world attention to America's cultural and intellectual accomplishments. JFK followed rather than led his wife's cultural tastes, but he appreciated talent even in fields where he possessed no real knowledge. Hosting a dinner of American Nobel Prize winners, he told his guests, "This is the most extraordinary collection of talent . . . that has ever been gathered together at the White House—with the possible exception of when Thomas Jefferson dined alone." Significantly, although some cynics sneered that the popularization of high culture would inevitably lead to its vulgarization, Kennedy firmly rejected the idea that culture and democracy were irreconcilable.

To many critics, the chief executive's preoccupation with "image" spilled over into too many areas. The space program was a case in point. Early in his second year in office the administration and the United States received a solid boost in prestige when astronaut John Glenn became the first American to circle the globe while in outer space. His accomplishment elated the President, as it did Congress and the public, who watched Glenn's triumphant launch and landing on television. Significantly, his feat gave credibility to the President's pledge to land a man on the moon before 1970.

Kennedy's bold commitment stemmed directly from the damage done to America's reputation as the world's leader in science and technology in 1957 when the Soviet Union sent an unmanned "Sputnik" into outer space. Fear—bordering occasionally on panic— that the Russians would convert their knowledge into military weapons capable of destroying the United States severely undermined Eisenhower's credibility as a master of military matters. The "missile gap" controversy was but one of the offshoots of the Soviet success. The Russians maintained their advantage for several years, orbiting two men for much longer periods before Glenn's flight occurred.

Kennedy was determined that the United States should not be

content with being second best in space exploration. In May 1961, shortly after Alan Shepard rocketed a modest 300 miles in suborbital flight, the President seized upon the excitement generated by Shepard's venture to announce his goals for the American space program. The ability to land and return a man safely from the moon was clearly paramount. "No single project in this period," he declared, "will be more impressive to mankind, or more important for the long-range exploration of space; and none will be more difficult or expensive to accomplish."

Not all scientists agreed with the emphasis on manned flights. The early American satellites launched in 1958, although tiny in size, had produced a bonanza of scientific knowledge. The very first had discovered the Van Allen radiation belts, a part of the magneto-sphere that surrounds the earth. The cost of the small, unmanned satellites was minimal compared to the expense of sending men into orbit. Still, as William L. O'Neill put it, "science had been a hitchhiker in the early space probes." The emphasis was on engineering feats capable of first catching up with and then surpassing the Soviets' ability to launch much heavier payloads into the outer atmosphere. The Soviets clearly possessed rockets with much greater thrust. In the ability to gather raw scientific data from space, however, the United States was behind little if at all.

But the manned flights, the "space spectaculars," viewed over television and cast as a competition with the Russians were far more glamorous. The first astronauts were bona fide heroes at a time when heroes were still in vogue. The estimated cost of $20 billion for putting a man on the moon was immense, but the competitive feature appealed so much to Congress and to the public that the legislators were willing to vote the money. The National Aeronautics and Space Administration (NASA) went first class. Its space center, located at Houston, in Vice President Johnson's state, after a celebrated search for the "best" location, was virtually a monument. The President wisely urged Budget Director David Bell to scrutinize the costs carefully: "This program has so much public support that unless there is some restraint there is a possibility of wasting some money."

Meanwhile, the much less expensive unmanned satellites con-tinued to produce highly valuable information. A Mariner 2 passed within 21,000 miles of Venus, radioing data back to Earth, and the commercially developed Telstar satellite made it possible to transmit television images all over the world. However, NASA Director James E. Webb, a wizard at public relations, consistently stressed that the manned lunar landing program should have top priority, and the President agreed. "Unless we are prepared to do the work and bear the burdens to make it successful," he told Congress, "there is no sense in going ahead."

In 1969 the United States achieved Kennedy's goal of putting a man on the moon. But the verdict is not conclusive as to the benefits gained. It is possible that the money (more than $25 billion; well over the estimates during Kennedy's time) could have been spent better for more mundane projects. Scientifically oriented unmanned space probes might have produced more useful knowledge at a fraction of the expense. But to Kennedy, as Sorensen explained, the space race was symbolic. American prestige was at stake, and this consideration dominated his policies in space as well as in other areas.

Spending for the space program provided a valuable plus for the economy. Although Kennedy did not emphasize the security aspects involved in a moon-shot, the desire to beat the Russians triggered the same favorable response in Congress as requests for increased defense spending. Few legislators dared to vote against funds to be used for national security, and defense and space needs consumed well over half the annual budget during the Kennedy years. In some instances entire industries, as well as individual companies, operated mainly for one customer—the federal government. Since the federal establishment provided the funds, in effect it became the innovator and risk-taker, while the companies reaped comfortable, though usually not excessive, profits. In addition, through government-sponsored research projects the firms gained sophisticated technological knowledge that could be converted into commercial use.

Most federal money, both for research and for production, went to a relatively few large corporations. Attempts to spread the flow of funds, especially to small companies, were only mildly successful. The fact was and is that only a relative handful of firms possess the technological expertise and systems competence to handle the demands of highly sophisticated defense or space projects. Appreciating the benefits of lucrative government contracts, major defense and space suppliers carefully cultivated good relations with Washington. Many companies hired retired high-ranking military officers whose contacts with defense officials could be useful. Despite the efforts of the cost-conscious Secretary of Defense, Robert McNamara, most contracts were negotiated, not let by competitive bidding. The former method involved cost-plus-fixed-fee agreements, which offered little or no incentive to reduce expenses.

Firms that lost lucrative contracts often complained bitterly and charged that politics dictated their failure to receive the award. McNamara's selection of General Dynamics Corporation instead of Boeing to develop and build the billion-dollar TFX aircraft led to extensive congressional hearings. The Secretary boldly reversed the judgment of military officers who wanted two separate models, one for Air Force use, the other for carrier-based Navy pilots. He chose to satisfy, but not exceed, the essential requirements for a plane that both services had agreed on and refused to accept the argument that a bi-service program was not feasible. As he explained to a congressional committee, he was not buying the "best." Rather, he declared, "we should buy only what we need . . . ." °

McNamara's persistent attempts to cut waste in defense activities frequently brought him into conflict with the armed services as well as military suppliers and occasionally congressmen. His creation of a single Defense Supply Agency to eliminate costly duplicate purchasing by the separate branches of the military produced substantial results, but his efforts to close or reduce nonessential military installations were often frustrated by political considerations. On balance the New Frontiersmen managed to increase marginally federal control of the expensive defense and space operations, but the "military-industrial complex"—the conjunction of an immense military program and a large arms industry—which Eisenhower had warned about in his farewell presidential address, continued to fare handsomely during the Kennedy administration.

Business generally had regarded Kennedy's election with some suspicion but no real alarm. His reliance on liberal advisers caused

---

° The TFX, later dubbed the F-111, proved to be a costly failure. Plagued by operational difficulties, the aircraft fell far short of meeting McNamara's optimistic expectations.

some worry, but his appointment of men like McNamara, Dillon, and Hodges to positions that would directly affect fiscal policy was received with favor and relief. Many business executives anticipated, incorrectly as it turned out, that the President's conservatively oriented father would influence his son's attitude. There was also widespread belief that his narrow margin of victory would temper any inclinations he might have to pursue heavy spending programs. Corporate officials engaged in defense and space contracting were optimistic, since Kennedy had urged a buildup in these areas.

By the end of JFK's first year in the White House, business spokesmen were becoming frostier in their attitude toward the administration. Although they were pleased with the end of the mild recession that existed when Kennedy took office, some of his early actions disturbed them. Business executives responded coolly to the President's call for business groups to establish "codes of ethical practices." Secretary of Commerce Luther Hodges's attempt to change modestly the ground rules that governed relationships between his department and the Business Advisory Council (BAC), an exclusive and self-perpetuating organization of blue-ribbon corporate executives that had extended advice to the government since 1933, provoked a much sharper reaction. The BAC voted to reconstitute itself into the Business Council and end its old relationship with the Commerce Department. It assured the President that it would be available to assist any government agency that requested help, but it pointedly declared that it would operate independently.

Some of the President's initial legislative requests, especially the change in the minimum wage law and his desire to eliminate tax-deferred privileges on income earned by American firms operating in developed countries, rankled various business groups. So did his proposal to restrict deductible expense accounts. Yet in two of the most sensitive areas of business-government relations—antitrust and labor—Kennedy did little or nothing to justify any serious business alarm. Neither he nor his brother the Attorney-General evidenced much interest in an aggressive campaign against big business. And although he had enjoyed strong support from organized labor during his campaign, he seldom used his office in a way calculated to disturb the existing labor-management balance. He did attempt to raise the prestige of labor by inviting union leaders to the White House and by appointing more of them to top-level government advisory committees. But significantly, he requested no new labor legislation. Nevertheless, relations between the administration and the nonmonolithic business communities deteriorated during 1961, and the President knew it. When the momentum of recovery waned during the winter months, the situation became even more difficult.

A slumping stock market during early 1962 further aggravated the uneasy feeling about the state of the economy. Then on April 10, 1962, Roger M. Blough, president of United States Steel, the giant of the industry, called on Kennedy. Blough informed the chief executive that his firm was increasing its prices six dollars per ton across the board. When seven large steel manufacturers followed suit, a furious Kennedy publicly denounced the price increase as "a wholly unjustifiable and irresponsible defiance of the public interest." Privately, he made his celebrated statement, "My father once told me that all steelmen were sons of bitches, and I did not realize until now how right he was." His crack, leaked to the public as "all businessmen" instead of "all steelmen," caused an immediate furor in the business communities. Ironically, Blough's action coincided with the annual White House reception for congressmen and their wives. The year before, the event had occurred at the time of the disastrous landing at the Bay of Pigs. "I'll never hold another congressional reception," the harassed President remarked.

Kennedy reacted so angrily to the price increase in part because he felt that Blough, by handing him a mimeographed statement already released to the press, was directly challenging him and his office. It smacked of an arrogant attitude towards the Presidency and represented a threat to all of his administration's economic programs. Only days before Blough's surprise visit, the industry and the United Steelworkers of America had concluded a new contract, three months before the old one expired. The agreement was estimated to cost the companies only 2.5 percent, a figure well within the limits of productivity gains by the industry and hence deemed by the Council of Economic Advisers to be noninflationary and too small to justify raising prices. When United States Steel acted to the contrary, the administration quickly decided to challenge the increase.

Using a "fact book" on steel compiled by the Council of Economic Advisers, government officials privately called acquaintances holding executive positions or directorships with the steel companies and made public statements condemning the action. McNamara directed defense contractors to buy steel from manufacturers who did not raise prices. The Justice Department subpoenaed documents relating to the increase. Democratic congressmen joined in by threatening investigations and possible legislation to protect the public interest. The President and his advisers considered even stronger steps—holding off the issuing of new depreciation schedules that would give tax benefits to the steel firms, possible antitrust action, establishing a presidential fact-finding panel, encouraging proxy fights for new directors, and asking for emergency legislation to roll back the prices. Hints of such possibilities were appropriately "leaked" to the press.

To the relief of the administration, none of the stronger, and politically risky, actions became necessary. Inland, Kaiser, and Armco—key members of the steel industry—decided to maintain prices. Their decisions started a chain reaction of companies rescinding the price increases, culminating on April 12, when US Steel announced that it too would roll back its prices to their previous level.

Although no one can be sure whether it was market pressure or government pressure that forced the companies to drop their plans to raise prices, the impact of the episode was profound: it significantly damaged the already frayed relations between business and the Kennedy administration. Many business executives questioned the wisdom or necessity of the steelmen's action, but most defended the right of company officers to raise prices when in their judgment such a move was necessary to assure adequate profits. The administration's response seemed heavy handed and coercive, and it badly frightened free enterprisers. To many businessmen, Kennedy's "SOB" remark reflected an attitude that worried them. So did the use of the FBI, whose agents imprudently called one individual for information in the middle of the night. Rumors of antitrust action or tax penalties against the steel companies alarmed business leaders even more. A *Business Week* survey of executives found that the general mood among the business communities was that the "damage is irreparable." Within a short time, buttons emblazoned with "S.O.B."—Sons of Business or Save Our Business—began to appear. Business cards, bumper stickers, and sly jokes mixed wit and venom to attack the New Frontier.

While some of Kennedy's advisers quietly continued to ponder ways to cope with the longer-range price problems in steel, JFK attempted to refute charges that he had engaged in a "brutal exercise" of presidential power during the crisis. Speaking to the annual meeting of the United States Chamber of Commerce in late April, he reminded his listeners that since government relied heavily on business earnings for its revenues, it could not afford to create an atmosphere that penalized profits. And he urged the executives to work with the government to develop a climate of "understanding and cooperation."

Plummeting stock prices, however, compounded the administration's problems with business. After reaching a record high in late December 1961, the market slid gradually downward. The decline accelerated in April, became even more severe in May, and climaxed on May 28, when a wave of selling produced the sharpest drop in stock values in one day since October 29, 1929, the infamous Black Tuesday. Wall Street wags cracked, "When Eisenhower had a heart attack, the market broke . . . if Kennedy would have a heart attack, the market would go up."

Fair-minded stock analysts admitted that the ingredients for a bearish market had existed for some time. Stock prices had risen to an artificially high level in anticipation of continuing inflation despite depressed corporate earnings during the recession of 1960–61. As a result, prices, relative to earnings, were overvalued. The leveling out of inflation in 1961–62, for which the New Frontier gladly took credit, contributed significantly to the decline in prices.

Although Sorensen and others heatedly denied, and indeed strongly resented, charges that the President had "overused" his power in the steel episode and hence had caused the market slump, the administration worried over the situation as the price indexes continued to fall. During May the CEA produced numerous position papers suggesting possible government steps to bolster the market, citing the overall strength of the economy and noting the differences between 1929 and 1962. Council Chairman Walter Heller assured his chief that the New Frontier was not to blame. But as he added in one memo, "I'd feel better if the market were going up."

The executive actions taken during the steel episode certainly seem to have provided the extra momentum for the already falling stock prices. Although the public resented the steel price increases, many Americans also regarded the President's subsequent blows on behalf of the national interest as being delivered with a heavy bludgeon rather than a deft rapier. Investing in the market involves irrational as well as rational judgments. Confidence, while unmeasurable, is one of the critical intangibles for investors, and, rightly or wrongly, it was shaken by Kennedy's performance.

Although some businessmen were convinced to the contrary, the President at no point entertained any intention of launching an all-out attack against them. He firmly believed that he could not attain his foreign and domestic goals without the cooperation of the powerful corporations that dominated the American economy. Sorensen warned him that "No Democratic President—in fact, no President in either party who believes in progress, promoting the public interest and a strong Presidency—can offer *any* program that will not be opposed by one or more vocal business groups; nor would withdrawing *most* of our program (or our enforcement of existing programs) be sufficient to satisfy *most* business critics." Kennedy realized that the problems involved in wooing business would be large, but he intended to try, and even Sorensen agreed that it might be desirable at least to attempt to soften business antagonism.

The chief executive focused directly on the tension between his administration and business in an impressive speech at Yale University in mid-June. In his address—described by Heller as "the most literate and sophisticated dissertation on economics ever delivered by a president"—Kennedy spoke candidly about business confidence. The economic slumps in 1929, 1954, 1958, and 1960, he noted, occurred when business had full confidence in the administration in power. What was needed, he declared, was a serious dialogue between business and government that would produce useful collaboration in promoting economic progress. It was time to stop the trend toward meeting present problems with old clichés, "before it lands us all in a bog of sterile acrimony."

Big business, especially, appreciated the benefits it enjoyed from

a congenial working arrangement with big government and welcomed the administration's overtures at reconciliation. Influential
business leaders, including Blough of US Steel, worked to temper,
not exacerbate irrational hostility towards Kennedy. On the other
hand, as Heller informed JFK in mid-July, after a meeting with the
members of the Business Council, "they consistently wanted the
President to act like a conservative Republican."

In the next few months, the New Frontier backed up its words of
friendship with deeds. Liberalized depreciation allowances and an
investment tax credit provided valuable incentives for firms to
modernize plants and equipment; lower margin requirements for
buying stock on credit helped stimulate activity on the securities
markets; a new trade bill—Kennedy's major legislative triumph in
1962—offered the prospect of lower world tariffs and increased
American exports. In addition, the President supported drug legislation in a weakened form palatable to the drug industry and backed a
communications satellite bill that allowed private firms to participate, rather than making the "Comsat" venture exclusively a
government-owned program.

In April 1963, when the steel companies again raised prices, they
shrewdly chose to do so "selectively," not by an across-the-board
price boost. The presidential response was decidedly different from
what it had been a year before. He announced that he was watching
the situation with great interest and declared his continued opposition to a blanket price increase. But he understood, he added, the
necessity for selected price adjustments. Kennedy obviously had no
wish to resume the battle with the steelmakers. Cynics chortled that
the "President had learned his lesson," but Sorensen credited JFK's
mild reaction to the fact that in 1963 there was "no affront to his
office and no abuse of his good faith." A little of both factors was
likely involved, but so was Heller's judgment, expressed in a
summary memo of the steel situation, that Big Steel exercised
restraint in raising prices. Regarding the inflationary impact of the
price increases, he concluded that "In short we have come off well,
but not unscathed." When additional selective price increases in
steel followed during the early fall, the CEA chairman again
hesitated to urge any drastic action by the President. "Government-
business relations are better than in a long time; any condemnation

of steel or intimation of possible 'future price crackdowns,' could,"
he explained, "impair confidence, with possibly bad economic and
political effects." He recommended, and the President agreed,
treating the situation in a low-key fashion.

The danger of the September price increases, as Heller unhappily realized, was that they could not be justified under the
wage-price guideposts, the core of the New Frontier's program to
prevent inflation. Announced in the January 1962 *Annual Report* of
the Council of Economic Advisers, the guideposts insisted that while
free collective bargaining between management and labor was the
proper vehicle for settling industrial disputes, wage and price
determinations should be tied to productivity advances in order to be
noninflationary.°

Neither the unions nor management expressed much enthusiasm
for the guidelines concept. Labor maintained that they unfairly
limited wage increases while rising prices and corporate profits more
than absorbed the fruits of greater productivity. Management
complained that the government was inclined to accept excessive
settlements while using the standards to restrict price advances in
conspicuous industries like steel. The primary weapon that the
Kennedyites wielded to enforce the guidelines was "jawboning"
(rhetorical persuasion) although the 1962 steel episode showed that
more coercive methods could be employed if the government were
willing to risk charges of dictatorial tactics. The guidelines worked
relatively well for Kennedy. Under the New Frontier the rate of
inflation was considerably less than during the Eisenhower administration. After 1966, however, when sharply increased spending for
the Vietnam war unleashed strong inflationary pressures, they
functioned much less effectively.

Stable prices helped to provide a climate of stability highly

----

° The following is a simplified example of a noninflationary productivity
increase: If 1,000 automobiles were produced in one year at a total cost of $2,500,000,
and the next year 1,025 cars could be manufactured at the same total cost, the
productivity increase would be 2½ percent. Consequently, the firm could raise the
wages of employees by 2½ percent, sell the cars to customers at the same price, and
still make the same profit. Although the Kennedy Council of Economic Advisers
prescribed no specific percentage for acceptable wage increases, the 3 percent average
increase in overall industrial productivity between 1947 and 1960 was generally
accepted as the allowable standard.

valued by business. Corporate profits began to rise impressively during the last half of 1962, and the stockmarket, after bottoming in late June, rallied strongly. During 1963, both edged toward record highs, and the Kennedy administration's popularity among the business communities rose with them. Businessmen began to realize that, as one financial columnist wrote, "To accuse Mr. Kennedy of being anti-business is almost akin to accusing Senator Goldwater of being pro-Communist." Neither the President nor business executives ever felt particularly comfortable with one another, but they recognized that a *quid pro quo* arrangement was valuable for each.

One policy of Kennedy's that business swung behind with slowly mounting enthusiasm was his decision to cut taxes in order to stimulate economic growth. As explained previously, Heller had urged him to do so during 1961, but he had refused. At the time of the stockmarket crash in 1962, Heller and the Council of Economic Advisers, along with nongovernment economists like Samuelson and Robert Solow, again pushed relentlessly for lower taxes to reduce "fiscal drag." Sensitive to recurring complaints that he was a reckless spender, it was difficult for JFK to accept the idea of a deliberately incurred federal deficit, an inevitable result of the loss of tax revenues. But he was at least equally stung by charges that he had done little to reduce the still unacceptably high rate of unemployment or to help the poor. There were several alternatives available for creating jobs and fostering prosperity. One was, as John Kenneth Galbraith argued, a massive federal spending program. Another, favored by Labor Department officials and others, was to attack "structural" problems in unemployment, those caused by technological advances that displaced workers. Conservatives meanwhile promoted the traditional concept that decreased government spending and a balanced budget would build business confidence and generate private investments that would create jobs.

None of the alternatives, however, promised to contribute as much to a faster growth rate as did the Keynesian-oriented approach advocated by Heller and the CEA. Their arguments convinced Kennedy to ask Congress to reduce taxes. Cold war considerations were important. The President feared that unless the United States increased its rate of growth it would be unable to maintain its position of dominance in its economic rivalry with the Soviet Union.

Although initially, reducing taxes would cause a larger federal deficit, it was hoped that by lessening the heavy drag on private purchasing power, initiative, and incentive, the tax cut would stimulate prosperity enough to produce subsequent larger taxable incomes and budget surpluses. Concern over unemployment was even more critical to Kennedy's decision. His adoption of the Heller strategy signaled a significant shift in goals, from budget balance each year or even over the business cycle, to balance at full employment.

The question of timing—when to ask the legislators for the tax cut—became the President's next problem. In August, Heller argued the quicker the better: "Five years of economic slack plus a 1962 slowdown that may turn into a recession are ample reasons for acting now." But Wilbur Mills, the Arkansas Democrat who wielded awesome power as chairman of the House Ways and Means Committee, and other congressmen showed little enthusiasm for a "quickie" tax cut. As a result, later in the month Kennedy told the public that he would wait until the following year to recommend a full-scale reform bill with major reductions in both corporate and personal income taxes.

The plan he submitted in January 1963 provided for cuts of $13.6 billion—$11 billion for individuals, the rest for corporations— plus partial or full closings of flagrant tax loopholes, which were expected to produce a gain in revenue of $3.4 billion, leaving a net reduction of $10.2 billion. Somewhat surprisingly, a cautious majority of the American public at first opposed tax reductions that would increase the national debt through a budget deficit. Heller's unpolitic remark before a congressional committee, blaming the attitude on "the basic Puritan ethic," added to the difficulties of winning popular support. During his first two years in the White House Kennedy often seemed reluctant to fight energetically for his legislative program, but in 1963 he was willing to use the Presidency as a "bully pulpit." Gradually, he began to gather friends for the tax cut. The bill remained unpassed and in doubt at the time of his death, but Kennedy had, nevertheless, helped significantly to educate the public about the merits of the "new economics." Although hardly new or novel, Kennedy's tax plan, subsequently enacted under Johnson, stimulated the longest continuous boom in American history.

During his last year in office, Kennedy also became much more involved in the civil rights struggle. Even so, he did so largely in response to events beyond his control. In 1962, as in 1961, he had refused to make civil rights a focal point of his administration. The Justice Department functioned more actively to enforce the voting rights of southern blacks than it had under Eisenhower, and the President symbolically continued to bolster the morale of blacks, but his inherent moderation and his reading of congressional attitudes caused him to hold back from committing his administration fully. Shortly after becoming President, Kennedy had publicly stated his position about civil rights legislation: "When I feel that there is a necessity for congressional action, with a chance of getting the congressional action, then I will recommend it to the Congress."

While Kennedy vacillated in the White House, southern Negroes, especially the young, stepped up their pressure against segregation and discrimination. Impatient with white leadership, black direct-actionists moved aggressively to take charge of their movement. Loren Miller bluntly delivered their message: "To liberals a fond farewell, with thanks for services rendered, until you are ready to re-enlist as foot soldiers and subordinates in a Negro-led, Negro-officered army under the banner of Freedom Now."

Although the majority of Negroes then still favored equality through integration, some, notably the Black Muslims, argued for parity with whites through segregation. Their views, flamboyantly expressed by the charismatic Malcolm X, were not popular in the segregationist South, since they argued that much of the southern United States should be given to Negroes in payment for their hundreds of years of work as exploited laborers. Malcolm X's statements, widely publicized in the media, were harsh, offending, and frightening to whites. He said out loud what millions of Negroes thought privately, and he helped to raise their pride in being black. Yet, only a relative handful joined the Muslims. Most preferred to follow the nonviolent, integration-oriented groups, such as Martin Luther King's Southern Christian Leadership Conference, SNCC, CORE, or the NAACP.

Virtually all the civil rights activism at the time centered in the South, and there even the modest efforts of the Kennedy administration to enforce voting rights or protect demonstrators caused the

President's popularity to decline. It plummeted much more sharply in 1962 when the New Frontier became embroiled in the attempt of a Negro Air Force veteran, James H. Meredith, to attend the lily-white University of Mississippi. Governor Ross Barnett, an unreconstructed racist, declared that Meredith would not be allowed to enroll, despite a federal court ruling to the contrary. At one point the governor, who Mississippi newspaper editor Hodding Carter, Jr., accused of deliberately trying to foment civil strife between whites and blacks, personally blocked Meredith's entry into the college board offices. After numerous fruitless telephone conversations with Barnett, Kennedy decided to act. He called the Mississippi National Guard to federal service, dispatched Army troops to nearby Memphis, Tennessee, and sent Deputy Attorney General Nicholas Katzenbach and federal marshals to assist Meredith in registering for classes.

The scene that followed was ugly. Students and sympathetic supporters attempted to drive the marshals out of the university's administration center. Leading the mob was a bizarre retired Army general, Edwin Walker, who had recently left the service after being reprimanded by the Kennedy administration for indoctrinating his troops with right-wing propaganda. Standing on the pedestal of a Confederate monument, Walker harangued the crowd with shouts of "Protest! Protest! Keep it up!" Although he insisted that he did not advocate violence, Walker declared that he would give the mob his "moral support" by leading their march against the federal marshals. Someone in the throng attempted to ram a bulldozer through the main door of the administration building. The bulldozer stalled, but the students systematically began to burn and wreck the trucks and station wagons used to transport the marshals to the campus. Ironically, 200 Mississippi troopers stood idly by while the riot developed. The trapped federal officials retaliated by firing a barrage of tear gas to drive the rioters back. The chaos lasted for fifteen hours before 5,000 soldiers and federalized National Guardsmen could be summoned to restore order. By then, two men were dead from gunfire, and hundreds of others were injured.

Southerners, predictably, bitterly resented the President's handling of the Meredith affair. At first he tried, as Sorensen urged, to make the defiance by Mississippi authorities "be against the majesty of the United States, not John F. Kennedy." But Barnett's unyielding refusal to obey a federal court decree to admit Meredith and his deliberate failure to use his state's law enforcement personnel to maintain order constituted a direct challenge not only to the law but also to the President personally. In the end Kennedy had little choice but to use federal troops. But he also hastened to try to heal the wounds created, resisting recommendations to "punish" Mississippi by cutting off federal funds and urging that Barnett be fined for resisting the court order, not turned into a martyr by imprisonment.

Meredith remained at Mississippi until he graduated, his safety protected by a dwindling number of troops and marshals. University students and faculty who extended a hand of welcome or who called for moderation were slandered, intimidated, and threatened. Though the pressure on him was intense, Meredith's gutty performance, backed up by the willingness of the Kennedy administration to insure his rights, represented a small but significant opening in what Professor James Silver, the Mississippi historian, described as "the closed society."

Early in the next year, prodded by the introduction of a civil rights bill by House Republicans and by the growing agitation from civil rights groups, Kennedy decided it was at last time to ask Congress for legislative action. Even so, the measure he presented in late February 1963 was exceedingly modest in scope, mainly providing for a speedup in the prosecution of voting cases and authorizing federal funds for school districts beginning integration. What happened during the next few months pulled Kennedy for the first time into the mainstream of the civil rights movement. The center of activity for racial controversy shifted to Alabama, where in late 1955 Martin Luther King, Jr., had launched his nonviolent campaign for equal rights. Sparked by the charismatic leadership of the articulate Baptist minister, blacks in Montgomery had staged a highly successful boycott of Montgomery buses to protest discriminatory seating practices. Having seen what massive protests could accomplish, in 1960 black activists began a series of "sit-ins" in countless southern facilities to force an end to segregation.

In April 1963, King and his Southern Christian Leadership Conference decided to concentrate on Birmingham. In an effort to eliminate segregation in snack bars, rest rooms, and retail stores and to abolish discriminatory hiring practices for such jobs as salesgirls and secretaries, King joined the local leader, Reverend Fred Shuttlesworth, in mounting massive demonstrations. Police commissioner Eugene "Bull" Connor countered by unleashing snarling police dogs and using high-pressure hoses and electric cattle prods against marchers. Recounted in detail by newspapers and shown on television around the world, Birmingham became a painful eyesore and moral canker for the United States. Although the local Negro community had been far from united when the protests in their city began, the police brutality jarred the passivity of the ghetto dwellers. Despite King's pleas for nonviolence, rioting and fire bombing turned Birmingham into a near battlefield. Yet, when Negro leaders and white businessmen worked out a compromise agreement, the mayor called the white negotiators "a bunch of quisling, gutless traitors." On May 10 Governor George C. Wallace announced his refusal to "be a party to any such meeting to compromise the issues of segregation." Two days later bombs exploded at the motel where King had been staying and at his brother's home, rudely shattering the uneasy truce.

The sickening events in Alabama shocked and upset Kennedy. He dispatched federal troops to nearby positions and made ready to federalize the National Guard if needed, but he emphasized that he would act only if state and local law enforcement failed. Meanwhile, the Justice Department worked diligently to secure an agreement between the two sides. As they had done in Mississippi at the time of the Meredith episode, Department officials systematically contacted business and civic leaders in Alabama, pressuring them to use their influence to "cool" the situation and allow reason to prevail. Yet little reason was displayed. Governor Wallace, a cocky former prizefighter who had transferred his pugnaciousness into the political arena and who belligerently declared his commitment to segregation "today, tomorrow, and forever," created his own disturbance. In early June he defied a federal court order by personally blocking the door to prevent two Negroes from registering at the University of Alabama, the last nonintegrated major university in the country. Kennedy quickly responded by ordering the state National Guard into federal service. After making his dramatic gesture, Wallace coolly stepped aside, and the students enrolled.

Passions in Birmingham subsided slowly. They flared up again in September when a bomb killed four black children at Sunday school. The nation was horrified. As was typical of such incidents in the Deep South, the killers were never brought to justice. King and his associates won only limited tangible gains from their demonstrations and boycotts in Birmingham. But their energy and blood were not expended in vain. As Eric Sevareid wrote, "A newspaper or television picture of a snarling police dog set upon a human being is recorded in the permanent photo-electric file of every human brain." He was right, and more Americans than ever began to realize the indignities and inhumanities heaped daily upon Negroes. A wave of moral outrage swept the country.

Ironically, the actions of the Birmingham authorities were perfectly legal. Negroes had no federally guaranteed right to eat in the lunch counters, work in stores, or even demonstrate peacefully in the streets. Just as during the Reconstruction, protection or extension of political and legal rights initially dominated efforts to aid blacks. But by 1963, a great many media, civil, and religious spokesmen were demanding that Congress act to provide social and economic rights as well. A caucus of Republican senators agreed. Hurrying to catch up with public sentiment, JFK decided by the end of May that the time for bold legislation had arrived. Speaking to the nation on the evening of the crisis at the University of Alabama, he delivered an emotional plea for "the nation to fulfill its promise." Emphasizing the moral issues involved, he declared, "We preach freedom around the world, and we mean it, and we cherish freedom here at home, but are we to say to the world, and much more importantly, to each other that this is a land of the free except for the Negroes; that we have no second-class citizens except Negroes; that we have no class or caste system, no ghettos, no master race except with respect to Negroes?"

A week later, as he had promised, Kennedy sent his new civil rights proposal to Congress. Vastly broader in scope than the one he had submitted three months earlier, it still fell far short of his rhetorical commitment. Although the President agreed to include a provision to cut off federal aid to institutions practicing discrimination, he wanted such action to be at the discretion of the executive branch and not mandatory. As NAACP leader Roy Wilkins observed about the Kennedy administration, in matters of economic leverage, the President and his advisers "ran away from it like it was a rattlesnake." The critical section of the bill dealing with Negroes' rights to service in public accommodations was watered down to include only enterprises having a "substantial" effect on interstate commerce. Fair-employment practices were omitted from the measure, although Kennedy compromised by endorsing legislation already pending. Furthermore, no stronger voting rights proposals were included.

On the other hand, the bill gave the Attorney General power to seek desegregation of public education on his own initiative when a lack of means or fear of reprisal prevented the injured party from doing so. And the public accommodations section, although far from comprehensive, would still strike a telling blow against segregation. Defending the President's cautious strategy, Sorensen emphasized that Kennedy was "not interested in a 'moral victory' on a legislative issue—he wanted a legislative victory on a moral issue." Even those disappointed by the weakened nature of the bill agreed that it went far beyond any previous presidential request concerning civil rights.

Despite strong public support for the measure, Kennedy knew very well that getting it passed would be extremely difficult. Southern senators could be counted on to filibuster, and obtaining cloture to halt the maneuver was always hard, since it required a two-thirds vote. Senators from states where civil rights were not so paramount an issue held the key. That meant mobilizing the maximum amount of public pressure. Kennedy recognized that his strong advocacy of civil rights would probably hurt him politically since he already enjoyed the backing of liberals and Negroes. But he believed that inaction would, in the long run, bring an even greater penalty.

To his credit, once he had firmly committed himself to the cause of civil rights, the President met with literally thousands of people to urge their support. The Leadership Conference on Civil Rights did yeoman work mobilizing its member organizations. White church groups in particular proved highly effective in generating backing. To dramatize to Congress the importance of the civil rights bill for black Americans, Negro leaders determined to mount a March on Washington, reminiscent of a tactic proposed in 1941 to prod

Roosevelt into issuing an executive order establishing a Fair Employment Practices Committee. The earlier effort was cancelled when Roosevelt complied with the Negro demands. But in August 1963, 200,000 Negroes and whites, mobilized with remarkable skill by veteran protest leader Bayard Rustin, marched through the nation's capital. The order, dignity, and patience the huge throng displayed provided reason enough for the event to be remembered, but the soaring rhetoric of King made the occasion a particularly unforgettable experience. "I have a dream," he declared, "that one day even the state of Mississippi, a desert state sweltering with the heat of injustice and oppression, will be transformed into an oasis of freedom and justice."

His impact on the vast crowd was enormous, but far from moving them to the violence that so many feared might erupt, his words conveyed the spirit of love and brotherhood: "When we let freedom ring, when we let it ring from every village and every hamlet, from every state and every city, we will be able to speed up that day when all of God's children, black men and white men, Jews and Gentiles, Protestants and Catholics, will be able to join hands and sing in the words of the old Negro spiritual, 'Free at last! free at last! thank God almighty, we are free at last!' "

Kennedy, who was skeptical about the good that the march could accomplish and concerned that lawlessness by some of the demonstrators might start a riot and seriously alienate Congress, responded to the event without enthusiasm. Fearing an adverse reaction, he refused to address the crowd. He also declined to meet with the leaders of the march before it occurred for fear that if they presented demands he could not meet, the demonstration might turn into an anti-Kennedy protest. He was obviously pleased when the march went so peacefully. As he belatedly pointed out, it was something of which "the nation [could] be justifiably proud." But it was important to the President that future protests be minimized lest they antagonize Congress, ignite a white backlash, and hence destroy hopes of passing the civil rights bill. For King and other seasoned civil rights leaders this restriction proved difficult. Having motivated the Negro citizens to action, they could not easily tell them to be placid.

Kennedy recognized their problems and appreciated their

willingness to follow his wishes. He got along well with most of the established Negro leaders. Roy Wilkins of the NAACP and Whitney Young of the Urban League were more congenial to his tastes than King, though he greatly respected the Georgia minister. King came on strong with a moral fervor that was sharply different from JFK's own style. Whether the President or his brother knew that the FBI was "bugging" King's telephone will be known for sure only when certain classified files are opened. It is indisputable, however, that the administration advised King to disassociate himself from persons alleged to be Communists or close to Communists. Harris Wofford, one of the chief executive's top civil rights advisers, insisted later that neither JFK nor his brother conveyed any doubt about Dr. King himself. They advised him to move away from the Communists "because of their confidence in King and their desire to keep him from being vulnerable." According to Wofford, "J. Edgar Hoover was in a regular campaign to convince Kennedy that King was immoral, and, if not subversive, the captive of subversives." But as Assistant Attorney General Burke Marshall informed Senator Peter H. Dominick, a Colorado Republican, in mid-1963, based on all available information from the FBI and other sources, there was no evidence that any of the top leaders of major civil rights organizations, including King, were either Communists or Communist-controlled.

Kennedy's attitude toward civil rights was really no mystery. It reflected quite naturally his private and political personality. He honestly sympathized with the underprivileged; he wanted to do something for them. But he viewed violence, or demonstrations that might lead to violence, as counterproductive to the attainment of equal rights and a threat to his other goals as President. Single-minded zealotry was simply alien to his style. Similarly, southern bigots appalled and disgusted him. The fact that some of his own appointees in the South were among the least fair-minded on race relations was particularly galling. Robert Kennedy's running feud with Judge William Harold Cox of Mississippi, a man appointed by JFK, underscored the frustrations involved in trying to appease southerners on the one hand and trying to push civil rights by legal means on the other. But it was a typical Kennedy type of strategy.

The President's solution to racial controversy was sober, sensible negotiations, helped along by government pressure, but always within the framework of moderation. His displeasure with the Civil Rights Commission's independent policies, which he manifested repeatedly, revealed his annoyance with those he believed were going too far too fast on their own with too little concern for negative consequences.

One of Kennedy's primary beliefs—often overlooked amidst the emotion of the times—was his firm feeling that economic gains for Negroes were absolutely vital if equal rights were really to mean anything for black Americans. He prodded federal agencies and departments to take action in this regard and planned an attack on poverty for 1964. Later in the sixties, particularly after the front lines of the civil rights struggle shifted from the South to the North, Kennedy's emphasis on securing tangible gains for Negroes appeared to make better sense than it had earlier. James Farmer of CORE, who was critical of Kennedy during the New Frontier years, commented that only after the President's death did he realize how important he had been to civil rights. By 1967, Farmer explained, he could see that there was "no question but that the President's attitude and the position he took on issues as well as his speeches helped us a great deal in building up the head of steam in the civil rights movement."

Still, Kennedy was not the gigantic figure in civil rights that some of his admirers claimed. Sorensen's book made Theodore Hesburgh, a member of the Civil Rights Commission, wonder, "Is he writing about the guy that I had to do business with?" It is possible to sympathize with Hesburgh's feelings, but it is difficult to escape the fact that moderate as Kennedy was about civil rights, he conveyed a sense of caring to the Negro masses far more successfully and more poignantly than any President before or after. One may deprecate his accomplishments and magnify his faults, but one cannot deny that in some mystical way the majority of Negroes identified with John Kennedy, and indeed, with his brothers. The fact that his civil rights bill was bogged down in Congress at the time of his death testifies to his failure in congressional leadership but does not lessen his symbolic value to the civil rights movement.

Kennedy's desire to build strong ties with the emerging nations of the world, especially in Africa, unquestionably influenced his attitude toward civil rights at home. Because he wished to look good and be successful abroad, he tended to start with foreign policy problems and work back to domestic affairs. He was disappointed by his own lackluster performance in handling international affairs during his first year in office; nevertheless foreign relations remained his paramount interest and greatest concern. The tensions he experienced over Laos, Cuba, and Berlin, compounded by his frustrating meeting with Khrushchev at Vienna, left their mark on the President's thinking. He feared that the Soviet premier might regard him as weak and indecisive. He and his advisers also worried about the potent anti-Communist sentiment in Congress and among the general public. By assuming, in George Kennan's words, "a strong and flamboyant anti-communist demonstrative posture," important political dividends could be reaped at home, and the Soviets could be impressed that the New Frontiersmen meant business. JFK recognized that such a stance would increase the chances for a major confrontation with the Russians. But he would not run the risk of being labeled soft on Communism. Thus when Kennan, the ambassador to Yugoslavia, begged him in mid-1961 not to announce a "Captured Nations Week," a pointless gesture that governments in Eastern Europe could not help but regard as unfriendly, the President refused.

The State Department's continuing failure to provide incisive analyses and viable alternative courses of action prompted Kennedy to order a major shake-up of the department late in 1961. Ironically, the principal victim of the "Thanksgiving Day massacre" was Chester Bowles, a thoughtful and articulate liberal noted for his unwillingness to accept the doctrinaire view of foreign policy in general and the cold war in particular. The President admired Bowles and appreciated his talents. But he regarded him as discussion- not action-oriented. Bowles was a believer in the power of ideas whose idealism rankled many of the hardheaded realists who surrounded the chief executive. His criticism of the Bay of Pigs operation added to his list of enemies. In addition, Bowles and Rusk clashed philosophically on how State should be run. Bowles wanted a heavy infusion of new blood into the tradition-laden department and got his way to a considerable degree in the initial appointment of ambassadors to serve the New Frontier. Rusk preferred to rely on the old department hands. As he frostily told Bowles, "I don't agree that we should grab the first fresh face we see and bring him into the State Department." Many of the career diplomats made little effort to hide their own disdain for Bowles and his ideas.

Even though Bowles had powerful friends within the liberal community, Kennedy chose to revitalize the State Department from below rather than by replacing the Buddha-like Dean Rusk. It would have been a major embarrassment to depose the man he had chosen to head the department less than a year before. Although some of the President's close associates believed that he had lost some of his initial respect for the Secretary's judgment, Kennedy nevertheless appreciated Rusk's loyalty and his willingness to accept second place under a chief executive who clearly intended to be his own Secretary of State. Rusk's counsel on critical issues was reserved for the President's ears alone. In meetings, the Secretary's views, other than a general belief in continuing the policies of his predecessors, remained a mystery. Publicly at least, he never questioned the cold war dogmas. Bland to a fault, a master of banal clichés, outwardly imperturbable, and a team player of the first rank, he kept whatever imagination and emotion he possessed carefully in check.

So it was Bowles, not Rusk, whom the President ousted. Ironically, Bowles, who humbly agreed to accept a rather vague assignment as Kennedy's Special Adviser for African, Asian, and Latin American Affairs, provided the type of unstereotyped, fresh thinking that Kennedy prized. His failing, as Schlesinger trenchantly explained, was that "The New Frontier put a premium on quick, tough, laconic, decided people; it was easily exasperated by more meditative types." An administration that was reminiscent of Theodore Roosevelt's ringing cries for vigor, manliness, and individual preparedness preferred to keep its worldly philosophers out of the front lines. George Ball, a resourceful and cool lawyer with varied government experience who was, like Bowles, closely identified with Stevenson, became the new Under Secretary. While it was hoped that Ball could improve the policy-management aspects of the department, three trusted White House staff members transferred to State were clearly intended to foster some of the innovative initiative that Kennedy badly desired. Walt Rostow became counselor and chief of the critical Policy Planning Council, Richard Goodwin was named Deputy-Assistant Secretary for Inter-American Affairs, and Fred Dutton was assigned as Assistant Secretary for Congressional Relations.

Significantly, Averell Harriman, over seventy years old but still full of drive and razor-sharp mentally, took over as Assistant Secretary for the Far East. A former ambassador to the Soviet Union and a one-term governor of New York, he was willing to accept the rather modest post because he was more interested in power than in status. He was known as "The Crocodile" for his habit of abruptly cutting off conversations that seemed stupid or pointless. It had taken him time to win Kennedy's confidence, and the President had initially appointed him an ambassador at large as something of a sop to his desire to serve and in recognition of his long and distinguished public service. He was regarded at first by the youthful New Frontiersmen as something of a has-been, but his assignment to the important Far East position signaled his emergence as a force to be reckoned with in the administration.

The reorganization of the State Department underscored Kennedy's intention of refurbishing his battered prestige in world affairs. He and his cohorts liked to think big; they viewed the entire globe, not just the United States, as their arena, and the challenges involved fascinated them. The ebullient Rostow remembered thinking, during the early days of the administration, that the situation, especially in foreign affairs, looked as if "our job was to deal with an automobile with weak brakes on a hill. It was slowly sliding backward. If we applied enormous energy, we could gradually slow that downward slide and bring the car to a halt. If we continued to apply the same stubborn energy, the car would begin to move forward and, in time, we would get it up to the top of the hill." The essential quality for Rostow, as for other administration stalwarts, was the will to succeed. Believing that the United States had the necessary resources to surmount all obstacles throughout the world, they intended to supply the "stubborn energy" necessary to motivate the will.

By the end of the sixties, Asia would be the United States' number-one foreign concern, but in 1962, Europe remained, as it had been since World War II, the center of attention. By the late fifties the nation's European allies, after years of relying heavily on the

United States for economic succor and military leadership, had begun to grow ever more restive with their position as the tail of the American comet. Having regained their economic prosperity, they disliked the growing control over their economies exercised by huge American companies. They confidently believed that Europe could be a third super force in the bipolar world of the United States and the Soviet Union that had existed since 1945. They especially resented their dependence on American nuclear weapons for their defense. Their pride was at stake. It was humiliating to have to tell Moscow that "Washington will defend us." But fear also played an important role. On the one hand the United States might get involved in a nuclear shoot-out elsewhere and drag its European allies into the fray without their consent. On the other, who could guarantee that if the Soviet Union made demands on Europe that America did not regard as worth an all-out war, the United States would use its nuclear arsenal to defend its allies? To eliminate such worries, some Europeans argued that each nation should possess and command its own nuclear capabilities. American strategists were horrified at the thought, arguing that the proliferation of nuclear powers would increase the threat of the Soviets' simply picking off the small nations one by one, since there would be little risk of other nations going to their aid. In addition, the possibility of a nuclear holocaust started by accident or miscalculation became infinitely greater. Washington also clearly recognized that independent European nuclear forces would diminish American influence.

The imperious French leader Charles de Gaulle provided the greatest spark for the movement by the European nations to reassert control over their destinies. But if he had not existed, he would have had to be invented, for he exemplified an idea whose time had come. By aggressively articulating France's desire for equality with the United States and by pushing the development of French nuclear arms, de Gaulle provided substance to the thoughts of other Europeans.

While French scientists struggled to build their own nuclear bomb and other countries debated the wisdom of pursuing a similar course, the Europeans also went ahead with plans to capitalize on their economic potential. In 1958, France, West Germany, Italy, and the three Benelux countries formed the European Economic Community (EEC), or Common Market, with the goal of turning themselves into an economic union over a twelve-to-fifteen-year period. Rebuffed in its efforts to join the Common Market, Great Britain countered in 1959 by establishing the European Free Trade Association (EFTA) in collaboration with Sweden, Norway, Denmark, Austria, Switzerland, and Portugal. Officially, the United States welcomed the efforts of its European friends to strengthen their economies, but it realized that the two competing groups could lead to conflicts that would seriously undermine the unity of the Atlantic Community against the spread of Soviet-inspired Communism. Equally threatening, the EEC and EFTA would be able to wield substantially more power, to the possible economic disadvantage of the United States.

Kennedy worried that American exporters might be locked out of the lucrative European markets, dangerously worsening this country's already serious balance-of-payments dilemma. In the last three years of the Eisenhower administration, American spending abroad for goods and services, foreign aid, and investments exceeded income by more than $10 billion. Speculators, believing that the value of the dollar was weakening, increasingly sought to exchange their surplus dollars for gold from America's gold reserves. The New Frontier's basic strategy for correcting the threat to the dollar and to the country's international credit position was to increase exports, thus reducing the adverse balance of payments and helping to slow—or, it was hoped, to stop—the gold drain. The President consequently made a trade expansion bill his major legislative target for 1962. Although some of his advisers would have preferred that he emphasize a controversial political issue such as Medicare or federal aid to education, the chief executive believed that the power to negotiate substantial tariff reductions was vital for domestic prosperity. The expected entry of Britain, America's leading trading partner, into the Common Market made the need even more imperative.

Often accused of not fighting for his legislative recommendations, JFK waged his battle for the trade bill with skill and vigor. And despite the opposition of some business interests and labor unions who feared the competitive impact of larger foreign imports, Congress agreed to his request. The President termed the new act, "the most important international piece of legislation . . . affecting economics since the passage of the Marshall plan." Unfortunately, the promise was more than the reality. Washington's hope that America's special friend in Europe, Britain, would be admitted to the Common Market—allowing it to act as a spokesman for the American point of view—was dashed when de Gaulle blackballed Britain's petition to join. The EEC proved to be stubborn about lowering trade barriers. The so-called Kennedy Round of negotiations began in 1964 and lasted until 1967. Although the bargaining reduced tariffs on 6,300 items by an average of 35 percent over a period of five years, the results did not live up to American hopes and expectations.

Kennedy's plan to bolster the Atlantic Alliance as a bulwark against the Soviet threat to Europe was loosely labeled the "Grand Design," after the title of the book published in 1962 by free-lance journalist Joseph Kraft. Written with the acknowledged cooperation of administration officials, Kraft's work concentrated on the economic aspects of the Alliance. But the New Frontiersmen recognized that military and political questions would be equally, if not more, difficult to resolve. The sticky problem was how to bring the European powers directly into the operation and control of the nuclear deterrence. Great Britain had long possessed its own nuclear warheads but had found the expense of building the vehicles to launch the explosives so great that it openly depended on the United States to provide the missiles necessary to deliver the explosive. In 1962, without prior consultation, the United States decided on its own to cancel work on the Skybolt missile that London had been counting on. Humiliated and angry, the British reluctantly accepted a substitute method of launching its warheads, but the affair emphasized that Great Britain was not really an independent nuclear power. France, however, intended to be. The thought of the French having such awesome power at their disposal caused deep anguish among the West Germans. Chancellor Konrad Adenauer, eighty years of age but still a commanding personality, required constant assurances of American affection. If the Germans, less than twenty years after they had reduced Europe to chaos, decided to follow the French example and build their own nuclear arsenal, the Kennedy administration knew that the Atlantic Alliance would be irreparably shattered.

To forestall such a disaster, the New Frontier attempted to placate Europeans by endorsing a proposal made by the Eisenhower administration in 1960 for a Multilateral Nuclear Fleet (MLF) of ships carrying nuclear weapons manned by crews drawn from the various NATO nations. In reality, as John Spanier wrote, the "MLF was no solution at all . . . because, while granting Europe the form of nuclear participation, it withheld the substance of that participation since the United States retained the veto over the use of the fleet's nuclear arms." Only the West Germans expressed much enthusiasm for the proposal, and they did so only with the stipulation that the United States should give up its veto. Kennedy, himself, was lukewarm about the MLF, accepting it only as the best available method to reconcile the desire of the NATO countries for a greater individual say in their defense with the goal of a united Europe. Certainly he hoped to preclude the development of an independent French nuclear force. Although he admired de Gaulle's personality, presence, and political skill and saw him as a great figure in history, JFK was also irritated by the French leader's intransigence and his insistence on "going it alone," a luxury France could enjoy because it was protected by the American nuclear umbrella.

To no one's surprise, the MLF never became a reality. Kennedy knew that neither Congress nor the American public would accept the placing of other fingers on the American nuclear trigger. The veto power could not be surrendered; hence the MLF was doomed. But there were other ways in which Kennedy might have responded affirmatively to Europe's determination to occupy a more equal position. His offer to negotiate bilaterally with the Russians over Berlin in 1961 alienated both de Gaulle and Adenauer, who felt that they should be part of any discussions. The President could have accepted the French leader's plea to establish a joint directorate on military strategy. The administration might also have provided stronger assurances that it understood and sympathized with European concern over American economic penetration of the Continent and that it would cooperate with efforts to lessen the impact.

Most of all, Kennedy could have articulated more emphatically his recognition that the bipolar world was changing, that the Soviet Union no longer constituted the same type of threat to Europe that it once had, and that America's European allies deserved to be elevated from their status as junior partners. When he failed to do so, Gaullism, the concept more than the man, gathered an irreversible momentum. During the rest of the decade, as the United States became increasingly preoccupied with its problems in Southeast Asia, the Atlantic Alliance deteriorated even faster.

The passing of the bipolar world occurred when not only Europe but also China began to flex muscles that potentially approximated, if not quite equalled, the strength of the United States and the Soviet Union. Despite their mutual identification with Communism, the Russians were not especially pleased to see the Chinese grow so tall. Sharing a long and difficult-to-defend frontier, the possibilities for conflicts of interest between the two powers were infinite. Chinese criticism of Soviet policies, particularly those that suggested the possibility of détente with the West, grew increasingly common. As sensitive to charges of "softness" towards the Americans as Kennedy was to complaints about his "softness" towards Communism, Khrushchev moved to cover his flank against the carping of Mao Tse-tung and his associates by aggressively rattling sabers over Berlin and belligerently baiting Kennedy at Vienna. And when the Berlin crisis eased, the Soviet leader, perhaps believing that the arms buildup implemented by the Kennedy administration had weakened Soviet security, kept the pressure on by resuming the testing of nuclear weapons in the atmosphere.

In his belief that Khrushchev had been deceitfully planning the tests even while Soviet and American officials were attempting to negotiate a treaty banning nuclear tests, Kennedy's first reaction, Sorensen related, was "unprintable." A few days later, in early September 1961, the President ordered the resumption of underground testing, which carried no danger of deadly fallout. He refused, however, despite heavy pressure from the scientific and military community, to authorize atmospheric tests. But after American scientists concluded that the Soviet exercise, which ended in November, had produced important weapons progress (Khrushchev boasted that a fifty-megaton superbomb had been detonated), Kennedy reluctantly announced in early March of the following year that unless the Soviets agreed to a test ban treaty by late April, the United States would initiate tests in the atmosphere. As he explained to the American people in a radio-television address, "In the absence of any major shift in Soviet policies, no American President—responsible for the freedom and safety of so many people—could in good faith make any other decision."

Kennedy's decision was influenced at least as much by political considerations, both domestic and foreign, as by military necessity. McNamara startled Rusk and Bundy while deliberations were going on by suggesting that the tests were not really necessary. Jerome Wiesner, the President's scientific adviser, believed that although they would "contribute to our military strength, they are not critical or even very important to our over-all military posture." Public opinion polls, however, showed that Americans favored the United States' resuming testing on its own, and Congress reflected that pressure. Speculating on why the Russians would risk the wrath of the world community by conducting new tests, Kennedy concluded that "The Russians are not fools. . . . They must believe they will gain most by appearing tough and mean." Although he had doubts about the value of the American tests, he rejected British Prime Minister Harold Macmillan's plea not to resume testing by explaining that the Soviets would attribute such a decision to weakness rather than goodwill. So, as George Kateb later wrote, "Feeling challenged, fearing to be thought fearful, Kennedy decided to do what he hated to do, and had little faith in. He could not escape the tyranny of appearances."

A few months after the United States resumed nuclear testing, the Cuban missile crisis provided the administration with a golden opportunity to show just how tough it could be. Aware that the Russians had been supplying large quantities of arms to the Castro regime, the United States believed that it had a pledge from the Soviets that the weapons would be defensive in nature. In press conferences in late August and mid-September 1962 Kennedy flatly warned that action would be taken to protect American security if Cuba became "an *offensive* military base of significant capacity for the Soviet Union." Then on October 14 an American reconnaissance plane routinely photographing Cuba discovered uncamouflaged sites of Soviet missiles capable of attacking the American mainland with nuclear warheads. Greatly alarmed, the Ex Comm (the Executive Committee of the National Security Council), taking care to conceal its activities in order to avoid public panic, began a series of meetings to consider what to do about the threat.

The Soviets' motives for deploying the missiles in Cuba remain obscure. Officially, the Russians explained that they only wished to protect the island from attack. It is quite likely that American involvement in the Bay of Pigs affair combined with the recurring demands of the political far right to "remove the communist menace that was only 90 miles away" provided hard-liners in the Kremlin with a compelling argument for taking steps to protect the Castro regime. It is doubtful that the Soviet Union believed that the location of the missiles in Cuba would alter the strategic balance of power *militarily*. As McNamara noted, "It makes no great difference whether you are killed by a missile fired from the Soviet Union or from Cuba." The Russian generals undoubtedly knew that the United States possessed a sizable edge in the number of nuclear warheads it could deliver against the Soviet Union. So while the Soviets gained an element of flexibility by locating missiles in Cuba, "the military equation," as Deputy Secretary of Defense Roswell Gilpatric later noted, "was not altered." From the Russians' point of view, however, the missiles could, conceivably, decrease the probability of an American invasion of Cuba.

A more viable explanation of the Soviet action was that it had an international political function. It provided the Russians with a relatively cheap way of appearing to support Castro and, at the same time, of rebutting Chinese criticism that the Soviet Union was not vigorously supporting "liberation movements." As Barton J. Bernstein observed, "Blocked in Berlin and condemned by the Chinese as unduly conservative, the Soviet Union, by placing missiles in Cuba, could gain prestige in the Communist world and perhaps also be in a stronger position for the next round of negotiations on Berlin." Soviet expert Charles Bohlen, then the American ambassador to France, theorized that Khrushchev intended to come to the United Nations in November and confront the United States with a virtual ultimatum on Berlin. Khrushchev may also have hoped that by locating the missiles in Cuba he could blunt attacks on him from within the Kremlin by those who wanted a larger military budget and disliked his advocacy of a peaceful coexistence. But the Soviet leader badly miscalculated the American reaction.

Although President Kennedy missed part of the crucial meetings of the Ex Comm because of campaign trips in connection with the impending congressional elections, he made it abundantly clear that some action had to be taken to remove the missiles. As Robert Kennedy explained in his account of the crisis, *The Thirteen Days*, his brother "could not accept what the Russians had done." Out of the Ex Comm's far-ranging and open discussions emerged a number of possible courses: private negotiations with Khrushchev without public announcement of the presence of missiles; a public announcement and then negotiations, possibly in the United Nations; an air strike and invasion; a "surgical" air strike against the missile; quarantine or blockade of Cuba; or a private approach to Cuban leader Fidel Castro.

The Joint Chiefs of Staff urged an invasion to seize the missiles and topple Castro's hated regime. They opposed a "surgical" air strike as unfeasible and too risky. They agreed, however, with Dean Acheson and Paul Nitze on the merit of a general air strike, one not restricted to the missile sites alone. Robert Kennedy heatedly disagreed, declaring that his brother would not go down in history as another Tojo and arguing that such an action would destroy America's moral position in the world. Furthermore, since the Russians manning the missiles would be killed, a strong Soviet response would be almost certain. There was also the possibility that the air strike might miss the missiles.

As the debate proceeded, Kennedy became convinced that a quarantine—a forceful action but less dangerous than a military attack—was the proper choice. By refusing to allow Soviet ships to sail to Cuba without first being searched by American personnel for "offensive" weapons, it would demonstrate the United States' determination to halt the Soviet threat while retaining the option of a subsequent air strike or invasion. The Joint Chiefs argued that the quarantine might not force the removal of the missiles, but Robert Kennedy, Sorensen, and McNamara supported the concept, and the majority of the Ex Comm members gradually swung behind the proposal.

On Monday, October 22, the President revealed his plan to deal with the missile threat, first privately to congressmen from both parties, then to the public in a nationwide broadcast. He emphasized that the Soviet government had repeatedly assured the United States, both publicly and privately, that the arms buildup in Cuba would retain its original defensive character. It was clear, he declared, that the Soviets had lied. The presence of clandestinely placed "offensive" missiles was "a deliberately provocative and unjustified change in the status quo which cannot be accepted by this country, if our courage and our commitments are ever to be trusted again either by friend or foe." On the diplomatic front, in the Security Council, United Nations Ambassador Stevenson confronted the Soviets with photographic evidence of the missiles, and Rusk obtained unanimous support for the administration's policy from the Organization of American States. Strangely, Valerian Zorin, the Soviet Ambassador to the UN, either from ignorance or deceit, at first denied the presence of the missiles in Cuba.

Tension mounted to a nerve-racking peak on Tuesday, when Khrushchev branded the quarantine "outright banditry" and warned Kennedy that his actions were pushing mankind "to the abyss of a world missile-nuclear war." The Soviets, he declared, would not accept the quarantine, and Soviet ships, if halted, would protect their rights. A press officer of the Soviet UN delegation told his American counterpart, "This could well be our last conversation. New York will be blown up by tomorrow by Soviet nuclear weapons." Although such a statement could easily be attributed to irrational panic, information that construction on the missile bases in Cuba was proceeding at full speed could not be so easily discounted.

But with the world seemingly teetering on the brink of World War III, common sense began to prevail. On Wednesday five large Soviet ships, thought to be carrying missiles, stopped in the Atlantic short of the quarantine zone. On Thursday Khrushchev responded favorably to UN Secretary General U Thant's letter calling for peace, and other Soviet vessels turned back. Hopeful as these actions were, the missiles still remained in Cuba. The rush to confrontation had been slowed, but the immediate cause of the problem remained unresolved.

On Friday the Soviets provided the first indication that the missiles were "negotiable." In an unorthodox diplomatic maneuver, the top Soviet intelligence officer in the United States suggested a possible deal to John Scali, an American Broadcasting Company correspondent. The Soviet Union would remove the weapons, promise not to return them, and allow the United Nations to verify their removal; in return the United States would issue a public pledge not to invade Cuba. Scali immediately passed the offer on to the State Department. Rusk, after consulting with the Ex Comm, sent back word that the administration was interested but that time was short. "Remember when you report this," he told Scali, "that eyeball to eyeball, they blinked first."

That evening, Kennedy received the first of two messages from Khrushchev, which in a rambling way suggested, but did not explicitly offer, a similar bargain. To most of the Ex Comm members the proposal seemed attractive, although some argued that the United States should apply more pressure and demand more concessions. While considering their reply to the Soviet premier, new developments cast a cloud of gloom on the situation. A Soviet ship had left the quarantine line and was headed for Cuba. The FBI reported that Russian officials in New York were destroying sensitive documents. Especially troubling was news that an American reconnaissance plane had been shot down over Cuba and the pilot killed. But most important of all, Khrushchev had dispatched a second letter, which raised the ante for withdrawing his missiles by demanding that American missiles in Turkey also be removed.

Once again the threat of war loomed large. Roger Hilsman of the State Department described Saturday, October 27, as the "blackest hour of the crisis." To his credit, the President, fearing rash action or errors, ordered all atomic missiles defused. In retaliation for the shooting down of the American plane, the Ex Comm at first decided on an air strike against the Cuban missiles. But when Robert Kennedy shrewdly suggested that the government ignore the second Khrushchev letter, which concerned the American missiles in Turkey, and simply answer the first one, the air strike was postponed to give the Soviets time to respond. Ironically, months before, Kennedy had directed that the obsolete and useless missiles in Turkey be removed. Although irritated that they had not been, he was unwilling, as Robert Kennedy explained, to order their withdrawal "under the threat from the Soviet Union." The younger Kennedy's ploy got around this problem.

Khrushchev broadcast his reply to the President's message

publicly the following morning without a mention of the Turkish missiles. A model of conciliation, he declared that he had "given a new order to dismantle the arms which you described as offensive, and to crate and return them to the Soviet Union." After referring to the UN inspection of their removal and the American pledge not to invade Cuba, he added a welcome thought about the future. "We should like to continue the exchange of views on the prohibition of atomic and thermonuclear weapons, general disarmament, and other problems relating to the relaxation of international tension." Kennedy quickly wired his appreciation, and the crisis was over.

As the world breathed a huge sigh of relief, speculation raged as to the reason Khrushchev had backed down. It is impossible to say why definitively, but the most likely explanation was America's overwhelming nuclear superiority, plus the fact that the Soviet leader, like Kennedy, was honestly horrified at the thought of a nuclear war that would have killed perhaps 100 million Russians, a like number of Americans, and untold numbers in other nations. To most Americans, Kennedy's tough conduct of the affair was magnificent. Bohlen called it the greatest moment in his administration. British leader Macmillan would later say that the President had earned his place in history by this one act alone.

But to earn one's place in history is not necessarily to prove that one's actions were wise. Doubts persist about Kennedy's handling of the Cuban missile crisis. Critics such as Richard J. Walton, Louise FitzSimons, David Horowitz, and Barton J. Bernstein have condemned his willingness to risk nuclear holocaust in the face of something less than an immediate, overwhelming threat to the nation's existence. "What, we may ask," wrote Bernstein, "would have happened if Khrushchev had not backed down . . . ? If the missile crisis was Kennedy's greatest triumph, as many scholars and memoirists contend, how many similar victories can America afford to seek?"

If, as McNamara and Gilpatric suggested, the missiles did not alter the nuclear equation, why did Kennedy insist on running the risk of starting World War III to obtain their removal? Why did he simply not ignore their presence? The key to his actions rests, as it did with his decision to resume atmospheric testing, with his appraisal of appearances, more than pure reality. He believed that

Khrushchev was testing his—and America's—will and courage. As he later explained, the missiles "would have appeared to [change the balance of power], and appearances contribute to reality." Kennedy reasoned that if the missiles had remained in Cuba, the rest of the world would believe that Khrushchev had successfully challenged the United States, and the Soviets would have gained an international political—though not military—victory.

Actually, most of America's allies were neither terribly upset by the presence of the missiles in Cuba nor particularly happy with Kennedy's bold response. West Europeans cared little for Cuba and were accustomed to living next door to Soviet missiles. The British backed Kennedy but feared miscalculation that would lead to war. The sensitive de Gaulle, whom Kennedy "informed" but failed to "consult" about his strategy, later pointed to the missile crisis as an example of how the NATO alliance interfered with national sovereignty, since it could drag members into a nuclear holocaust without their approval or even against their will. Ironically, whereas the Kennedyites feared a loss of prestige and credibility among America's allies unless the missiles were removed, the opposite resulted. Rather than strengthening America's global alliances, the handling of the crisis actually weakened NATO.

Domestic political considerations were equally compelling to Kennedy's thinking. Sorensen once explained that "Politics pervades the White House without seeming to prevail. . . . It is instead an ever-present influence—counterbalancing the unrealistic, checking the unreasonable, sometimes preventing the desirable, but always testing what is acceptable." Politics meant more than the impending congressional elections. The New Frontiersmen were keenly conscious of the impact of the crisis on the outcome of the legislative contests. But they were also aware that if the administration failed to deal firmly with the Cuban threat, Republican charges of "tragic irresolution," implying that the President was weak and spineless in protecting American interests, would make it even harder for the administration to conduct foreign policy effectively.

Kennedy's choice of a public confrontation rather than private negotiations in the missile crisis raises troublesome questions. Adam Yarmolinsky of the Defense Department recalled that the use of straight diplomacy was barely considered; neither was the possibility of economic leverage. The "flexible response" developed during the New Frontier to replace the Eisenhower doctrine of "massive retaliation" provided the Kennedy administration with a variety of military alternatives, and 90 percent of the crucial thirteen-day period was spent studying military issues. Political scientist Graham Allison, who examined the government's deliberations in minute detail, contended that "bureaucratic momentum" by the national security managers dictated the pursuit of a military "solution" to the missile problem. He concluded that the leaders of both the United States and the Soviet Union "only barely" managed to control the forward thrust of their bureaucracies towards war.

Unquestionably, bureaucratic momentum has contributed heavily to the development of the international tension since World War II. In the missile crisis, the important thing was that Kennedy—and Khrushchev—did prevail. One can agree with the critics that Kennedy placed too much weight on "prestige" in the crisis and walked too close to the precipice of nuclear war for comfort. But JFK deserves more credit than he often receives for repeatedly, throughout his administration, opting for a more moderate, less adventurous course in foreign affairs than that recommended by the hawkish cold warriors among his advisers. Although he valued their counsel, he appreciated far better than they did the full scope and ramifications of American actions. Many military leaders, for example, were openly disappointed when Khrushchev's message of conciliation ended the prospects for an American attack on Cuba. The President recognized that once a war began, the admirals and generals were vital, but he frequently questioned their judgment in strategic matters. After Curtis LeMay of the Air Force strongly maintained at one Ex Comm meeting that the Russians would do nothing if the United States launched an air strike on their missile sites in Cuba, JFK told O'Donnell, "Can you imagine LeMay saying a thing like that? These brass hats have one great advantage in their favor. If we listen to them, and do what they want us to do, none of us will be alive to tell them later they were wrong." Kennedy's real triumph in the Cuban missile affair was over his advisers.

After gaining the concession from Khrushchev, JFK refused to rub the Russian's nose in the dirt. When someone suggested that he go on television to announce his victory, he tartly replied, "I want no

crowing and not a word of gloating from anybody in this government." The President understood that the Soviet premier would be
having leadership problems with his own hawks as well as with the
Red Chinese. JFK also wanted to do nothing to further the illusion
that all the United States had to do was to be tough with the Russians
and they would collapse. As he told Arthur Schlesinger, Jr., the
Cuban situation had unique aspects, favorable to the American
position, that would not necessarily be present in other crises. The
Soviet Union remained a formidable and dangerous adversary, and
one not to be pushed around easily.

The impact of the Cuban crisis lingered long after the missiles
were removed. In the congressional elections held a little over a
week later, the President's party gained four seats in the Senate and
had a net loss of only two in the House, a much stronger showing
than the party in power usually makes in mid-term elections.
Representative Bob Wilson, chairman of the Republican Congressional Committee, claimed that the missile episode had cost the GOP
as many as twenty House seats. He angrily accused the administration of deliberately refusing to announce in September that it knew
that Soviet missiles were in Cuba. By waiting until nearer to election
time, Wilson maintained, the Democrats hoped to benefit from the
natural tendency of the public to rally around the President in a time
of national crisis.

Although spokesmen for the New Frontier denied the charge,
the Kennedy administration was guilty of managing the news once it
became certain that Soviet offensive missiles were on the island. By
manipulating announcements, passing certain key bits of information
to selected reporters, and appealing to the loyalty of newsmen not to
reveal critical information, the government incorporated the media
into its overall scheme to dislodge the missiles from Cuba. Assistant
Secretary of Defense for Public Affairs Arthur Sylvester subsequently
admitted that news management was an important weapon during
the strained situation. "It's inherent in [the] government's right, if
necessary," he argued, "to lie to save itself when it's going up into a
nuclear war."

The real significance of the missile crisis concerned the United
States' long-term relations with the Soviet Union. Walt Rostow
exulted that the episode could emerge as "the Gettysburg" of the

cold war. Macmillan told the House of Commons that the crisis represented "one of the great turning points in history." Though Kennedy regarded the episode as a significant cold war victory for the United States, he was more restrained in his judgment. Future historians, he explained, looking back at 1962 might mark it as a time when the tide *began* to turn. For the present, the President clearly recognized that the confrontation between East and West continued. He did not think, he told newsmen, "we are about to see a whole change in Communist policy." Kennedy hoped that Khrushchev understood far better than before that the New Frontier was determined to avoid any shift in the balance of power.

The President sensed that the Soviet leader, like himself, had been sobered, indeed frightened, by the imminence of a nuclear war when the interests of their two countries clashed in Cuba. As he wryly observed, "You can't have too many of those. One major mistake either by Mr. Khrushchev or by us . . . can make this whole thing blow up." Kennedy's fear of being tied to the use of nuclear weapons in every crisis situation had been one of the reasons he had pushed the military so diligently to develop a "flexible response." Worry about a nuclear war triggered by accident or miscalculation— spurred by popular movies like *Dr. Strangelove* and *Fail-Safe*—had also caused him to tighten the system of command control over nuclear weapons. After the Cuban missile affair, he considered it imperative to try with renewed vigor for a test ban treaty with the Soviets.

A general disarmament treaty would have meant even more safety for the world, but since nuclear arms were the greatest danger, it was important to start there. The task was not an easy one. In both the United States and the Soviet Union swollen military establishments and key industrial producers of defense hardware routinely opposed any form of disarmament and distrusted any whisper of détente. Technical differences, such as whether there should be on-site inspections of test facilities, presented additional sticky problems, but persistent off-the-record talks led to formal negotiations during the early summer and a treaty by late July 1963. According to the terms, underground tests could continue since there would be no on-site inspections. Atmospheric tests, however, were ruled out. Other nations with nuclear weapons were invited to join in the ban. The British agreed to do so; France and Red China, the two newcomers to the nuclear club, refused. The treaty, as Kennedy frankly admitted, was very limited in scope. But as one of his favorite quotations, an old Chinese proverb, explained, "The journey of a thousand miles begins with a single step."

Winning senatorial approval, the President realized, would not be easy. Consequently he used every opportunity, including a very effective television appeal to the public, to woo support. Secretary of Defense McNamara backed the treaty wholeheartedly, and the Joint Chiefs of Staff provided important, although carefully guarded, help. In spite of vocal opposition from many retired high-ranking military officers, some nuclear scientists, numerous defense contractors, and several influential senators from the southern-conservative-Republican bloc, public sentiment gradually swung overwhelmingly behind the treaty. The Senate ultimately voted its approval by a convincing 80–19 margin.

Kennedy took another modest step toward establishing a détente with the Russians by agreeing to sell them surplus wheat. Previously, the President had taken little interest in East-West trade questions, and although he spurned the notion that "a fat Communist was a good Communist," he believed that the wheat sale would be economically beneficial for the United States and would help to convince the Soviets that good relations could benefit both countries. Despite complaints from some congressmen, problems over financing the sale, a threatened boycott by longshoremen, and other assorted obstacles, he firmly insisted that the transaction was in America's best interest.

In other small ways Kennedy tried to hasten the mild thaw in the cold war with the Soviets. He enthusiastically agreed to the installation of a private "hot line" between Washington and Moscow in order to ensure instant communication between heads of state in time of crisis and continued his fairly active private correspondence with Khrushchev. He also ordered the removal of obsolete American missiles, regarded as threatening by the Russians, from Turkey, the United Kingdom, and Italy. In an important speech on world peace delivered at American University in June, the President declared that it was time "to reexamine our attitude toward the cold war. . . . We are not here distributing blame or pointing the finger of judgment.

We must deal with the world as it is, and not as it might have been had the history of the last 18 years been different."

Despite such gestures, however, Kennedy never really relaxed his basic cold war posture. He viewed the growing friction between the Chinese and the Russians skeptically, explaining that their disagreement was "over means, not ends" and warning that "A dispute over how to bury the West is no grounds for Western rejoicing." Although anxious to obtain a détente with the Soviets, his efforts to do so were based essentially on his belief that the argument over which ideology, ours or theirs, would prevail was not really central to relations between East and West. Rather, the Communist countries' attempts to upset the balance of power by imposing their system on others by force was the real cause of friction. It followed, therefore, that to bargain successfully with the Russians or their allies, the United States should always operate from a position of strength and respect. To ensure its own security, it was vital that America maintain its credibility as being willing to use its strength to block Communist, or Communist-sponsored, aggression whenever it threatened areas where the United States had committed its prestige.

The President's actions in Southeast Asia fleshed out the skeleton of his reasoning. Convinced that the Communists were instigating the revolution in South Vietnam, Kennedy continued to back the corrupt and inefficient Diem regime until well into 1963. He did so with considerable misgivings, sharing the concern of many of his advisers who doubted that Diem would be willing, in Rusk's words, "to take the necessary measures to give us something worth supporting." Although increasingly disenchanted with Diem, Kennedy also concurred with his Joint Chiefs of Staff that if the Communists prevailed in Laos and South Vietnam, "We would lose Asia all the way to Singapore."

For a time the situation in Southeast Asia seemed to brighten. After over a year of perplexing negotiations, the rival factions in Laos agreed to neutralize that country. According to the Geneva treaty signed in June 1962, all foreign military personnel were to withdraw. Official American advisers did leave, but both the United States and the Communists continued covert operations within Laos. Nevertheless, the agreement eased the danger of a major military confrontation in Laos.

In Vietnam the glowing reports forwarded in 1962 by General Paul Harkins, the American military commander, inspired a growing optimism. Although his command accepted the vastly inflated "kill" figures reported by the South Vietnamese Army (ARVN) without bothering to check them, Harkins's statistical tabulations of "VC killed" convinced many Washington officials that the Communists must be losing. McNamara spoke of "tremendous progress," which allowed planning to begin for the withdrawal of all American units. Kennedy, in his January 1963 State of the Union address, remarked that "the spearhead of aggression has been blunted in Vietnam."

Many American newspaper and television correspondents painted a very different picture with their depressing accounts of the war's progress. Their pessimistic reports infuriated military officials. When Admiral Harry Felt, Commander in Chief in the Pacific, met reporter Neil Sheehan, he snarled, "So you're Sheehan. Why don't you get on the team?" The difference in opinion between the military and the dissident newsmen occurred because the latter paid less attention to body counts than to the attitudes of the Vietnamese people. In the view of reporters like David Halberstam, unless and until Diem carried out his pledges of political and social reform, the chance of a South Vietnamese victory was very small or nonexistent. In contrast, although officers like Harkins paid lip service to the importance of winning the allegiance of the people, they basically saw the struggle in military terms. Most either failed to appreciate the necessity of subordinating military measures to a political and social program or else left it to someone else to do.

Until the late spring of 1963, the United States officially clung to Diem, despite growing displeasure with his leadership. As one journalist quipped, the American dictum was "sink or swim with Diem." Massive Buddhist demonstrations against his government, however, caused Washington to reappraise its position. On at least one occasion Diem's troops fired into a crowd of demonstrators. Several Buddhist monks dramatized their opposition by burning themselves to death. In August Diem's erratic and vastly unpopular brother, Nhu, unleashed a new wave of vicious assaults against Buddhists throughout the country only days after the Vietnamese leader had assured the American ambassador that his government was working for reconciliation with the Buddhists. For the Kennedy administration, the attacks were the last straw. It would no longer support Diem. But, significantly, the President did not at the same time question the basic commitment of preventing a Communist victory.

Washington cabled the new American ambassador to Saigon, Henry Cabot Lodge, that "Diem must be given a chance to rid himself of Nhu and his coterie and replace them with best military and political personalities available." If Diem refused, Lodge was instructed to turn to "appropriate military commanders." Lodge replied that it was foolish to go to Diem first and then to the generals, arguing, "it is in effect up to them whether to keep him." The ambassador, consequently, approached only the generals.

No coup developed at the time, however. The generals were uncertain of American support and even feared that they might be betrayed to Diem and Nhu by opponents within the American mission in Saigon. Kennedy, too, began to have second thoughts. Outgoing Ambassador Frederick Nolting argued that the United States had no choice but to support Diem as the only viable leader. Perplexed, the President hurriedly sent another fact-finding mission to Vietnam in early September. Upon returning to Washington, its principals, General Victor Krulak of the Marines and Joseph Mendenhall of the State Department, reported to the National Security Council. Krulak declared that the "war was going beautifully, that the regime was beloved by the people and that we need have no undue concern even about Nhu." Mendenhall disagreed: "South Vietnam was in a desperate state, . . . the regime was on the edge of collapse, and Nhu had to go." Kennedy listened politely, then asked, "Were you two gentlemen in the same country?" Trying to obtain a clearer view of the cloudy situation, JFK then dispatched McNamara and Taylor to review the progress of the war. Their report in early October emphasized the "great success" during the past year and insisted that the bulk of the 16,700 American troops then in Vietnam could be removed by the end of 1965. Harkins was even more optimistic, assuring Washington only a day before the ARVN generals moved against Diem that "on balance we are gaining in the contest with the V.C." and that "the general trend has been and continues upward."

Nevertheless, Kennedy was convinced that Diem must go; but

he still worried that the coup might fail. The White House wired Ambassador Lodge that the plotters should "show a substantial possibility of quick success; otherwise we should discourage them from proceeding since a miscalculation could result in jeopardizing U.S. position in Southeast Asia." The actual decision of whether to try to stop the coup was left to Lodge. He believed that the overthrow would succeed and assured the generals that the United States would look favorably upon their efforts. His judgment was confirmed on November 1, when the conspirators struck and, in less than twenty-four hours, easily took control of the South Vietnamese government, murdering Diem and his hated brother Nhu in the process.

The publication of *The Pentagon Papers* (the secret government documents describing American operations in Vietnam leaked to the press in 1971 by Daniel Ellsberg as an act of moral opposition to the war) left no doubt that despite official and unofficial denials, the Kennedy administration, including the President, knew and approved of the scheme for deposing Diem. The murder of the South Vietnamese leader and Nhu, however, was most emphatically against the wishes of the American government. JFK, Schlesinger reported, was "somber and shaken" by their deaths. "No doubt he realized that Vietnam was his greatest failure in foreign policy, and that he had never really given it his full attention." Ironically, less than a month later, Kennedy, too, was dead.

Purposefully or not, Kennedy's actions seriously deepened the United States' involvement in the Vietnam war. Whether he did so deliberately and consciously in an attempt to "discipline the communists" by "teaching them a lesson" in Southeast Asia, or whether he took only the required minimum steps to stave off defeat, not win a victory, is a moot point. Certainly Kennedy never completely understood the internal complexities of the Vietnamese struggle. American knowledge about the country, its people, culture, and history was frightfully limited. Information about the political situation in the country and the status of the fighting itself was consistently confusing and contradictory. Furthermore, the Department of Defense, the Central Intelligence Agency, and the Agency for International Development often seemed to be more interested in pushing pet projects than in coordinating their activities. Many in the administration were anxious to use Vietnam to prove to the Communists that guerilla wars were not the wave of the future. As Roswell Gilpatric of the Defense Department recalled, "Once it became plain that President Kennedy was going to allow a certain growth in our presence in Indochina . . . a lot of the more adventurous, innovative, imaginative types began to home in on that." Yet, although bureaucratic momentum and bungling affected Kennedy's specific decisions, they cannot ultimately be blamed for dictating his basic policy in Vietnam. As far as general strategy was concerned, the President acted with few illusions.

Fear that the Soviet Union or the Chinese Communists might miscalculate or misjudge American intentions obsessed Kennedy. Appearances were consequently important, indeed vital, and maintaining the credibility of the United States was imperative. Anything that damaged American prestige weakened the chances of keeping global peace and undermined the ability to lead effectively at home. Like Laos, Vietnam was an extremely messy situation. But in contrast to Laos it was much more militarily accessible for the United States and offered no obvious immediate possibility of negotiations. Therefore, although he recognized the difficulties involved, he felt that America's military presence there, until conditions permitted a satisfactory settlement, was essential for United States prestige. Anything less would risk a Communist victory, and that Kennedy was not prepared to do.

It is an oversimplification to say that he believed in the "domino theory"—that if Vietnam went Communist, all of Southeast Asia would fall like a row of dominoes—or that he was immovably wedded to the containment of Communism any place in the world. To a degree he accepted both concepts, but more as pragmatic strategy than as articles of faith. Nor did he accept the thesis that all Communists or all Communist countries were controlled by Moscow. He realized fully that Yugoslavia, for example, was not. His worries centered on the Soviet Union and Red China as powerful and dangerous adversaries. The essence of his concern was whether there was to be an accommodation or a showdown with the two major Communist powers. The latter alternative, since it so obviously included the danger of nuclear war, had to be avoided if at all possible. Accommodation, although slow and frustrating, was much the safer course. But it demanded infinite patience and willingness to sacrifice. Korea had been part of the accommodation principle. It was deliberately a "no-win" engagement. The United States had restricted its force to the minimum needed to attain its basic objectives: a halt to the Communist advance geographically, a demonstration to friend and foe alike that the United States would keep its commitments, and negotiation from strength to end the conflict.

Americans had come to accept Korea as a cold war victory. For Kennedy, the goals in Vietnam were basically the same. Whether or not the Vietnam war was a civil war—a burning question for so many in later years—was less important than the need to maintain America's credibility as a deterring force against aggression sponsored by the Soviets or the Red Chinese. To do otherwise would undermine the confidence of America's allies and increase the danger of a miscalculation or misjudgment by Moscow and Peking.

Although Kennedy insisted publicly that it was up to the South Vietnamese themselves to win the conflict, as *The Pentagon Papers* revealed, he and his senior advisers considered defeat unthinkable. Believing that sending in formal units of American ground troops to support the repressive Diem regime would provoke sharp criticism at home, the President filtered large numbers of "advisers" into Vietnam in small groups designed not to attract attention. The advisers were allowed to engage in combat and secretly to sponsor guerilla raids and amphibious landings against North Vietnam. These actions helped to secure the New Frontier's goal of "maintaining credibility." But most significantly, they also gradually transformed Eisenhower's "limited-risk gamble" into a broad and potentially unlimited commitment.

# V

---

## *The Unfulfilled Promise*

AT THE time, the Kennedy administration's policies in Vietnam commanded no consuming public interest. Never during the New Frontier did the Vietnamese conflict provoke riots or demonstrations. The news media argued only about the methods of conducting the war, not about the basic commitment. The consensus supporting the government's efforts to check Communism continued to be strong and healthy with only a modest fraying around the edges, and although the situation in Southeast Asia was exasperating, it was never Kennedy's number-one problem. In fact, during his last months in office, legislative matters occupied his time far more than Vietnam. And while the verdict was not in before his death, there were signs that for the first time since his early days in the White House, Kennedy was gradually regaining the initiative in his relations with Congress.

He had begun his administration by submitting an ambitious legislative program, which included, with the glaring exception of a civil rights proposal, the bulk of the Democrats' 1960 campaign promises. On the surface, his legislative record during his first two years looked impressive. Congress, Sorensen boasted, "enacted four-fifths of Kennedy's program." Measuring the administration's success with Congress by pointing to the high percentage of the President's total requests passed was deceiving, however. It gave equal weight to both minor and major proposals and included foreign policy legislation—normally much less partisan in nature—as well as domestic requests. Furthermore, some acts remained the chief executive's in name but were amended so extensively as to change sharply the substance of the original bill. Obviously, too, the "box score" approach conveniently ignored bills not submitted for fear they would not pass.

During 1962 only the Trade Extension Act could be considered a major act in which the President got substantially all that he wanted from Congress. The Revenue Act of 1962 granted business a billion dollars a year in special tax credits to encourage new outlays for plants and equipment, but the measure omitted the administration's proposals for withholding income taxes on dividends and interest and softened the Treasury's plan to tighten allowable expense-account deductions. The legislators refused to go along with the chief executive's desire to impose strict production controls on wheat and food grains, agreeing merely to extend the existing voluntary controls for another year, and they turned down the White House's request for stand-by authority to initiate a $2 billion antirecession public works program when economic conditions dictated its need. Congress also handed the administration a major loss by defeating its plan to create a Department of Urban Affairs with Robert Weaver as the first Secretary and the first Negro cabinet member in history. The House Rules Committee, led by its determined conservative chairman, Howard Smith, blocked bills for commuter transit assistance, construction grants and student loans for medical schools, youth employment, and aid for migrant workers. Especially significant, Congress again failed to enact two of the key Democratic campaign promises in 1960: Medicare and federal aid to education.

Part of Kennedy's problems on Capitol Hill stemmed from weak leadership in the House of Representatives. Speaker Sam Rayburn died of cancer late in 1961, and his successor, John McCormack of Massachusetts, was far less able to enforce discipline on the administration's behalf. Yet, as noted in an earlier chapter, even before Rayburn's death, the President had seriously disappointed many of his congressional allies, who found him excessively timid and ineffective in applying pressure skillfully enough to gather and hold reluctant votes.

His unwillingness to battle for controversial, emotion-laden issues frustrated many liberal Democrats. In 1962 he deliberately made the relatively safe, unexciting trade expansion bill his number-one priority instead of engaging in a bare-knuckled fight for Medicare, civil rights, or federal aid to education. Arthur Schlesinger, Jr., who had urged a more aggressive course, wrote that later he realized that Kennedy, fearing that the politics of conflict might seriously tear the American social fabric, had chosen the politics of consensus in an attempt "to prevent unreason from rending the skin of civility." Even allowing for overdramatic adulation for a dead President, there is little reason to doubt that Kennedy did act according to the way he read the political signs, and opinion polls at the time revealed no "clamoring for action." Senate Majority Leader Mike Mansfield, referring to the "strangely quiescent" mood of the country, explained, "It isn't demanding much of this or that."

Equally important reasons for Kennedy's cautious approach were the slim Democratic working majorities in both chambers and his apparent lack of confidence in his ability to lead the legislators. In raw numbers the Democrats held an imposing edge, 262–174 in the House and 64–36 in the Senate, but the advantage melted away to virtually nothing on crucial social-economic issues when members from the South refused to support the administration. Kennedy recognized the dilemma, quoting Jefferson, "Great innovations should not be forced on slender majorities." The critical measure of Kennedy's leadership of his party and of Congress was how well he was able to hold the loyalty of conservative Democrats. He worked hard, meeting privately with every committee chairman, inviting small groups of legislators to the White House for coffee hours, and holding briefing sessions on key domestic bills for Democratic members and on foreign policy measures for bipartisan groups. As Carroll Kilpatrick, the veteran Washington reporter observed, "The President's power struggle with Congress was almost equal to that of his struggle with the Communist leaders abroad." But though he expended enormous energy, JFK seemed relatively ineffective in his dealings with the handful of men who wielded the real power on Capitol Hill. Even Sorensen admitted that at first Kennedy was perhaps overly deferential with those who only a short time before had outranked him in Congress.

Urged by some to "go over the head of Congress," Kennedy declined to "spend" his popularity by appealing flamboyantly to the public to support his bills when the legislators refused to do so. The

President did attempt on occasions to educate the people. His speech in late 1961 before the National Association of Manufacturers about the need for new trade legislation was impressive and persuasive. So was his Yale address on economic myths a few months later. But cogent, restrained "lectures" of this nature were far removed from emotional appeals to the mass of voters to pressure their senators and representatives. He preferred instead to compromise and negotiate with Congress and consequently repeatedly signed bills that contained amendments with which he basically disagreed. Like Truman in the late 1940s, Kennedy frequently sacrificed domestic goals in order to protect support for foreign policy, his paramount concern.

By 1963 conditions looked considerably better for a determined campaign to enact some of the controversial pieces of legislation that Kennedy had declined to push previously. For one thing, JFK's popularity was remarkably high, with 76 percent of the voters approving of his presidential actions, according to the Gallup poll of January 1963. The Democrats' encouraging showing in the 1962 congressional elections constituted at least a mild endorsement for the New Frontier and helped to lessen the sting of Kennedy's razor-thin margin of victory in 1960. By gaining four Senate posts and losing only a handful of spots in the House, the Democrats managed to break the customary pattern of the majority party's losing a significant number of seats in mid-term contests. Furthermore, the *Congressional Quarterly* calculated that Kennedy actually gained in "hard-core" supporters in the lower chamber. Equally important, JFK's success in handling the steel and missile crises had raised his self-confidence immensely. Experience was also a factor. In theory at least, both the President and his "team" knew how to deal with Congress more effectively; the rough edges in congressional liaison had been smoothed by two years of practice. In addition, the Democratic leadership in both the Senate and the House, new during the preceding Congress, was also more seasoned. Most significant of all, Kennedy sensed that the public was ready to support modestly liberal social and economic legislation.

As he believed it would, Congress gave his 1963 recommendations careful consideration. But the solons moved with frustrating slowness. Delay, rather than outright denial, characterized the first session of the 88th Congress. At the time of Kennedy's death, only a relative handful of his critical proposals had actually become law, notably the nuclear test ban treaty and federal aid to medical schools and mental health. Congress had again refused to act on his plan for general aid to elementary and secondary education, but both houses had agreed to a college aid bill. It was in conference and the prospects for final clearance were good. The rest of the administration's major bills were seriously bogged down.

The large number of controversial measures submitted during the year unquestionably contributed to their slow progress through Congress, but Kennedy also made some questionable tactical moves. For example, his decision to name a blue-ribbon committee headed by World War II hero General Lucius Clay to "examine the scope, operation, and purpose of American overseas aid" helped to turn the annual debate over foreign aid appropriations into a particularly bitter and time-consuming affair. Angered by sharp cuts in his aid bills in 1961 and 1962, the President gambled that a prestigious investigating committee would report favorably and help to rebuild congressional and grass-roots support for the program. Such a tactic had produced good results for Eisenhower in the fifties. A number of Kennedy's advisers, however, worried about just how sympathetic the Clay committee, heavily weighted with conservative, private-enterprise-minded citizens, might actually be. Their concerns proved to be justified. Although Clay and his associates declared their approval of "properly conceived and administered" assistance programs, they also bluntly charged that the United States was trying to do too much for too many countries and urged that aid be extended only to nations whose attitudes were consistent with American beliefs and policies. Foreign aid, the committee concluded, should be conducted on the basis of enlightened self-interest.

The Clay committee's report accentuated the existing inclination of Congress to chop aid funding sharply. Hoping to stave off what appeared increasingly inevitable, the President agreed to a modest reduction but fought valiantly and energetically for the bulk of his recommendation. Ignoring the altruistic aspects of the aid program, he reminded the legislators that at least 80 percent of all aid dollars were actually spent for goods and services in the United States, not abroad: "Foreign aid is in our economic self-interest. It provides more than a half a million jobs for workers in every State. It finances a rising share of our exports and builds new and growing export markets. It generates the purchase of military and civilian equipment by other governments in this country. It makes possible the stationing of 3½ million troops along the Communist periphery at a price one-tenth the cost of maintaining a comparable number of American troops."

Ultimately, Clay and his committee rallied vigorously, though to no avail, to the President's side in a belated attempt to stop the legislators from emasculating the aid program. Kennedy had asked for $4.9 billion; Clay suggested a reduction to $4.3 billion; Congress ultimately voted only $3 billion. The final action came after his death, but JFK already knew that his program had been effectively torpedoed. Resigned to the disappointment, the President remarked that Eisenhower's people were right—the only way to sell foreign aid was on the grounds of military security. It was a mistake, he explained, to call the program AID, because it sounded like charity. "It should have been the International Defense Fund, or something like that."

As the exhausting congressional session wore on, attention focused mainly on the tax and civil rights bills. When at first his tax proposal failed to stimulate much enthusiasm, Kennedy appealed directly to the people. By carefully explaining the individual benefits that typical families could expect to receive, he succeeded in reversing early public opposition to the tax cut. By early fall opinion polls reflected solid support for the bill. To rally congressional favor for the measure, he took two important steps: He promised Wilbur Mills, the unchallenged expert on taxation in Congress and powerful chairman of the House Ways and Means Committee, that tax reduction would be accompanied by an "ever tighter rein on Federal expenditures"; and he implied that he might be willing to compromise on proposed tax reforms in order to get speedy action on a tax cut.

The administration had hoped to tighten some of the more egregious tax loopholes, the special advantages for certain interests and the generous personal itemized deductions, which were estimated to have lowered the government's potential revenue by perhaps $40 billion in 1962. Kennedy brooded over such glaring inequities as the fact that more than one-quarter of the Americans with incomes over $5 million a year paid no income tax at all in 1959. But in 1963, he agreed to sacrifice reform in order to obtain what he considered more important—a tax cut to stimulate economic growth and provide jobs. His reasoning was actually quite sound. Reform would produce more equity but would actually affect a relative handful of the more affluent. It would not help the millions of low- and middle-income taxpayers; the tax cut would. In late September the House approved a tax bill amended to exclude most of the proposed reforms. At the time of JFK's death, Senator Harry F. Byrd of Virginia, the tight-fisted chairman of the Senate Finance Committee, had the measure in limbo while conducting what he promised would be "comprehensive and lengthy hearings," but prospects for its ultimate passage looked reasonably favorable.

It was more difficult to predict the fate of the civil rights bill. Southern congressmen opposing the measure were well organized and brilliantly led by Senator Richard Russell. (Even Roy Wilkins of the NAACP referred to him as "the distinguished Senator from Georgia," carefully adding, "—and except in the field of human rights, he *is* distinguished"). Russell admitted that the nation faced a "social revolution" but argued, "The tempo of change is the crux of the whole matter. . . ." As a last resort the southerners figured to use a Senate filibuster in an attempt to block passage of a civil rights bill, but since southern chairmen dominated two of the key committees that would consider the measure, the House Rules and the Senate Judiciary, there was no guarantee that the bill would even get to the floor of either chamber.

To his credit, once Kennedy finally decided to push for a significant civil rights measure, he was willing to put his prestige on the line. He threw down the gauntlet to Congress in a dramatic message on June 19. "I ask you to look into your hearts—not in search of charity, for the Negro neither wants nor needs condescension—but for the one plain, proud and priceless quality that unites all as Americans: a sense of justice." He carried the fight to the American people by major speeches, news conferences, and White House press releases, even though he knew that his actions were costing him his popularity in the South. He also showed finesse in maneuvering the bill through the legislative minefield. When northern civil rights enthusiasts in Congress sharpened and expanded the administration's bill until the President feared that the measure might sink under its own weight, he summoned congressional leaders to the White House to urge a reconciliation of differences. His appeal spurred a compromise which enabled the measure's supporters to maintain a united front and which Attorney General Robert Kennedy declared was even better than the administration's original bill.

By his handling of the civil rights and tax proposals, Kennedy demonstrated that he had learned some valuable lessons during his first two years in the White House. Yet, there was no guarantee that either bill would have passed the Congress without the shock and incentive of the President's assassination. It is true that leaders of both parties later assured those who asked that the measures would have become law under Kennedy. But considering the martyrdom attached to JFK in the period immediately following his death, any less-positive statement would have been both tasteless and unpolitic.

Despite the stalemate in Congress, the frustrations of the Diem affair, and the tragic death of a prematurely born son, Kennedy was happier and more confident during the last few months of his life than at any time since he had been in the White House. To his close associates he seemed to be coming into his own as President. His health was much improved, thanks to successful treatments for his chronically aching back. He regarded the Senate's ratification of the test ban treaty in September as a major political gain, believing that it marked the development of a new consensus in the upper house that boded well for his programs in the future. There were also encouraging signs that the logjam in Congress over his domestic proposals would eventually break up.

On the horizon lay the 1964 election, and, like most successful politicians, JFK relished the thought of taking to the hustings. Contact with the people exhilarated him. Although physically exhausting, it recharged him emotionally. In September 1963 he tested the political waters with an extended tour of western states, most of which he had not carried in 1960. Officially, he billed the trip as a nonpolitical visit to conservation projects. As a quintessential easterner, Kennedy always looked and felt out of place talking about conservation, nature, and wildlife; press secretary Pierre Salinger dryly informed the press that the President had actually seen a moose from the window of his room at Jackson Lake Lodge, Wyoming. Nevertheless, JFK received a friendly reception on his tour that easily exceeded his expectations—especially when he deserted the conservation theme and spoke on foreign policy and the pursuit of peace.

Looking ahead, although Kennedy anticipated that the Republicans would ultimately select a relatively moderate candidate, the possibility that they might actually nominate their front runner of the moment, conservative stalwart Barry Goldwater, delighted him. The President liked the affable Arizona senator personally, but he disagreed with him on virtually every major issue. A Kennedy-Goldwater race would draw the lines sharply between the liberal and conservative positions on problems facing the nation. Since Goldwater usually spoke his mind with little thought about how his ideas might be interpreted and tended to oversimplify complex and difficult problems, the President reasoned that he would be considerably easier to defeat than some Republican dark horse candidate. He particularly looked forward to publicly debating Goldwater as a means of boldly emphasizing their differences to the voters.

Although he cautioned his staff not to talk to the press about the prospective GOP candidate, Kennedy could not resist the opportunity in late October to aim some whimsical barbs at his likely opponent. Asked to comment on Goldwater's charge that the New Frontier was managing the news to perpetuate itself in office, the President declined, explaining that Goldwater "has had a busy week selling TVA and giving permission to or suggesting that military commanders overseas be permitted to use nuclear weapons, and attacking the President of Bolivia while he was here in the United States, and involving himself in the Greek election. So I thought it really would not be fair for me this week to reply to him."

Kennedy did not expect his reelection bid to be easy and freely predicted a "hard, close fight" in most states, but he expected to win more handily than he had in 1960. Although detailed planning for the campaign was only in its infancy, certain basic themes to be emphasized were obvious. An overriding consideration would be the goal of presenting in dramatic terms evidence that the New Frontier was winning the struggle against Communism. This objective had figured in the administration's handling of the various hot-spot crises, in speeding up the pace of the space program, in beefing up the strength of the armed services, and in administering foreign aid. The enthusiastic response that Kennedy received to his comments about national security on his western tour vividly confirmed its merit as a campaign issue.

As for domestic issues, the New Frontiersmen believed that they held winning cards. The condition of the economy was certain to have a major impact on the voters. The tax cut, if passed, would, it was hoped, stimulate rapid economic growth, which would create new investments and thus new jobs. The pending civil rights bill was hurting the President's popularity badly in the South but figured to help his and other Democrats' chances in the big industrial states of the North. The administration planned to resubmit Medicare and federal aid to education to Congress during the election year. Even if they failed to pass, the President would be able to point out to the elderly and to the millions of parents with school-age children that he had tried to help.

The administration was also putting the finishing touches on an ambitious plan to attack poverty conditions in America. The President had seen poverty firsthand while campaigning in 1960. The deserted coal mines and sadly depressed villages of West Virginia in particular left an indelible imprint on his memory, and the call for an "economic drive on poverty" began to appear in his campaign speeches. Area redevelopment and manpower training projects became important parts of his first legislative program, while one of his first executive actions as President was to accelerate the distribution of food stamps to the needy.

Reading Michael Harrington's vividly descriptive—and indignant—book, *The Other America*, helped to crystallize his determination to do even more to combat poverty. Walter Heller and the Council of Economic Advisers convinced Kennedy that a tax cut would help the poor by creating new jobs, but John Kenneth Galbraith and others also impressed him with arguments that federal spending programs designed to combat the specific problems of the poor were necessary to strike at the heart of poverty conditions. During the spring of 1963 the CEA analyzed the latest available statistical information about those in a poverty status. Unhappily, as a Heller memo informed the President, between 1957 and 1961 the percentage of hard-core poor had been reduced by only one percent, while the total number of persons in the poverty range had actually increased. "This contrasts sharply," he noted, "with the 1947–57 record, when the percentage in poverty status dropped from 28.0% to 21.5%."

Urged to go ahead with its preliminary planning, the CEA worked throughout the summer and fall to develop possible ideas for an attack on poverty. Kennedy's interest in a comprehensive, across-the-board program remained strong. Only three days before his assassination, Heller asked him if he wanted to shift emphasis. "No," Kennedy replied, "I'm still very much in favor of doing something on the poverty theme if we can get a good program, but I also think that it's important to make clear that we're doing something for the middle-income man in the suburbs, etc. But the two are not inconsistent with one another. So go right ahead with your work on it."

The chief executive realized that trying to enact such controversial domestic measures as Medicare, federal aid to education, and a war on poverty in 1964 would be a political gamble. During 1963, his popularity index had tumbled—from 76 percent in January to slightly under 60 percent in the fall—as he had begun to speak out more aggressively on emotional issues like civil rights. The South, not surprisingly, accounted for the heaviest part of his loss in voter approval. But if he had learned anything during his three years in the White House, it was that trying to play too cozy with the conservative southerners had some serious drawbacks. He needed more nonsouthern Democrats in Congress to pass the kind of program the New Frontiersmen favored. Hence he planned to push measures in 1964 that would be popular in regions other than Dixie.

Kennedy frankly recognized that his chances of winning in most of the southern states were nil, but he believed that he had good prospects in Florida and Texas, the two most populous states and the ones where the old traditions and customs had undergone the most change. Rumors to the contrary, he had no intention of dumping Lyndon Johnson as his running mate. As he had been in 1960, the voluble Vice President would be valuable in persuading southerners, especially in his native Lone Star state, to vote Democratic.

Kennedy's preoccupation with carrying Texas prompted him to

go there in November on an openly political visit. He went hoping to unite the Democratic party in the state by welding together the two feuding factions identified with conservative Governor John Connally and liberal Senator Ralph Yarborough. His itinerary included San Antonio, Houston, Austin, Fort Worth, and Dallas, the latter in spite of scattered warnings that the ultraconservative city was rife with bitter anti-Kennedy sentiment. Only a month before a hostile crowd had spat on and jostled Adlai Stevenson when he was there for a United Nations Day speech. But on a politically oriented tour it would have raised embarrassing questions had Kennedy skipped the state's second largest city, so he scheduled a three-hour stay to include a motorcade and a luncheon speech at the impressive new Trade Mart.

Texas gave the President and his wife a rousing welcome, impressing even skeptics. Although angered by a scurrilous and tasteless advertisement in the *Dallas News* accusing him of being pro-Communist and other crimes, JFK was visibly pleased by the huge, friendly crowds that greeted him at his first three stops. Just after his plane landed at Dallas, he remarked, "This trip is turning out to be terrific. Here we are in Dallas, and it looks like everything in Texas is going to be fine for us." Minutes later, as his motorcade threaded its way slowly through the enthusiastic thousands who jammed downtown Dallas to cheer the President, Lee Harvey Oswald shot and killed John F. Kennedy with a high-powered rifle.

The President's assassination stunned not only the United States but the entire world. Never before had the death of any individual caused such an outpouring of grief in so many far-flung spots: in Ireland, where only months before Kennedy had reaffirmed his heritage during a triumphant visit; in West Berlin, where JFK had thrilled thousands by declaring, "Today, in the world of freedom, the proudest boast is *Ich bin ein Berliner*"; in the emerging states of Africa, where Guinea's Sékou Touré declared, "I have lost my only true friend in the outside world"; in India, where people cried in the streets of New Delhi. From London, Ambassador David Bruce reported that "Great Britain has never before mourned a foreigner as it has President Kennedy." In Moscow, Premier Khrushchev hurried to the American embassy to sign the condolence book. Although there were exceptions—Red China's *Daily Worker* featured a savage cartoon entitled "Kennedy Biting the Dust" and Madame Nhu, widow of the late Vietnamese official, bitterly charged Kennedy with the responsibility for the murder of her husband—the global response was overwhelmingly one of sadness. Arthur Schlesinger, Jr., who recorded in memorable words the dismay and anguish of persons famous and obscure, correctly wrote, "The people of the world grieved as if they had terribly lost their own leader, friend, brother."

In the United States a state of numbness seeped over the country. It is impossible to convey in words the gloom and agony that existed. Stunned, Americans tried to comprehend how such a crime could have occurred. It was so senseless and so unreal. Most people, whether Democrat or Republican, whether they revered or disliked the President personally, were unquestionably saddened by his death. For some, it was more than the killing of a man; it was a severe blow against the very concept of a country where public figures were free to move about, even to mingle with huge crowds, without fear of injury. Such things happened in the "banana republics" of South America but not in the United States. Yet, it had happened here.

Many businesses closed early, and so did most schools the day the President was slain. But amidst the anguish, life went strangely on. Some events planned for the weekend between the assassination and the funeral were cancelled; others continued as scheduled. The National Football League played its Sunday games to huge crowds, but television networks cancelled regular shows—and received countless complaints for doing so. Nevertheless, millions watched their sets endlessly during the long weekend, seemingly mesmerized by the endless line of mourners who passed by the President's body as it lay in state in the Capitol rotunda. Untold thousands waited in bitter weather for hours, day and night, for their brief chance to see the slain leader.

Jacqueline Kennedy, whose avid interest in the arts had helped to prime the New Frontier's emphasis on American cultural development, planned the funeral ceremony itself with an eye on historical precedent and image, but with uncommon good taste. Viewed by millions on television, it provided a needed catharsis for those who had lived in a state of shock for three days.

As the world grieved for Kennedy, it also puzzled over the mysterious circumstances surrounding his death. Two days after shooting the President, Lee Harvey Oswald was shot and killed by a small-time Dallas gambler, Jack Ruby. Incredibly, the incident took place before millions of television watchers, as the cameras recorded the Dallas police transferring Oswald from one jail to another. To many, the murder of the man accused of killing Kennedy smacked of an execution to seal Oswald's lips. It was widely believed that Kennedy's assassination was part of a conspiracy. To some the fact that Oswald had lived for a time in the Soviet Union, had married a Russian girl, and headed a Fair Play for Cuba committee suggested a Communist plot. Others, pointing to the signs of rampant right-wing extremism in Dallas, such as the harassment of Stevenson, the hostile advertisement in the newspaper, and reports that some Dallas schoolchildren clapped for joy when they learned of the President's death, were convinced that ultraconservative elements had schemed to kill the chief executive.

To find the truth, a blue-ribbon commission headed by Chief Justice Earl Warren spent months probing the slayings. In late September 1964 it issued a report stating that Oswald alone killed John F. Kennedy, that Ruby acted on his own in killing Oswald, and that no other individuals were involved in any way. Most of the American public accepted the findings without question. The commission's massive report provided a bonanza of information for those fascinated enough to plow through the twenty-six published volumes of testimony and evidence. A good many people were, and several challenged the conclusion that there was just one assassin. Disbelievers such as Mark Lane, Sylvia Meagher, and Penn Jones, Jr., took the report apart piece by piece and also searched for new evidence. The report itself offered some serious reasons for doubt. Marred by numerous errors and filled with large quantities of marginally relevant and often trivial material, it left some obvious questions unanswered. Critics charged that the Warren Commission seemed convinced from the start that only Oswald was responsible for the crime and that the evidence was used merely to verify what the commissioners wanted to believe. In 1967 Jim Garrison, the flamboyant district attorney in New Orleans, declared that he had absolute proof that other individuals besides Oswald were involved.

His claim attracted headlines, but his case fell flat in court, adding a touch of pathetic humor to the tragic affair and helping to keep the assassination pot boiling.

Trained historians, perhaps preferring to wait until the passage of time allows the dust to settle on the affair, or perhaps scared off by the impact of false conspiracy charges, have largely hesitated to probe the circumstances of the assassination. Most have been content to leave the task to citizen-scholars, opportunists, and eccentrics. One historian, David R. Wrone, who did examine with care both the commission's findings and the writings of the report's critics, concluded that the physical evidence seemed "incontrovertible that there was more than one assassin." Although this assertion indicated the existence of a conspiracy, he found "no evidence in the published material that would link the conspiracy . . . to the military, business, or intelligence bodies of America, France, or Russia. Nor is there evidence linking the conspiracy to a left-wing group."

That judgment seems reasonable but not conclusive. And it may very well be completely wrong. Significantly, however, it points up the failure of the Warren Commission to conduct an investigation so exhaustive, so painstaking thorough, and so judiciously fair as to silence the speculation and rumors. Admittedly, the commission was faced with a herculean assignment, but it did not do its job well.

The assassination contained all the ingredients of high drama: a young, handsome, popular leader cut down by violent murder in the prime of his life, leaving behind an elegantly beautiful widow, two attractive children, and a large and loyal band of mourning family and friends. Unfortunately, it also contained much of the stuff from which soap operas are made, and the post-Dallas treatment of JFK and the Kennedy family in general often seemed like a blend of serious drama and television serials. The slain President became an instant martyr, and martyrdom, as it often does, tended to confuse reality with romance. Allusions to the legendary kingdom of King Arthur and his dashing knights of the Round Table (prompted by Kennedy's publicized fondness for the musical play *Camelot*) suggested that the Kennedys and the New Frontier had brought a type of nobility to America. "Time," James Reston wrote, "seems to be trying to amend to John Fitzgerald Kennedy. Robbed of his years, he is being rewarded and honored in death as he never was in life.

Deprived of the place he sought in history, he has been given in compensation a place in legend."

For a year or two after his death even sober and serious students of his administration lavished praise upon Kennedy. Richard Rovere credited him with organizing "a generation of public servants who will be serving Presidents (and perhaps being Presidents) into the next century" and for "making thinking respectable in Washington. . . ." Political scientist William G. Carleton observed, "In modern times romantic heroes have become rare. Kennedy is the first in this tradition in a long time, and he is the only American in its top echelon." A year after the assassination, Reston brilliantly captured the essence of national feeling in his article, "What Was Killed Was Not Only the President But the Promise." "What was killed in Dallas was . . . the death of youth and the hope of youth, of the beauty and grace and the touch of magic. . . . He never reached his meridian: we saw him only as a rising sun."

Kennedy-mania resulted in a rash of actions to name airports, streets, schools, bridges, monuments, and geographic locations after JFK. Coarse likenesses of the dead President helped to sell paperweights, desk sets, and trinkets of all types. His book *Profiles in Courage*, which had won the Pulitzer Prize, again became a best seller. By featuring a story—no matter how trivial—about the man or his family, a magazine could count on boosting its sales. Books of all types and quality described his life from cradle to grave in minute, often fraudulent, and at times even vulgar, detail.

In 1965 the memoirs of his close associates began to appear. Schlesinger's and Sorensen's were major works, semischolarly and filled with valuable new information about the New Frontier. Salinger's *With Kennedy* was more limited in scope but still useful. Much less so was the account of the President's personal secretary, Evelyn Lincoln. (O'Donnell and Power's *Johnny, We Hardly Knew Ye* appeared much later, in 1972.) To no one's surprise, the books were overwhelmingly uncritical of their leader, rather like viewing him through a stained-glass window.

By the later sixties, however, the afterglow began to fade. For one thing, the early appraisals had simply been too ardent, too laudatory. For another, many of Kennedy's ideas and policies that drew praise earlier began to undergo serious reevaluation. Looking closely at his record, critics found much to fault. Roosevelt-style liberalism seemed conservative and ill prepared to cope with new perplexities, and they recalled that Kennedy had been rather reluctant to join even the liberal vanguard. The cold war consensus existed no more, but Kennedy was remembered as essentially a cold warrior. Civil rights, meaning integration and nonviolence, had given way to black power and intermittent riots, and the memory of Kennedy's cautious course remained to haunt his reputation. Most of all, Vietnam stirred moral outrage among millions of people, and Kennedy was identified as one who significantly enlarged the American commitment in that bedeviled land. His classic heroic image clashed with the growing antiheroic mood.

British journalist Henry Fairlie, in his best-selling *The Kennedy Promise: The Politics of Expectation*, argued that Kennedy's policies led to the "politics of confrontation" abroad and promised more than they could deliver at home. His political ability did not equal his ambition. Based more on an "elite consensus" than on "mass support," the New Frontier depended too much on superficial calls to action rather than on substantive programs. Even more critically, by trying to do too much overseas, Kennedy put the country on the road to rebellion against its own political institutions. Midge Decter accused the Kennedy administration of trying "to impose an image of itself on American society and American history: an image of itself as the rightful, by virtue of intrinsic superiority, American ruling class." Garry Wills, in *Nixon Agonistes*, raked the dead martyr over the coals with irreverent brilliance: "Style" replaced "ideology" under Kennedy, but the style was aggressive. "America, youthful, vigorous in a nondoctrinal way, would charm or bluff people over to its (nondoctrinal) cause." Most critics concentrated on JFK's foreign policy. Revisionist historians like William Appleman Williams and Walter LaFeber, who had earlier rewritten the traditional interpretation of the beginning of the cold war, turned their attention to Kennedy and found him to be a continuing link in the ruling establishment dedicated to an open, global marketplace and ready to use force when necessary to keep it open. The list could go on almost indefinitely with variations of interpretation as numerous as the writers themselves. But the point is obvious. The Kennedy halo slipped quickly when the consensus of the early sixties, particularly regarding the cold war, cracked under the intense pressure exerted by Vietnam abroad and the intensifying struggle for civil rights at home.

By the early seventies the impact of the efforts to cut Kennedy down to size were pointedly reflected in the teaching materials used in American elementary and high schools. Reviewing twenty-two textbooks, John Berendt found that students were learning that JFK was just a mediocre President. His "record at home was not impressive," declared one. "When it came to policy there was not much that was new about the New Frontier," said another. Most, observed Berendt, methodically robbed Kennedy of the humor and personality that were his trademark.

Each age writes its own history of the past in the light of its own needs and prejudices, a process already clearly demonstrated in the case of John Kennedy. As even more years pass the wisdom of decisions he made will appear greater or lesser according to their long-range influence. Thus interpretations will likely change many times during the course of decades and centuries. The problem is, of course, that the method of evaluating the record of a President unfortunately lacks the definitive quality of an election tally sheet, a baseball box score, or a business balance sheet. Since it is a very human task, it is not a very precise art.

Kennedy's tangible accomplishments, as even his admirers admit, were not very impressive. Although both Sorensen and Schlesinger commended his success in obtaining a high percentage of congressional approval of his legislative requests in 1961 and 1962, the overall tone of their pleading is to judge his Presidency by his intentions rather than by his achievements, noting that he had so little time. Appraising the Kennedy record, political scientist Richard E. Neustadt stressed that recent Presidencies have suggested a certain rhythm: intensive learning dominates the first two years; the fourth brings the test of reelection; assuming victory in the election, the seventh and eighth are years in which eyes turn to the coming nominations and the next administration. Thus, "the key years are the third, the fifth, and the sixth. Kennedy had only one of these." As Schlesinger put it, "It was as if Jackson had died before the nullification controversy and the Bank War; as if Lincoln had been killed six months after Gettysburg or Franklin Roosevelt at the end of 1935 or Truman before the Marshall Plan." By JFK's own standards of presidential greatness those chief executives who achieved their stated programs deserved the larger credit. He disagreed with historians' ranking Theodore Roosevelt, a marvel at using the White House as a "bully pulpit" but not very successful in getting important legislation through Congress, higher than Truman and Polk, who accomplished their legislative purposes but were less able to bring the public with them.

One suspects that considering what he concretely achieved—not proposed or hoped to achieve—Kennedy would rank his own domestic record as disappointing. Although his programs were designed to aid and advance the welfare state, Kennedy was decidedly not—to the pain of critics on the left—a leader in the class struggle or even a committed and zealous social reformer. He clearly shunned anything resembling radical change to the American social-economic framework, even though—to the disgust of critics on the right—he willingly, and usually enthusiastically, used federal authority and funds to ease the misery of the underprivileged. In essence Kennedy moved cautiously in the comfortable ruts worn by Roosevelt, Truman, and even Eisenhower. His tax-cut plan reflected an economic approach dubbed the "new economics," but it was a logical extension of the Keynesian concepts that had been gaining increased acceptance for a quarter of a century. Medicare and federal aid to education were the heirs of similar proposals made by Truman. The New Frontier's civil rights program was thrust upon the President by circumstances more than choice. His campaign against poverty had solid roots in the welfare programs of the Great Depression. Although the public appeared to agree with Kennedy's moderate approach, not one of his major controversial domestic programs became a reality while he lived.

Looking at the President's record in foreign affairs presents the same problem: how to balance what was with what might have been. Judging him by what he actually did, Kennedy emerges as essentially a cold warrior who (1) was in search of fresh ideas on how to make American diplomacy function more efficiently; (2) increased and diversified the military strength and capacity of the United States, thus creating more possibilities for different forms of foreign adventurism; (3) consistently showed an overriding concern not to appear weak or soft for fear of leading adversaries into misjudgment or miscalculation; (4) was open and receptive to new ideas on how to end the cold war and was eager to negotiate for peace but always from a position of strength; and (5) repeatedly decided on a more moderate course of action than that suggested by his military and civilian advisers.

His tangible record in foreign policy was checkered. The Bay of Pigs was a fiasco. Berlin and the Cuban missile crisis took the world to the brink of war, but, by the standards of Kennedy and his advisers, were cold war victories, since they showed America's resolve to contain Soviet expansion. His policies for Africa and Latin America seemed sensible, but the results, particularly in the latter area, were disappointing. His attempts to strengthen the Atlantic Alliance were hopeful but far from realized at the time of his death. The test ban treaty and other understandings reached with the Soviet Union were less of a breakthrough in reducing the dangers of a nuclear confrontation than his admirers claimed, but they were, nevertheless, positive accomplishments.

Kennedy's paramount blunder was Vietnam. His decisions deepened American involvement and constituted a major step toward entrapping the United States in a land war in Asia. That military strategist's nightmare in turn led to severe threats to many of the very things that Kennedy, ironically, sought most to protect: the health of America's social and economic institutions, civility in American political life, the morale of the United States armed services, and the unity of the Atlantic Alliance. Some of his close associates later stressed that he had privately declared his intention to get the United States out of Vietnam if he was reelected in 1964. But in view of Kennedy's conviction that it was imperative to prevent a Vietcong victory in order to maintain American credibility in the eyes of the major Communist powers, one is inclined to be skeptical that he would have dared to do so.

It is fair to say of Kennedy that he tried to do *too* much in foreign policy, and that the eager-beaver types who surrounded him aggravated his own inclination for vigorous action. He inspired their loyalty, their affection, and their enthusiasm to a remarkable degree, and they reveled in their tasks. Enormously confident of the wisdom of their views, the New Frontiersmen encouraged the President and each other never to stand still to such a degree that the campaign slogan of "moving America forward" seemed to be coupled with the dictum of "When in doubt, do something."

Intelligent and eager to learn, Kennedy appeared to grow in stature, particularly during his last year in office. Nevertheless, perhaps he was too young for the job of President. A patrician used to getting his own way, with more experience and maturity he would probably have gained a more sensitive and judicious view of reality. Yet, America in 1960 seemed ready for youth—Nixon, too, was a relatively young man, only a few years older than JFK—and Kennedy's refreshing zest for life and public service was one of his most engaging and remembered qualities. Indeed, in any final accounting of John Kennedy's performance as President, one cannot ignore the impact of his personal charm. A deeply serious man with an extraordinary sense of humor, his dry wit, his shunning of the corny, his emphasis on culture and intellect, his ability to make light of and poke fun at himself, his easy fatalism, all became a part of the New Frontier because they were so much a part of him.

But the fact remains that Kennedy achieved few concrete results. What he deserves to be remembered for most of all was his faculty for generating a strong emotional response among the American people—hatred among some, but love and affection among many more. Looking back at JFK from the perspective of the 1970s, a sensitive black woman in her thirties poignantly recalled the Kennedy magic: "Like a good book the life of John F. Kennedy steals inside and has somehow made me different. I never met him though it's hard for me to believe. . . . Everyone I knew loved him with a sort of possessiveness. It seemed as if they fancied themselves having a 'hot line' to his desk at the White House." Columnist Walter Lippmann long maintained that the great issues of life and politics in a prosperous nation are not material but spiritual. If Kennedy's tangible accomplishments were less than spectacular, his ability to motivate, to inspire, and to give Americans a sense of national direction was, nonetheless, remarkable. When he called upon people for dedication and purpose, most listened, understood, and believed.

# VI

## Transition to
## the Great Society

J OHN F. KENNEDY was the eighth American President to die
in office, and the sixth in little less than a hundred years. In four
cases the chief executive was assassinated. The fact that Kennedy's
death occurred in Vice President Johnson's home state was an irony
appropriate to a decade that seemed to be patterned after a Greek
tragedy. Johnson was with Kennedy on that fateful autumn day in
Dallas, riding in an open car only a short distance behind him. When
the shots that struck the President and Texas Governor John
Connally were heard, Secret Service agent Rufus Youngblood
roughly pushed Johnson to the floor of the car, courageously covering
him with his own body as a protection against further gunfire. A
short time later, with Kennedy officially declared dead, Dallas police
drove Johnson to the presidential airplane at Love Field. There, on
November 22, 1963, he took the simple oath that made him the
thirty-fifth man to hold the highest office that the people of the
United States can bestow.

Despite the numbing impact of the assassination, the transition
from Kennedy to Johnson was remarkably swift and smooth. Johnson
was better prepared than any Vice President in the country's history
to assume his new duties. Realizing that an activist like LBJ could
scarcely avoid being depressed by the frustrating powerlessness of
the Vice Presidency, Kennedy had taken great pains to keep his
subordinate involved in important government affairs. Johnson
served as a member of the National Security Council and chaired
both the National Aeronautics and Space Council and the President's

Committee on Equal Employment Opportunity. He dutifully attended meetings of the cabinet and the weekly conferences where the President briefed Democratic congressional leaders. In addition, Johnson journeyed over 100,000 miles to 30 countries as the chief executive's special representative, and made some 150 speeches. Many of the trips were basically goodwill missions, but others were for more important purposes, such as one to Berlin in 1961 to demonstrate America's determination to remain in that threatened city and one to Saigon in the same year to appraise the Vietnam war.

Personally, Kennedy had treated Johnson with great respect and kindness, and the two men got along well together. The same could not be said for the Vice President and JFK's staff. Despite Kennedy's insistence that everyone in the White House be courteous and considerate of LBJ, some of the New Frontiersmen made little effort to conceal their disdain for the Texan. Certainly Johnson was quick to regard trivial incidents as grave insults. In particular he resented the publicity that Robert Kennedy received from friendly members of the press. Chafing in relative obscurity, Johnson feared that the younger Kennedy would begin to emerge in people's minds as the logical successor to his brother in 1968, when the Vice President would still be young enough to make a serious bid for the top post.

Although he occasionally complained privately about his treatment, Johnson was, nevertheless, completely loyal to Kennedy. When LBJ reported the disgust of middle-class Democrats with stories about high living by the chic New Frontiersmen—particularly the celebrated midnight plunges by fully clothed guests into the swimming pool at Bobby Kennedy's home—he usually coupled his comment with an expression of understanding for the weight of the President's many burdens. Although he exerted surprisingly little influence over Kennedy's legislative program, Johnson was available to do the President's bidding, and JFK knew it. Some of the Vice President's assignments would have taxed the patience of a person much less accustomed than Johnson to the exercise of power. Old friends chortled at the thought of his spending hours discussing the policies of the National Zoo! Though faithful, there was no question that he was, as Leonard Baker later wrote, in an "eclipse." His office was insignificant—Benjamin Franklin had sneered that the holder should be called "his superfluous excellency"—and the man he served seemed dazzling.

Events in Dallas changed all of that.

Taking over the reins of government in a time of such trauma required great finesse. Johnson, the man deprecated for his lack of grace and taste, demonstrated both qualities. While intelligence agencies probed for any signs of a plot against not just Kennedy but the government of the United States as well, the new President moved quickly to ensure a smooth transfer of power. He mixed calls of comfort, such as to JFK's mother, with essential government business, interviews with selected reporters, conferences with congressional leaders, and a bit of diplomacy with foreign leaders, like Charles de Gaulle, who attended Kennedy's funeral. Winning confidence in his leadership was his first order of business, and during his first days in office Johnson attempted to touch all bases in a frenzy of activity. He lectured the governors of the fifty states on the need for their support. He sought the counsel of former Presidents Eisenhower and Truman. He spoke in person or by telephone with business, labor, and civil rights leaders, government workers, and elder statesmen. "People," he told them, "must put aside their selfish aims in the larger cause of the nation's interest. They must start trusting each other; they must start communicating with each other; and they must start working with each other."

Most of all he unabashedly attempted to cloak himself with the "mantle of Kennedy" as quickly and as completely as possible. His goals for America, he assured listeners, were the same as the slain President's. Ignoring memories of past grievances between himself and the Kennedy staff, he pled with them to stay on in his administration. "I need you more than John Kennedy did," he told them. When Arthur Schlesinger, Jr., submitted his resignation, Johnson rejected it as nothing more than a gesture. "If you act on it," he declared, "I'll have you arrested." When Schlesinger explained that every President should have the right to select his own people, LBJ replied that he now regarded the Harvard history professor as one of his own men. Despite the difficulty of working for another chief executive, the Kennedyites remained at least long enough to smooth the transition to a new administration. Some, like Schlesinger, performed few substantive duties, but they provided the symbol of continuity that Johnson wisely craved. Others, like Rusk, McNamara, McGeorge Bundy, and Lawrence O'Brien, became key figures on the Johnson team.

Reconciliation extended in other directions as well. James Rowe, a brilliant Washington lawyer, who along with attorneys Clark Clifford and Abe Fortas had been among Johnson's closest and most trusted advisers in the fifties, was summoned to the White House. He and LBJ had disagreed bitterly during the 1960 campaign and had parted on cool terms. The new President candidly apologized to Rowe for their past differences and asked for support and advice. When Rowe started to protest that their break had been his fault, Johnson cut him off, asking, "Damn it, can't you be content to be the first man the thirty-sixth President of the United States has apologized to?" To old adversaries like Joseph Rauh, the longtime wheelhorse of the liberal Americans for Democratic Action, he behaved in a similar way, appealing for help and assistance in a time of national need. He called Everett Dirksen, the minority leader in the Senate, to ask him to urge his party to forget partisan politics, "so that we could weather the national crisis in which we were involved and unite our people." Graciously, the conservative Republican from Illinois assured him that he would.

Five days after the assassination, Johnson delivered his first address to Congress. It moved many of those in the packed House chamber to tears. His low-key opening words—"All I have, I would have given gladly not to be standing here today"—were, as Tom Wicker of the *New York Times* wrote, "exactly the right statement, delivered in exactly the right tone." LBJ hammered home the themes of his message: national unity and continuity, the continuation of the policies and programs begun by John Kennedy. The emotional high point of his speech came when he turned to civil rights. "No memorial oration or eulogy," he declared, "could more eloquently honor President Kennedy's memory than the earliest possible passage of the civil rights bill for which he fought." After the applause died down, he continued: "We have talked long enough in this country about equal rights. We have talked for one hundred years or more. It is time now to write the next chapter—and to write it in the books of law." As a southerner, the first in the White House since Woodrow Wilson, Johnson's words had a special meaning. By pushing civil rights, he was staking out his claim for what had eluded him for so long: recognition as a national, rather than a sectional, leader. And by using the emotion engendered by the assassination—"Let us here highly resolve that John Fitzgerald Kennedy did not live or die in vain"—he was making it tough on Congress to deny what he wanted.

Johnson's first week in office gave him tremendous momentum. He captured the nation's confidence and appeared to be clearly in command of the situation. "There *was*," he later wrote, "a consensus—a broad, deep, and genuine consensus among most groups within our diverse society which would hold together, I hoped and prayed, long enough for important tasks to be accomplished." The consensus had been forged over a long period of time through the give-and-take of compromise. In Congress LBJ had been a master of the process, one of the most accomplished in American history, probably the best since Henry Clay. But compromise meant primarily bargaining on domestic matters. One won half a loaf today and hoped to enlarge the share next year or in five years. Foreign policy was a different matter. There, consensus had developed less through compromise than on the widely accepted basis of national self-interest. Diplomacy was primarily the realm of the executive branch, and although the Senate ratified treaties, it seldom horse-traded the way Congress did on domestic measures. So while Johnson possessed great experience and expertise in maintaining the consensus on domestic questions, he was less sure about how to preserve it when challenged on foreign issues.

Fortunately, when Johnson became chief executive he faced no pressing international crises. The world, like the United States, seemed to be in a state of shock over Kennedy's assassination. "Texas was always a joke," British historian Denis W. Brogan chided. "Now Texas is a bad joke." As Philip Geyelin noted, "It was no help to LBJ that a great many foreigners focused their criticism on Texas. . . ." Still, the world's relative quiet enabled him to center his energies on what he knew best—domestic affairs, and on what he did best—passing legislation.

To demonstrate at once his determination to break the logjam of bills in Congress, he insisted that the legislators complete action during 1963 on the foreign aid bill and the plan to sell wheat to the Soviet Union. The Senate gave its approval, but a great many representatives left for the Christmas holidays before a final vote on the measures could be taken. When Speaker John McCormack recommended doing nothing until the following year, Johnson refused. He dramatically ordered the members of the House to return to Washington, shrewdly blunting their irritation by inviting them to a festive reception at the White House on December 23. Standing on a chair in the State Dining Room, he urged his guests to act on the bills. The next morning the House gave him what he wanted. LBJ's performance added new luster to his reputation as a master of legislative maneuver. Close observers, however, noted that the vote reflected no switch of sides by Republicans, but rather that more Democrats responded to the plea to return to the capital. Nevertheless it was a victory for the new President.

By the time 1963 slipped sadly away, Johnson had basically decided on his legislative strategy for the following year. The tax cut and civil rights were to receive priority. The President knew that both would demand a maximum effort, but their passage would greatly enhance his chances of being elected President in his own right. Johnson also determined to add a third measure to his list of "must pass" legislation: an act formally declaring war on poverty.

LBJ reasoned that the life or death of the tax cut was tied to the federal budget. If he could convince fiscal conservatives in Congress that he intended to hold spending down, their support would insure passage of the bill. Kennedy had set an arbitrary limit of $101.5 billion on the new budget to be submitted in January. Never before, not even during World War II, had the budget exceeded the century mark. Johnson decided that political necessity required that the total be kept under $100 billion. Told by his advisers that a budget of $108 billion was actually needed and was defensible, he agreed. But, as he stressed to Walter Heller and Budget Director Kermit Gordon, it was essential to placate Senator Harry Byrd, the chairman of the Senate Finance Committee, if there was to be any hope of getting favorable action on tax reduction. If you don't get the budget below $100 billion, he went on, "you won't pee one drop." To Heller and Treasury Secretary Douglas Dillon in particular it was absolutely imperative to cut taxes as an economic stimulus, even if it meant whittling down the budget, and when the President submitted his budget to Congress in early January, it was a surprisingly low $97.9

billion. The lower figure reduced the projected federal deficit for the year by about half. To dramatize the government's commitment to a comprehensive economy drive, the President soberly declared that unneeded lights in the White House would be turned out, an exercise so overpublicized that it became a ludicrous episode.

The civil rights bill appeared to be even more difficult to pass than the tax plan. But while Johnson had some reservations about the absolute wisdom of tinkering with the tax structure, he was unequivocally committed to doing something significant to help minorities. The old saying that converts are more zealous than those born into their religion seemed to apply to LBJ and civil rights. Even as Vice President, his actions and statements were beginning to convince many blacks that LBJ was not a typical southerner about race. As his aide Hobart Taylor had told Johnson the previous summer, members of the Negro community who had heard his recent speeches in St. Louis and Detroit were saying, "I was wrong about Lyndon Johnson."

In his first days as chief executive, LBJ met individually with key leaders in the black community to assure them that he intended to press for the civil rights bill "with every energy I possessed." The dramatic statements on the subject in his first speech to Congress publicized his commitment. To suggestions that he go slow on such an emotional issue or modify the bill, he quoted advice "Cactus" Jack Garner had given him years before: there comes a time in poker and politics when a man has to "put in all his stack." Johnson decided that the civil rights issue was that time for him. Although he recognized that lining up votes to invoke cloture against a southern filibuster would be difficult, he decided against diluting the bill in an attempt to pick up additional support.

The President's decision to add the poverty program as a "must" for 1964 was really not surprising. It appealed strongly to his deeply felt sympathy for the poor and doubtless reminded him of the efforts of his patron, Franklin Roosevelt, to alleviate suffering among the impoverished during the depression years, when Johnson was just beginning his public career. On the day following Kennedy's assassination, when Heller asked the new chief executive what he wanted to do about the antipoverty campaign the New Frontier had been planning, Johnson replied, "I'm interested. I'm sympathetic. Go ahead. Give it the highest priority. Push ahead full tilt." As the official history of the program later recorded, if Kennedy had an "intellectual" appreciation of the plan, LBJ had a "gut" reaction to the basic idea, and he determined to make it the "cornerstone of his administration."

Once the President had given the full-speed-ahead signal, the next problem for administration planners was how to coordinate existing projects, like Area Redevelopment, and pending proposals, like the Youth Conservation Corps, into a coordinated and comprehensive program. Government agencies could be counted on to fight jealously any attempt to infringe upon their established domains. One possibility was to select a small number of "pockets of poverty" as demonstration areas. A "development corporation" in each could choose its programs from the wide variety of possibilities offered by competing federal agencies and coordinate the overall operation. Dubbed the "community action" concept, it became the heart of the administration's effort, although the idea of using only a limited number of areas was dropped as incompatible with the "unconditional war on poverty" declared by Johnson in his State of the Union message in early January.

In presenting the program to Congress the President used business terms to explain its purposes, emphasizing that it was a sound investment to salvage unemployable youths. The *Annual Report* of the Council of Economic Advisers, released a few days later, supplied an array of grim facts and figures to back up the chief executive's appeal. Using a poverty yardstick of $3,000 per year for a family of four, it reported the shocking statistic that in 1962, 9.3 million families, or 20 percent of the population, were below the poverty line. The proportion was even higher among certain groups—Negroes, the poorly educated, southerners, the elderly, families headed by women, and rural residents.

Two weeks later, in his budget message, Johnson tried to calm the anxieties of those who rebelled at the idea of Washington bureaucrats' extending their control still further over individual communities: "I propose a program which relies on the traditional time-tested American methods of organized local community action to help individuals, families, and communities help themselves." Community action programs would be locally initiated. Their goal would be to "focus" federal, state, and local resources and services—health, housing, welfare, agricultural—"on the roots of poverty in urban and rural areas." Asking for roughly a billion dollars to begin the campaign against poverty, he explained that he would shift dollars from the defense portion of the budget in order to keep his promise to hold the line on federal spending.

While Johnson was launching the crusade publicly with his messages to Congress, within the administration a battle was under way over who should administer the program. Secretary of Labor Willard Wirtz led the fight to assign the operation to a cabinet department or existing agency. Budget Director Gordon, Heller, and others contended that a new and independent agency would likely be more innovative. Johnson agreed with the latter argument on the grounds that "The best way to kill a new idea is to put it in an old-line agency." He also concurred with the suggestion made by Gene Patterson, vice chairman of the Civil Rights Commission, not to call the poverty program by that name because it had a deprecatory, pejorative sense. Instead it became officially the Economic Opportunity Program, although the term "Poverty Program" had so caught on that it was difficult to shake.

On February 1, the President named Kennedy's dynamic brother-in-law, Sargent Shriver, to add the directorship of the Office of Economic Opportunity (OEO) to his existing duties as head of the Peace Corps. Shriver plunged immediately into lengthy conferences with both government officials and private persons in a crash program to develop a plan of attack. The conferees accepted the community action concept fully but readily acknowledged the wisdom of delegating many specific responsibilities to various federal departments: jobs and training to Labor, education and health to HEW, rural programs to Agriculture. They also agreed on a three-point strategy: to emphasize individual economic independence, to build around the theory that poverty was cyclical, and to focus on the young.

Shriver and his associates turned next to forming a task force of experts to draft the specific legislation for the program and the President's message presenting the bill to Congress. The frenetic rush to complete the job caused one participant to describe it as "the beautiful hysteria of it all." Differences of opinion among the 137 participants were frequent and often caustic. When Michael Harrington, author of *The Other America*, the book that had inspired much of the intense concern about poverty, criticized the billion-dollar appropriation request as "nickles and dimes," Shriver answered dryly, "Well, I don't know about you, Mr. Harrington, but this will be my first experience at spending a billion dollars, and I'm quite excited about it."

An intense bureaucratic conflict among the twenty-one government agencies dealing with America's welfare system paralleled the work of the task force. The agencies administered some two hundred projects, many of them overlapping and interlocked, and they struggled furiously to protect their individual prerogatives. Shriver, although extremely gifted at inspiring those who worked for him and in producing enormous quantities of work, was not especially experienced or skilled in administrative and bureaucratic infighting. Johnson, however, was, and he functioned as a superb peacemaker, soothing tempers and making the critical decisions. Convinced that the task force proposals had too much of a military flavor, he insisted that the emphasis on military training camps be dropped, but primarily he was more interested in the ends than the means.

By mid-March the Economic Opportunity Bill was ready to send to Congress. It contained one exciting but controversial new idea, the Community Action Program, plus several less-original concepts: a Job Corps for youths 16–21, job-training programs for adult heads of households, work-study funds for college youths, grants to farmers and rural businesses, loans to individuals or companies willing to hire hard-core unemployed, and the Volunteers for America (VISTA) program for those willing to work with the poor. The bill provided Johnson with a potent political weapon in an election year. Unlike the tax cut and civil rights bills, which were warmed-over from the New Frontier, the war on poverty was clearly branded LBJ, and he left no doubt that he intended to fight for its enactment. "It gave him," James Sundquist wrote, "the excuse to stand on the same Southern courthouse steps [Gainesville, Georgia] where Roosevelt stood and pledge himself to carry on the war on want that FDR had started."

By the time Congress adjourned in October 1964, the big three of the President's legislative program had all been enacted, as well as a good many other significant bills, including the Urban Mass Transit Act, the Housing Act, the Nurse Training Act, the Wilderness Areas Act, an expansion of the food stamp program, and a wheat price-support bill. It was a remarkable performance, and Johnson received and deserved high praise for his role in prodding Congress to act after its sluggish and unresponsive performance in 1963. Yet, few observers believed that Johnson's acknowledged mastery of the legislative process or his legendary persuasiveness could have produced such results alone. The tremendous ground swell for the passing of the tax and civil rights measures as tributes to John Kennedy's memory was unquestionably important. In addition, any new President can count on a "honeymoon" period when legislators will usually cooperate with his wishes, and Johnson took full advantage of his.

Since 1964 was an election year, partisan politics were prominent, but that, too, probably worked to Johnson's benefit. With LBJ virtually certain to head the ticket in the fall, many Democrats were receptive to the argument that their chances for reelection would improve if they helped the President and the party roll up an impressive record to present to the voters. Johnson's success in persuading his fellow southerners to back his programs proved to be especially important, and the increased number of southern Democrats voting with their northern colleagues tipped the balance on many critical ballots.

The tax-cut bill was a case in point. Knowing that Senator Byrd's influence would determine the outcome, the President not only cut the size of his proposed budget dramatically to please the crusty Virginian but also flattered the senator by giving him an advance peek at the lowered figures before making them public. Delighted that at last a chief executive was committed to doing some real economizing, Byrd became virtually a secret ally of the President in securing passage of the bill. He had been a vociferous advocate of balanced budgets for too long to go so far as to vote for the measure, but his willingness to support it—quietly—was invaluable. Reportedly, he even told Johnson the night before the final vote, "I'm going to have to vote against the bill, but I'll be working for you behind the scenes."

LBJ's finesse with the southerners also provided the key to

passing the antipoverty act. With their heavily urban constituencies, northern Democrats backed the bill enthusiastically, but the southerners had a past record of deserting the party on similar measures. A few months before, enough of them had joined with the Republicans to defeat the extension of the Area Redevelopment Act and to block a youth employment program. The President moved to halt southern defections by shrewdly tabbing Representative Phil M. Landrum of Georgia, a man with impeccable conservative credentials and recognized parliamentary skills, to sponsor the bill. When a group of southerners objected to the reported plan to appoint Adam Yarmolinsky as deputy director of the program, Johnson quickly sacrificed him. The complaint against Yarmolinsky was that he was a radical, but, ironically, he continued to work in the Defense Department with access to military secrets without serious objection. By compromise and cajolery, LBJ held enough southerners in line to pass the bill comfortably. In the House 60 of 100 voted for the measure, while in the Senate, 11 of the 22 men from Dixie supported the President. It was questionable whether a program put together in such haste and frenzy could hope to work, but if nothing else, the widely publicized bill meant that the existence of real poverty in the United States was no longer a well-kept secret.

With the civil rights bill, Johnson's "southern connection" was little help. If anything, it was a handicap. Kennedy, as a northerner, could have accepted significant compromises in order to secure passage. As a southerner anxious to prove his liberal commitment to civil rights, such a course was next to unthinkable for LBJ. The key to the eventual enactment of the measure was the support of the Republicans. Shortly before Kennedy's assassination, the GOP leader in the House, Charles Halleck of Indiana, agreed to back the bill. With Johnson keeping the pressure on for passage, it cleared the House by a lop-sided margin of 290–130 in early February.

Everyone expected, however, that the fight in the Senate would be much harder. Although a clear majority of members favored the bill, a determined southern filibuster stalled action for over two months. Senator Richard Russell cleverly marshaled his forces into three talking platoons, one holding the floor while the other two rested. Meanwhile, ardent church leaders—Protestant, Catholic, and Jewish—joined liberal spokesmen and the President in urging the

Senate to close down debate and approve the bill. Their efforts were invaluable. One disgruntled Republican from the West complained, "Oh, I will have to vote for it in the end because you've got those damned pastors on my neck!"

What finally turned the tide was Everett Dirksen's decision to join hands with northern Democrats in passing the bill. The mellifluous-voiced minority leader quoted from Victor Hugo: "Stronger than all the armies is an idea whose time has come." He studied the document sentence by sentence and proposed a series of minor changes calculated to enable reluctant Republicans to vote yes. His amendments defined the limits of federal enforcement power and paid lip service to the rights of state and local authorities. Although some liberals were unhappy, most agreed with Senator Jacob K. Javits of New York that the purposes of the bill remained substantially intact. Johnson and the Democratic leadership in the Senate passed the word that they could live with the modifications. Dirksen's efforts earned him praise as the architect of the Civil Rights Act. Enough previously hesitant Republicans voted with northern Democrats to reach the two-thirds mark required to invoke cloture and halt the filibuster. After that, the final acceptance of the bill by the Senate was a foregone conclusion.

Whether the measure would have passed without Johnson's leadership remained an interesting but moot question. What mattered was that the first major civil rights act since the immediate post–Civil War period had passed under the administration of a southern President. It was an impressive triumph. Despite their bitterness, southerners accepted the outcome quietly with little of the overt defiance that had been predicted. The President, as the fall elections would confirm, had lost favor with the average citizen in the Deep South. But he had gained the confidence of millions of northerners.

Indeed, nothing surprised veteran Johnson-watchers as much in his first few months in office as his rapport with the American public. Many had frankly expected that once the "togetherness spirit" fostered by the assassination had faded, LBJ's style would badly rankle nonsoutherners. With his sure-handed public touch, however, almost everything he did seemed to strike a responsive chord, and he moved from one triumph to another with striking virtuosity. His speech before the United Nations General Assembly won favorable worldwide attention when he firmly called for an end to the cold war "once and for all"; his war on poverty and civil rights program stamped him as "one who cares"; his skill in resolving the differences over work rules avoided a crippling nationwide railroad strike and established him as a practical man of affairs.

Yet even in that halcyon period when he publicly seemed poised and self-assured, privately he revealed signs of insecurity. Stories began to circulate that in the days immediately after Kennedy's death Johnson had been unable to go to sleep without someone's remaining in the room with him. Accounts of his obsessive belief that the "liberals" and "intellectuals" were against him became juicy tidbits of gossip on the Washington cocktail circuit. Worries about his accent and mannerisms, telling drawbacks to his hopes of winning the nomination in 1960, continued to plague him in the White House. Especially galling was the knowledge that he was an "accidental President," who had inherited by assassination what he had been unable to obtain on his own. He told intimates that there were those—the archliberals, the Ivy League set in their smart Georgetown salons, the Kennedy crowd—who would never accept him as President. "You just wait," he told a friend, "and see what happens when I put one foot wrong."

The credibility gap that would gradually become one of his most painful problems began to manifest itself early in ways both important and insignificant. Reporters knew, for example, that he drank Scotch, but at his instructions, the White House insisted that he drank bourbon, an American product. While attempting to bring the budget below $100 billion in late 1963, he played with the press like a Yo-Yo, deliberately feeding them incorrect figures that caused them to misinform their readers. When he dropped his plans to make Adam Yarmolinsky deputy director of the Office of Economic Opportunity in order to satisfy the demands of some southern congressmen, he flatly—and falsely—denied that he had ever intended to appoint him to the position.

Johnson wanted badly to get along with the press, but he also wanted reporters to see things his way. In January 1964 he told several of them, "If you play along with me, I'll play along with you. I'll make big men of you. If you want to play it the other way, I know how to play it both ways too, and know how to cut off the flow of news except in handouts." Particularly during his first months in office, he consciously and assiduously courted members of the media. But if they subsequently wrote stories about him or his administration that he disliked, he was furious. *Time* magazine published an unflattering story about him in early April that stung him to the quick. It told of a gay and ebullient LBJ loading four reporters into his cream-colored Lincoln Continental and driving around his Texas ranch at 85 miles an hour while sipping beer from a paper cup. The tale was a sharp blow to his attempts to project the image of a responsible and serious public leader. But it also happened to be true. Johnson was not only outraged; he also felt betrayed. He seemed to believe that by wooing the press he could insure that he would be favorably portrayed. But reporters knew that if they were too glowing in their praise of the chief executive or repeatedly parroted his views, they risked losing their own credibility. Press and President were natural antagonists, and for a free press to be effective it could be no other way. As his first press secretary, Pierre Salinger, tried to convince him, good publicity could seldom be manufactured; it followed good works.

Johnson compounded his difficulties with the news media by a penchant for secrecy that baffled Washington observers. The gap between what press and public would like to know and what a government, in good conscience, feels it can release and confirm for general knowledge is a familiar story, particularly in the years since World War II. But in Johnson's case his devious denials and fetish for unwarranted secrecy eventually deepened the inevitable gap into a chasm. The same man who would brazenly pull up his shirt to reveal for the cameras the very private matter of a scar from his operation went to great lengths to prevent the public from learning in December 1963 that he had asked historian Eric F. Goldman to form a group of the "best minds" in the country to assist him in planning policies. Eventually, it became impossible to maintain the secret any longer, and Goldman became part of the White House staff.

Although the President honestly wanted to tap the ideas of the country's thinkers in developing his programs, it was also true that Goldman, as his "intellectual in residence," served as Johnson's way of saying, "See, I too have ties to the intellectual community, just as

Kennedy did." Sadly, the experiment was not a smashing success. When Goldman left the White House thirty-three months later, his considerable ego badly bruised, he was bitter with Johnson, and the President reciprocated the feeling. As one of LBJ's associates explained, it was difficult for Johnson to work with intellectuals because it was simply unnatural to his personality, his environment, and his background. When many of them joined the vanguard of opponents to his Vietnam policies, he became intensely resentful, blowing his dislike of their views completely out of proportion.

A proud and vain man, consumed by the desire to be a great President, Johnson drove himself relentlessly. Critics had chided Eisenhower for spending too much time relaxing. The reverse applied to Johnson. For him virtually everything had a political purpose. He liked to say that his father had once admonished him that no man belonged in politics unless he could walk into a room of people and know at once who was for him and who was against him. LBJ confidently believed that he possessed such an instinct, and he literally devoted his life to honing his natural political talents. Other men had hobbies or merely enjoyed loafing, but not Johnson. He enjoyed his family and drew pleasure from raising cattle and developing his ranch, but politics was both his vocation and his avocation. Cultural interests he left to his wife. If he entertained, as he and Lady Bird did frequently and with considerable charm, the guest list invariably centered on those whose interests were heavily political.

He studied, analyzed, catalogued, and remembered the strengths and the weaknesses, the likes and dislikes of fellow politicians as some men do stock prices, batting averages, and musical compositions. He knew who drank Scotch and who bourbon, whose wife was sick, who needed new post offices built to ensure reelection, and who was in trouble with organized labor, and he invariably recalled who owed him for a past favor. When he read, he did so to get specific, useful information, not for pleasure or for philosophical insight. Correspondent Hugh Sidey once queried a number of Johnson's aides about his reading habits in the hope of doing an article on the subject. Sidey had written a piece earlier about JFK's rapid reading speed and his love for reading virtually everything he could get his hands on. Not wanting to put their chief in a bad light compared to

Kennedy, the staffers assured Sidey that Johnson, too, was an omniverous reader. Asked to mention some of the recent books that he had read, each pondered and finally came up with an identical answer, British economist Barbara Ward's *The Rich Nations and the Poor Nations*. As they knew but were not about to admit, Johnson read few books. A compulsive worker, fourteen- and fifteen-hour days were standard fare for him, and he liked to boast that he slept at most only six hours per night. During periods of intense pressure and activity, his favorite method of resting was to lapse into extended bull sessions—usually about politics. The exuberant outburst by his aide Jack Valenti that the President had "extra glands . . . that gave him energy that ordinary men simply don't have" was overly extravagant, but LBJ's capacity for sustained work was indeed incredible.

He consistently stressed the need for good administration in government. Impressed by the scientific budget system initiated by Robert McNamara in the Defense Department, he wanted the entire federal establishment to adopt such a system. Yet, personally, he was not a very tidy administrator. He tried to do so much himself that he often got small things mixed up with big ones, just as he tried to do things faster than he could persuade people of the need. No detail was too small for his attention. He used the telephone—an instrument which seemed to fascinate and delight him—dozens of times a day in his obsession to know everything that was going on in his government. He insisted that lengthy and prolix reports be accompanied with crisp, incisive, and short (preferably one page) summaries. Although he possessed an enormous knowledge of government programs and a ready command of facts and figures, his historical perspective was limited largely to the years covering his own public service. Johnson had keen analytical ability and a knack for asking the right questions when probing an issue. In gathering data for use in making critical decisions he practiced what some observers referred to as the "principle of triangulation,"—always trying to get three different views and opinions. As Franklin Roosevelt did, LBJ liked to assign two staff people to the same job without telling either one about the other and to play advisers off one another so he could get both sides of a picture.

For those who worked closely with him, life was exhilarating and challenging but never easy. He pushed his aides at the same break-neck pace as he drove himself. Getting a few days, or even a few hours, off from the White House was a difficult, nearly impossible task. Reporter Chalmers Roberts recalled that late one hot Saturday afternoon in July, Johnson became highly indignant when he learned that one of his aides, Walter Jenkins, had gone to the beach. Just because Jenkins's wife had gone to the beach, the President snorted, didn't mean that his aide "had to go running after her."

LBJ followed up assignments impatiently, often demanding that staff members provide him with complete and thorough reports in an almost impossibly short time. For the Johnson men all-night sessions were common. The frequent tongue-lashings he inflicted on his staff were particularly trying. Sometimes they came collectively: "How can you be so goddamn stupid! Why can't I get men with the brains of the Kennedy bunch?" More commonly a single individual caught the brunt of his anger, departing, as Eric Goldman put it, "white-faced and shaken, swearing that he could not stand it another day." LBJ was very intolerant of a bad job, but he also used profanity and exaggeration to let off steam, and most of his aides came to realize that he exploded both to relieve himself of anxiety and to prod them to do better jobs on their assignments. Cushioning the impact of his verbal abuse were his habit of praising staff members extravagantly, sometimes only minutes after he had chewed them out, and his genuine interest in the overall well-being of his aides and their families.

George Reedy, one of LBJ's closest aides, observed that "a President moves throughout his days surrounded by literally hundreds of people whose relationship to him is that of a doting mother to a spoiled child. Whatever he wants is brought to him immediately. . . ." This type of environment magnified and accentuated the best and the worst of Johnson's personality traits. All chief executives use the "carrot and stick" approach to a degree; under LBJ it was simply more extreme. Although his aides were highly competent, they were tenser than Kennedy's had been. And despite Johnson's praise, they sensed that he was not fully confident of their ability to function independently. As a result, department and agency officials were often reluctant to trust an answer they received from his staff and insisted on receiving directions directly from the President.

Although he had insisted that Kennedy's staff remain with him, in order to use their talents and to display publicly the continuity in the White House, Johnson quickly showed privately that he did not intend to follow blindly in JFK's steps. He vetoed a number of appointments to key posts that Kennedy had approved in his last days. Not unnaturally, LBJ relied more and more on his own longtime associates. The Johnson men were mostly Texans who had demonstrated their readiness to subordinate their beliefs to his, even when their assumptions about legislative and social matters were different.

In Johnson's first months in office Walter Jenkins, a middle-aged man with a perpetual tired look, functioned essentially as chief of staff, though with drastically less power than Sherman Adams had wielded in the Eisenhower administration. Jenkins attended meetings of the cabinet and National Security Council, forwarded presidential directives to departments and agencies, and screened names for high-level appointments. He had been with Johnson since 1939, and his family and the Johnsons were extremely close. Sadly, in October of 1964, in the middle of the election campaign, Jenkins was arrested as a homosexual. Since homosexuals were believed to be susceptible to blackmail, one who had access to the most delicate of national secrets was considered a security risk. And although an FBI report declared that there was no evidence to suggest that Jenkins had compromised security "in any manner," the man who had served Johnson loyally for twenty-five years was forced to leave the administration.

His departure made Bill D. Moyers even more important to Johnson. Then only in his late twenties, blessed with great intelligence and charm, Moyers had been with Johnson off and on since his late teens. He was efficient, a man perfectly suited to the image of an administration that was getting things done. He was also a committed liberal with strong ties to the Kennedy camp. At first, he took charge of coordinating domestic programs. Later, when the President's problems with the press became particularly troublesome, the articulate young man became press secretary. Johnson's fondness for Moyers was well known; at times LBJ alluded to him as the son he never had. Closeted with the President for long hours of conversation, Moyers, more than any other aide, influenced the President's thinking. If, as Eric Goldman wrote, he was not exactly the President's "no" man—and Goldman believed that one could not say no to Johnson and stay in the inner circle very long—Moyers at least mastered "the art of the occasional sidewise suggestion, which sometimes diverted the presidential course." Harry McPherson explained that only Moyers "made Johnson think of himself when young." When Moyers, who wanted more independence than he could have in the White House, left Washington in 1967 to accept a lucrative position in publishing, Johnson was unable to conceal his hurt feelings.

Jack Valenti, Horace Busby, and George Reedy were Johnson loyalists who helped to ease his transition into the White House. Valenti was an effusive and quick-witted Texas public-relations man and jack-of-all-trades who accompanied the President most of the time. He was especially valuable as a speech writer, a personal contact man, and as the most frequent butt of the President's jibes. Busby, also a Texan, was a tireless worker who wrote speeches and handled special projects. He was perhaps more attuned to LBJ's mind than anyone else, and the chief executive valued greatly his pungent memos about domestic affairs and politics. Reedy was a non-Texan, tenaciously loyal to his chief. Better than anyone else, he knew LBJ's concept of news. When Pierre Salinger resigned as press secretary in the spring of 1964 to run for the Senate from California, Reedy, a former newspaperman, was the logical choice to replace him. Unfortunately, he and the reporters who covered the President did not get along well. His relations with the press deteriorated to such a point that he was switched to other duties and replaced by Moyers.

Later in the administration, Marvin Watson, Harry McPherson, Douglass Cater, and Joseph Califano became vital cogs in the Johnson staff. Watson handled appointments, guarded access to the President, and expedited paper work. A former steel company executive with archaic views towards labor, he was close-mouthed and, to some, close-minded, but his loyalty to LBJ overrode any philosophical disagreement on policies. Like Watson, McPherson was a Texan, as liberal in his views as Watson was conservative. He was an intelligent and sensitive lawyer with considerable literary talent, and he increasingly carried the load as speech writer. Cater, too, worked as a speech writer, especially on education and health matters. An Alabama liberal, Harvard educated, and for years the Washington editor of *The Reporter*, Johnson's wrath bothered Cater more than it did most of his associates. But Cater had long regarded LBJ as a uniquely gifted individual. He sympathized with the President's philosophy and thrilled to the challenge of making a contribution. Califano was a Brooklyn attorney whose ability to learn quickly and administer effectively enabled him to move up rapidly in the ranks of the Defense Department under McNamara. He impressed LBJ, who used his talents increasingly and finally trans-ferred him to the White House. By 1966 Califano became the key aide for coordinating the administration's domestic program. Tough, tireless, and demanding, he drove those who worked for and with him as hard as the President did. Califano's way of resolving long-winded debate was simply to announce that LBJ wanted a program paper by ten the next morning; Califano would need it by nine. The President expected it; therefore, an all-night work session was imperative. It was a tough way to make a living, but it produced enormous quantities of work.

Johnson chose aides who explicitly suited his moods and demands. He preferred young men, and the average age of his staff was in the thirties. With the exception of Moyers, none really achieved a public image. Indeed, Johnson resented his aides' receiving too much publicity; keeping a low profile was essential to staying in the President's good graces. When a series of stories identified Valenti as LBJ's closest associate, the President moved him farther away from the oval office. Hugh Sidey described the Johnson aides as "cautious bureaucrats, adept at shuffling memos and doing the mechanical things . . . demanded around the White House, but . . . not given charters for original thinking." His judgment was too harsh. LBJ badly wanted new ideas. But he also wanted them to be so merged with his own thinking that when they became public they were identified as his own. Most dangerous of all, Johnson failed to cultivate independent sources of information, depending too much on a relative handful of close advisers. They in turn, as George Reedy has made clear, hesitated to disagree with the President, or, even

when playing devil's advocate, to sustain the point to a convincing—
or sufficiently irritating—level. They told him primarily what he
wanted to hear. The situation, as Reedy noted, was by no means
unique to Johnson's Presidency. But with the mounting pressures of
the Vietnam war and the burning cities at home it became especially
critical.

In contrast to those who counseled him about domestic affairs,
LBJ's closest advisers for foreign policy and national security were
largely men who had come into government under John Kennedy.
Rusk continued as Secretary of State until the end of the Johnson
administration, and McNamara stayed on at Defense until 1968.
JFK's White House adviser on national security affairs, McGeorge
Bundy, remained until 1966, when Walt Rostow, another original
New Frontiersman, replaced him. LBJ leaned heavily on these men
to help compensate for his limited experience in foreign affairs, but it
would be incorrect to attribute the critical decisions made during his
administration to anyone but the President. Although as a senator his
focus had been overwhelmingly on domestic policies and politics, as
a representative he had been extremely active in matters involving
national preparedness, and Kennedy had been insistent that as Vice
President Johnson be included in deliberations concerning foreign
trouble spots. The new President was very much his own man in
diplomatic affairs, and he possessed strong convictions about America's role in the world.

Throughout his Presidency, several basic principles guided
Johnson's approach to foreign relations. First, to a very large degree,
he regarded foreign policy and domestic policy as indivisible. A
foreign decision which severely damaged his popularity at home, and
hence his ability to govern, would in turn destroy his capacity to
conduct diplomacy effectively. This belief influenced his actions
greatly in 1964 when he was running for reelection, dictated his
handling of the Dominican Republic crisis in 1965, and, as opposition
to the Vietnam war became increasingly intense and prevalent,
prompted him not to campaign for reelection in 1968. Johnson
believed that a successful foreign policy depended on taking care of
America's needs at home. If the United States failed to handle its
civil rights problems and its poverty wisely and fairly, it would sorely
damage its moral position as the leader in the world struggle against

tyranny. "The over-riding rule I want to affirm," he explained in 1966, "is that our foreign policy must always be an extension of our domestic policy. Our safest guide to what we do abroad is always what we do at home. . . ." As historian Walter LaFeber noted, the President easily applied his ideas to Vietnam: "I want to leave the footprints of America there. I want them to say, 'This is what the Americans left—schools and hospitals and dams. . . .' We can turn the Mekong [River area] into a Tennessee Valley."

Second, Johnson maintained a tough-minded view about the need to protect and preserve national interest. Thus, his support of foreign aid was conditioned by his belief that sheer charity and benevolence were sure ways to lose respect. Favors should be done for those who supported the United States and demonstrated by their deeds that they were appreciative. In the early fifties he had been annoyed by the unwillingness of the British and the French to give more help in the Korean war and by France's lack of toughness in Vietnam. As President he deeply resented the tendency of America's allies to criticize, not aid, the United States' efforts to save South Vietnam. Just before Christmas 1967, when Australian Prime Minister Harold Holt drowned, Johnson made the long and fatiguing trip to his funeral because Holt, more than any other leader in the world other than the South Vietnamese, had aligned himself with Johnson on Vietnam, and the President treasured his support. Rostow defined national interest as maintaining "a world environment within which American society can continue to develop in conformity with the humanistic principles that are its foundation." Johnson's actions as President suggested that he agreed with his aide's definition.

Third, LBJ feared that foreigners might miscalculate American intentions and American will. In his hard-nosed view of foreign affairs, diplomatic niceties mattered much less than what a country did. Negotiation and treaties were only good if one had the determination to back them up. Failure to do so, as he keenly remembered from his days in the House, had produced World War II. A willingness on the part of the United States to act had saved Korea. As he made clear to Kennedy on his return from Vietnam in 1961, it was imperative for America to live up to its commitments in

Southeast Asia. If we "throw in the towel" and "pull back our defenses to San Francisco and a 'Fortress America' concept," he declared, "we would say to the world in this case that we don't live up to treaties and don't stand by our friends. This is not my concept." To LBJ the Communist powers were totalitarian aggressors. Peace could not be preserved and American interests protected by appeasing them any more than the Munich agreement in 1938 had satisfied Nazi Germany's lust for conquest or prevented World War II.

During the five years that Johnson occupied the White House, the Vietnam war completely overshadowed all foreign policy considerations. Although in 1964 American involvement had not escalated to a point where it would dominate his attention as it would later, the war was already a highly worrisome situation. One of his first acts as President was to confer with Ambassador Henry Cabot Lodge, who had flown from Saigon to Washington for a scheduled meeting with Kennedy. Lodge reported that the situation looked grim. Vietcong "incidents" had increased sharply during November. Johnson listened, told him to "do the best you can," and sent him back. Two days later the President approved a plan to accelerate "non-attributable hit-and-run" attacks against North Vietnam as well as "operations up to 50 kilometers into Laos." The initial optimism about the Southeast Asian war that followed the overthrow of the Diem government faded quickly. After an inspection trip to Vietnam in December, Secretary McNamara pessimistically reported that the new regime was "indecisive and drifting." Unless the situation could be reversed in the next two to three months, he declared, more forceful moves would be needed to prevent Communist control of South Vietnam.

When conditions continued to deteriorate, Johnson agreed on February 1, 1964 to initiate Plan 34A, a variety of secret sabotage and psychological activities designed to pressure Hanoi into halting its activities in the South. The new operations included parachuting sabotage teams into the North, commando raids by sea against transportation targets, bombardments of coastal installations by PT boats, and kidnapping North Vietnamese citizens for intelligence information. Asian mercenaries were hired to conduct the raids under the direction of the American military. To collect information for Plan 34A operations, patrols by American destroyers were also initiated in the Gulf of Tonkin.

Meanwhile, the government of South Vietnam remained in a state of confusion, with General Nguyen Khan replacing the junta that deposed Diem. Throughout the spring of 1964, the President's advisers began to weigh seriously the advantages of bombing raids against North Vietnam, both as a means of drying up the flow of men and materials from the North and as a way of boosting morale in the South. The belief that North Vietnam was vulnerable to aerial attack became increasingly prevalent among military as well as civilian planners in Washington. Johnson, however, refused to consider such action. Busily engaged in legislative matters and concerned about forging the greatest possible support for his election campaign, he was in no mood to take measures that would so obviously signal an escalation of American involvement in the war.

The President correctly read the mood of the American people as being basically satisfied with American foreign policy. Republican spokesmen, such as Governor Nelson Rockefeller of New York, former Vice President Richard Nixon, and especially Senator Barry Goldwater, complained vehemently during 1963 and early 1964 that the Democrats were not "winning" global confrontations with the Communists, though they were unable to explain why the GOP had not rolled back the Iron Curtain with Eisenhower in the White House. More importantly, the Republicans also failed to produce a ground swell of popular opinion in favor of risking a general war in the pursuit of victory. Coexistence and a nuclear balance of power were the alternatives. When Khrushchev greeted Johnson's Presidency with something of a peace offensive, LBJ responded warmly, assuring the Soviet leader that he was "wholly committed to the search for better understanding among peoples everywhere . . . ." The only immediate tangible results were some mutual reductions in the production of enriched uranium, but the communication lines between the two heads of state were clearly open and tension between the two countries was less than it had been for many years. The message Johnson conveyed to the American public and the world in his first few months in office was that he intended to seek peace, not victory. But he also made it clear that he would do so while meeting American commitments from Vietnam to Berlin and while protecting the nation's interests and honor.

Johnson had barely settled into the White House routine when an outburst of hostility against the United States in Panama provided him with the opportunity to demonstrate how he would react to a crisis situation. In 1903 President Theodore Roosevelt had used the threat of American military force to help Panama break away from Colombia and form an independent country. The new state then quickly agreed to allow the United States to build and operate a canal connecting the Atlantic and Pacific oceans. A ten-mile-wide strip of land enclosing the canal was leased to the United States in perpetuity. Sanitarily and efficiently operated by the Army, the Canal Zone became a "Little America" surrounded by Hispanic culture. To Panamanian nationalists the Zone was a constant reminder of their servile position. They clamored for higher rent for the use of their land and for the removal of irritating symbols of American dominance.

Over the years the United States slowly and grudgingly agreed to various Panamanian demands and raised the annuity paid on the canal. In 1962 Kennedy agreed that the side-by-side flying of American and Panamanian flags would extend to all sites where the American flag was normally flown. To the ultranationalistic Americans living and working in the Canal Zone, many of whom were second- or even third-generation Zonians, any concession was highly irritating. Early in January 1964 an incident at Balboa High School involving flag flying touched off a brief demonstration by Panamanian students. More mature agitators quickly joined in, and within hours Molotov cocktails and sniper fire turned the disturbance into a riot.

For both Johnson and President Roberto Chiari of Panama the situation was political dynamite. Under strong domestic pressure to stand up to the United States, Chiari blamed Communist agents for the violence but felt compelled to rupture relations with Washington. For Johnson, the threat to the longtime symbol of American security, the Canal Zone, was bad enough. Since the flare-up occurred at a time when American fear of Communist-inspired Castro-like revolutions in Latin America was intense, Johnson knew that if he made serious concessions to the Panamanians under the pressure of violence, he would be reinforcing the Republicans' claim that the Democrats were soft on Communists. Consequently, he took a tough stand, insisting that law and order be restored as a prerequisite to negotiations on the basic differences. His hard-nosed attitude worried some observers, who feared grave damage to American prestige in Latin America, and it frustrated efforts by the Organization of American States to settle the dispute. In March, however, he softened his position enough to clear the way for the restoration of relations with Panama and the beginning of quiet, long-term negotiations between the two countries. They were still going on when Johnson left the White House, but the immediate danger had at least been defused.

In many ways the Panamanian incident was a tragicomedy. But it illustrated very well an American dilemma of the 1960s. Minuscule nations with little or no military power could make the United States writhe with their pinpricks. If Washington retaliated by using its full force, the United States' international prestige and its claim to moral leadership would be seriously damaged. Furthermore, wholesale military operations against a small offending power could, if the Soviets or the Red Chinese chose to make the affair a major confrontation, lead to World War III. On the other hand, if the United States did nothing, it lost face and tempted still other small nations to try their luck at twisting Uncle Sam's beard. Also, taking no action gave the political right wing in the United States a golden opportunity to win new adherents. So, despite its awesome military strength, the United States often found itself helpless to use its power to control events, as Johnson found out with the Panamanian incident. His response demonstrated his keen sensitivity to domestic considerations as well as his tendency to be unyielding in the face of foreign pressures and to attend to minute details himself.

Liberal Democrats worried that the President's handling of the situation was a bit too tough, and since it came only weeks after he had placed his fellow Texan Thomas C. Mann in complete control of Latin American affairs for the administration, they feared that Johnson might be less sympathetic to the social and economic reform goals of the Alliance for Progress. A career diplomat and ambassador to Mexico under Kennedy, Mann believed that the United States was not sufficiently encouraging private investment in Latin America. He was much less disturbed about military regimes' holding power, as long as they were anti-Communist and maintained stability, than were most of the New Frontiersmen. In March 1964 the administration accepted a military coup in Brazil without serious dissent then or later, even when the regime proved to be one of the most repressive in the hemisphere. Under Mann's influence the United States began to redefine the political objectives of the Alliance. The new emphasis centered around fostering economic growth and being neutral on internal social reform, protecting American private investments in the hemisphere, showing no preference for representative democratic governments in contrast to military governments, and diligently opposing Communism.

Kennedy's celebrated *Alianza* was generally acknowledged to be in grave trouble even before his assassination. Under Mann and Johnson the downhill trend continued, but at a faster pace. One bitter critic, historian Robert F. Smith, charged that "By the end of 1964 it was quite evident that the alliance was hardly more than the dollar diplomacy of the 1930s with a new facade. All of the old vocabulary had reappeared, and all of the traditional concepts of business diplomacy had been restated. The business of America was still business; not the restructuring of societies." Even if one grants that Smith was excessive in his charges and that Johnson genuinely wanted to improve social conditions in Latin America, Smith's overall judgment of the Alliance remained correct: it was a failure. Yet, Johnson alone was really not to blame. As Jerome Levinson and Juan de Onis caustically explained in their penetrating study, *The Alliance That Lost Its Way*, "Between the overambitious idealism of its development goals and the pointless obsessiveness of its concern for security, the United States really undermined the Alliance before it could get started."

Although the Atlantic Alliance was by no means in as bad condition as the Alliance for Progress, it also needed some shoring up at the time Johnson came to power. De Gaulle, having effectively stunted the growth of Kennedy's Grand Design for Europe, graciously attended his funeral and conferred privately with his successor. Their meeting was cordial, but the imperious Frenchman remained unmoved by the Johnson "Treatment." France went increasingly its own proud way. Britain, West Germany, and the other members of the Western European community declined to be pack bearers for de Gaulle, but they, too, began to behave more independently. Despite strong protests by Johnson, the British and French carried on extensive trade with Cuba, which bolstered the Castro regime appreciably. Attempts to reshape and reorder the Atlantic world depended heavily on the problem of how to share American nuclear weapons with the European powers. Although, as noted previously, Kennedy had begun to sour on the plan before his death, the Multilateral Nuclear Force (MLF) remained a possibility until late in 1964, when it was quietly dropped, leaving the perplexing nuclear dilemma unresolved. In his memoirs, *The Vantage Point*, Johnson simply ignored any dealings with America's European partners before 1966.

Although Johnson was never free of international headaches, during his first months in office there were no crises comparable to the Berlin or Cuban missile episodes. It was almost as if fate had favored him with a period of grace in which to make the transition, develop his initial program, and establish his fitness to hold the office before the year's political campaign got under way in earnest.

Wanting to personalize his administration and its goals, he struggled during the spring of 1964 to coin a slogan. In a televised interview in mid-March he told reporters, "I have had a lot of things to deal with the first hundred days, and I haven't thought of any slogan, but I suppose all of us want a Better Deal, don't we?" "Better Deal" failed to catch hold, but Johnson already had his eye on one that would—"The Great Society." It appeared first in an unused draft of a speech prepared a few weeks before by Richard Goodwin. Intellectual, skeptical, and, to some, abrasive, Goodwin was a brilliant young lawyer who was secretly writing speeches for the President, just as he had done earlier for Kennedy. He had been instrumental in bringing the Alliance for Progress to life early in the New Frontier. Recognizing Goodwin's prowess as a writer and thinker, Bill Moyers called him to LBJ's attention.

Although Johnson never used the draft in which the Great Society theme first appeared, he liked the ideas expressed well enough to begin weaving the phrase into his speeches and extemporaneous statements. Then in his commencement address at the University of Michigan on May 22, he drove it home with full force.

Like most people of his generation, he could never escape the imprint of the Great Depression. But he appreciated that the needs of the future were different from those of the thirties. The country as a whole was affluent, but something more was required:

"For a century we labored to settle and to subdue a continent. For half a century we called upon unbounded invention and untiring industry to create an order of plenty for all of our people.

"The challenge of the next half century is whether we have the wisdom to use that wealth to enrich and elevate our national life, and to advance the quality of our American civilization.

"Your imagination, your initiative, and your indignation will determine whether we build a society where progress is the servant of our needs, or a society where old values and new visions are buried under unbridled growth. For in your time we have the opportunity to move not only toward the rich society and the powerful society, but upward to the Great Society . . . .

"Will you join in the battle to build the Great Society, to prove that our material progress is only the foundation on which we will build a richer life and mind and spirit?"

Johnson's Great Society speech seemed to tap the very well-spring of the public mood. The abundance of America made it possible for people to be concerned about both the *quantitative* and the *qualitative* aspects of their lives and society. By articulating such feelings and by demonstrating with his initial actions as President that he was willing to face the problems and try for solutions, LBJ had established his image as a bold and forceful leader.

Significantly, the impact of Kennedy's assassination had caused Americans to rally strongly behind Johnson in an impressive display of national unity. He in turn had skillfully used the momentum of support generated by the tragedy to good advantage. The absence of severe foreign crises during his first months in office enabled him to immerse himself in his first love, domestic politics, where an almost unbroken record of accomplishment bolstered his confidence and fed his enormous pride and ego. Ironically, however, his achievements in domestic affairs contained the seeds of tragedy for his administration and, indeed, for America. Success at home reinforced his conviction that strong, activist leadership could overcome obstacles. If he, as President, could but focus the awesome power and sophisticated expertise of the United States on problems, surely they must yield. Unfortunately, he seemed unable—or unwilling—to differentiate between domestic and world politics. But as he was later to find out, the North Vietnamese were not very susceptible to the Johnson "Treatment," and, short of an all-out escalation of the American military effort that would inevitably risk starting World War III, they were remarkably capable of withstanding the force of American technology.

# VII

---

## *The Years of Triumph*

ALTHOUGH Johnson was immensely pleased by the warm response of the American people to his leadership during the difficult months of the transition, he still worried about being an "accidental President." The stigma could be removed only by winning the office in his own right in the 1964 election. Victory alone, however, was not enough to satisfy the ambitious Texan. Determined to be remembered in history as a great President, he was anxious to triumph by a margin that would be regarded as a popular mandate for his Great Society. To enact the sweeping legislative program he had in mind required an unusually cooperative Congress. If he could win big, it would provide an invaluable argument to convince reluctant congressmen to go along with the administration. If his margin was sufficiently large, in close congressional races it might also tip the scales in favor of the numerous Democratic candidates friendly to the President.

The President could scarcely have written a scenario more perfectly suited to his desire for a smashing victory than what actually developed. For two decades Republican conservatives had been charging that GOP candidates simply "me-tooed" their Democratic opponents. According to the conservative thesis, it was essential to wrest control of the party away from the eastern Establishment and return it to the "real Republicans," who had been denied a dominant voice in party leadership. The eastern clique— Wall Street lawyers, advertising men, and executives in blue-chip corporations—accepted the same brand of liberal internationalism and big government power as did the liberal Democrats. Small-town, rural, and independent business-oriented Republicans were ignored. Starting with the nomination of Wendell Willkie in 1940, the eastern Establishment had tapped a "me-too" candidate every four years to represent the party. Thomas Dewey, Dwight Eisenhower, and Richard Nixon suited the mold. Robert Taft, the conservative Ohio senator who had captured the hearts of the Republican rank and file during the late thirties, was repeatedly denied a chance to be the party's nominee. Although war-hero Eisenhower had been elected, the others had lost. The reason, in the view of conservatives, was quite simple: millions of Americans felt unable to identify with the candidate of either party. As a result, they stayed home or "went fishing." If, however, they had someone to support who stood for what they believed in, these "silent" voters would become vocal. And they would elect a conservative as President. The real problem, according to this line of reasoning, was not how to elect a conservative—the supposed horde of silent voters would handle that—but how to get one nominated.

A grass-roots campaign to accomplish that goal began almost as soon as the 1960 election was over. Kennedy's hairbreadth margin over Nixon added incentive for Republicans who believed that a conservative could win. For a candidate, most looked to Barry Goldwater, the affable and handsome senator from Arizona. President of his family's department store, civic leader, World War II Air Force pilot, talented photographer, shortwave-radio ham, and lover of Indian lore, he had somehow found time to enter politics in the late forties. He was elected to the Senate in 1952, and his basic conservative instincts and his breezy, off-the-cuff manner of speaking to audiences soon began to attract attention. His bluntness was an important part of his charm, but it also often got him into trouble. Although the tenor of his remarks and writing ran consistently to the right, in detail he frequently contradicted himself. In part that resulted from his tendency to "shoot from the hip" when questioned; in part from his indiscriminate use of ghost writers. "Oh hell, I have ghosts all over the place," he once told columnist Stewart Alsop. By 1963 his supporters were forced to employ microfilm and punch cards to catalogue and classify words said and written by and for the voluble senator.

Goldwater's rise in popularity among conservatives coincided with the resurgence of right-wing extremism in the United States, a recurring phenomenon with roots stretching back to the colonial era. McCarthyism had been the most recent manifestation of the politics of unreason. Far from dying after the Wisconsin senator was discredited personally, the militant anti-Communist movement quietly regrouped and reorganized during the late fifties. Early in the 1960s the "thunder on the right" began to be heard once again.

The number of organizations that identified with the radical right ran into the hundreds. Many were only local, others were regional, and a few were national in constituency. Many of the groups focused on a particular target: stores carrying goods made in Communist countries, the training of Yugoslav pilots in the United States, or foreign aid. Numerous citizens belonged to several different organizations, but the combined membership of all the groups, although extremely vocal, was relatively small. What made the right-wing extremists effective was not the strength of their active participants but the much greater number of Americans who were in sympathy with at least some of their goals.

The largest and most fascinating of the groups was the John Birch Society, a secretive, conspiratorial organization that surfaced in 1961. Obedient to a single leader, New England candy maker Robert Welch, the Birchers organized in cells like Communists, arguing that one could only fight fire with fire. Named for an Army officer shot late in World War II in China by Communist forces, the society stressed chauvinistic patriotism, urged the impeachment of Supreme Court Justice Earl Warren, and questioned the loyalty of distinguished Americans. In his book, *The Politician*, Welch declared that Eisenhower and his Secretary of State, John Foster Dulles, had been dedicated Communist agents. During the early sixties, the Birchers preferred to shirk the headlines as an organization, relying instead on various "fronts" or supporting other radical-right groups to promote their favorite hates. Later, they became less secretive, openly wooing members with enticing newspaper ads and educational forums.

Other right-wing extremists adopted different tactics to combat what they disliked. Eccentric, extreme fanatic groups, notably the Minutemen, secretly organized on a paramilitary basis, training their

small cadres in guerilla warfare and stockpiling weapons in anticipation of the day when the "patriots" would have to take to the hills to
resist a Communist-run America. Much more influential were the
anti-Communist "schools" and "seminars" conducted by roving
evangelists such as Reverend Fred Schwartz and Reverend Billy
James Hargis, who used Christianity as a vehicle for educating the
masses about the mysteries of Communism and its secret aims.

Certain stock appeals attracted followers of the various elements. Nostalgia played a major role, featuring the theme that
old-fashioned patriotism and the simple virtues of small-town, rural
life in an older America had been subverted by urban intellectuals
with their cosmopolitan—and hence suspect—ideas. Deep changes
in the social structure of America since the thirties had markedly
disturbed the position of old, established, privileged groups. Franklin
D. Roosevelt was a particular anathema since he had so significantly
fostered the growth of the welfare state. As right-wing favorite Dan
Smoot, a former FBI agent turned radio-TV commentator, explained,
"I equate the growth of the welfare state with socialism and
socialism with communism." In this way foreign policy was conveniently tied to domestic issues. Exacerbating the change in the
internal social structure were a succession of frightening international crises, which emphasized the fact that the United States was
no longer isolated from the rest of the world. "Godless Communism"
was not only to blame for problems abroad but at home as well.
Indeed, one of the predominant characteristics of right-wing extremists was their tendency to worry almost exclusively about the internal
threat from the Red menace. Although acknowledging the dangers
from the external Communist powers, they put far more emphasis on
the domestic conspiracy they believed was selling out the United
States to the United Nations and to welfare-state socialists.

Although not a member of any ultraright group himself,
Goldwater steadfastly refused to repudiate their support and maintained friendly relations with several of the organizations. Enthusiastic as the right-wingers were for his candidacy, they were not in a
position to lead the drive to secure him the Republican nomination.
That vital task was orchestrated by a small but dedicated core of
party regulars. Led by F. Clifton White, a shrewd political techni-
cian who had headed the Young Republicans between 1950 and

1960, they quietly organized to gain control of delegates in states that did not have presidential primaries. Top Republican officials largely ignored the activities of the "Draft Goldwater" movement, enabling White and his cohorts to line up supporters who elected delegates committed to the Arizona conservative at successive levels of party nominating conventions—precinct, county, and state.

In the states that held primaries, Goldwater did less well, but he won the critical race in California. New York Governor Nelson Rockefeller, the early favorite for the nomination, shattered his own chances by divorcing his wife and marrying a young divorcée with several small children. The old saw, "If a man can't manage his family successfully, how can he manage the country?" played nicely into the hands of the Goldwater forces. By the time Rockefeller officially withdrew from contention after his narrow defeat in California and threw his support to Pennsylvania Governor William Scranton, another eastern liberal, Goldwater had the nomination sewed up. About the only excitement at the nominating convention was provided by the repeated verbal clashes between the boisterous conservatives and the disillusioned liberals and moderates. The results were always the same: the gloating conservatives won handily. They overwhelmingly endorsed a platform carefully attuned to the sensitivities of the South, where Goldwater was expected to run especially strong, and easily defeated an attempt by liberals to renounce extremist groups such as the John Birch Society.

The ultraconservative mood of the Republican convention alienated liberals and moderates and vastly increased Johnson's hopes for a landslide victory. Having no serious challengers for the Democratic nomination enabled the President to devote his efforts to unifying his party. His biggest worry was whom to select as the vice-presidential nominee. Sentiment was strong to name Robert Kennedy, but Johnson, anxious to move out of the long shadow of his martyred predecessor, refused. Although the two men were not openly hostile to one another, a distinct antipathy did exist. Furthermore, LBJ found the idea of Bobby waiting in the wings as a crown prince ready to resume the quest for the New Frontier to be unnerving. Confident that he could win without a Kennedy on the slate, Johnson privately informed the Attorney General that he would not be his choice. As a cover, the President announced that no cabinet member or any official who sat regularly with the cabinet would be considered. Slightly shaken at first, Kennedy recovered his aplomb quickly, quipping, "I'm sorry I took so many nice fellows over the side with me." Trying to build interest in what he knew would otherwise be a dull nominating convention, Johnson then proceeded to play one of the little teasing games he enjoyed so much, hinting at first one and then another individual as his likely preference for a running mate. Declaring that he wanted a "prudent" and "progressive" man for Vice President, LBJ waited until the last minute before "recommending" Senator Hubert H. Humphrey to the delegates, who, of course, quickly nominated the loquacious Minnesotan.

The Republicans counted heavily on a white backlash against increasing black activism to enhance their chances of victory. Despite Goldwater's repeated claims that he opposed racial discrimination, he had voted against Johnson's civil rights bill in the Senate. That endeared him to southern voters and helped to persuade archsegregationist George Wallace, the feisty Alabama governor, to abandon his threatened third-party bid for the White House. Aware that a northern backlash would cut sharply into his vote, Johnson urged civil rights leaders to stop, or at least sharply curtail, demonstrations until after the election. Most cooperated, but they were in no position to dictate to millions of blacks. Riots, relatively small in comparison to those that occurred in following years, broke out in Harlem and other northern cities during the summer. Since Wallace had picked up a disturbingly high percentage of the vote as a candidate in Democratic presidential primaries in Indiana, Wisconsin, and Maryland, Johnson knew that it was absolutely imperative not to appear to be condoning the race riots. He vigorously assured the public that "American citizens have a right to protection of life and limb—whether driving along a highway in Georgia, a road in Mississippi or a street in New York City." Despite its initial promise, the white backlash strategy failed to bear the fruits that the Goldwater forces expected. Wallace's primary election successes proved to be more symbolic than real, and, judging by opinion polls taken in the last stages of the campaign, northern voters appeared to be against, not with, Goldwater on the basis of his stand on racial issues. In the South, the Republican did benefit, but the impact was substantially mitigated in all but the Deep South by the loyalty to Johnson of virtually all important southern Democratic leaders.

Meanwhile, liberal and moderate northern Republicans hesitated to identify enthusiastically with their party's presidential candidate. Belatedly trying to woo their support, Goldwater assured a gathering of party leaders that he would conscientiously administer the Civil Rights Act of 1964. He also declared that he would support NATO and the United Nations, favored strengthening the Social Security system, wanted to expel no one from the GOP, and had no wish to be supported by extremists. His efforts to "clarify" or modify his past positions, however, caused few liberal or moderate Republican officials, including Eisenhower, to give him more than token backing. A good many refused to do even that.

Nor did Goldwater's attempt to get into the political mainstream register on the American public. The Democrats capitalized repeatedly on Goldwater's propensity for making careless, simplistic comments on complex issues. They tore into his "victory over communism" theme with a vengeance. His impromptu suggestion to give NATO commanders discretionary control over nuclear weapons made it relatively easy for his opponents to "hang the bomb around his neck." A stinging television spot pictured a small girl picking petals from a daisy and counting them; the scene then switched to a countdown of a nuclear explosion. Meanwhile a narrator punched home the message: Johnson was for peace and military restraint; Goldwater had voted against the nuclear test ban. Although Republican protests caused the Democrats to drop that particular ad, others were equally effective in convincing a large part of the public that Goldwater was a dangerous warmonger. A Negro in Philadelphia declared, "Well, if Johnson wins, things will be O.K. They say the other guy might have us go to war with Russia." The wife of a Maryland airline engineer voiced a widely held view when she explained, "If Goldwater is elected, you don't know what to expect. He seems too quick to speak without thinking. He might bring us closer to war."

Goldwater had no more luck getting across his ideas on the danger of big government. Democrats shrewdly reduced his criticism of the swollen federal establishment to an attack on Social Security, charging that he would end the system. When the Republican candidate talked ideology alone, he sounded impressive. But when forced to discuss issues and programs, such as Social Security, he failed dismally. An elderly widow in Wisconsin expressed her frank worry about Goldwater as President: "He makes so many rash statements and then has to explain them." Constantly forced to be on the defensive, he seldom succeeded in his attempts at explanation or clarification. A comment by a Goldwater aide in the New Hampshire primary campaign typified the Republican candidate's dilemma: "Don't print what he *says*," the staff member snapped at reporters, "print what he *means*." Even Goldwater's catchy slogan, "In Your Heart You Know He's Right," backfired when the Democrats countered with, "Yes, Far Right," and jeered, "In Your Guts You Know He's Nuts."

Republican attempts to make law and order an effective issue were but marginally successful. Rapidly escalating crime rates generated genuine national concern and seemed to coincide with the growing number of Negro protests involving civil disobedience and especially with recent rulings by the Supreme Court. Beginning with its decision against segregated schools in 1954, the Court—presided over by a former Republican politician, Earl Warren, who had been appointed by Eisenhower the year before—launched an activist course, which consistently angered conservatives and very frequently irritated moderates as well. In case after case the justices antagonized southerners by enlarging the rights of Negroes. By other rulings the Warren Court substantially broadened the geographic base of its unpopularity. Its decision in 1962 that compulsory prayer in public schools was unconstitutional disturbed millions of Americans, convincing many that the Court was seriously damaging the nation's moral fiber. In another landmark case the same year, it firmly endorsed the one-man, one-vote principle, a potent blow against the overrepresentation enjoyed by the more conservative suburban and rural areas in state legislatures. Rulings protecting the rights of accused persons aroused bitter complaints that the Court was pampering criminals by making the task of law enforcement officials more difficult. But as Goldwater and his supporters found out, it was not easy to pin the blame for higher crime rates and "moral decay" on Johnson and the Democrats.

Not even the shocking news in mid-October that one of

Johnson's closest associates, Walter Jenkins, had been arrested as a homosexual in the basement of the Washington YMCA did much to strengthen the Goldwaterites' attack on Johnson personally as a wheeling-dealing, petty politician with shabby moral standards. Earlier, Robert Baker, a key Democratic party staff member in the Senate with extremely intimate ties to Johnson, had been charged with using his Senate job for financial gain. Jenkins plus Baker figured to make the Republican's case against LBJ much more plausible. But within forty-eight hours after the Jenkins affair became public knowledge, Khrushchev was deposed as Soviet premier, English voters turned the Conservative government out of office, and the Chinese Communists detonated their first nuclear bomb. Compared to such momentous events, the troubles of Lyndon Johnson's friends captured scant public notice. Furthermore, Goldwater's extremist reputation offset doubts about Johnson's integrity; hence the cruel joke, "It's a choice between a crook and a kook."

Although the Arizonan claimed that he wanted to stimulate debate about the fundamentals of government, very little serious discussion of issues actually occurred, certainly no more than in previous elections. Johnson flatly ignored his opponent's challenge for television debates, seeing no advantage in providing Goldwater with such an aura of respectability. Significantly, the President also bluntly, indeed ostentatiously, rebuked all hints that his administration had any plans to escalate American involvement in Vietnam, a disingenuous claim that was, as will be seen later, contrary to the facts. Johnson fully appreciated the advantage of being the "peace candidate" in contrast to the bellicose-sounding Goldwater.

Compared to many past campaigns, the 1964 affair was dull, enlivened only by Goldwater's occasional gaffes and by Johnson's fear-and-smear strategy. The results, however, were decisive and far-reaching. Johnson's margin of victory was awesome. Over 43 million people voted for his consensus brand of politics, a record-breaking 61.0 percent of the total. In defeat Goldwater carried only his native Arizona and five states in the Deep South, leaving the Republican party in a state of chaotic disarray. As columnist Walter Lippmann observed, "The returns prove the falsity of the claim . . . that there is a great, silent majority of 'conservative' Republicans who will emerge as the Republican Party turns its back on 'me-tooism' and offers them a 'choice.' The Johnson majority is indisputable proof that the voters are in the center."

The message that Goldwater's defeat boded no good for the GOP was drummed home in the congressional elections. Although the results certified that the Republican party was becoming firmly established in the previously solidly Democratic South, Republican leaders worried that elsewhere even more of the public were identifying with the Democrats. The percentage of Americans calling themselves Republicans had been falling steadily for more than two decades, and Goldwater's lopsided loss threatened to intensify the trend. As Johnson had hoped, his avalanche helped the Democrats increase their margin in the Senate by two (68–32) and gain a whopping 37 seats in the House (295–140). Not since 1936 had they enjoyed such a commanding advantage.

Johnson's huge margin of victory did much more than simply strengthen his hand with Congress. Significantly, it also further inflated his conception of presidential authority. Since such a large proportion of the electorate had endorsed his leadership, he felt increasingly certain that his view of America and of the world was right and proper. Thus, he felt no constraint against ordering, three months after his election, the systematic bombing of North Vietnam, despite the fact that during the campaign he had repudiated such a policy. It is perhaps unfair to say that Johnson deliberately lied about what he might do in Vietnam in the future, but at best he was not candid on the subject with the American people. And once safely assured of four more years in the White House, the confident President was ready and willing, both at home and abroad, to use his power aggressively to back up his convictions.

Clearly he had a golden opportunity to convert his dream of a Great Society into a reality. Haunted by the narrowness of his election, Kennedy had been reluctant to push relentlessly for controversial measures. LBJ, on the other hand, enjoyed a convincing mandate and was eager to tackle big problems like civil rights, poverty, health care, and education. According to opinion polls, the public was overwhelmingly optimistic about the future, but Johnson perceptively recognized that politics and national moods go in cycles. Although he was riding an upward crest, he knew that he would have to work fast to take advantage of his opportunity to move the country a significant distance domestically. Shortly after his inauguration, he assembled key administration officials who handled legislation for various departments and told them, "Now look, I've just been reelected by the overwhelming majority. And I just want to tell you that every day while I'm in office, I'm going to lose votes. I'm going to alienate somebody. . . . We've got to get this legislation fast. You've got to get it during my honeymoon."

Johnson knew that it was imperative to present Congress with a carefully developed blueprint for implementing his Great Society early in the new session. His experience in Congress and in the executive branch taught him that the traditional process of relying on federal departments and agencies to formulate legislative ideas was unlikely to produce the innovative and imaginative new approaches that he wanted. Too little fresh thinking occurred, and ideas almost inevitably became bureaucratized along established channels. By the time proposals were forwarded to the Bureau of the Budget, which coordinated presidential programs, most of them had become a cautious compromise designed so as not to rock the boat. Furthermore, many of the serious problems facing the country—the dilemma of the cities, for example—encompassed aspects outside the established framework of any one department or agency. A better vehicle for developing programs was clearly needed.

During 1960, Kennedy had used a number of task forces to examine certain critical problems on an off-the-record basis. Drawing heavily upon intellectuals and party dignitaries, as well as individuals experienced in government operations, the groups were, to a considerable degree, window dressing for the campaign. Nevertheless, JFK's staff found several of the task force reports extremely useful in developing legislation for 1961. Bill Moyers and Budget Director Kermit Gordon suggested that Johnson use the task force concept to brainstorm for the 1965 legislative program, and the President readily agreed.

The task forces, consisting of both government and nongovernment people, began work in midsummer 1964. With few exceptions, they worked without public notice. Secrecy was essential because Johnson wanted candid advice, and just as the delegates to the Constitutional Convention of 1787 were able to change positions without public embarrassment because their deliberations were private, the members of the task forces enjoyed the luxury of being able to criticize existing policies or even individuals without being subjected to pressure by Congress or by interest groups. In order not to stifle creative thinking, the President instructed the task forces not to worry about political or fiscal matters. Those problems, he explained, were his and the Budget Bureau's responsibilities. Thus even though the people on the task force that developed the Model Cities program believed it to be politically unfeasible, they went ahead and recommended the plan.

The fifteen task forces in 1964 operated essentially on an ad hoc basis, but their efforts proved to be so effective in formulating the President's 1965 legislative campaign that the concept became institutionalized for the rest of the Johnson administration. The White House staff collected ideas from every possible source from within and without the government. Johnson's aides continued to make frequent trips to academic institutions, for example, to sample fresh thinking even after the President became increasingly at odds with much of the intellectual community because of its criticism of his policies in Vietnam. The staff asked questions such as "What is the administration doing wrong?" "What problems have been overlooked?" and "What pressing needs are begging for attention?" As the ideas accumulated and were sorted, certain items were singled out for in-depth examination. Sometimes the staff hired a consultant with special expertise in the area of concern. In other cases they assigned the issue to one agency or department, set up an interagency task force, or established an outside task force.

Both the charter and the composition of outside task forces were always cleared in detail with LBJ. He frequently vetoed suggested members, particularly if there was too heavy a concentration from one geographic area. Johnson's insistence that appointments, even for relatively minor posts, be approved by him was well known in Washington, and the membership of the task forces was no exception. Mindful of the heavy concentration of federal officials from the East Coast, he persistently urged his staff to seek out talented men and women from other parts of the country. Once a task force completed its work and turned in its report, the presidential staff, assisted by the Budget Bureau, summarized it in one or two pages for presentation to LBJ.

The old joke that the way to pigeonhole a problem is to give it to a task force was essentially untrue with Johnson. He accepted a high proportion of the recommendations submitted to him. When he turned one down, it was usually because of budgetary considerations or because he felt that he would be unable to get the measure out of congressional committee. But from 1965 on, the great bulk of his legislative proposals resulted from task force recommendations, and the task force concept was one of the most significant of his administrative innovations.

Most observers considered LBJ's domestic program to be basically a continuation of the welfare programs of the thirties. Johnson, however, saw the Great Society as going well beyond the work of his great hero, Franklin Roosevelt. Johnson stressed opportunity, not handouts. Like Thomas Jefferson, he deeply believed that each person should have a full and complete chance to help himself. Government's job was to make sure that everyone in the Great Society started on equal footing, that children were not handicapped by poor or insufficient medical care or education, and that no one was discriminated against because of race. Under these conditions, poverty would disappear because people would pull themselves up.

Johnson's approach combined a heavy dose of the government-fostered welfare state, commonly identified with twentieth-century liberalism, with a measure of the self-help doctrine so attractive to conservatives. As a philosophy it reflected both his background and his basic temperament. As a strategy it shrewdly suited the consensus politics that Johnson believed in so fervently. The response of the voters in the 1964 election convinced him that he could obtain the legislative measures essential to making the Great Society a reality.

In his 1965 State of the Union message Johnson devoted less than one-fifth of his address to foreign affairs. Vietnam received only a brief mention, and in stark contrast to the previous year, he did not refer to John F. Kennedy even once. He spoke with the confidence of a President elected in his own right, and he made it abundantly clear that progress in domestic affairs would receive top priority.

During the frenetic spring days of 1965 Johnson pushed his legislative program relentlessly. "I want to see a whole bunch of coonskins on the wall," he told associates. But two skins in particular were designated as absolutely critical—Medicare and aid to elementary and secondary education. President Truman had begun the process of educating the public for both programs, but they had evoked such intense emotion and bitter controversy that neither had ever come close to passage. As late as 1963, supporters were frankly pessimistic about their chances of being enacted. The 1964 election results, however, dramatically changed the odds. In a classic bit of political irony, the most hostile opponents to both Medicare and federal aid to education helped to clinch their passage by nominating Goldwater. Johnson's landslide victory carried into Congress, especially to the House, a host of Democrats who were openly sympathetic to the proposals. Every one of the fifty-six freshmen Democrats who were not from the South and who voted on the education bill of 1965 voted yes; and they supported Medicare 58–7.

Johnson's tactics for the first session of the 89th Congress were shrewd. Like a football coach telling his team to attack the other side's strongest point of defense head-on, he deliberately elected to go after Medicare and education first. If he could win the hardest battles first, he reasoned, the momentum would carry over, making it relatively easy to enact the rest of his legislative program. Three days after his State of the Union address, the President sent Congress a strong appeal to pass a law providing health care for older Americans. Kennedy had introduced a similar bill, but to the dismay of liberals he had not really gone all out to gain its adoption, at least in part because he knew that without the support of Wilbur Mills, chairman of the House Ways and Means Committee, the plan had no chance of becoming law. During the early sixties, senior citizens groups and the AFL-CIO actively promoted the measure, but the American Medical Association (AMA) countered their efforts with a massive, well-financed advertising campaign, which hammered effectively at the theme "Socialized Medicine and You." The doctors' lobby declared that "social insurance is the common European system, while public assistance [charity] is the traditional American approach," and maintained that incorporating health care for the elderly into the Social Security system would be "a foot in the door" for total socialized medicine. Furthermore, the AMA warned, such a program would dangerously undermine the "sacred" doctor-patient relationship.

By 1965, however, the rapidly escalating costs of health care and the greater awareness of the need to provide some dignity for the growing ranks of retired Americans caused the AMA's cries of "wolf" to backfire. Overblown rhetoric, such as capitalism is endangered by "the concept of health care as a right rather than a privilege" and the campaign against Medicare is a battle for the "American way of life," actually helped rally both the public and Congress to support the measure. One quality that made Wilbur Mills so consistently effective was his ability to keep abreast of the times. Determined that no bill recommended by his committee should lose on the House floor, he ran Ways and Means with calculating caution. Seeing the ground swell of enthusiasm for Medicare, he observed that he was "acutely aware of the fact that there is a problem here which must be met."

Recognizing that passage of Medicare was probably inevitable, the AMA and the Republicans boldly switched tactics, protesting that the problem with the Democrats' bill was that it did not go far enough in providing assistance to the aged. Seeking to reap a political gain by offering more coverage than the Democrats while at the same time preserving their long-standing ideological commitment to voluntarism, the Republicans shrewdly submitted an amendment providing voluntary federal insurance to cover not only hospital-related expenses but doctors' fees and drug costs as well, with those eligible paying half of the insurance premium and the government paying the balance.

In a brilliant legislative maneuver, Mills seized upon the Republicans' proposal to develop a two-tiered bill that went far beyond the administration's original plan. In its final form the act provided compulsory hospital insurance financed primarily by Social Security taxes, but it also offered voluntary insurance to cover physicians' and surgical fees with the government and the beneficiaries sharing equally in the premium costs. Significantly, Congress also accepted another proposal by Mills: to provide generous federal grants to states that enacted programs making medical payments for certain categories of poor and medically indigent persons *below* the age of 65. The plan—termed Medicaid—attracted little attention at the time, but by the end of the decade it was costing the federal government almost as much as Medicare.

Immensely pleased by the passage of the health care package,

Johnson flew to Independence, Missouri, to sign the bill in the presence of the eighty-one-year-old Truman. "No longer," the happy President declared, "will older Americans be denied the healing miracle of modern medicine. No longer will illness crush and destroy the savings that they have so carefully put away over a lifetime so that they might enjoy dignity in their later years."

The program's popularity with the aged was unmistakable, but the new law was not without its drawbacks. Although Medicare-Medicaid helped to improve health care for the aged and many of the poor, it also sharply raised the demand for medical services and hence contributed heavily to the soaring medical prices for all Americans. In particular, the ability of many already highly paid members of the medical profession to benefit from the federal largesse aroused the ire of critics. The crux of the problem, historian Allen J. Matusow explained, was that Medicare-Medicaid, like other essentially conservative Great Society reforms, "aimed at far-reaching reform without change in existing institutions or challenge to vested interests. The government in effect turned the program over to the medical profession, paid its fees, and imposed only the feeblest regulations on it."

On January 12, only five days after sending his Medicare request to Congress, LBJ dropped his second blockbuster on the legislators by asking for $1.5 billion in aid for elementary and secondary schools. Kennedy's attempt to pass a comparable measure in 1961 had foundered on the thorny issue of federal aid to parochial schools. Having been badly burned, JFK declined to put the prestige of his office on the line the following year to support the many educational bills that various congressmen introduced. In 1963, however, he had proposed an omnibus measure comprising almost two dozen different types of programs calling for federal funds to improve and expand education. Separated from his comprehensive proposal, two bills— aid for vocational education and for college facilities construction— passed late in the session. But the explosive question of federal appropriations for elementary and secondary schools remained in limbo.

Raising the quality of education coincided logically with the Johnson administration's war on poverty. The poor almost universally suffered from inadequate education, as the excellent 1964 task force report on education prepared under the direction of John Gardner, then president of the Carnegie Foundation and later Secretary of HEW, made clear. Almost everyone agreed that better education was desirable, but writing a law that Congress would accept was political dynamite. One sticky problem—the question of funds for racially segregated schools—had been settled by the Civil Rights Act of 1964, which outlawed separate black and white school systems. But the old dilemmas—should tax money go to parochial schools and how to divide funds between the various states—remained as formidable obstacles.

The parochial school issue revolved around the First Amendment to the Constitution—the separation of church and state. Trying to work out a compromise between opposing sides, Anthony Celebrezze, the Secretary of HEW, expounded homely analogies that made sense to at least some of the antagonists. If, he argued, it was constitutionally permissible for a student from a parochial or private school to go to a public library and check out a book for class, why not bring the books—or other equipment/supplies—to the school? He also used the example of an individual's going to a religious service on a subway subsidized by public tax revenues. Lyndon Johnson was especially critical to the resolving of the religious problem. Unlike the Catholic Kennedy, he could afford to endorse the concept of providing aid to parochial schools. The question was could he convince enough congressmen.

Senator Wayne Morse of Oregon and Assistant Secretary Wilbur Cohen of HEW were the heroes who finally devised ways to break the logjam. The irascible Morse, a highly talented logician, had introduced an education bill the year before that proposed to use the long-established principle of giving federal funds to "impacted" areas (localities whose public schools were overburdened by the children of servicemen stationed at adjacent military bases) to provide federal aid to "poverty impacted" school districts identified on the basis of unemployment and welfare statistics. Johnson told Cohen, who was a brilliant administrator and a marvelous craftsman at writing legislation, to work something out so that the administration would not be caught between the Catholics and the Baptists. Building on the foundation laid by Morse, Cohen and his assistants developed a simple but logical formula for awarding money to schools, either public or private. It was based on the number of students from families whose annual incomes were less than a certain minimum figure. In its final form, for each child in poverty, the 1965 formula provided the school district with a basic grant equal to 50 percent of the state's per-pupil education cost.

Although poor rural areas in the South stood to gain the most, southern archconservatives like Howard Smith, chairman of the House Rules Committee, condemned the passage of the bill in strong terms and with dire predictions for the future. "We apparently have come to the end of the road so far as local control over our education in public facilities is concerned," he declared. "I abhor that. . . . This is the day that the bureaucrats in the Education Department have looked forward to . . . ." Representative Adam Clayton Powell, Jr., of New York saw things differently: "This is the precise moment in history for which we have waited. Let us ring our bells of freedom and liberty throughout the land." The canny Morse was less flamboyant. "Let us face it," he explained, "we are going into federal aid for elementary and secondary schools . . . through the back door."

Regardless, Johnson was elated. Reflecting on his year as a teacher in Cotulla, Texas—a small town on the outskirts of Houston—he insisted on journeying "back home" for the bill-signing ceremony. In the dilapidated little building near his ranch where he had first gone to school, he affixed his signature in the company of assorted dignitaries, including congressmen, government officials, seven Mexican-Americans from his classes in Cotulla, and seventy-two-year-old Mrs. Kate Deadrich Loney, who had been his first teacher.

As Johnson had gambled that they would, the Medicare and education bills established a rhythm of accomplishment for his legislative program. "Johnson asketh and the Congress giveth," aptly described the Washington scene during 1965. True to his prediction, the flood of bills began to recede somewhat during 1966. Nevertheless, during its two years of life, the 89th Congress set an unparalleled record in passing significant legislation.° In scope and

° Major laws enacted during 1965–66 included: Aid to Elementary and Secondary Education, Aid to Higher Education, Arts and Humanities Foundation,

scale the "Johnson Congress" erected an imposing framework for the Great Society. A big question remained, however: would succeeding Congresses and administrations provide the necessary funds to flesh out and vivify the skeleton?

The nation's vigorous economic growth provided solid reasons for optimism. John Kennedy had taken office in the midst of a very mild recession. By early spring 1961, however, the economy had begun to turn around, and it maintained a modest upward trend throughout the rest of the New Frontier. As Walter Heller and other expansionist-minded government officials had predicted, the tax cut enacted in early 1964 gave the economy a tremendous boost. During 1964 the gross national product increased by an impressive 7.1 percent and zoomed even higher during the next two years (increases of 8.1 percent in 1965 and 9.5 percent in 1966). The boom generated higher tax revenues in each year, giving Congress the happy chore of disposing of the additional funds. Although the federal budget remained unbalanced, the deficit dropped from $4.8 billion in 1963 and $5.9 billion in 1964 to $1.6 billion in 1965 and $3.8 billion in 1966. A relative handful of fiscal conservatives argued that some of the increased federal income should be used to chip away at the huge national debt, but most economists argued that such an action would end the economic upswing and bring on a recession. Few Americans were willing to risk that unpleasant possibility. Government economists operated on the basis of budget balance at "full employment"—actually defined as unemployment of no more than 4 percent—and insisted that small deficits caused no real harm. The statistics on unemployment and inflation reinforced their position. As the economy hummed, the rate of unemployed declined from 5.7

International Education, Scientific Knowledge Exchange, Cultural Materials Exchange, Medicare, Vocational Rehabilitation, Manpower Training, Teachers Corps, New G.I. Bill, Heart-Cancer-Stroke Programs, Mental Health Facilities, Health Professions, Medical Libraries, Child Health, Community Health Services, Military Medicare, High-Speed Transit, Water Desalting, Traffic Safety, Highway Safety, Tire Safety, Water Research, Urban Mass Transit, Federal Highway Aid, Clean Air, Water Pollution Control, Clean Rivers, Voting Rights, Social Security Increase, Anti-Poverty Program, Aid to Appalachia, Child Nutrition, Child Safety, Mine Safety, Law Enforcement Assistance, National Crime Commission, Drug Controls, Juvenile Delinquency Control, Narcotics Rehabilitation, Bail Reform, Truth-in-Packaging, Protection for Savings, Housing Act, Model Cities, Rent Supplements, and a host of measures designed to beautify America and protect recreational and historic sites.

percent in 1963 to 5.2 percent in 1964, 4.5 percent in 1965, and a gratifying 3.8 percent in 1966. The rate of inflation remained at less than 2 percent through 1965, increasing to 3.8 percent in 1966. In addition, the nation's troublesome balance-of-payments position improved encouragingly.

As the economy continued to surge forward month after month, Keynesian economics—or, as it was commonly called, the new economics—became much more widely accepted. Yale economist James Tobin optimistically declared in 1966 that the immense economic gulf that had separated academics from businessmen, bankers, congressmen, financial journalists, and editorial writers had been greatly narrowed. Practical men of affairs were beginning to see, Walter Heller explained, "that positive federal action to maintain high and rising levels of demand poses no threat to economic freedom and is, moreover, philosophically neutral. . . ." That was all very true, but as new economists themselves readily agreed, success in regulating the economy depended on continuous "fine-tuning" of interest rates, federal tax levels, and total federal spending. Much of the essential "tinkering" demanded congressional cooperation. If the legislators failed to respond promptly to executive recommendations to change tax or spending levels, not even the wisest economic advisers could hope to maintain growth within the bounds of manageable rates of inflation. Since political considerations "back home" inevitably influenced the legislators' willingness to act, the delicate machinery of economic management could easily be upset. In the last part of the Johnson administration this lesson was brought home forcefully.

In 1965 and early 1966, however, the President and his economic advisers gratefully accepted the fiscal dividends provided by the booming economy as a means of bringing the Great Society closer to reality. Prosperity helped in two vital ways: by creating new jobs and by generating additional federal income that could be used to fund new social programs. Congress, which frequently approves new federal activities but then starves them to death by providing little or no money for their operation, funded the programs it authorized during 1965 and 1966 quite generously. Outlays for education and manpower, for example, increased from $2.5 billion in 1965, to $4.5 billion in 1966, and $6.1 billion in 1967. Spending for health, community and regional development, and welfare services also increased. But total obligations for the Office of Economic Opportunity, the principal vehicle in the war against poverty never reached $2 billion per year under Johnson. At that level, the war was reduced pretty much to a skirmish.

Cynics also questioned exactly who would benefit most from the allocation of more public resources to social services—the poor or the economic interests. The skeptics knew that on many occasions during the twentieth century, enlightened executives of America's largest corporations and banks had shown a remarkable knack for accommodating quickly and shrewdly to changing trends, frequently making use of the changes for their own purposes. With national sentiment running overwhelmingly in favor of Johnson's Great Society, and with their own profits breaking records, the smart thing to do was to join the crusade. And just as the 1964 tax cut—once congressional amendments had emasculated proposals to close loopholes—provided the biggest bonanza to prosperous corporations and wealthy individuals, so many of the social programs provided opportunities for gain for many of the nation's largest economic enterprises. The omnibus housing measure and the rent subsidy plan helped a number of families escape the slums but also substantially benefited builders and landlords. The Appalachia program devoted the greatest part of its funds to road building. Although that increased the mobility of labor, boosted the tourist trade, and encouraged industry to locate new plants in the miserably backward area, it also meant lucrative contracts for road builders.

Ardent liberals and radicals objected to the conservative financing scheme for Medicare. Participants were scheduled to pay a premium each month—$3 when the plan began—which would be raised as medical costs increased. Even more important, the bulk of funds for the program were scheduled to come from payroll taxes, a notoriously regressive form of taxation.

The war on poverty was attacked as "fundamentally conservative." By concentrating on "education, training, and character building," wrote Christopher Jencks, the government assumes "that the poor are poor not because the economy is mismanaged but because the poor themselves have something wrong with them." Critics also attacked the generous salaries paid to local poverty officials and excoriated the government for its extensive use of major corporations, like Litton Industries, Philco, and International Telephone and Telegraph, to operate the job camps established to train unemployed youths.

Johnson accepted without serious qualms the fact that business would likely enjoy some pleasant fruits from the Great Society. The President frankly wooed the leaders of the blue-chip companies that exerted such a powerful influence on the American economy. Kennedy had done so, too, but LBJ was much more successful in winning their confidence. Firmly believing that businessmen were afraid of big government, he consciously attempted to ease their fears and secure their help. His homey observation that "the average businessman is kind of proud when he goes home that he can go in and see his little daughter at night, and not have people sayin' they are thieves and Al Capones," reflected an understanding of business that enabled him to develop a warm rapport between Wall Street, Main Street, and the White House.

That the President, almost all members of Congress, and the great bulk of the American public hoped to blunt the growth of radicalism by reallocating larger funds to social services is indisputable. As it was, much of the middle class soon began to grow restless and resentful about the administration's repeated emphasis on poverty and civil rights. The Community Action Program, an innovative project designed to give the poor a chance to shape their own destinies through "participatory democracy," proved to be particularly unnerving. When the poor talked in committee meetings about organizing against the political and economic structure, critics castigated CAP as amounting to the state financing "guerilla warfare" against itself. The repercussions were not long in coming. By late 1966 a significant number of congressmen, including many of the President's strongest supporters, were bluntly telling the administration that an alarmingly high number of their constituents were complaining that the Great Society was *only* for the poor and *too little* for the middle class. But since the President's program had raised the expectations of the underprivileged enormously, any cutback in the antipoverty campaign was certain to increase tensions among the poor.

The mounting frustrations of the middle class were in part a backlash against the new mood of strident and frequently violent militancy manifested by black Americans. Most whites outside the South had rejected Goldwater's subtle appeal to racism—cloaked in support for "states' rights"—during 1964, but during the succeeding years black actions increasingly clashed with white views of how the civil rights movement should be run. The change coincided both with the growing tendency by members of the radical wing of the movement, notably SNCC and also many members of CORE, to reject American society and its economic system and with the spread of black protests, previously centered almost exclusively in the South, to the North.

Beginning in 1964 blacks began to protest against segregated schools in northern cities. While no formal "black" or "white" schools existed, "de facto" segregation resulted from residential segregation. In February over 400,000 black students boycotted the New York City public schools, demanding that busing be used to break the pattern. Similar boycotts developed in Chicago, Boston, and elsewhere. In other communities, picketing and sit-ins were used. Regardless of the tactics, white parents overwhelmingly opposed busing. The middle and working classes reacted angrily. Education was their children's ticket to a better life, and they feared that black children bused in from the ghettos would seriously lower educational standards. Black parents just as staunchly believed that white schools provided better education; therefore, their children should have the chance to benefit from attending previously all-white schools. Court decisions did not order school authorities to correct racial imbalance caused by residential segregation, but they declared that they were not prohibited from taking such steps. These rulings allowed blacks to keep the pressure on school boards to do so. Given the mood of white parents this issue inevitably caused strong and continuing bitterness on both sides.

Efforts in the South during election year centered on registering voters. A particularly ambitious effort, the Mississippi Summer Freedom Project, highlighted the rapidly deteriorating cooperative effort between blacks and whites in the civil rights movement. Over one thousand young white volunteers, most from prestigious northern colleges, accepted an invitation for self-sacrifice by paying their own expenses to work in Mississippi with blacks. Although they were provided with two weeks of training at Oxford, Ohio, few of the white youths were ready for what they faced. Mississippi prepared for the "invasion" by passing new laws to "preserve public order." A report summarizing the results of the Summer Freedom Project testified to how little order was actually preserved: 3 persons killed, 80 beaten, 3 wounded by gunfire in 35 shootings, more than 1,000 arrested, 35 black churches burned, 30 homes and other buildings bombed, numerous mysterious deaths among other blacks, and only 1,200 new voters registered in the entire state. Furthermore, relations between the idealistic white volunteers and the blacks they lived and worked with were severely strained. Many blacks felt that the whites exuded a sense of moral superiority. Sexual problems between the workers compounded the tensions. The root of the difficulty probably lay in the fact that blacks were beginning to wear out psychologically from always turning the other cheek when physically abused. As black psychiatrist Alvin F. Poussaint explained, blacks suppressed their rage publicly, as the principles of nonviolence dictated, but directed it at each other and white civil rights workers. The whites could leave if things got too dangerous in Mississippi, but the blacks could never escape their blackness. The murder of three summer workers brought their predicament home to blacks with resounding force. Because two of the victims were white, national attention zeroed in on Mississippi. The FBI investigated the case and ultimately arrested twenty-one persons, including the sheriff of Neshoba County. But the circumstances surrounding the deaths of other blacks in the state attracted no great interest and remained unsolved.

Mississippi also made news at the Democratic National Convention when the Mississippi Freedom Democratic Party (MFDC) challenged the right of the lily-white "regular" delegation to represent the state. The Johnson forces, alarmed by the threat of a white backlash, moved quickly to effect a compromise: two delegates-at-large for the MFDC. To black militants the proposition seemed to be further proof that they could ill afford to trust white liberals.

Although Johnson received an awesome 90 percent of the black votes on election day, his endorsement by the black community was less universal than it appeared on the surface. A good many disillusioned blacks simply refused to vote. But a great many more in the South were unable to cast a ballot because they had been denied the right to register by state officials. It was obvious to both civil rights officials and the Johnson administration that federal action was necessary to stop southerners from using evasive tactics to keep blacks off the voting rolls. The President promised the Urban League the month following his election that he was not through pushing for full equality: "Great social changes tend to come rapidly in periods of intense activity before the impulse slows. I believe we are in the midst of such a period of change. Now, the lights are still on in the White House tonight—preparing programs that will keep our country up with the times." The pressing need, the Justice Department informed the chief executive, was a new law to guarantee voting rights, and in his State of the Union address Johnson urged Congress to eliminate "barriers to the right to vote."

While the administration pondered specific legislative proposals, Martin Luther King, Jr., fresh from a trip to Sweden, where he had accepted the Nobel Peace Prize for 1964, determined to apply some additional pressure. He announced that he was launching an all-out drive to register three million southern blacks. As the focal point of his effort, he picked Selma, Alabama, a city of 15,000 blacks and 14,000 whites with a voting roll 97 percent white and 3 percent black. Selma appeared to be a perfect spot to dramatize the issue. George Wallace was expected to be a special attraction. In previous civil rights confrontations the governor had performed as a classic racist. In addition, Dallas County sheriff, James Clark, could scarcely have been better cast for the role by Hollywood. Six feet tall and two hundred pounds, the hulking Clark lamented, "all this nigger fuss here of late. We always git along. You just have to know how to handle them."

From early January until late March the activities in little Selma commanded the nation's attention. Sheriff Clark confronted the blacks who marched on the courthouse with nightsticks, electric cattle prods, bullwhips, and arrest. In the process he became almost a fixture on the nation's evening television news. In February King revealed plans for a March of Freedom early the following month from Selma to the state capital at Montgomery, fifty-two miles away. Governor Wallace prohibited the march and ordered state police to enforce his decree. When King and his supporters refused to turn around, the troopers and Sheriff Clark's volunteer posse bombarded them with tear gas, then assaulted them with clubs, whips, and wet ropes, chasing the bleeding victims back towards Selma. Two days later the civil rights forces tried a second time, accompanied by over four hundred white clergymen and laymen of all faiths who had poured into Selma. A court decree blocked the march, but the murder of the Reverend James Reeb, a white Unitarian minister from Boston, by four white toughs added to the national indignation raised by the earlier attack on the marchers.

The President faced a serious dilemma and he knew it. On the one hand he was reluctant to use federal troops in a local situation. On the other he had no desire to alienate the northern support he had won by his efforts in 1964 by failing to do something to show support for King and his courageous legions. Efforts to work out a peaceful solution suitable to both sides stalled, and King scheduled another attempt to march to Montgomery for March 21. When George Wallace requested a conference, LBJ quickly agreed, figuring to use the occasion to give the Alabaman the Johnson "Treatment." The meeting was cordial but not particularly productive. Johnson appealed to Wallace to build for the future of all the people in his state. Stop the race baiting, the President urged, and work for constructive harmony. The governor, however, refused to budge, and on his return to Alabama compared the coming Selma march to the Communist "street warfare" that "ripped Cuba apart, that destroyed Diem in Vietnam, that raped China—that has torn civilization and established institutions of this world into bloody shreds." The state of Alabama, he declared, would not expend the required $350,000–$400,000 necessary to protect the "so-called demonstrators." The funds would be used "for the care of our sick and infirm, both white and Negro." It was up to the federal government, Wallace wired Johnson, to provide protection. Frankly relieved to have a specific request to intervene, the President quickly federalized units of the Alabama National Guard and dispatched federal marshals and the FBI to cover the march, which then proceeded without incident.

A few days before the uneventful march, the President appeared on television, pleading for his voting rights bill before an unusual joint evening session of Congress. Comparing Selma with Lexington, Concord, and Appomattox as turning points in "man's unending search for freedom," he ended his emotional address by solemnly repeating the refrain of the civil rights marchers' hymn, "We shall overcome."

A solid bipartisan coalition enacted the bill five months later, after overriding the usual delaying tactics by unyielding southern legislators. Earlier civil rights acts had authorized federal officials to attack the denial of voting rights in the courts, and, since the beginning of the Kennedy administration, the Department of Justice had actively pressed such cases. But the court proceedings were frustratingly slow. The new law, which applied to state and local elections as well as to federal, authorized the executive branch to appoint "examiners" to register voters and eliminated literacy tests. It singled out the South for attention by restricting its application to areas where literacy tests were used and where fewer than 50 percent of the persons of voting age voted in a presidential election or (thanks to an amendment demanded by House Republicans) to "pockets of discrimination" anywhere the Attorney General could prove their existence to a federal court. The President dispatched examiners into the Deep South immediately after signing the bill into law, and in the next twelve months they registered over 400,000 new black voters in the affected states. By 1968 the total numbered over a million. In Alabama alone the numbers of blacks on the voting rolls more than doubled in a year to include 51.5 percent of the black voting-age population. Not surprisingly, one of the ways they used their new right was to vote Sheriff Jim Clark out of office in Dallas County, Alabama.

The events at Selma and the subsequent enactment of the Voting Rights Act marked the last great triumph for the nonviolent, integrated, civil rights movement. Men like King, Whitney Young of the Urban League, Roy Wilkins and Clarence Mitchell of the NAACP, Bayard Rustin, and A. Philip Randolph had made tremendous contributions and continued to be important figures. But they were unable to control a movement that was rapidly evolving into a type of revolution. More militant spokesmen sounded a different drumbeat, and, while no single leader or small group of leaders could speak for all blacks, it soon became obvious that a growing number were tired of waiting for Congress to act, were worn out with the psychological tensions of "loving their enemies," and were unable to contain their rage any longer.

Many blacks found the doctrine preached by Malcolm X particularly appealing. He argued shrilly that blacks must defend themselves; if attacked they must strike back. Malcolm X had broken with the rigorously segregationist Black Muslims in 1963. He continued to stress blackness, not integration, but indicated a willingness to work—cautiously—with whites who were sincere in their willingness to aid the black cause. He emphasized that blacks must direct their own destinies; whites who wanted to help must not presume to take charge. A magnetically charismatic man, he was austere in appearance and commanding in presence. His murder in early 1965, probably by Black Muslims, gave blacks an important new hero and martyr but cost them an exciting and highly capable spokesman for their cause. With his talents for leadership and his capacity for intellectual growth, he might have been the right person to unite militant blacks.

Malcolm X's ideas remained after his death and influenced the thinking of many blacks who argued that "it was time to quit kissin' Whitey's ass." The new mood showed up clearly in response to the publication of a hush-hush report, written primarily by sociologist Daniel Patrick Moynihan, entitled "The Negro-Family: The Case for National Action." Prepared for the Department of Labor, the document reviewed the "Negro American Revolution" and concluded that "Negro social structure, in particular the Negro family, battered and harassed by discrimination, injustice, and uprooting, is in the deepest trouble." A wealth of statistics emphasized the instability of all but middle-class Negro families: nearly a quarter of urban Negro women who had been married were divorced, separated, or living apart from their husbands; nearly one-quarter of Negro births were illegitimate.

The report clearly implied that white, middle-class standards were superior and exactly what the country must endeavor to provide for its black citizens. Floyd McKissick of CORE delivered a stinging rebuttal: "Just because Moynihan believes in middle class values doesn't mean that they are good for everyone. . . . Moynihan emphasizes the negative aspects of the Negroes and then seems to say that it's the individual's fault when it's the damned system that needs changing." Radicals viewed the report as another white alibi and an attempt to snuff out the growing pride in being black. Even moderate and conservative civil rights spokesmen regarded it as suggesting that "it was necessary for the improvement of the Negro community to come from within."

Important as the Moynihan report was to theorists, it attracted little notice among the mass of either black or white Americans, but violence did. During the hot summer months of 1965, one frustrated black community simply exploded. Not many Americans had ever heard of Watts, a dingy section of Los Angeles. Although as slums go it looked better than the deprived areas in eastern cities, it was, nevertheless, sadly out of step with the glittering good life in most of California. Unemployment among adult males was a shocking 30 percent. There was constant friction between the inhabitants of Watts and the city police. Officers in Watts called their nightsticks "nigger knockers." Not surprisingly, charges of police brutality were frequent. Los Angeles, under demagogic Mayor Sam Yorty, habitually ignored the needs of the section until looting and rioting erupted on August 11. A minor incident involving a police arrest started an affair that finally took 14,000 National Guardsmen to end. After five days, 34 people were dead, 4,000 more were under arrest, and much of the section was destroyed by fire. Los Angeles officials blamed civil rights workers, Communists, and other conspirators, but the real causes were unquestionably the poverty conditions that pervaded the ghetto.

Most significantly, once Watts gained national attention because of the riot, it got sizable federal help in the form of antipoverty money. In addition, volunteer social agencies moved in to set up centers for social services, and business provided funds to start black-owned firms. The message from Watts to the rest of the black communities in America seemed to be, if you want help, do something drastic to force authorities to act. Whites suddenly realized that the blacks were angry and that they were willing to take violent actions *outside* the South. It had been one thing for northern whites to support a nonviolent civil rights movement, particularly since it had been centered mainly in the South, but it was something else when the activity shifted away from Dixie. The white backlash that had failed to develop in 1964 began to emerge with a vengeance in late 1965 and 1966.

Lyndon Johnson refused to join the white reaction. Although he loathed the black radicals, he still believed that common sense and decency on the part of whites could defeat the attack on the American system. Deciding to act boldly, during 1966 he asked for legislation in three specific areas—juries, physical security, and housing. Congress agreed with the first two, but the housing question shattered consensus support for civil rights. The reason was quite simple: northerners were being asked to make illegal a discriminatory practice universal in the North—segregated residential housing. Seventeen states had fair-housing laws, but only a handful covered all housing. None attempted seriously to prevent the development of all-white suburbs. Real estate interests and conservative business organizations generated a scathing barrage of criticism, alleging that the housing bill threatened property values and free enterprise. Congressmen received a flood of mail in opposition. As proponents of the measure acidly charged, the North was revealing its hypocrisy in all its ugliness.

While the legislators debated, new crosscurrents buffeted the civil rights movement. For one thing, Martin Luther King, Jr., led his Southern Christian Leadership Conference into pronounced opposition to the American involvement in Vietnam, a position that cost him friends and support in the White House. Both SNCC and CORE agreed with King that the Vietnamese effort was diverting efforts to remedy racial strife at home by depriving the Great Society program of needed funds. But they broke with King sharply over the nonviolent, integrationist course he pursued. James Farmer retired as head of CORE at the end of 1965, and Floyd McKissick, who replaced him, assumed a considerably more militant posture. John Lewis, SNCC's most prominent spokesman, faded from sight, and Stokely Carmichael, a fiery and articulate radical, rapidly pulled the organization away from King's influence by expounding a new and appealing slogan, "Black Power."

The split had been coming for a long time, flaring into the open in early summer, 1966. James Meredith, who had integrated the University of Mississippi in 1962, decided to dramatize the "all-pervasive and overriding fear that dominates the day-to-day life of the

Negro in the United States, especially in the South and particularly in Mississippi," by walking from Memphis, Tennessee, to Jackson, Mississippi. Barely ten miles into Mississippi, Meredith was shot three times. As Johnson ordered the Attorney General into action to apprehend the assailant, King, McKissick, Carmichael, Young, and Wilkins hurried to Memphis to continue Meredith's pilgrimage. Harassed by taunts from jeering whites, sharp disagreements among the leaders seethed beneath the surface. Carmichael electrified the crowd and attracted the attention of the media with his cries of "Black Power." "The only way we gonna stop them white men from whuppin' us is to take over. . . . What we gonna start saying now is black power. . . . Ain't nothin' wrong with anything all black 'cause I'm all black and I'm all good. Now don't you be afraid. And from now on when they ask you what you want, you know what to tell them." The excited crowd answered in unison, "Black power! Black power! Black power!" Although King characterized the term as "unfortunate" and warned that "we must never seek power exclusively for the Negro," the slogan spread like fire throughout black America.

Black power meant different things to different people. To some it meant ousting whites from the civil rights movement and a basic separation of blacks from whites. To others it meant putting blacks in charge of the movement even while accepting help from whites as foot soldiers. Some radical blacks and many frightened whites connected the phrase with an attempt to initiate a violent revolution to overthrow the American social and economic system. Others accepted it as the determination of blacks to use pressure-group tactics as a political weapon to achieve their goals. To almost all the term signified a concentrated attempt to instill a sense of pride and identity in black people.

Regardless, the coining of the slogan coincided with a rising level of violence in race relations. Throughout the summer of 1966 blacks rioted almost daily: thirty-eight separate disturbances were counted. Cleveland experienced the worst single sustained outbreak, but officials in San Francisco, Chicago, Dayton, and Milwaukee regarded their situations as bad enough to ask for the use of National Guardsmen to assist police in restoring order. Cries of "Get Whitey" and "Burn, baby, burn" merged with charges of police brutality.

Although moderates, like the distinguished black sociologist Kenneth B. Clark, tried to explain that the nation had ignored "the rage of the rejected" until it simply exploded and argued that "Negroes generally are law-abiding in a world where the law itself has seemed an enemy," white Americans reacted angrily and bitterly to the sight of burning cities.

The image of a black youth hurling a Molotov cocktail and shouting "Black Power" effectively killed Johnson's 1966 civil rights legislation. Everett Dirksen, the Senate minority leader who had been so instrumental in passing the 1964 and 1965 bills, agreed with most of the administration's requests but opposed the open housing section as "absolutely unconstitutional." With blacks "burning down the goddamned town," whites were in no mood to pressure the Republican stalwart to change his position. Although the bill passed the House and enjoyed the support of a clear majority of the Senate, Dirksen's opposition was critical. Without his help, the two-thirds vote needed to invoke cloture and halt the southern filibuster against the measure could not be lined up, and the bill died.

Republicans running for office in the 1966 congressional elections recognized "crime in the streets" as a powerful issue and called for better police forces to enforce law and order. "How long," demanded House Republican leader Gerald Ford of Michigan, "are we going to abdicate law and order—the backbone of civilization—in favor of a soft social theory that the man who heaves a brick through your window or tosses a fire bomb into your car is simply the misunderstood and underprivileged product of a broken home?" Placed uncomfortably on the defensive, Democrats warned that education, jobs, and better housing plus the end of discrimination were absolutely essential to eliminating the roots of the violence. Even if the Democrats were right—and millions of Americans believed that they were—what they were calling for required money and lots of it. But by late 1966 federal funds were committed to other, more destructive purposes.

As the avowed "peace candidate" in 1964, Johnson had treated the troublesome conflict in Southeast Asia gingerly, although he had agreed to increase covert efforts to defeat the Vietcong early in the year. His biggest problem developed in late summer when North Vietnamese torpedo boats allegedly fired at the American destroyer

*Maddox*, one of the ships assigned to intelligence collection patrol close to the coast of North Vietnam. Angered, the President ordered another destroyer, the *C. Turner Joy*, to join the *Maddox* on patrol in the Gulf of Tonkin. What actually occurred then is hazy and may never be completely clear, but Washington at least believed or wanted others to believe that the North Vietnamese repeated their attack, this time on both ships, on August 4.

The President briefed sixteen congressional leaders hastily summoned to the White House and asked for a resolution condoning whatever action he deemed necessary in response. The assembled senators and representatives unanimously agreed. Senator William Fulbright, the Arkansas Democrat who frequently criticized American foreign policy, flatly declared, "I will support it." Neither then nor later did the chief executive advise Congress about two commando raids by the South Vietnamese against islands in the gulf held by the North Vietnamese, operations that at least suggested to Hanoi that the American destroyers were providing support. The legislators, both Democratic and Republican, seemed completely willing to accept Johnson's explanation of the situation without bothering to dig into the background. A resolution authorizing the chief executive to "take all necessary measures to repel any armed attack against the forces of the United States and to prevent further aggression" passed in the House 416–0 and in the Senate 88–2. Only Senators Wayne Morse of Oregon and Ernest Gruening of Alaska voted no. In view of the grant of power the resolution provided, the lack of serious challenge to the resolution seemed surprising in retrospect. It became a vital basis for Johnson's—and Nixon's—continued prosecution of the war in the face of subsequent congressional opposition. But at the time it provoked virtually no dissent and surprisingly little attention, either in Congress, the media, among intellectuals, or with the public in general.

Pentagon officials seized upon the resolution to push their ideas for air strikes against the North. Johnson had no intention of bombing North Vietnam at that stage of the election, but, significantly, plans were readied for prompt action if and when Hanoi responded to provocations in such a way as to make escalation a viable option. The chief executive acknowledged publicly in late August that some of his advisers wanted to bomb. But he insisted that the war should be fought "by the boys of Asia to help protect their own land." Yet, the continuing discussion about and planning for bombing the North suggest that such an action was inevitable once the President was safely reelected.

In November an interdepartmental working group directed by Assistant Secretary of State for Far Eastern Affairs William P. Bundy (brother of Johnson's White House adviser on foreign policy and son-in-law of former Secretary of State Dean Acheson) examined the case for opening up the war offensively against Hanoi. The group's report declared that although the main elements of Communist strength in South Vietnam were indigenous, they received substantial aid from North Vietnam and in a large measure obeyed orders from Hanoi. To be effective, increased American pressure against the North would have to persuade Hanoi "that the price of maintaining the insurrection in the South would be too great. . . ." The working group presented several options for consideration, including graduated air strikes against the North.

Under Secretary of State George Ball, independent-minded and intellectually courageous, sharply questioned the idea that bombing would do any real good. Ball was an Illinois lawyer with close ties to Adlai Stevenson. He had served off and on in the federal government since the early New Deal, and was highly respected for his skill in international economic affairs and for his willingness to defend persons attacked by McCarthy during the heyday of the red scare. Being a hard-nosed realist and a believer in power politics, and having an orientation that was heavily towards Europe, not Asia, Ball viewed the Vietnamese conflict as a foolish dissipation of American strength. He had few allies among other high-level administration officials, and until he left the administration in September 1966, he was the most consistent and dogged dissenter from the policy of escalating the war. But even in dissent, the Under Secretary remained essentially a team player, and when he retired to private life he flatly refused to make his departure a public protest against the President's war policies.

As in most subsequent cases when Ball opposed increasing American involvement in Vietnam, his arguments against bombing North Vietnam failed to convince his colleagues for long. By late January 1965 McNamara and McGeorge Bundy were arguing that unless the United States exerted stiff pressure on Hanoi the Saigon regime would collapse. As Bundy explained, "the time has come for harder choices." On February 6 Communist forces struck at the American military advisers' compound at Pleiku. Johnson immediately ordered four retaliatory air raids against targets north of the 17th parallel dividing North and South Vietnam. A week later, agreeing with his advisers that the situation in South Vietnam was so bad that America faced defeat unless conditions could be turned around, he approved Operation Rolling Thunder, the long-planned systematic bombing of the North.

As the air strikes got under way, Secretary of State Rusk launched a major public-information campaign demanding that Hanoi stop its offensive against the South. Negotiations were fruitless, he warned, unless the enemy halted its attacks. But without the bombing, Rusk did not expect much in the way of serious negotiations. As he told a visitor in June 1965, "four years of bilateral discussions" had produced no response from Hanoi other than telling the United States to "go to Hell." The sustained air strikes against military targets were counted on to bring the North Vietnamese to the conference table on terms clearly favorable to the United States. Rusk, who became increasingly rigid in his position on the Vietnamese conflict during 1965, believed that the compelling reason for the United States to fight in the war was to prevent its adversaries from underestimating democracy's willingness to do what it had to do to deter aggression. The leaders of the "other side," he explained, had declared a doctrine of world revolution which "ought to be as credible as [Hitler's blueprint for world conquest] *Mein Kampf*." Thus, while the war in Vietnam was "mean and frustrating," the United States had no choice.

Johnson, Rusk, and the key national security people—almost all of whom had been appointed by Kennedy—believed that Communism, directed by a "bellicose and boastful" Red China, threatened to engulf the whole of the Far East. Peking had detonated its first nuclear explosion the previous October and was openly promising Hanoi full support. The Chinese were also urging "wars of national liberation" and stirring up trouble in Thailand and Malaysia. In Indonesia President Sukarno was dependent on Communists to stay in power. North Korea remained a threat to South Korea. Johnson saw an ominous combination shaping up between Red China, North Vietnam, Indonesia, and North Korea, which would probably bring Cambodia in as junior partner and absorb Laos. "The members of this new axis," he wrote in his memoirs, "were undoubtedly counting on South Vietnam's collapse and an ignominious American withdrawal. . . . The entire region would then have been ripe for the plucking."

If the United States had confined its escalation to aerial operations, public opposition to the war would probably have remained relatively limited. What set off the increasing wave of intense and widespread criticism was the increased number of ground troops, which soon included draftees, involved in heavy day-to-day fighting in Vietnam. Rising opposition to the war at home paralleled the mounting lists of Americans killed or wounded in combat. April 1, 1965 was one of several cardinal dates in the long Vietnamese conflict. On that day President Johnson, fearful that the Saigon regime would collapse, decided to use American ground troops in *offensive* action against the Vietcong. Yet, disingenuously, he stated at a press conference only the day before, "I know of no far-reaching strategy that is being suggested or promulgated." A few days later when he approved sending an additional 18,000–20,000 men to Vietnam, he ordered that the decision be given as little publicity as possible in order "to minimize any appearance of sudden changes of policy."

Ironically, during the same month that Johnson's fateful decision planted America's boots so firmly in the Vietnamese quagmire, an incident in the Caribbean added serious new difficulties to his growing list of problems. On April 24 a revolution broke out in the Dominican Republic, long one of Latin America's most oppressed and depressed nations. In 1961 assassins had gunned down dictator Rafael Trujillo, who had ruled the country at his personal whim for many years. President Kennedy's quick deployment of American naval units helped prevent attempts by Trujillo's relatives to replace him. In 1962 a reform party led by Juan Bosch, a man genuinely committed to democracy, won 60 percent of the votes in a national election. His tenure in office, however, was short. Ten months later conservatives backed an army coup d'etat that deposed Bosch and installed a government headed by Donald Reid Cabral.

The United States resumed relations with the Dominican Republic shortly after Kennedy's death as part of the new policies toward Latin-American governments initiated under Johnson by Assistant Secretary of State Thomas Mann. American investments helped to prop up the sagging Dominican economy, but Reid Cabral proved incapable of holding the support of the groups that had put him into office. Pushing a financial austerity program, he sharply slashed the budget of the armed forces. That action cost him his last effective allies, and a small group of army officers easily overthrew the regime on April 24, 1965. However, the rebels failed to agree on who should lead the nation. Both Bosch and Joaquín Balaguer, a former Trujillo lieutenant distinguished for his relative honesty, had supporters. When a Bosch man received the nod as provisional president, dissident factions in the armed services led by Air Force General Elí Wessin y Wessin prepared to launch a counterplot. The American embassy, which at first had accepted the revolt as "just another revolution," regarded the possibility of Bosch's returning to power as contrary to the interests of the United States and encouraged the Wessin forces with modest material aid and considerable moral support.

By April 28 the fighting was widespread. United States Ambassador W. Tapley Bennett concluded that the rebel faction loyal to Bosch was winning. He frantically cabled Washington that American lives were in danger and urged armed intervention to "prevent another Cuba." Bennett provided a list of fifty-three Communists who were allegedly leading the revolution and forwarded accounts of embassies being ransacked and hundreds of people being shot and decapitated.

In Washington, Johnson and his team swung into action. The President ordered several hundred Marines into the Dominican Republic to protect American citizens, directed the State Department to ask the Organization of American States to convene, and conferred with congressional leaders. On the evening of the twenty-eighth he explained his actions to the American people via television, stressing the need to guarantee the safety of Americans caught in the revolution. As information about the events continued to pour into Washington, he warmed up to the view that the Communists had taken over the faction that appeared to be winning. By the evening of the twenty-ninth, convinced that to do nothing was to risk another Cuba, he instructed units of the 82nd Airborne Division to proceed to the Dominican Republic—the beginning of a troop buildup that at its peak totaled 22,000 men. It was no longer a case of protecting American lives, he explained to the public; Communist leaders, "many of them trained in Cuba," had taken over the "popular democratic revolution." Secretary Rusk agreed, declaring that "the Communists had captured the revolution according to plan, and the danger of a Communist takeover was established beyond any question."

Once American troops arrived in strength, the forces favored by the United States quickly took control. Attention then focused on diplomatic efforts to stabilize the embattled country. John Barlow Martin, ambassador to the Dominican Republic in 1962 and 1963, returned as Johnson's special envoy and put together a temporary government under General Antonio Imbert that turned out to be a military dictatorship. Embarrassed, Washington sent veteran diplomat Ellsworth Bunker to maneuver Imbert out of power and install a less authoritarian provisional regime. With the Johnson administration providing the Dominican Republic with more economic aid on a per capita basis than it gave to any other country in Latin America during the year after the revolution, Bunker managed to place a modest liberal, García-Godoy, in charge. Meanwhile private business, confident that the American government could be counted on to prevent a Castro-type revolution, resumed investing heavily in the country. In mid-1966 Joaquín Balaguer won the presidency in an election judged by outside observers to be relatively free and honest. Washington was pleased with the results, knowing that Balaguer could be trusted to ensure the anti-Communist stability deemed essential to America's interests.

Johnson's handling of the Dominican situation provoked serious challenge on several counts. His public statements were extravagant, often hyperbolic, and embroidered with descriptions of occurrences in sharp disagreement with on-the-scene observations and careful postmortems. Significantly, the President never claimed that the Communists had been active in launching the revolt, only that they had taken over the "popular democratic revolution" once it was under way. Unquestionably, Communists sought to capitalize on the disturbances, but the administration's case about the likelihood of Communists' actually seizing power was not convincing. Jerome Slater argued persuasively in his 1970 book, *Intervention and Negotiation: The United States and the Dominican Intervention*, that the Dominican Communists were split into three quarreling groups and had little popular support. But when Ambassador Bennett and his associates concluded that if Bosch's supporters held the upper hand in the revolution the Communists *would* prevail, Johnson, preconditioned by his cold war attitude and his obsession with Castroism, was unwilling to gamble that they *would not.*

Johnson wanted and finally got the Organization of American States to sanction his administration's action. But the approval was given so unenthusiastically that Johnson privately complained, "The OAS couldn't pour piss out of a boot if the instructions were written on the heel." To many Latin Americans the intervention smacked of Yankee gunboat diplomacy so characteristic of another era. It constituted in effect a bold doctrine—the Johnson Doctrine—that the United States had a legitimate right to intervene with armed forces in countries torn by civil strife in which the Communists might gain. Since American officials seemed unable to avoid classifying all social revolutions as Communist-inspired or controlled, the implications were frightening.

The simultaneous buildup of American troop strength in Vietnam and the United States' military operations in the Dominican Republic prompted journalist Philip Geyelin to write tartly, "Marines seemed to be landing everywhere at once." On April 1, when Johnson issued the order to employ American fighting men in offensive maneuvers, 27,000 troops were in Vietnam. By the end of the year, the number had risen to almost 185,000. Despite the obvious implications of such a massive increase in American personnel, the Johnson administration refused to admit any shift in American policy. In early June 1965 the press officer for the State Department announced that American ground forces would assist Vietnamese units in combat "when and if necessary." But the White House insisted that the primary mission of the United States ground troops continued to be to guard important military installations like air bases, although the units could be used, if the military situation demanded it, *to support Vietnamese forces faced with aggressive attack.*

The facts were, as newsmen candidly reported from Vietnam, that American ground forces were being used in purely offensive operations. The first search-and-destroy mission—a favorite tactic of the American military commander in Saigon, General William Westmoreland—occurred in the last days of June. Still, the President maintained that there was no change of policy whatever. Johnson's credibility, already suspect among many newsmen, sagged to a new low among those following the war closely. However, at that point, the American public was only beginning to become restive about the war, and the chief executive's formal speeches about Vietnam were well received by all but the hard-core peace faction. His televised address at Johns Hopkins University on April 7, 1965, for example, generated a warm and largely favorable response at home. After reaffirming America's commitment to an independent South Vietnam, Johnson pledged his readiness for "unconditional discussions" with the governments involved to bring an end to the fighting. The significant part of his speech, however, was his presentation of a bold proposal for the cooperative economic development of Southeast Asia. As soon as peace was achieved, he declared, he would ask Congress for a "billion dollar American investment" in the effort. Having decided covertly to increase the size of the stick being used by the United States in the war, Johnson now offered the carrot.

Hanoi, however, along with Peking and Moscow, gave the proposal a very cold shoulder. LBJ explained that he was not surprised: "I know the other side is winning; so they do, too. No man wants to trade when he's winning." Therefore, the United States had "to apply the maximum deterrent till he sobers up and unloads his pistol." The President remained convinced that the important thing was to maintain enough force to prevent the Communists from winning, but not so much pressure that it might bring the Red Chinese into the conflict on an active basis. In his view neither the "Goldwater solution"—the use of nuclear weapons—nor the proposals of Senator Wayne Morse and others simply to pull out of Vietnam altogether were satisfactory. LBJ tried to walk a narrow line: he refused to grant all the requests for troops that Westmoreland made, but he was determined to send enough to guarantee that the Communists would not triumph.

Not all the President's advisers agreed with the massive injection of American ground troops into the fighting. Ball warned his chief on July 1 that there was no certainty of beating the Vietcong or even forcing them to the conference table on American terms, "no matter how many hundred thousand *white, foreign* (U.S.) troops we deploy." And, he warned, once the United States embarked on a course entailing heavy casualties, "our involvement will be so great that we cannot—without national humiliation—stop short of achieving our complete objectives. Of the two possibilities, I think humiliation would be more likely than the achievement of our objectives—even after we have paid terrible costs." Johnson paid heed, however, to the counsel of others, such as Rusk, who maintained that if the Communist nations discovered that the United States would not keep its commitments, they might not "stay their hand." Furthermore, Rusk insisted, the rate of escalation in the fighting had been determined by the other side. The United States had shown "patience and forbearance"; it had no other choice but to respond to the increased tempo of Communist attacks with more force.

Even as the Johnson administration stepped up its military involvement in Vietnam, it continued to seek a way to convince Hanoi to negotiate. In July 1965 McNamara suggested a six-to-eight-week bombing pause as part of a diplomatic initiative. Although the Joint Chiefs of Staff opposed the idea, he pushed it throughout the fall. Rusk ultimately agreed with his colleague on the ground that it would again emphasize to the American people that the government was doing everything it could to find a peaceful settlement. The Secretary of State's reasoning reflected the very noticeable rise in opposition to the war during the autumn months, as American troops engaged in sustained bloody fighting. Although highly dubious that the attempt would be worthwhile, the chief executive reluctantly agreed, announcing the heralded "Johnson peace offensive" on December 23, 1965. With the bombing raids stopped, UN Ambassador Arthur Goldberg carried the American appeal for peace to Secretary General U Thant, while other diplomats conferred with leaders of countries throughout the world. Thirty-seven days later, after receiving no positive response from Hanoi, the President resumed the air strikes against the North.

Johnson was convinced that it was necessary to apply still greater pressure to persuade North Vietnam to go to the conference table. A few days after the end of the bombing pause he flew to Honolulu to confer with South Vietnamese Premier Nguyen Cao Ky, who had taken power eight months before. Although Ky's government had done little to reform the corrupt bureaucracy or to mobilize renewed support for the war among rural Vietnamese, it had at least been able to provide a semblance of authority. The talks between the American and South Vietnamese officials covered not only the fighting but also ways to improve the health, education, and economy of the Asian country. Ky promised to write a constitution "in the months ahead," have the people approve it, and follow with "genuine democratic elections." To the perpetually overoptimistic Walt Rostow the new government included "just the kind of second generation figures that I hoped in 1961 Diem would find and bring forward—young, intensely nationalistic, inexperienced, energetic." During the next few months, as Ky struggled against competing factions, Rostow remained satisfied that all was going well. Others were less confident. When Rostow suggested at a meeting that "we were not seeing a recurrence of 1963 but the pangs of a nation being born," an old friend retorted, "Walt, are you mad?"

According to Johnson's public statements, the President, too, was encouraged by Ky's efforts and by the progress of the war in general. Throughout 1966 he painted a picture of progress, reiterated the domino theory, and repeatedly insisted that he was ready to negotiate. It remained clear, however, that he intended to bargain only on American terms. When Robert F. Kennedy—by then a senator from New York—declared that he favored allowing the National Liberation Front (NLF), the political arm of the Vietcong, to participate in governing South Vietnam, Vice President Humphrey answered for the administration. Such a strategy, he tartly replied, would be like putting "a fox in a chicken coop."

Although the military issued intermittent optimistic statements about how well the war was going, Westmoreland significantly continued to ask for considerably more troops than the President was willing to authorize. Even so, by the end of 1966 well over 400,000

American troops were in Vietnam. Bombing attacks against the North were intensified during the year at the insistence of the Pentagon, despite evaluations indicating their ineffectiveness. The raids had not measurably lessened the enemy's ability to supply its forces in the South but had instead strengthened the North Vietnamese people's patriotic support of the Hanoi regime.

Late in 1966, Robert McNamara began to express to the President some of his growing pessimism about the American effort. The Secretary of Defense advised against continued bombing, urged more vigorous attempts to make peace, and even suggested developing a "realistic plan providing a role for the VC in negotiations, postwar life and government of the nation." He also expressed doubts that more troops would substantially change the situation and questioned the estimates of enemy losses reported by the military. All his comments were made to Johnson privately; publicly, McNamara remained a loyal supporter—then and later—of the administration's policies.

Although Johnson chose to disregard the recommendations of his respected Pentagon chief, McNamara's diminishing enthusiasm for the war added an important, though secret, voice to those challenging the United States' role in the war. The November congressional elections added heavily to the President's woes: the Republicans replaced forty-seven Democrats in the House and three in the Senate. Meanwhile, LBJ's own approval ratio, measured by the Gallup poll, declined from 66 percent in November 1965 to 44 percent in October 1966. Republican spokesmen claimed that the voters were repudiating his domestic policies by saying that he was "doing too much" and "moving too fast." That was undoubtedly a factor, as were the riots in the cities and the white backlash. But so was Vietnam. Dr. George Gallup, the polltaker, judged that the Vietnam war was "probably the prime reason why the GOP did so well." The chief executive took comfort from the fact that polls showed that a majority still believed that the United States was right to be in Vietnam, although the number of dissenters was rising rapidly. No longer could he write them off as a slender minority or a bunch of kooks. By the end of 1966 protests against the war clearly constituted a serious threat to Johnson's ability to lead effectively.

# VIII

## *The Years of Frustration*

"I JUST hope that foreign problems do not keep mounting," Lady Bird Johnson remarked during the summer of 1965. "They do not represent Lyndon's kind of Presidency." The irony of her comment soon became painfully apparent, as Vietnam increasingly consumed the energies of the chief executive as well as the resources of the nation. Like an acid eating at the vitals of America, the war destroyed the strong consensus on foreign policy that existed when Johnson entered the White House and both directly and indirectly aggravated the country's domestic troubles. Like two other Democratic Presidents he greatly admired, Woodrow Wilson and Franklin Roosevelt, Johnson was elected as a domestic reformer but found that war came to dominate his time.

Johnson was not so insensitive as to be unmoved by protests against the conflict. But as his hands became figuratively bloodier, he grew even more determined not to end the American involvement without a settlement that would guarantee a non-Communist South Vietnam. Anything else, he believed, would make meaningless the sacrifices of the Americans killed and wounded in the fighting. Convinced that history would judge the United States' role in Southeast Asia to have been correct, wise, and necessary, the President held relentlessly to his course in the face of opposition to the war that grew steadily more aggressive and widespread. Although public opinion polls taken during the Johnson years indicated that at no time did the majority of the American people favor simply walking out of Vietnam, by late 1966 public appearances by the chief executive were carefully restricted to functions where protesting demonstrators likely to embarrass him could be excluded with relative certainty. If not a captive in the White House, he was, at the least, unable to move about the country with the freedom that Presidents customarily enjoy.

The war protesters included Americans from a broad cross section of the population, but college students sounded both the first serious criticism and the loudest and most abrasive challenges about Vietnam. As they had done during the revolution against social values in the 1920s, the young were out in front, serving as the cutting edge; their elders, or at least some of their elders, hurried to catch up. The reasons were not hard to find. For one thing youth and idealism go hand in hand. For another, young men are inevitably called upon to fight and die in the wars older men decide to wage. Opposition to the war provided the necessary catalyst to pull together various strands of disillusionment with American society. This loose coalition, known as the Movement, had both political and cultural manifestations.

The abundance enjoyed by Americans in the 1950s provided the fertile soil which spawned and nurtured the young people who constituted the Movement. Following World War II, technology and economic growth appeared capable of making the American dream of prosperity for all come true. For the majority of the white population the decade was a period of remarkable material gain. Mass-produced products of an amazing variety filled the homes in the shining new suburbs that multiplied outside the dingy and decaying cities. Paralleling and accompanying the "good life" was a strong drive for conformity. Anyone who dared to challenge the benefits of capitalism or to question the wisdom of anti-Communism as an ideology walked on dangerous ground. Conformity was the watchword of society, and being "well-rounded" its highest distinction.

Even at the time not everyone agreed that America was rapidly becoming the promised land, although evidence to the contrary was largely ignored. The growing intensity of Negro protests emphasized that black Americans were not sharing equally, but since the disturbances centered almost wholly in the South, they were dismissed as more sectional than national. There were millions of poor people, but they made so little noise that their plight was little more than a footnote to the events of the decade. Intellectuals, such as David Riesman and Paul Goodman, only rippled the tranquil waters with their doubts that people were as satisfied as they appeared to be on the surface and their theories that a vast number of individuals were quietly alienated by the dull and meaningless lives they led. Writers and artists like Jack Kerouac, George Tooker, and the "Beat" poets of New York and San Francisco, who ridiculed American culture as bland and boring, attracted a handful of devoted followers but slight notice from the general public.

Among those who agreed most ardently with the criticisms of America were a small number of students from relatively affluent middle-class homes. Unlike many of their parents, they had seldom foregone basic needs. Spoiled and pampered in many cases, they nevertheless rejected the type of sterile future they could anticipate. Boredom, to them, was the cardinal sin. They regarded social norms as stifling, poverty in a land so rich as inexcusable, inequality among races as indefensible, and mindless anti-Communism as illogical and—given the existence of nuclear weapons—dangerous. Bureaucracy and technology were especially galling. Society was overdeveloped and plagued with immense bureaucracies in government, trade unions, and even in the universities most of them attended or had attended. Technology had produced frightening instruments, like computers, which were rapidly reducing human beings to little more than punch cards. ("Do not spindle, fold, or mutilate—I am a student," became a favorite slogan on college campuses inundated by computerized systems.) A small elite, or elites, made the key decisions in all institutions, and the governed had little or no choice in their destinies.

In the late fifties small numbers of university students and faculty, disgusted with both Western imperialism and the excesses of savage Soviet Marxism, began to seek alternatives. Referring to themselves as the New Left, they essentially regarded the Marxist-Leninist emphasis on the working class (a disciplined "vanguard" party) and society's economic relations as dated and irrelevant. Instead, they focused intensely on alienation and humanism, drawing heavily from the humanistic socialism of the young Marx and from the writings of pacifists and philosophical anarchists. Clubs formed at a number of top-flight universities, and activist journals designed to communicate the ideas of the New Left appeared and disappeared.

As Irwin Unger, a recent historian of the New Left, convincingly argued, it was a movement of "*white* middle-class youth." Although black activists goaded the consciences of white radicals and at times participated in New Left activities and decisions, the Movement was a phenomenon common to all affluent industrial countries, none of which, except the United States, had a serious racial problem.

John Kennedy's election in 1960 stirred members of the Movement momentarily. They liked his call for sacrifice and commitment. The Peace Corps and the Alliance for Progress seemed to be steps in the right direction. But Kennedy soon lost the support of the disillusioned. In confrontations over Berlin and Cuba he rattled nuclear sabers and talked a conventional, hard-nosed cold war line. At home he moved cautiously and very slowly. Soon the New Left concluded that Kennedy was just a younger, better-looking, more witty edition of the old stereotype.

Early in JFK's administration the Students for a Democratic Society (SDS) developed as a formal organization. Originally loosely connected with Old Left organizations like the Student League for Industrial Democracy (organized in 1930), SDS's ties with the Old Left became steadily weaker during the sixties. The New Left enthusiasts were simply far too radical and much too undisciplined to suit the tastes of old-line Marxists. The SDS viewed tightly knit organizations and designated leaders as dangerous manifestations of the undemocratic hierarchies or elites that characterized the type of institutions they opposed. Started at the University of Michigan, SDS held its first national convention in 1962 and issued the Port Huron Statement, an "agenda for a generation." Written by a brilliant young activist, Tom Hayden, the document frankly admitted that SDS members had been "bred in at least modest comfort, [and were] housed now in universities." But, it declared, they looked "uncomfortably to the world we inherit." In mild language Hayden ticked off the evils: rampant racism, international tension, anti-Communism as an ideology, bureaucracy, alienation, and helplessness. In subsequent years the SDS would be less temperate in its rhetoric. Its goals, however, remained much the same: the search for community, participatory democracy, social and personal relationships that meant sharing experiences, and lives unfettered by the cramping pressures of competitive careers and styles so characteristic to America. Capitalism, SDS members made clear, caused many, perhaps most, of America's problems. It supported racism abroad as well as at home and stifled the chances of real equality.

Since the university was the base for the radical solutions implied by the SDS and like-minded students, not surprisingly an academic institution became the site of the first major confrontation outside the civil rights arena. But significantly, the New Left demanded only "reform," not radical change. The University of California at Berkeley was huge and sprawling, heavily bureaucratized, and drowning in a sea of self-imposed regulations. Its attempt to restrict on-campus recruiting for off-campus political activism provoked student protests that simmered for months and finally erupted into the Free Speech demonstration in the fall of 1964. Mario Savio, an electrifying speaker, mobilized thousands of students with his warnings against the university's dehumanizing attitude. "Free Speech" easily converted to filthy speech at Berkeley, causing a countervailing protest from tax-paying Californians who wondered just what their sons and daughters were learning at state schools. Results of the episode were far reaching: a shake-up in the administration of the University of California, the radicalization of a significant number of students, the popularization of the slogan "You can't trust anyone over thirty," a powerful incentive for a taxpayer's rebellion against financing education, and an important issue for conservative Republican Ronald Reagan to use in his successful 1966 campaign for governor.

Paralleling and overlapping—a part of, yet not exactly the same as—the Movement was the counter culture. The former was essentially political. The latter, as Theodore Roszak explained in his highly sympathetic *The Making of a Counter Culture*, was a revolt against "objective consciousness" and the rational scientists, engineers, and statesmen who managed lives by coldly examining and arranging the objects of the world rather than feeling for them. Both the political activists and the counter culturists condemned the old culture of their parents because it tended "to give preference to property rights over personal rights, technological requirements over human needs, competition over cooperation, violence over sexuality, concentration of wealth over distribution, the producer over the consumer, means over ends, secrecy over openness, social forms over personal expression, striving over gratification, Oedipal love over communal love . . . ." But the counter culturists, in some cases frightened by encounters with police and exhausted by the strain of "causes," generally preferred to avoid confrontation politics. Although they considered themselves allies of the Movement and accepted its goals as their own, the counter-culture hippies increasingly eschewed political activism in favor of a more passive and introspective existence.

The counter culture rejected systematized knowledge, logic, and often even reason itself in favor of mysticism, shamanism, strange cults, African and Asian creeds, and sometimes their own version of Christianity. Whether clustered in decaying "crash pads" in large cities or living in agrarian communes in the country, drugs, music, and uninhibited sexual expression characterized their lives. So did bizarre clothing and long hair. They started free universities to circumvent the rigidity of established disciplines and curriculums. They initiated underground newspapers to communicate in a manner unfettered by Establishment restraints and "turned on" with drugs, rock festivals, "happenings," and "be-ins," where everyone did his or her "thing"—whatever it might be. Heroes were out; it was the era of the anti-hero. Yet certain individuals stood out even in the counter culture: Bob Dylan, Janis Joplin, and the Beatles in music; Timothy Leary as the high priest of the drug experience ("drop out, turn on, tune in"); Abbie Hoffmann and Jerry Rubin as particularly zany counter culturists with strong, if often erratic, ties to the political Movement.

Almost every nuance adopted or adapted by the counter culture shocked sober-minded, "straight" Americans. They regarded rock music as too loud, too strange, and the lyrics too hard to understand. Had most grasped the words and their meaning, they would have hated the music even more, since the lyrics frequently stressed drugs, sex, and revolution. Dirty clothes and long, unkempt hair suggested personal filthiness, free sexual expression clearly implied moral degeneracy, and the heavy use of dope represented a contempt for one's body and mind and an unwillingness to face personal responsibilities. Refusing to prepare for a vocation or simply not working were taken as signs of laziness and went directly against the grain of the American work ethic.

The political activists in the Movement were too committed to changing America by direct action to accept the counter culture's tendency to "drop out." Berkeley had shown that protests could shut down a campus. It could, the young radicals believed, also be used to bring about other changes. But although they could play an annoying, troublesome role, they could not really function effectively unless they could recruit a mass of supporters. The growing numbers of counter culturists were unreliable allies, and most college students were not members of SDS or any other radical organization. Consequently, to rally enough of the normally nonradical types to action required a genuinely popular cause. The escalation of the American war effort in Vietnam provided just such a one. Rising draft calls radicalized more bright young Americans than the teachings of Karl Marx, SNCC, or the SDS could ever hope to do. Hence in 1965 the Movement began to swell rapidly in size, although most of the new recruits were college students. Working-class youths held back. Most resented the hippie culture and the demonstrations against the Vietnam war. Conditioned by their early training to accept the fact that probably they would never have much say in making national policy anyway, they tended to conform, not rebel. Thus, the universities, the training camps of the country's future leaders, provided the breeding grounds for the war protesters.

During 1965 the first antiwar "teach-in"—half lecture and seminar, half political rally—occurred at the University of Michigan. Speakers attacked the intellectual bases of America's role in Vietnam, and students responded enthusiastically. Those who questioned the war at other colleges followed suit, but the Movement also sought more dramatic ways to emphasize its opposition to the conflict. Rallies and marches became popular tactics. Spokesmen for the Movement optimistically declared that alliances of progressive forces were developing around the world. Student protests in Japan, England, Germany, France, and other countries gave credence to their claim. Some Movement leaders stressed the need to organize communities outside the universities against the war, but their poorly planned attempts to form alliances with the working class, the dream of the traditional Left, bore few fruits. Trade unions rudely rejected their overtures. Equally frustrating were the young radicals' amateurish efforts to elect political candidates sympathetic to their cause. They contributed marginally to the election of SNCC worker Julian Bond to the Georgia legislature in 1965, but in other races their favorites lost badly.

The Movement failed to win converts from outside communities in part because it had no cohesion or coordination. Inherently skeptical of hierarchies, the New Left suffered from a lack of skilled leadership. Even more critical, however, was the Movement's refusal to respect the civility and compromise traditionally accepted by Americans. Although the young radicals lauded dissent and participatory democracy, they stridently repressed disagreement to their own views and attempted to deny opponents an opportunity to express contrary opinions. And while the Movement rhetorically assumed a righteous moral posture, many members proceeded to steal and damage the property of nonradicals. Such tactics severely alienated the very people the New Left was attempting to woo.

Beginning in 1966, peace demonstrations began to become more militant. Political moderates, frustrated by their inability to convince the government through reason, grew increasingly radicalized. Some simply refused to accept their draft orders to report for military service. An unknown number of men who were already in the armed services balked when ordered overseas and faced court martial rather than fight. Some Vietnam veterans, like Sergeant Donald Duncan, left the service and denounced American actions in Vietnam. A number of military men stationed in Southeast Asia deserted and made their way to neutral countries where they were granted asylum. Most common of all, thousands of Americans fled to Canada or Europe to avoid the draft.

Angry protesters attempted to disrupt the war effort at home by "sitting-in" the entrances of Selective Service induction centers, and some universities responded to student demands by severing their formal connections with Selective Service. Many opponents of the war deliberately violated the law by publicly burning or returning their draft cards to their draft boards. College protesters harassed on-campus job interviewers from companies with connections to the Defense Department, such as Dow Chemical, which manufactured napalm. Central Intelligence Agency and armed services recruiters suffered similar fates when they visited colleges. Protest marches grew much bigger during 1967. An estimated 300,000 people participated in New York City early in the year, and in November over 100,000 joined in an unsuccessful attempt to close down the Pentagon. The escalation of resistance created an obvious potential for violence, but throughout 1967 the protests remained peaceful for the most part, although police sometimes used excessive force when removing demonstrators and prowar hecklers frequently incited physical retaliation. Although outright violence remained a relative rarity, as the public became increasingly aware of the administration's half-truths and outright lies about the war, good manners went down the drain. Any attempt by government spokesmen—including the President—to speak in public in defense of American involvement in Vietnam could be guaranteed to draw a noisy crowd of demonstrators who would disrupt the occasion if they possibly could.

The antics of the war protesters repulsed millions of Americans who considered themselves "ordinary, average, hardworking citizens" and who were willing to trust the President's judgment that Vietnam was necessary to protect the security of the United States and its way of life. With the exception of a few isolated incidents, such as the flag-waving parade by New York City construction workers, most attempts to show support for the administration's war policies received little national attention. Individuals who spoke out for what was right, not wrong, about America were commonly ignored by the news media and not infrequently castigated as right-wing reactionaries. With their flamboyant styles and inflammatory rhetoric, the radicals were surefire headline makers, and television and the press provided them with extravagant, perhaps excessive, coverage. To a significant degree, the heavy publicity accorded the antiwar protests misled many observers into believing that support for radical politics was much wider and more deeply rooted than in fact it was. The truth became apparent in succeeding years. Torn by severe internal dissension, by the end of 1969 the New Left was in serious disarray. Subsequently, with the steady withdrawal of American fighting forces from Vietnam and the dwindling number of young men likely to be drafted, the antiwar movement's mass support likewise dissipated. By the end of 1972 the

New Left, although not dead, no longer basked in the spotlight or seemed to be a potent political force.

But in 1968, with the war in Vietnam raging and with draft calls high, the Movement seemed to be gaining strength rapidly. The more extreme members professed to see no alternative to violent revolution as a means of purging America of its evil institutions and restoring power to the people. It is difficult to convey the intensity of their hatred. In their view the Johnson administration typified the utter bankruptcy of the United States as it existed. The positive-government liberalism of the twentieth century was nothing more than a new, clever tactic of the ruling Establishment for manipulating people's lives. Anyone who stood in the way, either at home or abroad, and defied manipulation was ruthlessly crushed by the government. A student leader attending a tumultuous conference on Students and Society hosted by the Center for the Study of Democratic Institutions at Santa Barbara, California, in 1967 summed up the angry position of extremists: "What I mean by revolution is overthrowing the American government and American imperialism and installing some sort of decentralized power in this country. I'll tell you the steps that I think will be needed. First of all, starting up fifty Vietnams in Third World countries. This is going to come about by black rebellions in our cities joined by some white people. . . . The major thing student activists can do while all this is going on—I mean completely demoralizing and castrating America —is to give people a vision of something other than what they have now."

Although most intellectuals stopped well short of such a vitriolic recommendation for changing America, a sizable number applauded the efforts of student activists and joined in vocal denunciations of the administration and particularly its war policies. Their attacks further aggravated Lyndon Johnson's intrinsic distrust of the amorphous and ill-defined intellectual community. Linguist Noam Chomsky argued that intellectuals were "in a position to expose the lies of governments, to analyze their actions according to their causes and motives and often hidden intentions." Reading each day of fresh atrocities in Vietnam, Chomsky declared, each must ask, "What have I done" to prevent such horrors?

Attempts by the President to tap the "best minds" for ideas

failed to convince many scholars, writers, and artists that Johnson sincerely wanted their help. Unquestionably, many of them found it difficult to really like the President because of his style. Political scientist John Roche, who succeeded Eric Goldman as the White House intellectual in 1966, deprecated the intellectual critics of the President as "only a small body of self-appointed people who live in affluent alienation on Cape Cod and fire off salvos against the vulgarity of the masses . . . . The main problem is that an awful lot of these guys prefer style to performance." Roche had a point. The intellectual community is no more monolithic than the business community or the trade unions. Nor is it possible to define with even a modest degree of precision just who is or is not an intellectual. At best it is a very loose term, applied indiscriminately to scholars, writers, and creative and performing artists. But for his part, Johnson responded to the criticism of *some* intellectuals by generally regarding *all* as hostile to his administration.

The White House Festival of the Arts in June 1965 provided an apt example of Johnson's rapidly mounting animosity toward any who were identified, correctly or not, as intellectuals. Remembering how Kennedy had impressed intellectuals by hosting cultural events in the White House, Goldman proposed that Johnson hold the festival as a salute to citizens who promoted cultural activities in their local communities. The President liked the idea and gave his adviser the go-ahead. To highlight the festivities, distinguished men and women in various fields were invited to read or show or perform their works. Most accepted with enthusiasm, but poet Robert Lowell subsequently developed second thoughts. In a public letter he explained that although he admired most of the administration's domestic legislation and intentions, he regarded its foreign policy with "the greatest distrust and dismay." Therefore, he declared, he was withdrawing from participation in the festival. Johnson was furious, particularly when the *New York Times* carried the story on its front page. When a handful of other invited dignitaries endorsed Lowell's decision, the chief executive, enraged, railed at "those people" and lumped them, as Goldman sadly wrote, into "one repulsive conglomerate." The event itself was of minor importance; Johnson's attitude, however, was not.

Although the sniping by intellectuals at his policies angered the

President, he knew that they wielded little real power. The growing ranks of congressional "doves" troubled him much more. Publicly he claimed that the overwhelming 504–2 vote by the legislators in favor of the Tonkin Gulf Resolution in 1964 constituted clear authority for him to take whatever actions he deemed necessary to protect American interests in Vietnam, though he avoided any revotes on that supposed mandate. Consequently, he felt betrayed when congressmen like Senator William Fulbright turned against him on Vietnam. The influential chairman of the Senate Foreign Relations Committee had warned in earlier years that modern technology made it imperative for a President to have broad power to act quickly in foreign affairs, and he had firmly supported the Tonkin Gulf proposal. But during 1965, Fulbright changed his mind about Vietnam and decided that America was "losing its perspective on what exactly is within the realm of its power and what is beyond it." His persistent and stinging criticism infuriated the President, who privately castigated his tormentor as "a frustrated old woman" and declared that the southerner simply "cannot understand that people with brown skins value freedom too." Other congressmen who shifted positions on the war also earned Johnson's wrath. On the other hand, he accepted Wayne Morse's opposition rather calmly, since the pesky Oregon Democrat had consistently spoken and voted against increasing American involvement in Asia.

Johnson blamed opposition to the war on a variety of reasons: the recurrence of isolationism, a little racism ("the Vietnamese are not our kind of people" attitude), and mistaken judgment about the continuing danger posed by China and the Soviet Union. "Most of them," he once declared, "have set [*sic*] out all wars. They love liberty but only talk about it. They have no style or character; they are uncouth and they have no guts . . . ." As the conflict dragged on and the opponents of the war grew more caustic in their denunciations of his administration, Johnson reciprocated the bitterness, arguing vehemently that the efforts of the "cut and run people" strengthened Hanoi. "Fifteen to twenty percent of the people question everything about us. They engage in character assassination. They have none of the feeling for the independence of brown men that they have for people of their own race." Despite the annoying complaints of the "Nervous Nellies," he insisted that he had "not the slightest doubt that the courage and dedication and the good sense of the wise American people will ultimately prevail."

Johnson counted heavily on the popularity of his Great Society program at home to offset growing dissatisfaction with his war policies. But ironically, many of his strongest backers on Vietnam were the most alienated by his domestic programs. Generally speaking, the students and the intellectuals who formed the vanguard of opposition to the war approved of his attempts to secure equal rights for minorities and his crusade to eliminate poverty, though most felt that he did not go far enough. Conversely, middle-class WASPS (white, Anglo-Saxon, Protestant) and white ethnics—hard working, patriotic, and nonrebellious—who agreed that it was "better to stop the spread of Communism in the marshes of Southeast Asia than on the beaches of the West Coast," believed that the administration was doing too much for the blacks and the poor and too little for them. When riots broke out in major cities, many of those who were willing to go down the line with Johnson on the war in Vietnam became his severest critics on domestic policy. Thus while the polls continued to show that the majority of the people opposed simply pulling out of Vietnam, the President's personal approval rating with the voters stayed below 50 percent from 1966 until he left office.

The urban riots made the sixties the most violent decade in American history since the Civil War. The reasons why they occurred have been repeated so often as to become almost clichés: racism in American society; the existence of separate racial worlds; police behavior; the feeling of hopelessness and frustration among minority groups because of their inability to achieve significant political, social, and economic change; and the developing sense of racial identity and pride. Blacks won important legal gains with their nonviolent tactics between 1954 and 1964. But economically and politically they remained far removed from anything approaching genuine equality with whites. Unemployment rates for blacks were far higher, average earnings far lower. In a society that placed a premium on material possessions as a sign of personal success, the low economic status of most blacks translated easily into low self-esteem. During the Watts riot of 1965, Louis Lomax, the perceptive black writer, encountered a black looter removing a bulky sofa from a burning furniture store by balancing it on his head and shoulders. "Brother, brother," Lomax implored, "do you realize what you're doing?" "Don't bother me now," the burdened man replied, "I've got to hurry back to get the matching chair."

Between 1964 and 1967 over one hundred major riots demonstrated dramatically that blacks would no longer be content with legal gains in the South. And since most of the disturbances occurred in the North, they sorely strained the patience of the white middle class in the parts of the country that had strongly supported Johnson during the 1964 election. Northern whites had agreed that it was important to free the Negro from obvious and obnoxious restrictions in employment and in the use of public facilities such as restaurants, buses, schools, and rest rooms. Once that was done, however, it was up to each individual to make his own way. Despite the difficulties involved in growing up in a WASP culture, the Irish and Italians had pulled themselves up by their own bootstraps, and the Poles, Greeks, and Slavs were gradually doing so. Many white ethnics felt that they still lacked power, status, and intellectual voice, but they worked hard and suffered their frustrations silently and peacefully. Most believed that blacks should do the same. The flaw in the Bootstrap Theory was that none of the white ethnics had ever been slaves. Equally important, since they were white, they could melt relatively easily into the social landscape. Nevertheless, when the most apparent response by blacks to Great Society programs specifically designed to assist them was rioting, the white backlash that had been predicted in 1964 but had not developed blossomed with a vengeance.

Black riots were a significant issue in the 1966 elections. Republicans, as noted previously, capitalized heavily on the law-and-order issue and registered sizable gains in both houses of Congress. But blacks also won some important victories in the same election. Edward Brooke won handily in Massachusetts and became the first black in the Senate since the Reconstruction period. Blacks doubled their seats in state legislatures and for the first time had a major impact on elections in the South. Nevertheless, civil rights activists recognized that their struggle would be much more difficult in view of the changing national mood. New ideas and tactics were needed. Labeling the past dozen years as the "Second Reconstruction," historian C. Vann Woodward warned, "Veterans of the Second Reconstruction and planners of the Third would do well to face up to the fact that the one is now over and the other is still struggling to be born."

Although Johnson pushed hard for new civil rights legislation in 1967, few shrewd political observers expected the incoming Congress to react favorably. Basically, his proposals were the same as his unsuccessful 1966 bill but split into six separate laws. Only one passed, an extension of the life of the Civil Rights Commission. Congress also approved the chief executive's nomination of Thurgood Marshall, the great-grandson of a Maryland slave, to the Supreme Court. The first black American ever to sit on that august body, Marshall had served twenty-three years as counsel for the NAACP and later as a circuit court judge before Johnson selected him as Solicitor General in 1965.

The House also administered what many blacks regarded as a slap in the face by unseating Adam Clayton Powell, Jr., the flamboyant black representative from New York. For years he had wielded great power as chairman of the Education and Labor Committee, but his life style made him highly unpopular with a great many of his colleagues. He padded his pockets by putting his estranged wife on the payroll, even though she did not work in his office; he also cavorted with the beautiful young women he hired for his staff and traveled widely on sightseeing junkets at the taxpayers' expense. Many other congressmen committed similar or even worse acts, but they did so quietly. Powell sinned openly and often with considerable publicity. His ability to flaunt the rules and his knack for making the Establishment work for him made Powell a hero in the ghetto.

Finally, however, Powell went too far. Convicted of libel in New York, he refused to pay the judgment awarded to the plaintiff. To avoid arrest he simply stayed away from the state, living in comfort at his island retreat in the Bahamas. His enemies used the incident to strip him of his prestigious chairmanship. When he screamed racism, the legislators voted to unseat him. Furious, the voters in his district gave Powell, who did not make a single campaign appearance, 80 percent of the vote in the special election to fill his seat. Subsequently, a court ruling upheld his claim to be reseated, but his chairmanship was gone for good.

Actually, nothing that Congress or the administration did or did not do during the first part of 1967 caused the wave of urban riots that occurred during the summer. After the experiences of the preceding three summers, it was no surprise that they broke out. Urban officials built up their arsenals of antiriot weapons, prepared contingency plans, and devised riot-control tactics. On the more positive side, metropolitan governments also hurriedly attempted to improve relations between the police and black residents. In Chicago policemen gave talks to high school students; in New York officers took black and Puerto Rican youths to ball games and weekend camps. Other cities developed similar programs, and most provided police with crash courses in human relations. Many communities tried to find employment for ghetto adolescents, calling upon local businesses to provide some of the needed jobs and drawing upon Office of Economic Opportunity funds to create others. Despite such efforts, far too few youngsters found work or participated in the new recreational programs that were started. For many ghetto dwellers, the main evidence of their government's attempts to forestall violence was the sight of youngsters cooling off by splashing in the water sprayed from fire hydrants on sweltering summer days.

Such efforts were a classic case of too little and too late, and the troubles began with the arrival of hot weather. Minor outbreaks occurred as early as April and mounted in intensity as the temperatures climbed. In mid-July, Newark and Detroit virtually exploded. Newark was clearly a city ripe for trouble. The unemployment rate for nonwhites was over 10 percent, three times as great as for whites. The community's slums were particularly bad, even by the dismal standards of other northern ghettos. Blacks claimed that white city officials were consistently trying to oust them from Newark by rezoning black residential areas into business districts. City officials made the situation worse by largely ignoring black grievances, and promises from politicians and the business community of a "New Newark" were considered relevant only to white aspirations. When police allegedly beat up a black taxi driver, blacks took to the streets. Fierce violence, highlighted by sniper fire and fire bombings, continued for three days before state troopers and

National Guardsmen combined with local police to quell the disturbance.

The Detroit riot made Newark look like small potatoes. Although many of the Michigan city's 600,000 black citizens were reasonably affluent, its unemployment rate was as high as Newark's. In addition, Detroit had a long tradition of racial friction. Only a spark was needed to provoke another outbreak of violence. A police raid on a black speakeasy triggered looting and burning, which spread like wildfire. Governor George Romney rushed National Guard troops to the scene, but they lacked adequate training and discipline to deal effectively with the rapidly worsening situation. Police and guardsmen exercised little restraint and answered sniper fire with indiscriminate shooting, thus contributing to the overall confusion and terror. After two days, Romney reluctantly requested Army troops, and 4,700 paratroopers restored calm in a matter of hours. Forty-three persons were dead, hundreds injured, and thousands under arrest. Property damage estimates ran into the hundreds of millions, and at least 5,000 people were homeless.

In the 1967 outbreaks, as in earlier riots, the leaders of the established moderate civil rights organizations were of little help in providing mediation. Neither the NAACP, the Urban League, nor Martin Luther King's SCLC had a significant base in the northern or western ghettos. Compared to the movie-gangster rhetoric of Black Power spokesmen like Stokely Carmichael and H. Rap Brown, the older generation of civil rights leaders sounded tame. King argued that "our power does not reside in Molotoff cocktails, knives, and bricks . . . ." But such implements were in fact standard tools for the summer riots, and the language of Brown—"violence is as American as cherry pie," riots are a "dress rehearsal for revolution," and Johnson is "a mad, wild dog"—suited the mood of angry blacks far better.

The militants had several important advantages over the moderates in competing for black followers. They were free of the financial, political, and organizational responsibilities that often restrained moderates, and they were not expected to produce as much in the way of concrete results. In addition they were more colorful in their dress and style and especially in their rhetoric. Consequently, they were more newsworthy. Quite possibly, as historian Robert Fogelson observed, the media may well have been reflecting their audience's preferences by devoting so much attention to the black militants, since the militants offered "a rationale for the liberal's guilt, the conservative's prejudice, and the radical's aspiration."

The moderates knew that if they appeared too eager to cooperate with the Johnson administration, they would further destroy their already strained credibility with angry black ghetto dwellers. Johnson appreciated their problem. Once, after a friendly private meeting with a moderate leader, the President insisted that his caller tell newsmen upon leaving that he had demanded and received some action from the chief executive. "What about Annapolis?" Johnson suggested to his visitor. "The Naval Academy's only got a handful of Negro midshipmen. You brought that to my attention, and I said I would see to it that the Navy changed and got some more black faces in the officer corps. I'll do it right now." With that LBJ telephoned the startled Secretary of the Navy and told him that he wanted immediate attention given to the problem.

By 1967, many within the administration were anxious to make rioting more expensive for the rioters. One possibility was to indict extremists like Carmichael, who went around delivering such fiery bromides as, "Mao Tse-tung said, and I agree, that political power goes out of the mouth of a gun. The vote means nothing unless you've got the gun behind it." Attorney General Ramsey Clark scotched the idea, arguing that his staff had investigated the evidence carefully and that there were insufficient grounds for conviction; acquittal would simply make the bellicose Carmichael even more of a hero.

No one could seriously object, however, to appointing a commission to study the 1967 riots. It was an old tactic. Commissions had investigated the 1919 riot in Chicago, the Harlem riots of 1935 and 1943, and the Watts riot of 1965. Certainly a new investigation could do no harm. Most people close to the scene also doubted, however, that it would produce much in the way of positive results. Kenneth B. Clark, a distinguished black sociologist, referred to riot reports as "a kind of Alice in Wonderland—with the same moving picture re-shown over and over again, the same analysis, the same recommendations, and the same inaction." The President chose no radicals, either black or white, for the 1967 commission. Cochaired by Governor Otto Kerner of Illinois and Mayor John Lindsay of New York, the panel included two blacks, Senator Edward Brooke and Roy Wilkins, but essentially represented the white Establishment.

Despite its moderate composition, the commission's report bluntly admitted that white racism lay at the heart of the problem: "What white Americans have never fully understood—but what the Negro can never forget—is that white society is deeply implicated in the ghetto. White institutions created it, white institutions maintain it, and white society condones it." Examining twenty-four disorders in twenty-three cities, the commission and its staff compiled an impressive body of information about the genesis of the riots. Although some specific event triggered the actual outbreak of violence, the eruptions spread because of disturbed social atmospheres in the cities, with prior incidents involving the police being important in almost half the cases. The typical rioter was a teenager or young adult, male, a lifelong resident of the city in which he rioted, a high school dropout, usually unemployed or employed in a menial job, proud of his race, highly distrustful of the political system, and extremely hostile to both whites and middle-class blacks. The commission found that in several cities the principal official response following the riots had been to arm the police with more sophisticated weapons, and it warned that increased polarization between the races was clearly evident. The commissioners urged a massive commitment to improving housing, education, the welfare system, and employment opportunities for blacks.

Considering the costs in lives and property damage caused by the riots (130 persons killed and $714.8 million in estimated costs between 1965 and 1967, according to the report of the Senate Permanent Committee on Investigations), a massive program to implement the recommendations of the commission made sense. Congress, however, was more concerned with the criminal aspects and the need for more effective measures of repression. The legislators had displayed an incredible insensitivity to the problems of slum dwellers in the interim between the Newark and Detroit riots: the House refused to consider the administration's proposed $40 million grant program to help communities exterminate rats, a major grievance in the ghettos. Republican Representative Joel Broyhill of Virginia wise-cracked that "the rat smart thing" would be "to vote down this rat bill rat now," and a majority of his colleagues agreed.

Even if Congress had been responsive to attacking the underlying causes of unrest, the soaring costs of the Vietnam war made any major spending programs extremely unlikely, if not quite impossible. When civil rights spokesmen urged a $100 billion "domestic Marshall Plan" to pull blacks out of poverty, Senator Robert Kennedy candidly replied, "We're not going to appropriate the kind of sums you're talking about in the immediate future. If the Vietnam war is over, five years from now perhaps we might be doing that." By 1966 the conflict was costing more than $2 billion per month, leaving only comparative small change for the administration's campaign to foster economic opportunity for the poor.

Nevertheless, in the early days of the celebrated war on poverty optimism reigned supreme. Ethusiasts in the Office of Economic Opportunity flatly predicted that the struggle could be won by 1976, and in 1965 presented a comprehensive program for action through fiscal year 1970. Ever mindful that many congressmen were highly skeptical at best about the poverty crusade, the plan devised by Sargent Shriver and his cohorts emphasized the theme that the poor must be provided ways to help themselves; that simply enlarging federal money payments to the impoverished would not produce the desired results.

The OEO's original plan proposed three major channels of attack: a Public Employee Program to complement job-training efforts by providing permanent, federally financed, useful jobs for those capable of working; social programs featuring community action projects to change the environment of the poor through preschool and precollege programs, adult literacy courses, legal assistance, health and family planning, housing rehabilitation and construction, and counseling programs; and a universal negative income tax going to all the poor according to the single criterion of need. Under the last provision families with incomes below subsistence level would receive the difference between the two amounts from the federal government. For example, if the minimum necessary for subsistence for a family of four was set at $3,000, a family with an annual income of $2,000 would be paid $1,000. The poverty crusaders recognized the controversial character of the negative income tax but argued that it was much superior to increasing welfare payments. It offered the advantage of being flexible, easily implemented, and more economically administered than the existing welfare system with its horde of bureaucrats, and it would not destroy the incentive of recipients to find jobs that would pay them more. Furthermore, OEO staffers maintained, it was fair, because the last two tax cuts had gone almost totally to the nonpoor.

Hopes that the funds for such an ambitious program would be available and appropriated faded almost as soon as Shriver submitted the 1965 National Anti-Poverty Plan.° Whether Congress would have approved the specific programs and dollar outlays recommended under any circumstances is debatable. The rapid acceleration of spending for the Vietnam war made the question moot. In the budget for fiscal year 1967, which was being prepared in late 1965 when the antipoverty plan was submitted, the administration whittled down OEO's share from almost $4 billion to only $1.75 billion. Funds for most of the other proposals in the comprehensive plan were eliminated altogether. Requests for money by the poverty organization in subsequent years met similar fates. The hard fact was that the shooting war simply destroyed any real prospects for the administration's promised "unconditional" war on poverty.

Political opponents of OEO used the spending cutback to renew their attacks on the program, including no fewer than seven formal congressional investigations between 1965 and 1968. Republicans regarded the Economic Opportunity Act as a frankly political measure intended for partisan advantage. Yet they had to be careful in criticizing the program for fear of appearing to be in favor of poverty. Although lapel buttons declaring "I fight poverty—I work" and books and magazine articles filled with half-truths and innuendoes about the fallacies of the basic antipoverty concept were popular in some conservative circles, most active political figures focused their attacks on OEO's alleged waste of funds, its organiza-

° Funds recommended by the 1965 National Anti-Poverty Program were as follows (dollars in billions):

|             | FY 1966  | FY 1967  | FY 1968   | FY 1969   | FY 1970   |
|-------------|----------|----------|-----------|-----------|-----------|
| Total       | $1,428   | $9,228   | $12,065   | $14,334   | $16,924   |
| OEO Portion | $1,428   | $3,994   | $ 6,580   | $ 8,487   | $10,461   |

tional confusion, its violation of states' rights, and its supposedly partisan purposes. Senator Dirksen described the program as "the very acme of waste and extravagance and unorganization and disorganization" and branded it as a "colossal disgrace, and in some cases, an absolute fraud upon the taxpayers of this country." The cutback in OEO funds caused by the spiraling costs of the Vietnamese conflict enabled Dirksen and his allies to save their energy.

As a result, the antipoverty program never operated at more than half speed, if that. Although unemployment went down because of the economic boom, the hard-core jobless received only very limited help in finding work. General education received a generous increase in federal funds, but little money went into the type of project that would contribute significantly to aiding the poor. Operation Head Start for preschool children and Operation Upward Bound for older youngsters suggested what specific, innovative programs could achieve in this regard, but with their funds they could only scratch the surface. The guaranteed-income concept became better known and better understood, but it remained a theory, not a reality.

The budgetary limitations on the antipoverty funds added to the existing disillusionment and bitterness of the poor. OEO made their disappointment even greater by its outlandish campaign for "maximum feasible publicity" about the war on poverty. Only the Pentagon expended more effort than OEO on public relations. Thousands of beautiful brochures and tons of press releases helped to awaken millions of Americans to the deep social, economic, and physical roots of poverty and to punch home the message that there was no economic reason for poverty in this country. But to those in poverty the unrealized expectations made the earlier promises seem like a cruel hoax.

Despite the frustrations produced by the combination of over-selling and underfinancing, the Great Society's efforts to end poverty left an indelible mark. OEO's Community Action Program (CAP) mobilized the poor better than anything had ever done before. By involving poor people in programs as participants rather than simply as beneficiaries, those who had been routinely excluded from leadership began to assert themselves. In many communities CAP activities built an important consensus at the very time when race, politics, and war were pulling the country apart. People who struggled over the structure and content of local community action agencies frequently found that they had something in common. Poor citizens would never again be quite as passive about their problems. In the long run this new attitude promised to be a much more important outgrowth of the war on poverty than the fact that it brought some new services to some poor people.

Unfortunately, the huge amount of federal funds required by the Vietnam war hurt the poor financially not only by depriving them of the promised programs but also by generating price increases. Inflation began to worry administration officials as early as mid-1965, shortly after the escalation of American efforts in the conflict. As predicted, the 1964 tax cut produced a strong surge in economic growth. The federal funds pumped into the economy because of war spending acted as a potent additional stimulus, which produced dangerous inflationary pressures. Alarmed, the Council of Economic Advisers began during 1966 to explore the possibilities of cutting back nondefense spending and strengthening the wage-price guideposts. A tighter monetary policy helped initially to slow the rate of growth and keep inflation in check, but by the fall of the year the Council recommended even stronger actions. Johnson consequently requested Congress to suspend temporarily the investment tax credit and accelerated depreciation allowances that had been granted during 1962 as incentives for business to modernize plants and production facilities.

Looking ahead, the President's economic advisers forecast a modest slowdown in economic growth during the first half of 1967, but because they believed that the persisting danger of inflation was so strong, they considered recommending a temporary increase in income taxes beginning July 1, 1967. However, when the economy behaved even more sluggishly during early 1967 than had been expected, the administration refrained from asking Congress for a tax increase. By midsummer, however, the economy was racing forward at a breakneck pace once again. In addition, it seemed almost certain that spending for the war would go even higher. As a consequence, Johnson asked the legislators on August 3 to impose a temporary 10 percent surcharge on personal and corporate income taxes, warning that without the additional revenue the government would face a dangerously large deficit, which would unquestionably add to the wage-price spiral.

The House Ways and Means Committee, however, aggressively challenged the chief executive's claim that a tax boost was necessary and insisted on investigating the proposal with great deliberation. When it became obvious that the measure would not pass during 1967, the President cut nondefense spending sharply in order to achieve some fiscal restraint. Social welfare programs caught the brunt of the economizing, but there were not nearly enough reductions available to offset the billions being poured into Vietnam. Congress continued to dally over the tax question during the first half of 1968, squabbling with the administration on the form of the tax increase, how much spending should—or could—be trimmed, and who should do the cutting, the legislative or the executive branch. Not until June 28, almost a year after the President had requested action, did the tax bill finally become law. The delay was one cause of the jump in the federal deficit to $25.2 billion (compared to $3.8 billion in 1966 and $8.7 billion in 1967), far higher than had been expected. The legislators were guilty of poor judgment in being so slow in passing the tax increase, but the administration contributed to the laggard pace by concealing the magnitude of rising war costs.

As economists feared, the huge deficit fueled the already dangerously strong inflationary pressures. The Consumer Price Index, which had increased by a little over one percent per year during the Kennedy administration and by only slightly more in the early Johnson years, shot up by 3 percent in 1967 and by 5 percent in 1968. The government's vaunted wage-price guideposts helped to maintain relative price stability between 1961 and 1965, but once the defense budget skyrocketed, producing excessive demands on the country's overall productive potential, the standards could only moderate the speed of price advances. Voluntary in nature, the guideposts simply failed to inspire an adequate social consensus. They remained too much a "government policy," not a "public policy," and they were bitterly attacked by many companies and unions. Even during their heyday, some gross violations by management and labor undermined their effectiveness. After his inauguration in 1969, President Richard M. Nixon largely discarded the standards. He proposed to keep government intervention in the economy to a minimum, disdaining the use even of "jawboning"—rhetorical persuasion by the government to mobilize the power of public opinion against the market power of strong unions and powerful businesses—in maintaining the guideposts. Ironically, by 1971 the continuing inflation caused him to adopt *mandatory* controls over wages and prices. Their failure to work effectively made the soaring rate of inflation one of the most painful and dangerous legacies of the Vietnam war.

The war permeated almost everything; its impact was inescapable. When a group of white and black women were invited to the White House to discuss crime in the streets, black singer Eartha Kitt angrily took the floor to declare that young people were rebelling and using marijuana because of the war in Vietnam. According to the *New York Times,* Mrs. Johnson was stunned and embarrassed, and, "her voice shaking and with tears in her eyes," she replied, "I'm sorry I do not understand the things that you do. I have not lived with the background that you have . . . . But I think we have made advances in these things and we will do more."

The pressure of the war on the President kept mounting and building. Always short-tempered with aides, he became even more so. Those who left the administration received the sting of his growing petulance. When Bill Moyers questioned the war after leaving the White House staff, Johnson cuttingly told reporters, "Moyers is not a foreign policy expert. I never had one hour's discussion of foreign policy with Moyers." When McGeorge Bundy departed, the President compared him unfavorably with his replacement, Walt Rostow. When George Ball left, he was denounced privately for "leaking" documents to a writer hostile to the chief executive. Johnson became increasingly obsessed with leaks. In late 1967 when he flew to Australia for the funeral of Prime Minister Harold Holt, he decided to return via Rome in order to meet with the Pope. The visit was cloaked in secrecy, but the news somehow got out, enabling the Communists in Italy to organize demonstrations. LBJ was furious, blaming "disloyalty" and "unpatriotic sentiments in the Department of State" for the leak.

Johnson took great pride in the efforts of American fighting men in Vietnam, including his two sons-in-law. Their courage inspired him and strengthened his resolve not to give in to those who wanted the United States simply to pull out of the war. But he insisted that he remained open to negotiation. In late August 1966 he announced another peace offer had been sent to Hanoi. The United States would stop the bombing if the North Vietnamese would pledge to send no more troops south. In October he flew to Manila to discuss with Asian leaders a four-point response from the North Vietnamese. Hanoi demanded the withdrawal of all American troops, equipment, and bases from South Vietnam; no foreign military alliances for either Vietnam, pending final reunification; settling the internal affairs of South Vietnam in accordance with the program of the National Liberation Front; and peaceful reunification without foreign interference. The United States and its friends at Manila countered by demanding an end to aggression, the preservation of South Vietnam's territorial integrity, reunification in conformity with the principles of the 1954 Geneva accords, and the reciprocal withdrawal of all foreign troops within six months after the cease-fire. The specific statement on troop withdrawal represented an attempt to emphasize that America entertained no desire to retain permanent bases in Vietnam, and reflected the criticism by Soviet Foreign Minister Andrei Gromyko to Johnson shortly before that the United States had been "very general" in previous statements about removing its troops.

While in Manila, Johnson slipped away from the conference long enough to make a surprise visit to Cam Rahn Bay, one of the major American military bases in Vietnam. The experience exhilarated the President. As he later wrote, he had never been more moved by any group he had ever talked to in his life. Carried away by the warmth of his reception by the fighting men, he urged them to "come home with that coonskin on the wall." As British journalist Louis Herren observed, his statement hardly suggested a disposition to meet Hanoi even halfway in negotiations. His enthusiasm had not abated a few days later when he addressed American troops stationed in South Korea. Lauding the men for their courage in waging the battle for freedom, he bragged that "my great-great-grandfather died at the Alamo." The patriotic allusion happened to be untrue, but it served as Johnson's way of telling the men that he was one of them in spirit, that he understood and deeply appreciated their sacrifices.

He took great pride in his role as commander-in-chief. On one occasion a young serviceman helpfully informed the chief executive, "Sir, there's *your* helicopter." "Son," Johnson replied, "they're *all* my helicopters!" He agonized over having to send men to fight and possibly die. Seeing the 82d Airborne Division off for Vietnam from their base at Fort Bragg, North Carolina, he boarded one of the huge transport planes, looked at the paratroopers sitting in silence with their rifles sticking up between their knees, and quietly told them, "There are half a million men out there and they want you there. I know you will do well  . . .  I pray each of you comes back." When he finished, they shouted, "All the way, sir," the airborne chant. Deeply moved, Johnson wheeled about and went into the cabin of the plane. "Take care of those boys," he told the pilot. His admiration for such men was immense, and their efforts on the battlefield heightened his loathing of the "peaceniks" and "doves," who castigated his war policies. They were "Nervous Nellies," who enjoyed the luxury of debate and protest, picketing, and sit-ins in the safety secured and preserved by the American armed forces.

During his last years in office, Johnson's thoughts dwelled increasingly on the men in Vietnam. By seven o'clock each morning the preceding day's casualty figures had been compiled and delivered, along with summaries of the combat action, to the President's bedroom. He began each new day by reading what was happening in Vietnam. The number of Americans killed and wounded mounted steadily, but many of the President's advisers bubbled with optimism about the way the war was going. Walt Rostow wrote in December 1966 that the military situation was so "greatly improved" that he expected a "potentially victorious position by the end of 1967." General Westmoreland agreed, declaring that "the enemy's hopes are bankrupt." Yet he continued to request more troops. McNamara, however, grew even more disillusioned with the conflict during 1967, challenging the argument that either additional personnel or continued bombing would bring Hanoi to the conference table on terms the United States would accept. Systems analyses prepared in the Pentagon supported the Defense Secretary's position.

Johnson listened attentively to the conflicting views but sided with those who urged a more vigorous prosecution of the war, not a cutback. Although he refused to go along with all demands by the military to escalate ground actions, he did agree to extend the air war to a host of new targets, many of them close to Hanoi and near the Chinese border. McNamara opposed the air raids as not only expensive in money and pilot losses but also politically and morally wrong. "The picture of the world's greatest superpower killing or seriously injuring 1,000 non-combatants a week, while trying to pound a tiny backward nation into submission on an issue whose merits are hotly disputed, is not a pretty one," he privately wrote the President in May 1967. The following month McNamara commissioned an in-depth study of the American role in Vietnam since World War II. Conducted in absolute secrecy, the investigation took a year and a half to complete. The report—leaked in 1971 by Daniel Ellsberg, one of the researchers, and published in part by the *New York Times* as *The Pentagon Papers*—contained over 7,000 pages of narrative and documents.

Even as he stepped up military pressure, Johnson took pains to explore possibilities for negotiation. But, most significantly, he refused even to consider allowing Communists to serve in a coalition government in South Vietnam. Without this concession, repeated efforts to get peace talks under way simply failed to jell.

The President's stubborn determination to have things his way soured America's increasingly tenuous relations with its principal allies. Prime Minister Harold Wilson of Great Britain made little effort to conceal his displeasure about Vietnam. France's Charles de Gaulle had made his position on American involvement clear to Johnson's emissary George Ball in December 1964: the United States was overrating China's power and influence in the Far East, and it was wrong for the United States to involve itself deeper in the Vietnamese mess. "You cannot win it," the imperious Frenchman declared. The United States should sound out Peking and secure some type of settlement, for if America escalated the war, it would only alienate world opinion. When Johnson disregarded his advice, de Gaulle considered it only one more reason why France should follow an independent foreign policy. The French withdrew from NATO and insisted that American troops be removed from French soil. Publicly, the President kept his temper in check and refused to condemn de Gaulle. Privately, he was less restrained. At one point he contemptuously snarled about the French leader, "if he wants to jack off, he can."

The heavy commitment of United States military resources in Vietnam weakened the nation's capability to respond to emergencies that might develop elsewhere in the globe, but to the relief and surprise of many, the Soviets made no open attempt to take advantage of the situation. Negotiations to de-escalate the arms race continued between Washington and Moscow, with particular attention on the question of antiballistic missiles (ABM). The Soviets had developed a limited ABM system for defense by 1967, and the American military maintained that it needed one too. McNamara, however, insisted that the American answer to the Russian ABM should be more destructive power for its offensive missiles. He maintained that the Soviets would respect the ability of the United States to penetrate the Russian defensive missile screen; hence they would not be inclined to adventurism. The Chinese were another matter. They, too, had nuclear missiles, and neither Washington nor Moscow felt confident that Peking understood the nuclear ground rules. It was arguable that at least a thin American ABM system was necessary to guard against a Chinese, if not a Soviet, attack. Johnson and McNamara reluctantly agreed to begin construction on a limited defensive missile program at an estimated cost of $5 billion. Coming on the heels of the costly summer riots in the cities, the decision irked many Americans who believed that the money was badly needed to solve the country's painful domestic ills.

Despite the stalemate between the United States and the Soviet Union on further disarmament agreements, relations between the two countries generally improved. When Israel launched the Six Day War against Egypt and Syria in early June 1967, Johnson and Soviet leader Aleksei Kosygin exchanged assurances of nonbelligerency, putting the recently installed hot line between Washington and Moscow to good use. Three weeks later, when Kosygin journeyed to New York to attend the United Nations General Assembly, Johnson was determined to confer with him. The Soviet leader preferred not to go to Washington, and the President believed that New York was hardly the setting for quiet, relaxed talks. Kosygin declined to meet at a military base but agreed to Johnson's suggestion of a small state college in little Glassboro, New Jersey. Working frenetically, the Secret Service converted the college president's home into a communications center for the impromptu summit conference. The two-day session produced no spectacular results, but it was not expected to. As Johnson realistically observed, "When nations have deeply different positions, as we do on these issues [e.g., the Middle East, Southeast Asia, nuclear proliferation, and antiballistic missiles], they do not come to agreement merely by improving their understanding of each other's views. But such improvement helps." The meetings, the President explained, had made the world a little smaller and a little less dangerous.

At Glassboro, Kosygin passed on a message from Hanoi that it was ready to talk if the United States stopped bombing the North. After consultation with his advisers, Johnson asked him to tell Hanoi that the United States would do so, but the President added an additional qualification: American and Allied forces in the northern provinces of South Vietnam would not advance to the north during the talks if the North Vietnamese would reciprocate by pledging not to move their troops southward. Hanoi apparently concluded that there was no advantage to such a deal, for it failed to reply to the American offer.

Consequently, the fighting went on, and the American military high command optimistically concluded at the end of 1967 that the North Vietnamese and the Vietcong were losing the war. In his report to the President of January 27, 1968, General Westmoreland confidently wrote, "The year ended with the enemy increasingly resorting to desperation tactics in attempting to achieve military-psychological victory; and he has experienced only failure in these attempts." Four days later, the Communist forces launched their massive Tet (lunar New Year holiday) offensive, attacking 34 provincial and 64 district towns, as well as all autonomous cities, a dozen American bases, and the American embassy in Saigon.

Far from being too weak to mount a major attack, as Westmoreland's report had implied, the Vietcong was clearly still a power. Although the American command claimed that the enemy had suffered devastating losses in the attack—40,000 killed, at least 3,000 captured, and perhaps 5,000 wounded—the chairman of the Joint Chiefs, General Earl G. Wheeler, admitted after a hasty trip to

Saigon that the Vietcong had seized the initiative. They were "operating with relative freedom in the countryside" and had driven the South Vietnamese forces into a "defensive posture around towns and cities." In addition, the Vietcong's ability to strike at so many supposedly secure locations had critically crippled the Saigon regime's pacification program, aimed at winning the loyalty of the South Vietnamese rural masses.

Westmoreland, nevertheless, maintained that the Tet offensive had resulted in a major victory for the forces under his command. But he badly undermined his claim by urgently requesting 206,000 additional troops and more fighter squadrons. Pentagon officials estimated that his demands would add approximately $12 billion to the prevailing $30 billion annual cost of the war. It would also necessitate calling up thousands of reservists to meet the nation's military manpower requirements.

When Westmoreland forwarded his plea for reinforcements, Robert McNamara was in his final days as Secretary of Defense. Having turned "dove" on the war, he had decided to retire from the administration, and Johnson had named him president of the World Bank. The President was not very sorry to see him go. The day his new position was announced, McNamara telephoned the chief executive while LBJ was talking to a small group of newsmen. They could hear only Johnson's end of the conversation, but he pointedly revealed his feelings about McNamara's departure. "Yes, Bob," said the President, "I'm sitting here with tears in my eyes, too." But, as one of the listeners later wrote, "LBJ was as dry-eyed as any human being could be."

Clark M. Clifford, the new top man at the Pentagon, had been one of Johnson's two closest unofficial advisers for years. (The other was Abe Fortas, whom the President had appointed to the Supreme Court in 1965 and whom he would unsuccessfully attempt to promote to Chief Justice in 1968.) Clifford was an urbane, sophisticated lawyer with few peers as a Washington lobbyist. He had been a speech writer and special counsel for President Truman and had previously declined opportunities to join both the Kennedy and the Johnson administrations, preferring to continue his extremely lucrative law practice. He had a shrewd awareness of how government operated and an intimate knowledge of politics in general and

Democratic party politics in particular. At the time he became Defense Secretary, Clifford had a reputation as a "hawk" on the Vietnam war: he believed that the struggle was essential to contain China; he accepted the domino theory; and he had opposed earlier bombing pauses. But once he got to the Pentagon and started to investigate the conflict more carefully, he began to change his mind.

Johnson publicly agreed with the military men that the enemy had failed to accomplish its objectives with the Tet offensive. But privately he had doubts, and he appointed a study group headed by Clifford to review Westmoreland's requests with respect to their impact on the budget, possible future negotiating positions, and public opinion. Reading pessimistic reports prepared by Pentagon and Central Intelligence Agency analysts, the new Defense Secretary evolved into a strong force against any further escalation of the war. He concluded that despite the presence of half a million American troops, the Saigon regime did not control much more of South Vietnam than it did in mid-1965. Furthermore, the bombing raids on the North, although so intense that they made those during World War II look modest in comparison, were not producing results. Despite the bombing, infiltration from the North was three to four times as great as it had been in early 1967.

Members of the study group clashed sharply over what course of action should be taken. Their discussions intensified differences that had been simmering since 1966, especially between civilian and military officials. The Joint Chiefs of Staff, General Maxwell Taylor (Johnson's personal military adviser), Secretary of the Air Force Harold F. Brown, Rostow, and Under Secretary of State Nicholas Katzenbach sternly opposed any thought of cutting back the bombing. Clifford, supported by most of the civilian hierarchy at the Pentagon, argued that the war must be wound down, not escalated or maintained at its existing level. Secretary Rusk was, as usual, ambivalent. Although against any new American initiative for peace talks, he agreed that it might be prudent to restrict the air raids to south of the 19th or 20th parallel unless the enemy made any major new moves. Even many of the "hawks" had reservations about granting Westmoreland the additional 206,000 troops.

Meanwhile, the news media continued to hammer hard at the credibility gap of Johnson and the Defense Department, and public opinion polls indicated that disenchantment with the war continued to grow. Many reporters were no longer willing to accept the administration's truthfulness or its good faith. After years of disillusionment with government double-talk and, in many cases, outright prevarications about the conflict, they tended to deprecate any new official pronouncements about Vietnam.

During late February and March 1968, Clifford quietly rallied support within the administration for his position that the war should be reduced, not increased. By repeatedly reminding the chief executive that the cost of victory had risen sharply and by rigorously challenging the optimistic reports being sent by American officials in Saigon, he helped check the momentum for increasing the war effort. Political happenings were also making an impression on the President. Senator Eugene McCarthy, an outspoken and bitter critic of the United States' involvement in Vietnam, ran a surprisingly strong race against Johnson in the New Hampshire Democratic presidential primary on March 13. Three days later Senator Robert F. Kennedy announced that he would enter the race for the party's nomination on an antiwar platform, and on March 18, 139 House members proposed a resolution for a congressional review of the administration's policy in Southeast Asia.

Without warning, the President relieved Westmoreland of his command on March 22. Attempting to obtain some fresh thinking about the grim situation in Vietnam, Johnson next summoned the Senior Informal Advisory Group to Washington. The "Wise Men," as they were commonly called, included an imposing galaxy of former and present high government dignitaries, quite literally a "Who's Who" of the American Establishment: former Secretary of State Dean Acheson, former Under Secretary of State George Ball, General Omar Bradley, former White House national security adviser McGeorge Bundy, General Matthew Ridgway, former Secretary of the Treasury Douglas Dillon, General Maxwell Taylor, former Deputy Secretary of Defense Cyrus Vance, Supreme Court Associate Justice Abe Fortas, UN Ambassador Arthur Goldberg, and retired diplomats Arthur Dean, Robert Murphy, and Henry Cabot Lodge. Almost all of them had approved the administration's decision to intensify the bombing of North Vietnam in 1967.

After listening to detailed briefings, a solid majority of the group concluded on March 26 that the present policy had reached an impasse; that it could not achieve its objectives without the application of virtually unlimited resources, did not command citizen support, and needed to be changed. Shocked, Johnson concluded that the advisory group had made its decision more on the basis of the public's growing revulsion against the war than on what they learned in the briefings. He was right. Acheson, a man noted for his consistent hard-line anti-Communism, gave one of LBJ's aides an editorial from a newspaper that had previously supported the war. "The war," it declared, "had made us—all of us—lose sight of our national purposes." Russia was enemy number one, China, enemy number two; the world's vital strategic areas in their proper order were Western Europe, Japan, the Middle East, Latin America, and, only then, Southeast Asia. And, the editorial concluded, "The most critical priority of all, of course, is the home front." "This," Acheson exclaimed, "represents my views precisely. I could have written it myself."

On March 31, five days after the Wise Men presented him with their recommendations, Johnson stunned the nation by stating at the end of his television address on Vietnam, "I shall not seek, and I will not accept, the nomination of my party for another term as your President."

The surprise conclusion of his speech upstaged his announcement that he was ordering a sharp restriction of the bombing and proposing peace talks. Johnson was frankly skeptical that halting the air raids would coax Hanoi to the conference table. Six times before he had tried such an approach with no success. But this time it worked. On April 3 the North Vietnamese expressed their agreement. Quibbling about a location, despite Johnson's oft-repeated declarations that he was willing to meet "anywhere, anytime," delayed the beginning of the negotiations until May 10. After finally agreeing on Paris as a site, the two sides squabbled inconclusively for the rest of LBJ's term in office and throughout almost all of Richard Nixon's first four years in the White House.

The President's two critical decisions—to stop most of the bombing and not to run for reelection—were closely connected, although Johnson insisted in his memoirs that he had always intended to leave office at the end of his first full term. As far back as 1965 he had discussed the question with close friends. During late 1967 he had mentioned the fact to a handful of associates and had instructed Horace Busby to draft a statement announcing the fact for possible use in his 1968 State of the Union Message. Yet, as one of his longtime staff members, George Reedy, later observed, Johnson had used the threat of quitting many, many times as a political ploy to win sympathy—when he was majority leader of the Senate and as President in 1964 shortly before his nomination, for example. The President himself later admitted that his decision could have been undone up until the last minute by any one of a dozen things. If the Vietcong had suddenly launched a large new series of attacks, or if he had become convinced that his action would undermine the morale of American troops in Vietnam, he wrote, "I would have changed my mind." His determination to quit was by no means irrevocable until he made his startling pronouncement.

Almost certainly, Lady Bird Johnson's desire that LBJ step down while still in good health was critical to his decision. His two hospitalizations for surgery while President, on top of his serious heart attack in 1955, gave her good reason for concern. He, too, recognized that the pressures of the office were enormous and unrelenting, and placed a heavy strain even on his remarkable physical stamina. Most of all, however, Johnson decided to quit because of the war. He reasoned that his withdrawal might encourage Hanoi to begin peace talks that would help heal the painful and dangerous divisions within the United States. Contrary to the scathing charges against Johnson by some of his more egregious antiwar critics, the conflict troubled him deeply. He honestly hoped that his decision to retire would mark the beginning of the end of the struggle in Southeast Asia.

With Lyndon Johnson out of the race, the presidential campaign took on a drastically different complexion. "In 1968," wrote Theodore H. White, "it was as if the future waited on the first of each month to deliver events completely unforeseen the month before." Johnson's decision to retire by no means meant that he intended to desert the policies—either foreign or domestic—that he had fostered. Vice President Humphrey picked up the mantle of the Johnson team, pleading with proadministration Democrats to transfer their allegiance to his cause. Although he delayed until late April before formally announcing his candidacy, he declared, "I will not run away from the record of this administration. I will do everything in my power—if the Lord gives me strength—to carry the record of the Johnson-Humphrey administration to the people in the months ahead."

The nation barely had time to digest LBJ's decision to retire and Hanoi's acceptance of his invitation to talk before the murder of Dr. Martin Luther King, Jr., turned the spotlight on domestic problems. His assassination on April 4 by a racist, white ex-convict, James Earl Ray, in Memphis, Tennessee, ignited riots in over one hundred cities. Washington, D.C., looked like a battlefield. Looters smashed windows in buildings within three blocks of the White House, while smoke from scores of fires blanketed the city. In Chicago, Mayor Richard J. Daley ordered police to "shoot to kill" arsonists and "shoot to maim" looters. Appeals by civil rights moderates for blacks not to desecrate King's memory by violence had little effect. Robert Kennedy, speaking on a street corner in Indianapolis, had more. He quoted Aeschylus, "Even in our sleep, pain which we cannot forget falls drop by drop upon the heart until in despair, against our own will, comes wisdom through the awful grace of God," and declared that he knew how blacks felt, because he too had lost a brother at the hands of a white assassin. His success in calming the anger of his listeners testified to the remarkable rapport that the Kennedys enjoyed among black Americans.

The Johnson administration responded to the riots by alerting 350,000 troops and National Guardsmen for possible duty and by rushing Attorney General Ramsey Clark to Memphis to take charge of the investigation. The President declared April 7 as a day of national mourning for King. Congress responded to black wrath by passing the controversial Open Housing Act, which had been stalled for over two years. It might have become law anyway, but King guaranteed its passage with his life. The legislators also enacted ambitious measures for housing construction and urban development but acceded to demands for "law and order" by imposing stiff penalties for persons crossing state lines with the intent of inciting disorders.

Throughout the trying weeks following the assassination, Johnson maintained a calm, patient approach. Late in April the Poor

People's March being planned by King at the time of his death brought thousands of protesters to Washington, not to demonstrate and leave, but to camp on the mall near the Lincoln Memorial. Resurrection City, a shantytown constructed of plywood and canvas, added to the chaos and disarray in the capital caused by the recent riots. Ralph Abernathy, who succeeded King as head of the Southern Christian Leadership Conference, lacked both the magnetic personal qualities and the leadership ability of his predecessor. He talked about "educating the government," but the overall-clad field workers who met with congressmen and federal officials accomplished relatively little. The main goal of the Poor People's crusade had been to pressure for passage of the civil rights bill, but it actually became law before the marchers arrived. Lacking specific legislative objectives, the demonstrators were urged by militants, who infiltrated Resurrection City, to provoke a direct confrontation with authorities. Meanwhile, disgruntled whites argued that the government should disband the unsightly camp.

The President, however, refused to take precipitous action. Although he received little credit for his shrewd handling of the tense scene, his administration prevented violence by its tact and patience. In 1932 Herbert Hoover had handled a similar situation, the World War I veterans' Bonus March, by using Army troops to drive the protesters away from their camp. Johnson used much more finesse. After two months, police quickly and peacefully evacuated Resurrection City without serious incident.

Long before the Poor People's March faded into memory a new wave of violence erupted, this time on the nation's seething college campuses. At Columbia University radical students seized five buildings in protest against the school's participation in war research and in support of neighborhood opponents of Columbia's plan to expand its facilities. The strikers shut down the university and held the buildings for six days, destroying files and breaking furniture. College officials vacillated at first but eventually called in police, who roughly expelled the demonstrators. The incident triggered outbursts at schools across the country. In some cases, as at Cornell, black militants brandishing guns were the principal actors. In others antiwar agitators took the lead. Classes were disrupted, faculty and moderate students intimidated, and administrators harassed and occasionally threatened physically. The episode frightened millions of Americans and underlined the general malaise that gripped the United States. Accounts of violence or the threat of violence filled newspapers and television screens. The country seemed close to coming apart at the seams. In only three short years the celebrated Johnson consensus had been completely shattered.

Despite the chaos that punctuated the spring months, the political campaigning scarcely missed a step. The presidential candidacies of Eugene McCarthy and Robert Kennedy were critically important in defusing some of the explosive mood, especially among the young, since they offered modest alternatives to the war policies of the Johnson administration. Thousands of war protesters trimmed their hair, shaved their beards, and scrubbed their faces in order to work for the two professed peace candidates.

McCarthy's entry into the race came at the urging of a student-based antiwar movement forged by a thirty-eight-year-old political activist, Allard K. Lowenstein, who turned to the Minnesota senator after Robert Kennedy, Lieutenant General James Gavin, and Senator George McGovern of South Dakota refused to lead the campaign to stop Johnson. McCarthy was a scholar-poet, cool, pensive, shy, but not modest. He had voted for the Tonkin Gulf Resolution in 1964, but by 1966 his support for the war was rapidly wavering. In 1967 he deeply believed that the conflict was no longer morally justifiable and that the administration's offers to negotiate were not really sincere. He was convinced that *someone* must oppose the President in the Democratic primaries, and since Robert Kennedy was unwilling to do so, McCarthy decided that it was up to him personally to make the race.

His organization was a sharp contrast to the well-oiled machines that were commonplace during the sixties. Like the senator himself, it was often erratic yet usually efficient. And it was supremely dedicated. Young people, mainly college students, provided a horde of energetic volunteers for McCarthy's first test, the New Hampshire primary in March. Guided by a handful of canny political professionals like Richard Goodwin, Kennedy's and Johnson's old speech writer, "the kids" canvassed the Granite State from top to bottom. Sam Brown, a Harvard Divinity School student and a superbly talented mobilizer of student workers, explained why the young had rallied so eagerly to McCarthy: "Study in the universities is irrelevant. The war is on our minds. The rhetoric of the government is outmoded—the problem is how you affect the government." Brown and his confederates showed in New Hampshire that they could affect government. To the surprise of most political pundits, McCarthy carried 42.4 percent of the Democratic vote against Johnson's 49.5 percent. When McCarthy's write-ins on the Republican side were added in, he received almost the same number of total votes. It was unquestionably a stunning moral victory for him and the antiwar movement. To at least some degree it helped confirm Lyndon Johnson's decision not to run for reelection.

It also helped convince Robert Kennedy that he had underestimated the chances of stopping the President. Reassessing the situation, he made a last-ditch effort to secure the chief executive's agreement to soften his stance on negotiation terms with the enemy. If Johnson would do so, Kennedy reasoned that he would have no cause to enter the race. But he failed to reach a satisfactory understanding with the White House, and feeling certain that McCarthy could never win the nomination, he announced on March 16 that he would run. Many of his close advisers argued that he should avoid contesting McCarthy in the primaries. Such a strategy, they maintained, would keep the peace forces unified and enhance Kennedy's chances of winning at the convention. Kennedy refused. "I am not going to come out for McCarthy in the primaries," he declared, "I'm going to do it [run in the primaries] myself. I'm going."

Because he had declined to run earlier, Kennedy's decision to jump into the fray after McCarthy had blazed the way in New Hampshire provoked angry charges that Bobby was a callous and ruthless opportunist. Hurrying to regain the lead of the antiwar faction, especially among the young, the forty-two-year-old New York senator took to the campaign trail immediately. At first he sounded overly shrill and strident. But gradually he softened his style, becoming less somber and more engaging. He delighted audiences with his witty, self-deprecating banter, particularly his knack for mocking his own weaknesses. While speaking in agricultural Nebraska, a tiny piece of paper blew out of his hand. "That's my entire farm program," he quipped, "give it back quickly." He always drew laughs with jabs at his "ruthlessness," the term critics invariably used to describe him.

He carefully outlined his specific program: a nonexemption lottery instead of Selective Service, negotiation but not surrender in Vietnam, and income-tax incentives to stimulate private enterprise for public welfare. He was against overcentralizing power in Washington and for law and order, but also strongly committed to equal rights for all minorities. Obviously, his ideas were neither novel nor revolutionary. But Kennedy conveyed a sense of urgency and passion that no other candidate could match. He had always possessed a unique ability to arouse emotion. People either loved him or hated him; few were ever indifferent. His strongest appeal was in the ghettos, where he generated an incredibly warm response. His speeches to minority crowds were short and direct, coupling the standard liberal promises of equal opportunity, jobs, and school equality with appeals to his listeners to vote so they could help elect him.

The odyssey of Robert Kennedy lasted eighty-five action-packed days. He met McCarthy head-on for the first time in the Indiana primary in early May and rolled up a handsome victory after an expensive and hard-fought campaign. A week later he triumphed by a narrow margin in Nebraska. But later in the month McCarthy reversed the trend in Oregon, a state described as "one huge suburb surrounded by green grass." Moderately conservative, yet progressive-minded about government, Oregon had no sizable urban ghettos where Kennedy could work his magic. If he had had a choice, he would have preferred not to run in the primary. But Oregon law required all individuals judged by its secretary of state to be candidates, whether declared or not, to be listed on the primary ballot. Only by swearing an affidavit that he or she did not want to be President could a person's name be removed. Kennedy waged a vigorous battle, but McCarthy's attractiveness to Oregonians proved difficult to shake. The easygoing Minnesotan shrewdly left the heavy work to a knowledgeable, hard-working state organization, which contrasted markedly with his amateurish national staff, and he won impressively by a 20,000-vote margin. By doing so, he snapped the string of twenty-seven consecutive Kennedy—John, Robert, and Edward—victories.

The following week McCarthy and Kennedy faced each other for the last time, in the key California primary. The winner would collect 174 delegate votes, one-eighth of the total needed to capture the nomination. The loser figured to be knocked out of the race. Worried by McCarthy's success in Oregon, Kennedy decided to accept his opponent's challenge to debate, a confrontation he had previously refused. Their televised meeting probably did not shift many votes. The huge black and Mexican-American blocs in the state were far more critical to the outcome. True to form, Kennedy scored heavily with minority voters, rolling up large enough majorities in the big southern California ghettos to offset McCarthy's popularity in northern California. The New York senator grabbed 46 percent of the ballots to McCarthy's 42 percent, while a slate pledged to the Johnson administration picked up the balance.

At that point, fate dealt another of the bitter hands that made 1968 so tragic and utterly unpredictable. With his victory secure, Kennedy went to the Ambassador Hotel in Los Angeles to thank his exuberant supporters for their help. "On to Chicago," he shouted to the crowd as he left. Then, as the candidate departed through the hotel kitchen, Sirhan B. Sirhan, a young Jordanian immigrant, stepped out of the throng and shot him three times at close range. The horrified onlookers seized and subdued the assassin, but Kennedy's wounds were fatal.

For the third time in less than five years the United States suffered the trauma of a major national leader gunned down in the prime of life. The political campaign ground to a halt while the country paid its final respects to Robert Francis Kennedy. In death as in life, he generated enormous emotion. Thousands of people, softly singing the "Battle Hymn of the Republic" as the funeral train passed by, lined the tracks between New York City, where the funeral took place, and Washington, where he was buried near his brother in Arlington Cemetery. Millions more watched the somber ceremonies on television.

With Kennedy's death the hopes of those Democrats determined to repudiate the war policies of Lyndon Johnson sagged miserably. McCarthy remained a possibility, but his chances of getting the Democratic nomination had never looked particularly bright. They had depended on his winning enough primaries to show his strength as a vote getter. But he had defeated Kennedy in only one face-to-face contest. Although millions of voters admired his independent nature, his cool detachment, and his willingness to challenge Johnson when no one else would, many also believed that he was too indifferent about wanting the Presidency to make the type of strong chief executive that most Americans had grown to expect. The *New Republic* called it the "passion-for-office" test, and, despite the reaction against Johnson, undeniably a President of the strong school, McCarthy failed to strike enough of a spark to capture the nomination.

In contrast, Kennedy had appeared to have a very good chance. Like McCarthy, he appealed strongly to the young and to the antiwar movement. But unlike McCarthy he also had the overwhelming support of the minorities. And, although white working-class voters generally backed the war and were usually in the vanguard of the white backlash, they, too, liked Bobby Kennedy. Because they knew of his conservative, Catholic, anti-Communist background—the very thing that made him somewhat suspect to much of the intelligentsia—they understood that it was not easy for him to change from support of the conflict in Vietnam to opposition. Zealous, impulsive, and imbued with a never-ceasing drive to win and to excel, no one ever thought of suggesting that he would be anything but a strong President. He could be moody, but he was never detached. He threw himself into causes, expending his enormous energy with reckless abandon. His enthusiasm, so different from McCarthy's diffident cynicism, was infectious. So was his compassion. Blacks and Mexican-Americans sensed intuitively that he cared. He seemed constantly to be changing, learning, becoming more aware. His death was a personal loss to millions.

With Kennedy out of the race, Hubert Humphrey moved indisputably into the driver's seat. Although he had announced his formal candidacy too late to enter the primaries, he had quickly picked up a sizable number of delegates in state nominating conventions. With the power of the President and the administration behind him, the loquacious Vice President was in an enviable position. He could avoid the expense, fatigue, and animosity of the primaries and still go to the convention as the odds-on favorite. Kennedy's assassination made his position even more secure.

While the Democrats garnered most of the attention during the primaries, the Republicans used the time to close ranks and fill their war chest for the main event. Seemingly perilously close to extinction as a major party after the 1964 debacle, the GOP rebuilt and reorganized itself during 1965 and 1966. The hard work paid dividends in the 1966 congressional elections. Four men stood out as major contenders for the party's nomination for the Presidency in 1968. Richard Nixon and Governor Nelson Rockefeller were familiar figures, but Governor George Romney of Michigan and Governor Ronald Reagan of California were relative newcomers to national politics. Romney, who was a former president of American Motors, had a dynamic personality; he was fiscally conservative, but had a respected record in behalf of civil rights. Reagan, a handsome former movie and television star, effectively used his skill as a performer to argue his conservative philosophy in an appealing fashion. Without previous political experience he had defeated veteran Governor Edmund G. (Pat) Brown in 1966 and became the fair-haired boy of the Goldwater wing of the GOP.

Nixon spent the mid-sixties carefully cultivating a new image, though he denied that there was a "new Nixon." He read widely, did some writing, and gave generously of his time to help revitalize the GOP. To many interviewers he seemed mellower, less intense and rancorous, more receptive to new ideas. But his lust for politics remained. Considered politically dead after being defeated in his bids for the Presidency in 1960 and the governorship of California in 1962, he had bounced back by 1966 and was considered a prime prospect for the White House. His ties with the party professionals were still strong. They knew, trusted, and respected the former Vice President. Nixon firmly believed, however, that he had to break his reputation as a loser by winning the nomination via the primary route. Since he had no need to establish himself in the public eye, he decided against any premature, pell-mell rush for the nomination. Anxious to cultivate an image as a seasoned statesman, he announced that he was taking a "sabbatical" from politics during 1967 to travel throughout the world and to write.

Nixon's strategy helped to focus national interest on the other major Republican possibilities, especially Romney, the early front runner. Almost immediately after being reelected to his third term by an impressive margin in 1966, the Michigan governor began to travel and speak throughout the country. He achieved his goal of becoming better known, but his comments on national and international issues were often vague, confusing, and contradictory. His biggest blunder occurred when he declared that his earlier support for American involvement in Vietnam resulted from his being "brainwashed" by American briefers during his visit there in 1965. That apparent admission of naiveté raised serious doubts about his potential as a President. Fighting back, he reaffirmed his position that the war should not be Americanized, that the Vietnamese should work things out for themselves, that he favored direct negotiations between Saigon and the Vietcong, and that the bombing of North Vietnam should be cut back. His arguments appealed to many Americans, but Romney was unable to erase his reputation as a person inexperienced and unsure on foreign affairs. By February 1968 opinion polls indicated that he enjoyed so little support that he dejectedly withdrew from contention.

Romney's departure left Nixon, who had revealed his plans to enter a number of state primaries, with no announced opponent. The other hopefuls hastily reassessed their strategies. Rockefeller figured he would inherit the support of party liberals who had backed Romney, but he concluded that their strength would be insufficient to block Nixon. On March 21 he startled the nation by announcing that he would not campaign actively for the nomination, although he would accept a draft. He did not, he added, expect or wish to encourage such a call. "I find it clear at this time," he explained, "that a considerable majority of the party's leaders want the candidacy of former Vice-President Richard Nixon." Six weeks later Rockefeller reversed himself. By then, however, Nixon was in command of the situation. Reagan, meanwhile, decided to continue the course of action he had been following since early 1967—making frequent out-of-state speaking trips but denying that he was a candidate. Privately, he hoped that a deadlocked convention would turn to him as a fresh face. Romney's and Rockefeller's decisions crippled his expectations for such an outcome but left him unwilling to meet the Nixon steamroller head-on.

From beginning to end the Republican convention in Miami, Florida, mixed exuberant patriotism—as when actor John Wayne delivered an inspirational reading called "Why I Am Proud to Be an American"—with boredom. Novelist Norman Mailer described the mood perfectly: "On and on they came, the clean, the well-bred, the extraordinarily prosperous, and, for the most astonishing part, the entirely proper. Yes, in San Francisco in '64, they had been able to be insane for a little while, but now they were subdued, now they were modest, now they were looking for a leader to bring America back to them, their lost America . . . . The Wasp had come to take power."

The outcome did little more than confirm the obvious. Nixon destroyed Reagan's slim chance of capturing the nomination by securing the open support of southern conservatives led by Senator Strom Thurmond of South Carolina. Rockefeller's final hope for winning the top prize depended on opinion polls showing that he had a significantly better chance than Nixon did of defeating any Democratic nominee, but the polls failed to suggest such a clear-cut verdict. Nixon made some minor concessions to the Rockefeller forces on the platform—which promised de-Americanization of the Vietnam war—swept to an easy first-round victory, and picked Governor Spiro T. Agnew of Maryland as his running mate. Originally regarded as something of a liberal, Agnew's hard-line law-and-order position on urban riots had made him a hero among conservatives. His selection signaled Nixon's willingness to sacrifice black backing in favor of white votes in the South and border states.

Democratic conventions are traditionally more exciting than the Republican affairs, but the contrast in 1968 was extraordinary. Hubert Humphrey had the nomination effectively locked up well before the nominating sessions began, but his opponents refused to roll over and play dead. And since his position was clearly to defend the record of the Johnson administration, war protesters planned to make the Chicago convention the target of massive demonstrations. Mayor Richard Daley knew that trouble was likely, but he believed that his tough police force, backed by National Guardsmen and, if needed, regular Army troops, could cope with any problems.

During late August antiwar people flooded into Chicago by the thousands. Abbie Hoffman and his "Yippies" scheduled a Festival of Life as a contrast to the convention, which they characterized as a celebration of death. Other, less frivolous groups also planned events.

Daley handled the explosive situation in the worst possible way. Rather than issuing the demonstrators parade permits and allowing them to use city parks for their activities, he tried to keep the offensive, long-haired visitors out of sight. Police attempts to drive the gathering protesters out of Lincoln Park, three miles north of the hotel district that served as headquarters for the Democratic candidates, provoked bloody encounters even before the convention opened. The dissidents stubbornly kept returning, and the law enforcement authorities, using tear gas and clubs, repeated their sweeps of the park.

Conditions within the Chicago Amphitheater, site of the convention, were only slightly less tense. The most elaborate security measures in American political history were set up to screen out potential troublemakers. Delegates were issued special passes that were electronically scanned, and their packages and purses were routinely searched. Security officers trying to keep unauthorized persons off the convention floor often used excessive force. Media representatives seemed to be special targets for harassment and abuse; on one occasion a television reporter was knocked down by guards. Frequent scuffles added to the usual confusion in the jammed convention hall.

The platform fight over the Vietnam issue was the highlight of the formal proceedings. Delegates pledged to Kennedy, McCarthy, and Senator George McGovern favored a version calling for an immediate halt to the bombing of North Vietnam, and they urged that the South Vietnamese negotiate a political reconciliation with the Vietcong. But by roughly a 3–2 margin the convention adopted a plank that declared only that the United States should "stop all bombing of North Vietnam when this action would not endanger the lives of our troops in the field; this action should take into account the response from Hanoi." In effect it differed little from the Republican position and endorsed President Johnson's stand. The outcome of the heated struggle clearly indicated the strength of the proadministration forces, who were committed to the nomination of Hubert Humphrey, and his victory was a foregone conclusion.

While the delegates were debating the Vietnam question, events were unfolding in downtown Chicago that would steal the spotlight away from the convention business. The previous night, August 27, most of the antiwar groups had moved to Grant Park, adjacent to the huge Hilton Hotel. By the afternoon of the twenty-eighth the thousands of militant Movement people, Yippies, drifters, and simply curious onlookers had become a restless mob. Movement leaders herded most of them into a march to the Amphitheater. When police blocked their path, the crowd surged toward the Hilton Hotel, where Humphrey was putting the finishing touches on his acceptance speech for his expected nomination. Confronted by a cordon of police, many of the frustrated protesters threw sticks, bottles, and clods of earth. At that point, Daley's men in blue lost control. A flying wedge of police slashed into the crowd, hurling tear gas grenades and clubbing demonstrators, newsmen, and innocent bystanders. When those attacked fled into nearby Grant Park, side streets, and hotel lobbies, the officers pursued relentlessly. Persons caught were dragged, often by their feet, to waiting police wagons. Although acknowledging that the marchers were guilty of provocations, the National Commission on the Causes and Prevention of Violence, appointed by President Johnson, bluntly labeled the episode a "police riot."

The worst of the bloody battle was over in less than half an hour. A short time later millions of Americans were watching hastily edited films of the riots on television. Ironically, a strike by telephone workers in Chicago prevented live remote broadcasts except from the convention center itself. Mayor Daley's minions deliberately harassed camera crews who attempted to film activities for delayed broadcasts, but intrepid cameramen were nevertheless successful in filming the brutal beatings, gassings, and macings inflicted by the Chicago police.

Among the viewers were many of the delegates at the Amphitheater, who watched on tiny television sets on the floor of the convention. Appalled and angered, some argued that the proceedings should be adjourned immediately. Senator Abraham Ribicoff of Connecticut, making the nominating speech for Senator George McGovern, bitterly declared, "With George McGovern we wouldn't have Gestapo tactics on the streets of Chicago," a remark that brought Mayor Daley to his feet, savagely shouting obscenities easily lip-read by those watching on television.

Party officials insisted that the convention go on with its

business, and later in the evening the distracted delegates nominated Humphrey by a comfortable margin on the first ballot. Accepting the honor, the Vice President—who ironically had keyed his candidacy around the theme "the politics of joy"—put on a brave and optimistic front, urging Democrats to "take heart" and "make this moment of crisis . . . a moment of creation." Unlike Eugene McCarthy, who personally intervened to prevent police from beating a group of youths, Humphrey carefully avoided taking sides in what Norman Mailer called "the siege of Chicago." Convinced that he could not win without the power and money that tied him to Johnson, Humphrey, like the President, refused to condemn publicly the actions of Mayor Daley and his police. Privately, the Vice President knew that the week's chaotic events, explicitly and shockingly detailed on television, had severely, probably irreparably, damaged his chances of winning the election. "Chicago was a catastrophe," he later admitted to Theodore White. "My wife and I went home heart-broken, battered and beaten. I told her I felt just like we had been in a shipwreck."

Polls taken immediately after the depressing convention added to his gloom. Humphrey trailed Nixon by 8 to 12 points and was only 8 to 10 points ahead of Alabama segregationist George Wallace, who had decided to make a bid for the White House as a third-party candidate championing the cause of working-class whites. The Democratic nominee keenly realized that it was imperative to restore party unity by bringing the antiwar activists back into the fold while holding the support of the party regulars who backed the President.

As Vice President, Humphrey had steadfastly endorsed Lyndon Johnson's policies, loyally subordinating his own views to his chief's. He continued, until late in September, to reject the advice of those who argued that his only hope for victory was to move away from the President on Vietnam and become his own man. But at last, in a speech at Salt Lake City, he partially severed the umbilical cord to LBJ by promising that as chief executive he would risk an unconditional cessation of all bombing. It was a subtle but important shift from the prevailing American position that a complete bombing halt required a reciprocal act of good faith on the part of Hanoi. For Humphrey, the speech was a critical turning point in the campaign. From then on the antiwar forces began to rally to his support. Even

McCarthy gave him a lukewarm but very welcome endorsement. Gradually, the Democratic campaign began to gather steam. Humphrey's running mate, Senator Edmund Muskie, helped enormously, winning respect by his cool handling of hecklers who attempted to disrupt his speeches and, as a Polish-American, appealing strongly to white ethnic voters.

Plentifully financed, Nixon kicked off his campaign in early September with an elaborate and expensive campaign. He hammered hard at how the United States had lost confidence at home and prestige abroad under two Democratic administrations. In his carefully worded basic speech he lamented the fact that "the strongest nation in the world can be tied down in a war in Vietnam for four years with no end in sight," expressed his dismay at the lawlessness that gripped the country, and declared that "when the president of the United States of America for the first time in history cannot travel . . . to any major city in the country without the fear of a hostile demonstration, then it's time for a new leadership for the American people." He attracted huge, friendly crowds who loved "the speech" and responded so enthusiastically that Nixon worried that his followers might become overconfident.

George Wallace and his American Independence Party enjoyed remarkable success in getting on the ballot by petition in all fifty states. Stressing property rights and arguing that local government, not Washington, should handle local affairs, he attracted the law-and-order crowd, especially among the lower middle class, which felt threatened by the black revolution. For a time he appeared to be cutting deeply into the traditionally Democratic labor vote. He made a serious tactical error in October by picking retired Air Force Chief Curtis LeMay to be his vice-presidential running mate. The blunt-spoken general, an unrelenting and well-known "hawk" throughout his service career, almost immediately got the ticket in hot water with a reckless quip about bombing North Vietnam back to the Stone Age. Wallace quickly released a platform promising to win in Vietnam with conventional forces, but he never regained his lost momentum.

The last weeks of the campaign belonged to Humphrey. Slowly but surely he cut into Nixon's once-commanding lead. On October 31 Johnson provided a huge boost to the Vice President's chances by announcing a complete bombing halt over North Vietnam. Many Republicans suspected that the action was designed specifically to raise Humphrey's prospects, but, taking their cue from Nixon, most refrained from accusing the administration of such a motive except in a very gentle, back-handed way. By election day the two principals were neck and neck according to the polls, while Wallace had slipped badly.

The actual results testified to the accuracy of the pollsters' predictions. Humphrey and Nixon ended up in almost a dead heat, each with 43 percent of the vote, with Wallace collecting 14 percent. The Republican edged his rival by only 310,000 ballots out of more than 70 million cast, but the 32 states he won gave him 302 electoral votes against the 191 in the 13 states plus the District of Columbia Humphrey carried. Although Wallace captured five states, he failed to achieve his goal of preventing either of his opponents from gaining a majority of the electoral college. Had he been able to do so, the election would have been thrown into the House of Representatives, where Wallace could have bargained for favorable concessions for the South in return for his support. He came very, very close to that objective. A shift of only 43,000 votes in key states would have prevented Nixon from winning outright.

The election demonstrated convincingly that the Republicans had made a remarkable recovery from their unhealthy state in 1964. Yet they failed to capture either house of Congress, and antiwar Democrats won or held many seats. In the South the shift away from the Democratic party continued, with Humphrey able to win only Johnson's home state of Texas. Outside of Dixie, however, the old Democratic coalition of blacks, labor, Catholics, Jews, and city dwellers held together despite the appeal of George Wallace among union members. Blacks were particularly important for Humphrey, giving him an impressive 85 percent of their votes. It was no comfort to the Democrats, however, that Nixon's and Wallace's combined votes meant 57 percent of the electorate voted for the conservative candidates. It was uncertain whether that total reflected only a temporary white backlash against the violence of the preceding years or a flat rejection of the brand of liberalism popularized by Franklin D. Roosevelt's New Deal and continued by Truman, Kennedy, and Johnson.

More than anything else, one crucial fact stood out in 1968. Although violence and tumult punctuated the year and produced unpredictable political oscillations and extremes, in the end, the turmoil produced quite conventional results. Despite the bitter internal warfare within the major parties and the start of the most ambitious third party in forty-four years, the two-party system prevailed.

For Lyndon Johnson, Nixon's triumph was one more unhappy event in a generally frustrating year. Humphrey had irritated LBJ during the campaign by making statements about the Vietnam war that the President believed Hanoi would interpret as a major departure in American policy, but he sincerely regretted the Vice President's defeat. Johnson continued to believe that if he himself had run, he would have been reelected. Publicly, he ignored the fact that the election represented something of a repudiation of his administration. He blamed Humphrey's loss on the refusal of Saigon officials to attend the Paris peace talks and maintained that people speaking for Nixon had encouraged them in their decision by suggesting that, if elected, the Republican candidate would offer policies more favorable to the South Vietnamese. Had they kept their promise to participate, thus enabling the peace talks to be in progress on election day, the President later wrote, Humphrey, not Nixon, would have been the next chief executive.

Johnson was determined to leave his successor with "the best possible military posture in Vietnam" and consequently insisted on keeping strong pressure on the North Vietnamese throughout the year. The number of American troops in Southeast Asia reached its peak late in the summer of 1968. After the election, the President exercised special caution to guard against Hanoi's making some surprise move before Nixon took office.

Even as a lame-duck President, LBJ continued to pursue the possibilities of beginning strategic arms limitations talks with the Russians. Earlier plans for Johnson to visit the Soviet Union late in the year to initiate the negotiations had been scuttled in late August when Moscow, alarmed by a wave of liberalization under way in Czechoslovakia, had launched a lightning invasion, quickly occupied the country, and snuffed out the sparks of dissent. In late November, Johnson proposed a summit meeting with Soviet leaders in Geneva just before Christmas. Unhappily for the President, however, the Russians preferred to wait until the new administration assumed power.

Denied the chance to go out of office on a note of diplomatic triumph, LBJ busied himself ensuring that the records of his administration would be properly collected and transferred to the Johnson Library in Austin and coordinating the transfer of power to the Nixon administration. In public he seemed at times to be somewhat sullen. It was not easy for him to function without the anticipation of future battles to be fought and new goals to be won. "I do understand power," Johnson once said, "whatever else may be said about me. I know where to look for it and how to use it." As a lame-duck President, he could sense power slipping away, and the feeling was not pleasant. He spoke frequently of his achievements, declaring that what really mattered about his Presidency was not the ultimate judgment of history but whether there had really been a change for the better in the way Americans lived. His last State of the Union address to Congress was anticlimactic, but there was a deeply felt sentiment in the chamber as he talked of his long years in federal service. Finally, on January 20, a gray and chilly day in Washington, the awesome burdens of the nation's highest office were lifted from his shoulders. A private citizen for the first time in over thirty years, Lyndon Johnson left the bustling capital to return to his ranch in the gently rolling Texas hills he loved.

# IX

## The Legacies
## of Disillusionment

JOHNSON'S departure from the White House marked the end of an ambitious effort to move America forward in the well-worn tracks forged by Franklin Roosevelt and Harry Truman. Both Kennedy and Johnson proudly carried the banner of New Deal liberalism at home and cold war containment abroad. As a result, despite marked differences in their backgrounds and personal styles, their administrations were essentially pieces of the same cloth. Measured by new laws enacted and programs initiated, especially under Johnson, their record was impressive. Yet after eight years of their leadership, instead of being stronger and more unified, the United States was actually weaker and more divided.

Even if the sixties had been as tranquil a period as the later fifties, Lyndon Johnson's style alone would have caused him problems. His coarse, common mannerisms offended the sensibilities of intellectuals and media taste makers who believed that a President should make politics sound like a moral and intellectual challenge. Such faults were minor, however, compared to his incredible vanity, arrogance, and propensity for secrecy and dissembling. Subjected to the relentless attention that any chief executive invariably receives, everything about Johnson—his shortcomings as well as his many virtues—seemed excessive. He could be cranky or jovial, waspish or considerate, vindictive or generous, but he was never bland. Ambassador Henry Cabot Lodge described him perfectly: "The great problem is that this fellow is outsize, oversize; he's bigger than life, so his virtues seem huge and his vices seem like monstrous warts, almost goiters. It's because all you can do is photograph him at a particular angle at a particular time, and whatever it is you're seeing is all outsize."

President-watchers marveled at Johnson's almost inexhaustible energy. On one occasion guests at his Texas ranch were startled to see the President of the United States out in his yard at 6:30 in the morning picking up paper cups left from the previous evening's barbeque. The same restless drive characterized his conduct of national affairs. As he told listeners many times, he intended to use the power he had at his disposal to do things. Convinced that he knew what was best for America, he rarely hesitated in making tough decisions, even in the face of strong opposition.

His enthusiasm for improving the lives of Americans was insatiable. Far more than any previous chief executive, LBJ committed himself wholeheartedly to civil rights. He was, to use historian Carl Degler's term, one of those "other Southerners," who dissented from the stereotyped version of white southern racial behavior. Compared to John Kennedy, however, Johnson never really captured the hearts of the black masses, even though under his leadership their tangible gains were substantially greater than they had been under the New Frontier.

Unquestionably part of the progress in civil rights during the Johnson administration came because of tragedies. After the deaths of John Kennedy and Martin Luther King, Jr., Americans were ashamed of the image projected by the nation and were especially receptive to civil rights legislation. But, as moderate civil rights leaders overwhelmingly agreed, the fact that Johnson rose above his background to provide the federal commitment to the cause was vital. Kennedy was intellectually sympathetic to black equality, but he was unable to manipulate government the way Johnson could and much less willing to risk defeat on legislation. In addition, Kennedy was much more inclined to weigh the northern black vote against the southern white vote. Johnson simply plunged ahead. Once converted to the cause of racial equality, he did not mince words in trying to convince others. Talking to a group of Texas editors, he declared, "You sons-of-bitches have got to find out that the world doesn't belong to all one group of people, that this is the black man's world as well as the white man's world."

His frigid response to the Kerner Report (Commission on Civil Rights) after the 1967 riots was one of the rare times he seemed to retreat from his commitment. Believing that the document attacked him personally, in public he virtually ignored its informative findings and thoughtful observations. But at the same time he continued to push zealously for the Open Housing bill, and, with the added incentive of King's assassination, Congress finally passed the measure. By the end of Johnson's administration almost all that could be done to help blacks by removing legal obstacles had been done. What remained was to raise their economic status—government action could help to do that—and to change white attitudes, an infinitely more difficult task, but one which Johnson struggled energetically to accomplish.

In other domestic areas—education, health care, expanded opportunity and social welfare for the disadvantaged, transportation, safety, the environment, law and order, and consumer protection—Johnson pushed through an amazing array of legislation. In sheer numbers and in scope, the laws passed in his administration attacked more problems and affected the lives of more people than did the measures of any of his predecessors. As a leader in protecting and advancing the public interest, his record was unmatched. He maintained that his efforts went well beyond the New Deal because they centered on providing individuals with an equal chance to help themselves rather than on giving handouts. But his methods were much the same as those used during the preceding thirty years: the federal government acted both as a regulator to control excessive behavior and as a positive stimulator of the economy.

Johnson had no desire and made no attempt to alter the existing economic system. Rather he succeeded in stimulating economic growth in order to provide jobs and security for more people. The redistribution of income from rich to poor was not one of his objectives; increasing the total available for distribution was. By the end of his administration, the gross national product was moving rapidly toward a trillion dollars per year ($865.7 billion in 1968), but inflation was eating hungrily at the growth in per capita income, which rose from $2,219 in 1960 to $3,420 in 1968. The distribution of income changed but slightly, the poorest people receiving a little more, the wealthiest a fraction less.

Major corporations had solidified their position of dominance. They reaped the benefits of lucrative military and space contracts and enjoyed increases in profits which were markedly larger, percentagewise, than the rise in per capita personal income. Even so, large firms were less concerned about maximizing profits than in guaranteeing their chances of survival by reducing risks. Through advertising and cozy working relationships with the government and by taking over ownership of their suppliers to ensure the uninterrupted flow of essential materials, the corporate giants managed to manipulate the market in such a way as to maximize their prospects for future prosperity. The welfare of government and big business became so intertwined that whenever large companies employing a significant number of workers and engaged in critical federal contracts got into financial trouble, the government invariably stepped in to assure the continued operation of the beleaguered firm. The biggest businesses also continued to grow even bigger. By 1968 the 200 largest manufacturing corporations owned two-thirds of all corporate assets held by manufacturing concerns, an amount roughly equal to what 1,000 firms owned in 1940.

Labor union members, relative newcomers to the middle class, became consumers and increasingly turned socially conservative during the sixties. Workers tended to satisfy their ambitions by purchasing a wide variety of items that formerly had been considered the perquisites of the upper-middle or upper classes. Consumption helped to dull the alienation caused by work on assembly lines, but job boredom continued to be an important worry. It was time, sociologist David Riesman suggested, to design men back into the machines, rather than out of them, so that workers could gain satisfaction from their tasks. Although unions steadily accelerated their drive to organize white-collar employees, most of the labor organizations stubbornly resisted attempts by blacks to join in significant numbers. Union members were among the most ardent supporters of the war in Vietnam, consistently rejecting efforts by radicals to form an alliance against the "capitalist classes." Politically, labor continued to exert a strong influence, particularly on the Democratic party, but its opportunities to be a factor of importance among Republicans as well were on the increase.

Although Johnson made no effort to eliminate the practice by interest groups, such as big business and organized labor, of using their political and economic muscle to bargain for benefits, he did, with his moderate reforms, encourage blacks, consumer groups, and poor people to compete more effectively with the established power blocs. By cutting through the delaying tactics of the American Medical Association, he obtained Medicare. The Voting Act of 1965 enabled blacks in the South to become a formidable force in southern politics. To the anguish of the real estate lobby, the Open Housing Act took an important first step toward abolishing residential segregation. Legislation for Truth-in-Lending, Truth-in-Packaging, and Truth-in-Securities enhanced the ability of consumers to challenge producers. The Community Action Program, despite the bitter hostility it provoked among local and state authorities, began to involve the poor in decisions concerning their own lives and to make them more aware of their potential for organization and political bargaining.

The Johnson approach featured a whirlwind of activity: finding problems, devising methods to attack them, securing legislation to establish programs, and obtaining funds to finance their operation. It required enormous energy and drive, a rare skill in persuading Congress to go along, considerable executive ability, and a lot of good luck. The President provided the first three, and, initially, he enjoyed a large measure of the last. When the Republican party allowed Goldwater and his conservative cohorts to seize control, it handed Johnson a golden opportunity to rally Americans of a more liberal and moderate political persuasion. His overwhelming victory in 1964 swept scores of like-minded Democrats into Congress and generated a powerful momentum to enact the goals of the Great Society. Skeptics doubted even then that most people really loved or respected LBJ. But even if they did not, a solid majority in 1964, 1965, and early 1966 *approved* of what he was doing. As he anticipated, however, the relative boldness of his domestic program aroused a negative reaction from those who decided that he was going too far, too fast. Yet, he might have pulled it off had it not been for Vietnam.

The ugly war in Southeast Asia became the tragedy of Lyndon Johnson and America during the sixties. It touched everything. Cutting deeply into the nation's resources, the conflict starved and emasculated the President's social and economic programs. It prevented him from putting his best effort into the domestic areas where his talents were most effective. Ultimately, bitter opposition to the war caused him to retire from office, his work at home really only begun. In a sense, the war in Vietnam caused Johnson's symbolic death as surely as assassins' bullets killed John and Robert Kennedy and Martin Luther King, Jr.

Although deeply troubled by his inability to end the hostilities, Johnson adamantly refused to risk actions that might lead to a North Vietnamese–Vietcong takeover of South Vietnam, either by military conquest or by political infiltration through a coalition government. The "domino theory"—that a Communist win in Vietnam would expose all of Southeast Asia and subsequently all of the Far East to militant Communist aggression of the Red Chinese variety—influenced him heavily. So did the thesis that an insurgent victory in South Vietnam would inspire revolutionary movements around the globe to try their luck against governments favored by the United States.

Both the Kennedy and the Johnson administrations officially insisted that Southeast Asia was vital to American security, but the argument was tenuous at best. Much more important to the thinking of both Presidents was their belief that a Communist triumph in South Vietnam would dangerously affect the global balance of power psychologically and politically. They reasoned that if Washington failed to maintain its commitments to Saigon, America's allies elsewhere might conclude that their own defensive agreements with the United States were worthless. Even more critical, a failure of American will in South Vietnam might persuade the Soviet Union and Red China that the United States was irresolute, a miscalculation that could conceivably tempt the big Communist powers to engage in new foreign adventures that might lead to a nuclear World War III.

The Kennedy-Johnson strategy was vintage cold war containment, designed to keep differences between East and West within tolerable limits and help preserve the nuclear peace. The Communist issue in Vietnam continued to serve, as it had done since the end of World War II, as a valuable means of rallying public support for the United States' foreign actions. But in essence, containment was a synonym for a classic balance-of-power policy. Since the Soviet Union and Red China furnished supplies to North Vietnam and the Vietcong, Washington believed that it was crucial to contain aggression sponsored in any way by Moscow and/or Peking. Significantly, however, the United States made no overt attempt to root Communism out of Cuba, only ninety miles away, even while it was waging major military operations in far-off Vietnam. The reason was that the United States and the Soviet Union had reached a *quid pro quo* over Cuba during the missile crisis of 1962 when Kennedy promised not to invade the island in return for the Russians' removing their missiles. Washington thus accepted the Castro regime, at least for the immediate future, as part of the prevailing balance of power. No such understanding existed about Southeast Asia. There the United States believed that a symbolic stand against Communism was imperative even if in reality a non-Communist Vietnam was not vital to American security.

The containment policy worked well for Kennedy and Johnson in crises that could be favorably resolved at low cost and with relative quickness—in Cuba, Berlin, and the Dominican Republic, for example. But in Vietnam the American public lost patience when the conflict dragged on and on, extorting a heavy price in lives and resources. Since the United States fought in Vietnam ostensibly to fulfill commitments made to an ally, the wisdom of collective security received sterner challenges than at any time since the 1920s. The spirit and unity of the Atlantic Community, previously America's number-one priority, sank dangerously low. In addition, it is possible that the bitter experience of fighting an Asian ground war with conventional weapons lessened the opposition of the American people to the use of nuclear arms in any future test of wills. Most critical of all, so many government statements about the war proved to be misleading and often patently false that millions of Americans lost confidence in Johnson's leadership. As a consequence, the conflict deeply divided the American people and severely damaged national morale.

Even without the disrupting influence of the war, the sixties in all probability would have been a decade of intense social and cultural upheaval. After the relative tranquility of the late fifties, a swing toward activism was predictable. John F. Kennedy's 1960 campaign theme of "moving America forward" reflected the widely held belief that the country needed to be stirred up. The black revolution alone would have been potent enough to make the Kennedy-Johnson years anything but quiet, but as it turned out, the combination of strident antiwar protests and militant racial challenges stretched the people's capacity for civility almost to the breaking point. To dissidents the American government's support of a corrupt and undemocratic regime in Saigon paralleled the hypocrisy found at home: blacks still not enjoying rights theoretically ensured by constitutional amendments almost a century old, millions living in abject poverty amidst the most opulent surroundings in the world, and the general public unable to make institutions controlled by small elites respond to their needs and wishes.

Violence in Vietnam was matched by the "rediscovery of violence" at home. As the National Commission on the Causes and Prevention of Violence made clear, the phenomenon was neither new nor unique to the United States. But most Americans, proud of their heritage and accomplishments and lulled by the relative calm of the 1950s, were oblivious to the violence that had permeated the nation's history. Thus the outbreaks of the 1960s caused surprise as well as shock and frustration.

The assault against the established political, social, and economic system overflowed into an attack on Western culture in general and American mores in particular. Counter culturists questioned puritanical sex codes, the work ethic, the value of competition, and accepted modes of dress and manners. Some argued that knowledge, scientific inquiry, and disciplined training were of little value; what was important was to experience and to feel. Although the young formed the vanguard of change, the cultural revolution was too complex to explain as simply a generation gap. At the heart of the turmoil was a loss of optimism about the direction America was going and an increasing inclination among older people as well to challenge traditional values.

Radical Protestant theologians proclaimed that "God is dead," while a band of radical Catholic priests, notably Daniel and Philip Berrigan, led a militant opposition to the war. Less venturesome clergy revived the Social Gospel and engaged actively in civil rights demonstrations, rent strikes, and peace marches. Protestants and

Catholics alike hastened to simplify and clarify religious services in order to make them more relevant and understandable to worshippers.

Literature, theater, and movies helped both to mirror and to stimulate the changes taking place. Aided by new Supreme Court decisions on pornography that a work was acceptable if it did not violate "prevailing community standards" *or* if it had redeeming social or esthetic importance, books, plays, and films portrayed explicitly the expanded frontiers of sexual freedom. The Justices opened the door by ruling in favor of publication and distribution of older erotic books like D. H. Lawrence's *Lady Chatterley's Lover.* After that, virtually no work was deemed to be so pornographic as not to have some trace of social or moral value. Novelist John Updike used the new permissiveness to explore wife-swapping, while more pedestrian talents cranked out hard-core pornography masquerading under the guise of literature. Tom Wolfe was acclaimed for his writings on drug use and radical chic—the inclination of many of the "beautiful people" to adopt the ways of the "Now Generation" as a means of satisfying their egos and creating excitement. Many writers pessimistically described the modern world as an irrational mixture of tragedy and comedy, with life itself as a supreme farce.

In the theater the decade's smash box-office hit was *Hair*, billed as a "tribal-love-rock musical" and featuring a scene in which performers of both sexes disrobed. Its success inspired countless imitations, most of them far less cheerful in tone and considerably less artistic. The flamboyant Living Theater, combining radical declarations, sexual gestures, and unrehearsed encounters with the audience, found spectators in the sixties far more receptive than those of the previous decade. Although plays depicting sexual action stirred great controversy, the most shocking presentation of the period centered on politics. Barbara Garson's parody, *MacBird*, slashed savagely at Lyndon Johnson. Roughly following the plot of Shakespeare's *Macbeth*, MacBird (Johnson) violently deposed his leader (Kennedy) in order to gain power to carry out his evil designs (Vietnam).

Movie makers profited from "adult pictures" that specialized in sex and gore, while so-called family-entertainment films dwindled in number as audiences who would pay to see them shrank in size.

Pictures using cold war themes, especially those dealing with intelligence operations, like *The Ipcress File,* and the horror of nuclear war, such as *On the Beach* and *Dr. Strangelove,* offered both solid entertainment and somber warnings about the dangers to mankind inherent in sophisticated technology. The mood of the decade made anti-heroes into heroes, and the movie industry cooperated. *Bonnie and Clyde* told the bittersweet and violent story of bank robbers in the 1930s but reflected the spirit of the sixties.

Early in the Kennedy administration the chairman of the Federal Communications Commission, Newton Minow, charged that television was a "vast wasteland." By the end of the decade, little had changed. Although the networks periodically offered outstanding productions, most programming was run-of-the-mill. Unlike the movies, television was unable to make even a pretense of restricting its audience to adults in order to deal with subjects deemed unfit for children. Since sex scenes were excluded, the broadcasters emphasized violence, despite complaints that a steady diet of brutality had a dangerous effect on juvenile and adolescent viewers and possibly on mentally unstable adults as well. Ironically, even without fictional violence, the daily video coverage of the war in Vietnam provided ample evidence of the ways human beings abuse one another.

Art battered the concept that a clear line existed between mass culture and high culture. Pop art drew heavily upon the consumer culture for subjects. Andy Warhol attracted wide attention as an exponent of the pop art school with his painting of Campbell Soup cans. Admirers explained that pop artists selected examples from the affluent commercial world in order to illustrate society's "growing sameness." Some art critics applauded the way pop artists poked fun at the severity of abstract art, but many ordinary people wondered if they were being "put on."

Music was the special language of the young, carrying the message of the peaceful revolution occurring in human consciousness and values, and, coincidentally, making superstars like the Beatles, Jimmy Hendrix, Bob Dylan, Janis Joplin, and the Rolling Stones both immensely famous and very rich. Folk protest songs had long been popular with the small American Left, and in the sixties folk music enjoyed a massive revival of interest. Lyrics described the fear of being destroyed by nuclear explosions, lamented the banality of

going to school, railed against parental interference with teen-age
love, expressed the suffering of blacks, called for peace, and glorified
the use of marijuana and LSD. Singer Neil Diamond, however,
estimated that only 10 percent of the listeners ever really paid
attention to the words of popular songs. The rest liked the music for
entertainment value. That was particularly true for hard rock, which
drew upon folk, blues, and country music but embellished and
modified them with sophisticated techniques and modern electronic
technology. The noise level of hard rock was ear-splitting, but the
music generated a white heat of excitement.

During the late sixties, a new spirit of activism motivated many
women to demand new rights, both legal and social. Numerically the
ratio of women to men had widened even further, but females
remained a minority of the work force and of college graduates.
Compared to other industrially advanced countries, women in the
United States accounted for a strikingly low percentage of lawyers,
doctors, and college teachers, a proportion even smaller in the sixties
than it had been in the twenties. Radical feminists lashed out at the
family as an oppressive unit designed to subjugate women and called
for the abolition of both marriage and the family. Although the
overwhelming number of women disagreed with such revolutionary
proposals, many moderates added their voices to calls for an Equal
Rights Amendment for women, repeal of laws prohibiting abortion,
an end to discrimination in education quotas, free child-care centers,
deduction of child-care expenses from income taxes, and equal pay
for equal work. Homosexuals, too, began publicly demanding equal
rights.

In spite of the excitement caused by the revolt against established values, millions of Middle Americans rejected the main thrust
of the social-cultural revolution. Yet, many secretly welcomed
modest changes to the old codes. Conservatives and moderates began
to wear their hair longer and dress more colorfully. Liberalized sex
standards caused some who were distinctly not members of the
counter culture to do openly and without guilt what previously they
had felt compelled to hide. Unmarried couples living together
became commonplace, and many more people accepted the practice
without qualm.

Nevertheless, campus protests, the drug culture, ghetto riots, radical politics, and the erosion of authority appalled most rural, small-town, and suburban middle-class citizens and most working-class white ethnics. They were inclined to support the war in Vietnam, back police and law and order enthusiastically, and retain their belief that hard work was important for personal success. Attempts by young radicals to enlist allies from among the working class fell flat. As political analysts Richard M. Scammon and Ben J. Wattenberg explained, the great majority of voters were "unyoung, unpoor, and unblack; they were middle-aged, middle-class, and middle-minded."

Implicit in the bitter disagreement between Americans over the Vietnam war and cultural standards were growing doubts about the wisdom of New Deal liberalism and cold war containment, the basic principles of the Kennedy and Johnson administrations. Blacks and the poor believed that they were still not getting a fair share of the benefits. On the other hand, the middle and working classes increasingly felt that minority groups and those on welfare were receiving too much help compared to themselves. Middle-income earners labored hard and paid sizable taxes but received relatively few federal benefits. In contrast, the rich took advantages of tax loopholes, corporations enjoyed handsome government contracts and subsidies, and government regulatory agencies guarded the special interests they were supposed to police more than they protected the general welfare. Reports of government waste and fraud rankled Middle Americans, as did the huge, costly, and often irritating bureaucracy required to administer federal operations. During the sixties, the feeling grew that perhaps the "experts" in Washington really did not have answers to the multitude of problems confronting the country.

The counter culturists and the young radicals had been the first to question the wisdom of relying on technological expertise, but George Wallace had also based much of his appeal on attacks against intellectuals and social planners. Enamored by their ability to use their carefully honed skills to solve problems of all types, technician-intellectuals increasingly wielded a heavy influence on national policy. Unsentimental, laconic, and supremely confident, they not only manned the "think tanks" and the task forces but also frequently became the public officials who executed the orders of

Presidents. In their roles they mingled cozily with the older men of the Establishment who had long shaped vital decisions.

The technician-intellectuals reached new levels of importance during the Kennedy and Johnson administrations. But they also ran into stubborn obstacles to their wizardry. The Vietcong's ability to prevail against sophisticated "solutions" raised serious doubts about the limits of technology and the morality of destroying a village or a country in order to "save" it. Ronald Steel expressed the views of many when he wrote that Vietnam was "a war conceived, promoted, and directed by intellectuals fascinated with power and eager to prove their toughness and resolve." They were the "best and the brightest," as David Halberstam called them, and they had been counted on by Kennedy and Johnson to work wonders. But the conflict in Vietnam, combined with the persistent difficulties at home, revealed their limitations.

Most important of all, the events of the sixties shook the faith of the American people in the political system. Since Congress had surrendered so much of its authority to the executive branch during the previous thirty years, the public looked to the White House for direction. Kennedy and Johnson promised energetic, progressive leadership. During the first half of the decade, their rhetoric and many of their actions helped to inflate even more the already strong mood of optimism that prevailed in America at the end of the fifties. In contrast to the bland qualities of the "mild bunch," as one historian characterized the Eisenhower team, the Kennedy and Johnson administrations featured activism and vigor. They caused the expectations for a better life to rise dramatically among blacks, the poor, and, indeed, among Americans in general. Problems could be solved by technological expertise; the President had "the facts" and knew best; the federal government could manage the economy and produce prosperity. Kennedy's assassination momentarily slowed the momentum, but Johnson shrewdly used the tragedy to mobilize support to push the martyred President's programs. Johnson's landslide triumph over Goldwater in 1964, followed by his success in getting Congress to enact his Great Society legislation, carried the promise of positive-government liberalism to its zenith.

The bubble showed signs of bursting during 1965. Escalating the United States' involvement in Vietnam required a stiff increase in draft calls and diverted both money and energy from domestic needs. The war also confused and perplexed more and more Americans, and, because Johnson and his associates chose to conceal so much about the conflict, many people began to believe that the government was incapable of telling the truth. Johnson's credibility gap became immense. Assassinations, riots, burning cities, and protests against the war added to the feeling that the nation's leadership had failed. As disaffection mounted, the widely held belief that the United States required a bold, active individual in the White House became the subject of serious question. Kennedy and Johnson were fundamentally decent men, whose ambitions both reflected and influenced the American people. The two Presidents believed that they could shape the destinies of the United States and the world by a combination of will and pragmatic knowledge. Their dreams and hopes were shattered by intractable and sometimes absurd forces beyond their control, though often of their own making. By the end of 1968, America was in a sad state of disarray, plagued by violence and dissent at home, and mired in a deliberately no-win war abroad.

Even so, only the most optimistic revolutionary could claim that genuinely radical change to the American system was imminent. The political and social center, battered and bruised as never before, continued to hold together. Nevertheless, the impact of the sixties' disasters was undeniable. The legacies—punishing inflation, new cultural norms, greater racial bitterness, disillusionment with big government and technological expertise, and distrust of presidential power—would not be easily or painlessly forgotten.

# Bibliography

THE COLLECTIONS at the Kennedy and Johnson presidential libraries are indispensable sources of information about the respective presidential administrations. The Kennedy Library is temporarily located in the Federal Reserve Records Center at Waltham, Massachusetts, but will eventually occupy its own facility at Cambridge, Massachusetts. The Johnson Library is housed in a large and impressive new building on the campus of the University of Texas at Austin. Although only a relatively small number of the millions of papers held by both institutions were available for research when I visited them, additional collections are opened yearly. Both libraries are pursuing oral-history projects aggressively, and transcriptions of interviews with key administration and public figures provide a rich vein of information for scholars.

The published material about the sixties and about the two Democratic administrations is already voluminous. The list given here is by no means comprehensive but rather cites the works I found most valuable.

Two good general histories of the decade are available: William L. O'Neill, *Coming Apart: An Informal History of America in the 1960's* (1971) is opinionated, provocative, and a pleasure to read; David Burner, Robert D. Marcus, and Thomas R. West, *A Giant's Strength: America in the 1960's* (1971) is a briefer, judicious, and balanced appraisal. Ronald Berman, *America in the Sixties* (1968) is an important early intellectual history of the decade. Ronald Lora, ed., *America in the '60s: Cultural Authorities in Transition* (1974) provides a useful collection of essays and documents on social-cultural change. See especially Lora's thoughtful and succinct introduction. Other anthologies of value include Edward Quinn and Paul J. Dolan, eds., *The Sense of the Sixties* (1968); Peter Joseph, *Good Times: An Oral History of America in the Nineteen Sixties* (1973); and Herbert Mitgang, ed., *America at Random* (1970). John Brooks, *The Great Leap* (1966) is a useful account of how America changed between 1939 and 1964. For statistical information about the sixties, the annual edition of the official *Statistical Abstract of the United States* is invaluable.

On Kennedy before his election to the White House, by far the best study is James MacGregor Burns, *Kennedy: A Political Profile* (1960), a penetrating appraisal by a political scientist. For information about the Kennedy family Richard J. Whalen, *The Founding Father: The Story of*

*Joseph Kennedy* (1964) and Rose Fitzgerald Kennedy's delightful memoir, *Times to Remember* (1974) are useful. Nancy Gager Clinch, *The Kennedy Neurosis: A Psychological Portrait of an American Dynasty* (1973) is a bitterly critical psychohistory of the family. Although interesting, it is overly astringent and methodologically questionable. It should be used with Robert Coles, "Shrinking History," *New York Review of Books* (Feb. 22, 1973), an incisive examination of psychohistory. A helpful bibliographical tool is Martin H. Sable, *A Bio-Bibliography of the Kennedy Family* (1969).

Theodore H. White, *The Making of the President, 1960* (1961) is the standard account of the election of 1960. The best of White's quadrennial volumes on presidential elections, it provides both an arresting narrative and shrewd judgments on why Kennedy edged Nixon. Useful also are Theodore C. Sorensen, "The Election of 1960," in Arthur M. Schlesinger, Jr., ed., *History of American Presidential Elections, 1789–1968*, Vol. IV (1971), and the essays by various authors in Paul T. David, ed., *The Presidential Election and Transition, 1960–1961* (1961). V. O. Key, Jr., "Interpreting Election Results," in the latter work, is especially enlightening, as is Key, *The Responsible Electorate* (1966) and Philip E. Converse and others, "Stability and Change in 1960: A Reinstating Election," *American Political Science Review* (June 1961). Paul Tillett, ed., *Inside Politics: The National Conventions, 1960* (1962) contains important essays by political scientists about the composition of state delegations to the conventions and helpful information about campaign organizations. A sparkling personal account by one of Kennedy's dedicated workers is Jerry Bruno, *The Advance Man* (1971). The campaign speeches, remarks, press conferences, and statements of Senator Kennedy during the campaign are conveniently assembled in U.S. Senate Report No. 994, Committee on Commerce, *Freedom of Communications* (87th Cong., 1st sess.), Part 1. Part 3 contains the joint appearances of Kennedy and Nixon, including transcripts of their television debates. Nixon explains his campaign strategy and his decision not to contest the outcome of the race in *Six Crises* (1962). On the impact of Kennedy's religion and civil rights on the election, see the stimulating studies by Lawrence H. Fuchs, *John F. Kennedy and American Catholicism* (1967) and Russel Middleton, "The Civil Rights Issue and Presidential Voting among Southern Negroes and Whites," *Social Forces* (Mar. 1962). David T. Stanley, *Changing Administrations: The 1961 and 1964 Transitions in Six Departments* (1965) is informative on the transition of power between the Eisenhower and Kennedy administrations.

Useful starting points for studying Kennedy's presidential years are James T. Crown, *The Kennedy Literature: A Bibliographical Essay on John F. Kennedy* (1968); the official *The Public Papers of the Presidents: John F.*

*Kennedy, 1961, 1962, 1963* (3 vols.); and U.S. Senate Document No. 53, *Summary of the Three-Year Kennedy Record and Digest of Major Accomplishments of the 87th Congress and the 88th Congress, 1st Session, January 3, 1961, to December 30, 1963* (88th Cong., 1st sess.). The two general accounts of the administration, Arthur M. Schlesinger, Jr., *A Thousand Days* (1965) and Theodore C. Sorensen, *Kennedy* (1965) are outstanding. Detailed and highly informative, they are "must" reading for Kennedy scholars despite their overwhelmingly symapthetic view of the President and his efforts. Also consult Sorensen's later book, *The Kennedy Legacy* (1969). Kenneth P. O'Donnell and David F. Powers with Joe McCarthy, *"Johnny, We Hardly Knew Ye": Memories of John Fitzgerald Kennedy* (1972) and Pierre Salinger, *With Kennedy* (1966) are important, though less so than the books by Sorensen and Schlesinger. Two books by Kennedy's longtime personal secretary, Evelyn Lincoln, *My Twelve Years with John F. Kennedy* (1965) and *Kennedy and Johnson* (1968), are of marginal worth. Fascinating for the lighter side of JFK is *The Pleasure of His Company* (1966) by Paul B. Fay, Jr., a close friend of the President.

Aida DiPace Donald, ed., *John F. Kennedy and the New Frontier* (1967) is a particularly significant collection of writings about the Kennedy Presidency. For favorable accounts written by persons not in the administration, see Hugh Sidey, *John F. Kennedy, President* (1964) and William Manchester, *Portrait of a President: John F. Kennedy in Profile* (1962). Enlightening reflections about both Kennedy and Johnson are found in the memoirs of three veteran Washington newsmen: Arthur Krock, *Memoirs: Sixty Years on the Firing Line* (1968); Chalmers M. Roberts, *First Rough Draft* (1973); and William Lawrence, *Six Presidents, Too Many Years* (1972). Critical of Kennedy are Henry Fairlie, *The Kennedy Promise* (1973); Victor Lasky, *JFK: The Man and the Myth* (1967); and Malcolm E. Smith, Jr., *Kennedy's 13 Great Mistakes in the White House* (1968). Fairlie's excellent book is filled with many provocative observations, but Lasky's work is a hatchet job that borders at times on the ridiculous.

Kennedy's tragic assassination prompted scores of hasty and almost universally favorable appraisals of his tenure in the White House. The best include James MacGregor Burns, "The Legacy of the 1000 Days," *New York Times Magazine* (Dec. 1, 1963); William G. Carleton, "Kennedy in History: An Early Appraisal," *The Antioch Review* (Fall 1964); Richard E. Neustadt, "Kennedy in the Presidency: A Premature Appraisal," *Political Science Quarterly* (Sept. 1964); James Reston, "What Was Killed Was Not Only the President But the Promise," *New York Times Magazine* (Nov. 15, 1964); and Tom Wicker, "Kennedy Without Tears," *Esquire* (June 1964). Writing several years later, Midge Decter, "Kennedyism," *Commentary* (Jan. 1970), cast a harsh dissenting vote against such flattering portrayals of the slain leader.

Kennedy's assassination is examined in enormous detail, but unfortunately without answering all questions, in the official *The Warren Commission Report* (1964). David Wrone cogently evaluates and summarizes the writings of those who challenge the validity of the government report in an excellent article, "The Assassination of John Fitzgerald Kennedy: An Annotated Bibliography," *Wisconsin Magazine of History* (Autumn 1972). Also useful is John Kaplan, "The Assassins," *American Scholar* (Spring 1967), a review of books dealing with the assassination. Among the best of the many studies criticizing the Warren Commission's findings are Edward Jay Epstein, *Inquest: The Warren Commission* (1966); Penn Jones, Jr., *Forgive My Grief: A Critical Review of the Warren Commission Report of the Assassination of JFK* (1966); Mark Lane, *A Citizen's Dissent: Mark Lane Replies* (1968); and Sylvia Meagher, *Accessories After the Fact: The Warren Commission, the Authorities, and the Report* (1967). William Manchester tells the story of the tragic day in Dallas and the President's funeral in meticulous—some would say nauseous—detail in *The Death of a President* (1967). Also see Samuel C. Patterson, "Reactions to the Kennedy Assassination among Political Leaders, *Public Affairs* (May 15, 1967).

Lyndon B. Johnson's early years are recorded by William C. Pool, Emmie Craddock, and David E. Conrad, *Lyndon Baines Johnson: The Formative Years* (1965) and Alfred Steinberg, *Sam Johnson's Boy* (1968). J. Evetts Haley, *A Texan Looks at Lyndon: A Study in Illegitimate Power* (1964) is a vitriolic, often irrational, account of LBJ's pre-Presidential career, while William S. White, *The Professional: Lyndon B. Johnson* (1964) is overly flattering. On Johnson's skill as a congressional politician, see Robert L. Branyan and R. Alton Lee, "Lyndon B. Johnson and the Art of the Possible," *Southwestern Social Science Quarterly* (Dec. 1964). A fine study of LBJ as Vice President is Leonard Baker, *The Johnson Eclipse: A President's Vice-Presidency* (1966).

On Johnson as President, *The Public Papers of the Presidents: Lyndon B. Johnson, 1963–1964, 1965, 1966, 1967, 1968–1969* (10 vols.) are essential. Although Johnson's memoirs, *The Vantage Point* (1971), are exceedingly bland, they nevertheless contain much valuable information. Lady Bird Johnson, in *A White House Diary* (1970), offers little help in understanding her husband's policies but presents an interesting account of her role as First Lady. Historian Eric F. Goldman, Johnson's intellectual-in-residence early in the administration, provides a brilliant portrait of the President with special emphasis on his relations with the intellectual community in *The Tragedy of Lyndon Johnson* (1969). In conjunction with Goldman's book, see the article by English journalist Henry Fairlie, "Johnson and the Intellectuals," *Commentary* (Oct. 1965), which argues that attacks by intellectuals on Johnson were unwarranted. Books by Johnson aides other than Goldman have been neglected by many critics. Harry McPherson, *A Political Education* (1972) is an excellent study, gracefully written and very revealing about LBJ. So is George E. Reedy, *The Twilight of the Presidency* (1970), which focuses as much on the Presidency as an institution as on LBJ. George Christian, *The President Steps Down* (1970) deals only with Johnson's last months in the White House but provides important information.

Some of the best accounts of the Johnson Presidency are by journalists, notably Rowland Evans and Robert Novak, *Lyndon B. Johnson: The Exercise of Power* (1966); Hugh Sidey, *A Very Personal Presidency: Lyndon Johnson in the White House* (1968); and Louis Herren, *No Hail, No Farewell* (1970). Richard Harwood and Haynes Johnson, *Lyndon* 1973) is brief and entertaining and includes a fascinating collection of photographs. Michael Davie, *LBJ, A Foreign Observer's Viewpoint* (1966) and the bitterly critical Robert Sherrill, *The Accidental President* (1967) are of little value. An excellent collection of essays and documents by Marvin E. Gettleman and David Mermelstein, eds., *The Great Society Reader* (1967), contrasts Johnsonian liberalism with the avowed socialist position of the editors, which they explicitly enunciate in penetrating introductory essays to various sections of the book. Two brief but highly stimulating judgments of Johnson are by historians William Appleman Williams, *Some Presidents: Wilson to Nixon* (1972) and T. Harry Williams, "Huey, Lyndon, and Southern Radicalism," *Journal of American History* (Sept. 1973).

The essential studies of the 1964 elections are Theodore H. White, *The Making of the President, 1964* (1965); John Barlow Martin, "The Election of 1964," in Schlesinger, ed., *Presidential Elections* (cited above); and Milton C. Cummings, Jr., ed., *The National Election of 1964* (1966). Also valuable are Walter Dean Burnham, "American Voting Behavior and the 1964 Election," *Midwest Journal of Political Science* (1966), and Harold Faber, ed., *The Road to the White House* (1965). David S. Myers, *Foreign Affairs and the 1964 Presidential Election in the United States* (1972) examines a critical issue in the election. On Barry Goldwater, see his own works, *The Conscience of a Conservative* (1960), *Why Not Victory* (1962), and *Where I Stand* (1964), plus Richard Rovere, *The Goldwater Caper* (1965); Clifton White, *Suite 3505: The Story of the Draft Goldwater Movement* (1967); and Stephen Shadegg, *What Happened to Goldwater?* (1965). Lloyd A. Free and Hadley Cantril, *The Political Beliefs of Americans: A Study of Public Opinion* (1967) is informative about the public mood on various issues. The resurgence of the radical right is examined in valuable studies by Daniel Bell, ed., *The Radical Right* (1963); Benjamin R. Epstein and Arnold Forster, *The Radical Right: Report on the John Birch Society and Its Allies* (1966); and Richard Hofstadter, *The Paranoid Style in American Politics and Other Essays* (1967).

On the personnel who served on Kennedy's and Johnson's staffs and who held vital federal administrative positions, see Patrick Anderson, *The Presidents' Men* (1969); Lester Tanzer, ed., *The Kennedy Circle* (1961); Joseph Kraft, *Profiles in Power* (1966); Ben H. Bagdikian, "The 'Inner Circle' Around Johnson," *New York Times Magazine* (Feb. 28, 1965); and Charles Roberts, *LBJ's Inner Circle* (1965). David Halberstam, *The Best and the Brightest* (1972) is a brilliant and outspoken portrayal of the liberal intellectual technicians who helped to shape Vietnam policy. Presidential relations with the press are probed by Miles B. Johnson, *The Government Secrecy Controversy* (1967); James E. Pollard, *The President and the Press, Truman to Johnson* (1964); and James Deakin, *Lyndon Johnson's Credibility Gap* (1968). Also see David Wise and Thomas B. Ross, *The Invisible Government* (1964).

The best study of Kennedy's and Johnson's domestic policies generally is James L. Sundquist, *Politics and Policy: The Eisenhower, Kennedy, and Johnson Years* (1968). Less comprehensive but penetrating is Tom Wicker, *JFK and LBJ: The Influence of Personality Upon Politics* (1968), which is especially good on the interrelationship between Vietnam and domestic affairs in Johnson's case. Also see Carroll Kilpatrick, "The Kennedy Style and Congress," *Virginia Quarterly Review* (Winter 1963), and James MacGregor Burns, *The Deadlock of Democracy* (1963). Abraham Holtzman, *Legislative Liaison: Executive Leadership in Congress* (1970) is helpful regarding the role of Kennedy's staff in dealings with Congress. On Johnson's Great Society, examine articles by William Leuchtenburg, "The Genesis of the Great Society," *The Reporter* (Apr. 21, 1966); Robert Lekachman, "Death of a Slogan—The Great Society, 1967," *Commentary* (Jan. 1967); Kenneth McNaught, "American Progressives and the Great Society," *Journal of American History* (Dec. 1966); and Max Ways, "Creative Federalism and the Great Society," *Fortune* (Jan. 1966).

National economic policy is incisively discussed by Walter W. Heller, *New Dimensions of Political Economy* (1966). Also see the applicable sections of Herbert Stein, *The Fiscal Revolution in America* (1969) and Robert Lekachman, *The Age of Keynes* (1966), plus the works by Seymour E. Harris, *The Economics of the Political Parties: With Special Attention to Presidents Eisenhower and Kennedy* (1962) and *Economics of the Kennedy Years and a Look Ahead* (1964); Arthur M. Okun, *The Political Economy of Prosperity* (1970); E. Ray Canterbury, *Economics on a New Frontier* (1968);

and James Tobin, *National Economic Policy* (1966). Business-government relations are examined by Jim F. Heath, *John F. Kennedy and the Business Community* (1969) and Hobart Rowen, *The Free Enterprisers: Kennedy, Johnson, and the Business Establishment* (1964). The steel crisis of 1962 is detailed trenchantly by Grant McConnell, *Steel and the Presidency—1962* (1963) and less satisfactorily by Roy Hoopes, *The Steel Crisis* (1963). A discerning but generally favorable appraisal of the wage-price guideposts is John Sheahan, *The Wage-Price Guideposts* (1967). For labor relations, consult John L. Blackman, Jr., *Presidential Seizure in Labor Disputes* (1967). A concise examination of tax policy is Joseph Pechman, *Federal Tax Policy* (1966), but Joseph A. Ruskay and Richard A. Osserman, *Halfway to Tax Reform* (1970) is also useful. Two books by John Kenneth Galbraith on contemporary American capitalism, *The New Industrial State* (1967) and *Economics and the Public Purpose* (1973), are extremely enlightening. Also stimulating is Morton Mintz and Jerry S. Cohen, *America, Inc.* (1971), which contends that more and more wealth and economic power are being concentrated in the hands of a few large corporations.

Efforts to alleviate unemployment and aid to depressed areas are described capably by Arthur M. Okun, ed., *The Battle against Unemployment* (1965); Conley H. Dillon, *The Area Redevelopment Administration* (1964); Sar Levitan, *Federal Aid to Depressed Areas* (1964); and Joseph M. Becker, William Haber, and Sar Levitan, *Programs to Aid the Unemployed in the 1960's* (1965). Don Hadwiger, *Pressures and Protests: The Kennedy Farm Program and the Wheat Referendum of 1963* (1965) and "The Freeman Administration and the Poor," *Agricultural History* (Jan. 1971) examine farm policy. For a colorful account of the passage of the 1962 drug bill, see Richard Harris, *The Real Voice* (1964). On Medicare the following are especially valuable: Richard Harris, *A Sacred Trust* (1966); Robert S. Myers, *Medicare* (1970); and Allen J. Matusow, "Reform in the Great Society: The Case of Medicare," *Rice University Studies* (Fall 1972). The struggle for federal aid to education is told by Tom Wicker, *JFK and LBJ* (1969); Stephen K. Bailey, *The Office of Education and the Education Act of 1965* (1966); and Philip Mercanto, *The Politics of Federal Aid to Education in 1965: A Study in Political Innovation* (1967).

The subject of poverty has been especially popular. Books that helped reawaken American interest in poverty include John Kenneth Galbraith, *The Affluent Society* (1958); Leon H. Keyserling, *Poverty and Deprivation in the United States* (1962); and Michael Harrington, *The Other America* (1962). The last is reported to have been critical in whetting Kennedy's determination to attack poverty. Also see Dwight Macdonald's provocative essay, "Our Invisible Poor," *The New Yorker* (Jan. 19, 1963). Subsequent general studies of note include Ben B. Seligman, ed., *Poverty as a Public Issue* (1965) and Richard M. Elman, *The Poorhouse State* (1966). Daniel Knapp, *Scouting the War on Poverty: Social Reform Politics in the Kennedy Administration* (1971) focuses on the New Frontier. Good on the war on poverty launched by Johnson's Great Society are James L. Sundquist, *Politics and Policy* (1968); James L. Sundquist and David W. Davis, *Making Federalism Work* (1969); Joseph Kershaw, *Government Agency Poverty* (1970); Sar Levitan, *The Great Society's Poor Law: A New Approach to Poverty* (1969); Frances Fox Piven and Richard A. Cloward, *Regulating the Poor: The Functions of Public Welfare* (1971); Chaim I. Waxman, *Poverty: Power and Politics* (1968); and, especially, Daniel P. Moynihan, *Maximum Feasible Understanding* (1970).

The writings on civil rights in the sixties are extensive. For an understanding of Kennedy's approach to civil rights, Harry Golden, *Mr. Kennedy and the Negroes* (1964) is good but less valuable than Victor Navasky, *Kennedy Justice* (1971). Useful for the New Frontier's philosophy about civil rights is Burke Marshall, *Federalism and Civil Rights* (1964). The author served as Assistant Attorney General for the Civil Rights Division. On the role of the courts, consult Arthur J. Goldberg, *Equal Justice: The Warren Era of the Supreme Court* (1972); Archibald Cox, *The Warren Court: Constitutional Decision as an Instrument of Reform* (1968); and R. H. Sayler, ed., *The Warren Court: A Critical Analysis* (1968).

The shifting course of the struggle for black equality is detailed during the period 1954 to 1964 by Anthony Lewis, *Portrait of a Decade* (1964). Benjamin Muse cogently summarizes events between 1963 and 1967 in *The American Negro Revolution: From Nonviolence to Black Power* (1968). August Meier and Elliott Rudwick, eds., *Black Protest in the Sixties* (1970) is a helpful anthology of *New York Times* materials on black activities. Also see Meier, *The Transformation of Activism: Black Experience* (1970). Charles Silberman, *Crisis in Black and White* (1964) is a superb, thoughtful statement of racial attitudes in the middle of the decade. William Brink and Louis Harris, *Black and White* (1966) provides illuminating public opinion survey information.

On the nonviolent movement, David Lewis, *King: A Critical Biography* (1970) is excellent, but see also the eloquent *Why We Can't Wait* (1964) by Martin Luther King, Jr. SNCC is described by Howard Zinn, *SNCC: The New Abolitionists* (1964), but Allan J. Matusow, "From Civil Rights to Black Power: The Case of SNCC, 1960–1966," in Barton J. Bernstein and Matusow, eds., *Twentieth Century America: Recent Interpretations* (1969) is more perceptive. James W. Silver, *Mississippi: The Closed Society* (1964) is trenchant on racial problems in the author's home state, but also see Donald R. Mathews and James W. Prothro, *Negroes and the New Southern Politics* (1966).

C. Eric Lincoln, *The Black Muslims in America* (1961) is helpful about the foundations of Black Power. The *Autobiography of Malcolm X* (1965) is a classic. Also good are Eldridge Cleaver, *Soul on Ice* (1968) and William H. Grier and Price M. Cobb, *Black Rage* (1968). For the views of the man who made the phrase famous, see Charles V. Hamilton and Stokely Carmichael, *Black Power* (1967). Hugh D. Graham, "The Storm over Black Power," *Virginia Quarterly Review* (Autumn 1967), discusses the problems that Black Power raised for white liberals, and Christopher Lasch, "The Trouble with Black Power," *New York Review of Books* (Feb. 29, 1968), expresses the negative reaction of the white left. Floyd Barbour, ed., *The Black Power Revolt* (1968) is a convenient collection of statements on the subject. Lee Rainwater and William Yancey, *The Moynihan Report and the Politics of Controversy* (1967) reprints Moynihan's famous report and many of the reactions to it.

The demands for equal rights by blacks stimulated new feelings of assertiveness and self-awareness among Mexican-Americans and American Indians. See Matt S. Meier and Feliciano Rivera, *The Chicanos* (1972) and Edward Simmen, ed., *The Chicano: From Caricature to Self-Portrait* (1971) for information on Mexican-Americans. Two excellent books detailing the grievances of Indians are Vine Deloria, Jr., *Custer Died for Your Sins: An Indian Manifesto* (1969) and Alvin M. Josephy, *Red Power: The American Indians' Fight for Freedom* (1972).

A most valuable study of urban rioting during the sixties is Robert M. Fogelson, *Violence as Protest; A Study of Riots and Ghettos* (1971), which includes several articles about various aspects of the subject published previously in scholarly journals. Joseph Boskin, "The Revolt of the Urban Ghettos, 1964–1967," *The Annals of the American Academy of Political and Social Science* (Mar. 1969), probes the causes of the outbreaks. The *Report of the National Advisory Commission on Civil Disorders* (1968) presents a huge quantity of information, including valuable statistical data. Good on the Watts riot is Jerry Cohen and William S. Murphy, *Burn, Baby, Burn* (1966), while John Hersey, *The Algiers Motel Incident* (1968) focuses indignantly on a crucial episode during the 1967 Detroit riot. Edward C. Banfield, *The Unheavenly City* (1970) raises provocative and highly controversial challenges to the ability of liberal programs, such as many of those begun under the Great Society, to solve America's urban ills. On violence as an historical phenomenon in America, see Hugh Davis Graham and Ted Robert Gurr, eds., *The History of Violence in America* (1969) and Richard Hofstadter and Michael Wallace, eds., *American Violence: A Documentary History* (1970), which includes Hofstadter's brilliant essay, "Reflections on Violence in the United States."

The complex and confusing radical New Left Movement is chronicled clearly and perceptively by Irwin Unger, *The Movement: A History of the American New Left 1959–1972* (1974). Unger defines the New Left as a movement of white middle-class youth. Paul Jacobs and Saul Landau, *The New Radicals: A Report with Documents* (1966) is both a cogent narrative and a useful collection of documents. Other useful anthologies are Mitchell Cohen and Dennis Hale, eds., *The New Student Left* (1967) and Massimo Teodori, ed., *The New Left: A Documentary History* (1969). Perhaps the most thoughtful scholarly observer writing about the young white militant is Kenneth Kenniston, whose three major books on the subject, *The Uncommitted* (1965), *Young Radicals* (1968), and *Youth and Dissent* (1971), are essential reading. Also see the important article by D. Westley and R. Braungart, "Class and Politics in the Family Backgrounds of Student Political Activists," *American Sociological Review* (1966). Kirkpatrick Sale, *SDS* (1972) is an important study of the best known of the groups constituting the amorphous New Left. Two of the most useful accounts of protests at individual college campuses are Seymour M. Lipset and S. S. Wolin, eds., *The Berkeley Student Revolt* (1965), about the free speech incident at Berkeley in 1964, and Jerry L. Alvorn, et al., *Up Against the Ivy Wall: A History of the Columbia Crisis* (1968). A good presentation of the differences of opinion between younger and older activists on the proper way to reform American society is "Students and Society," *An Occasional Paper* by the Center for the Study of Democratic Institutions (1967).

The best-known studies of the counter culture are Theodore Roszak, *The Making of a Counter Culture* (1969) and Charles Reich, *The Greening of America* (1970), but sociologist Philip Slater's *The Pursuit of Loneliness* (1970) is briefer, clearer, and more thoughtful. Reich's overblown and naive work should be read in conjunction with Samuel McCracken's slashing review in *Change* (1971). O'Neill's *Coming Apart*, previously cited, includes an especially incisive assessment of the counter culture. On hippies, see Nicholas von Hoffman, *We Are the People Our Parents Warned Us Against* (1968). Harrison Pope, Jr., *Voices from the Drug Culture* (1972) is the best book on the use of drugs. The rejection of the counter culture by most working-class youth is described forcefully by Peter L. Berger and Brigitte Berger, "The Blueing of America," *New Republic* (1970), but also see Michael Novak's brilliant *The Rise of the Unmeltable Ethnics* (1973).

On Women's Liberation the most serious and judicious book is William H. Chafe, *The American Woman* (1972). Chafe covers the period from 1920 to 1970, with an especially trenchant appraisal of the sixties. Robert J. Lifton, ed., *The Woman in America* (1965) and Robin Morgan, ed., *Sisterhood Is Powerful* (1970) are worthwhile. See also the entire Spring 1964 issue of *Daedalus*, especially Carl Degler's profound essay, "Revolution Without Ideology: The Changing Place of Women in America."

The exciting and frenetic election of 1968 is recounted by Theodore H. White, *The Making of the President 1968* (1969), but a study by three English journalists, Lewis Chester, Godfrey Hodgson, and Bruce Page, *An American Melodrama: The Presidential Campaign of 1968* (1969), is more piercing. David S. Broder, "The Election of 1968," in Schlesinger, ed., *Presidential Elections* (previously cited) is valuable. Norman Mailer brings his talents as a novelist to bear on the nominating conventions and produces a near masterpiece of unique political reporting, *Miami and the Siege of Chicago* (1968). On the views of Eugene McCarthy, see his book, *The Year of the People* (1969). The efforts of Robert Kennedy to win his party's nomination are traced by Jules Witcover, *85 Days: The Last Campaign of Robert Kennedy* (1969) and David Halberstam, *The Unfinished Odyssey of Robert Kennedy* (1968). Also see Jack Newfield's sensitive *Robert Kennedy: A Memoir* (1969). There is no satisfactory study of Hubert Humphrey, but consult Robert Sherrill and Harry Ernst, *Drugstore Liberal* (1968) and Nelson Polsby, *The Citizen's Choice: Humphrey or Nixon* (1968). A revealing work about George Wallace is Marshall Frady, *Wallace* (1968). Joe McGinnis worked for the Nixon campaign, then described how the candidate was packaged and merchandized to the public in *The Selling of the President 1968* (1969). Garry Wills, *Nixon Agonistes* (1970) is by far the best portrayal of Nixon and offers stimulating judgments about Kennedy, Johnson, and New Deal liberalism as well. On Nixon's strategy to strengthen the Republican party, see Kevin Phillips, *The Emerging Republican Majority* (1970). Richard Scammon and Ben J. Wattenberg, *The Real Majority* (1970) is valuable for the reactions of Middle Americans to the radical protests and the counter culture when they went to the polls.

The literature on national security and foreign policy is immense and often more impressive than the writing on domestic affairs. Excellent studies by Alain C. Enthoven and K. Wayne Smith, *How Much Is Enough?* (1971) and Adam Yarmolinsky, *The Military Establishment* (1970) examine how the defense program of the United States was shaped during the sixties. Jean Edward Smith, "Kennedy and Defense: The Formative Years," *Air University Review* (Mar.–Apr. 1967), probes JFK's background on defense. On the alleged missile gap during the 1960 election, see Edgar M. Bottome, *The Missile Gap: A Study of the Formulation of Military and Practical Policy* (1971) and Roy E. Licklider, "The Missile Gap Controversy," *Political Science Quarterly* (Dec. 1970). Robert S. McNamara explains his philosophy of defense in *The Essence of Security* (1968). McNamara is the subject of books by Henry L. Trewhitt, *McNamara* (1971); William W. Kaufmann, *The*

*McNamara Strategy* (1964); and James M. Roherty, *Decisions of Robert S. McNamara* (1970), but the most informative study of the former automobile executive's approach to his duties is Robert J. Art, *The TFX Decision: McNamara and the Military* (1968). General Maxwell Taylor, chairman of the Joint Chiefs of Staff under Kennedy, discusses his conception of national security in *Swords and Plowshares* (1972) and *Responsibility and Response* (1967). On the critical role of research and development in national defense, consult H. L. Nieburg, *In the Name of Science* (1966) and Richard J. Barber, *The Politics of Research* (1964). Useful on the space program is Richard L. Rosholt, et al., *An Administrative History of NASA* (1966). Regarding the activities of the top-secret Counter Intelligence Agency, David Wise and Thomas B. Ross, *The Invisible Government* (1964) is provocative—and disturbing. Victor Marchetti and John D. Marks, *The CIA and the Cult of Intelligence* (1974), published with deletions secured by the CIA after a court fight, is valuable. Less helpful are Allen W. Dulles, *The Craft of Intelligence* (1963) and Lyman B. Kirkpatrick, *The Real CIA* (1968).

Probably the best single volume on foreign affairs during the sixties is Walt W. Rostow, *The Diffusion of Power* (1972). Rostow's analysis, which is exceedingly favorable to both Kennedy and Johnson, has been sharply challenged by revisionist historians in particular, but his command of the material is impressive. Also see his *View From the Seventh Floor* (1964). Two general studies of American foreign policy since World War II, Walter LaFeber, *America, Russia, and the Cold War, 1945–1971* (1972) and John W. Spanier, *American Foreign Policy Since World War II* (1971), include useful commentaries on the sixties. Other general accounts of American foreign policy of value include Theodore Draper, *Abuse of Power* (1966); Richard J. Barnet, *Intervention and Revolution* (1968); Seyom Brown, *The Faces of Power* (1968); and, especially, Ronald Steel, *Pax Americana* (1971). Walter LaFeber, "Kennedy, Johnson, and the Revisionists," *Foreign Service Journal* (May 1973), is illuminating, as are articles by John Kenneth Galbraith, "The Plain Lessons of a Bad Decade," *Foreign Policy* (Winter 1970–71); Richard J. Barnet, "The Illusion of Security," *Foreign Policy* (Summer 1971); and Graham Allison, Ernest May, and Adam Yarmolinsky, "Limits to Intervention," *Foreign Affairs* (Jan. 1970). Godfrey Hodgson argues that the Establishment has lost much of its earlier influence over the conduct of American diplomacy in "The Establishment," *Foreign Policy* (Spring 1973), while Henry Fairlie, "A Cheer for American Imperialism," *New York Times Magazine* (July 11, 1965), and Irving Kristol, "American Intellectuals and Foreign Policy," *Foreign Affairs* (July 1967), take sharp issue with much of the criticism leveled at United States foreign policy. The important study by Richard J. Barnet, *Roots of War* (1972), deserves special attention. Barnet argues that war making under Kennedy and Johnson must be analyzed through the National Security Managers' bureaucracy, the political economy of expansion, and the failures of the electoral process to control foreign policy. *The Arrogance of Power* (1966) and *Old Myths and New Realities* (1964) by J. William Fulbright are important for the views of the sophisticated chairman of the Senate Foreign Relations Committee.

Among works focusing primarily on the Kennedy administration, Roger Hilsman, *To Move a Nation: The Politics of Foreign Policy in the Administration of JFK* (1967) is the most informative. It is also highly favorable. McGeorge Bundy, "The Presidency and the Peace," *Foreign Affairs* (Apr. 1964), and Harlan Cleveland, "Great Powers and Great Diversity: The Perceptions and Policies of President Kennedy," *The Department of State Bulletin* (Dec. 23, 1963), view the New Frontier's foreign policy positively. Both authors, like Rostow and Hilsman, were high-level officials under Kennedy. Also laudatory is William Leuchtenburg, "President Kennedy and the End of the Postwar World," *The American Review* (Winter 1963). In contrast, Richard J. Walton, *Cold War and Counterrevolution: The Foreign Policy of JFK* (1972) and Louise FitzSimons, *The Kennedy Doctrine* (1972) are sharply critical, seeing JFK as basically a conventional cold warrior and the New Frontiersmen as far too concerned about image. Anthony Hartley, "John Kennedy's Foreign Policy," *Foreign Policy* (Fall 1971), maintains that the Kennedy administration was much too impatient in the conduct of foreign affairs. George Kateb, "Kennedy as Statesman," *Commentary* (June 1966), sees Kennedy's record as mixed.

On Kennedy's efforts to reorganize and invigorate the State Department, I. M. Destler, *Presidents, Bureaucrats, and Foreign Policy: The Politics of Organizational Reform* (1972); Chester Bowles, *Promises to Keep* (1971); and Richard A. Johnson, *The Administration of United States Foreign Policy* (1971) are good. Dean Rusk's thoughts about foreign policy as revealed in his public speeches are conveniently collected in *Winds of Freedom* (1963). If for no other reason than its engaging literary style, John Kenneth Galbraith, *Ambassador's Journal: A Personal Account of the Kennedy Years* (1969) is worth reading. JFK's exciting Peace Corps project is criticized by Marshall Windmiller's *The Peace Corps and Pax Americana* (1970) as the "colonial civil service of imperial America," and generally commended by Robert O. Carey, *The Peace Corps* (1970). Also see *Point of the Lance* (1964) by Peace Corps Director Sargent R. Shriver, a collection of speeches about the early days of the organization.

The most useful accounts of Johnson's foreign policy are the President's *The Vantage Point* and Rostow's *The Diffusion of Power*. Philip Geyelin, *Lyndon B. Johnson and the World* (1966) is very good for LBJ's first years in office. Robert W. Sellen, "Old Assumptions Versus New Realities: Lyndon Johnson and Foreign Policy," *International Journal* (Spring 1973), is cogent. *The Discipline of Power* (1968) by George W. Ball, who served as a foreign policy adviser to both Kennedy and Johnson, makes no attempt to chronicle events but is nevertheless significant.

Michel Tatu, *Power in the Kremlin: From Khrushchev to Kosygin* (1969) is excellent for American-Soviet relations, but also consult Arnold L. Horelick and Myron Rush, *Strategic Power and Soviet Foreign Policy* (1966) and Adam Ulam, *Expansion and Coexistence: The History of Soviet Foreign Policy, 1917–1967*. Edward Crankshaw and Strobe Talbot, eds., *Khrushchev Remembers* (1970) is fascinating. Kennedy's success in negotiating a test ban treaty with the Soviets is discussed by Arthur H. Dean, *Test Ban and Disarmament: The Path of Negotiation* (1966); Ronald J. Terchek, *The Making of the Test Ban Treaty* (1970); and Lincoln P. Bloomfield and others, *Khrushchev and the Arms Race* (1966). Also consult Harland B. Moulton, *From Superiority to Parity: The United States and the Strategic Arms Race, 1961–1971* (1972).

America's problems with its European allies are examined thoughtfully by Henry A. Kissinger, *The Troubled Partnership: A Reappraisal of the Atlantic Alliance* (1965). On Kennedy's "Grand Design" for Europe, see Robert Kleiman, *Atlantic Crisis; American Democracy Confronts a Resurgent Europe* (1964) and Joseph Kraft, *The Grand Design: From Common Market to Atlantic Partnership* (1962). John Newhouse, *De Gaulle and the Anglo-Saxons* (1970) is helpful about the United States' dealings with the imperious French leader. David Nunnerly, *President Kennedy and Britain* (1972) is a first-rate account, both incisive and comprehensive, of American-British relations under JFK. The friction between the two countries caused by the United States' unilateral cancellation of the Skybolt agreement is analyzed brilliantly by Richard E. Neustadt, *Alliance Politics* (1970). Jack M. Schick carefully examines the troubles in Berlin in "The Berlin Crisis of 1961 and United States Military Strategy," *Orbis* (Winter 1965), and *The Berlin Crisis, 1958–1962* (1971). For an enlightening description of Berlin as a source of aggravation between East and West with emphasis on the Soviet side of the controversy, see Robert M. Slusser, *The Berlin Crisis of 1961* (1973).

The most detailed study of American policy in the Congo during the early sixties is Stephen R. Weissman, *American Foreign Policy in the Congo, 1960–1964* (1974), but also see Ernest W. Lefever, *Crisis in the Congo: A U.N. Force in Action* (1965). The New Frontier's plans for improving America's image in Africa are discussed by William Attwood, Kennedy's ambassador to Guinea, in his *The Reds and the Blacks* (1967) and by G.

Mennen Williams, the assistant secretary of state for Africa, in *Africa for the Africans* (1969).

America's relations with Latin America during the sixties revolved around the ambitious Alliance for Progress. The premier account is Jerome Levinson and Juan de Onis, *The Alliance That Lost Its Way: A Critical Report on the Alliance for Progress* (1970). Also uncomplimentary is Abraham P. Lowenthal, "Alliance Rhetoric Versus Latin America Reality," *Foreign Affairs* (Apr. 1970). Other useful studies include William D. Rogers, *The Twilight Struggle: The Alliance for Progress and the Politics of Development in Latin America* (1967); Harvey S. Perloff, *Alliance for Progress: A Social Invention in the Making* (1969); and R. Harrison Wagner, *United States Policy Toward Latin America: A Study in Domestic and International Politics* (1970).

On the United States' response to Castro's rise to power, see Philip W. Bonsal, *Cuba, Castro, and the United States* (1971). The ill-fated Bay of Pigs invasion is described in detail by Haynes Johnson, *The Bay of Pigs: The Leaders' Story* (1964) and Karl E. Meyer and Tad Szulc, *The Cuban Invasion* (1962).

The best example of John Kennedy's approach to diplomacy in a nuclear world was the Cuban missile crisis of 1962. Especially valuable is Barton J. Bernstein, "The Cuban Missile Crisis," in Lynn H. Miller and Ronald W. Pruassen, eds., *Reflections on the Cold War: A Quarter Century of American Foreign Policy* (1974). *The Missile Crisis* (1966) by journalist Elie Abel is a readable and reliable narrative. Robert Kennedy, *Thirteen Days: A Memoir of the Cuban Missile Crisis* (1969) provides invaluable information about the thinking of the President and his advisers, but also see Dean Acheson, "Dean Acheson's Version of Robert Kennedy's Version of the Cuban Missile Affair," *Esquire* (Feb. 1969). Other worthwhile accounts include Jerome H. Kahan and Anne K. Long, "The Cuban Missile Crisis: A Study of Its Strategic Context," *Political Science Quarterly* (Dec. 1972); Arnold Horelick, "The Cuban Missile Crisis: An Analysis of Soviet Calculations and Behavior," *World Politics* (Apr. 1964); Roger Hagan, "Triumph or Tragedy," *Dissent* (Winter 1963); Alexander George, "The Cuban Missile Crisis, 1962," in George, et al., *The Limits of Coercive Democracy* (1971); Leslie Dewart, "The Cuban Missile Crisis Revisited," *Studies on the Left* (Spring 1965); and Robert Crane, "The Cuban Missile Crisis: A Strategic Analysis of American and Soviet Policy," *Orbis* (Winter 1963). A useful work on the aspects of international law involved in the crisis is *The Cuban Missile Crisis: International Crises and the Rule of Law* (1973) by State Department counsel Abram Chayes. Graham Allison, *Essence of Decision* (1971) examines the missile confrontation in depth and concludes that "bureaucratic momentum" determined American actions. Allison argues that foreign policy must be viewed in the context of organizational theory rather than ideology. His views are strongly contested by Stephen D. Krasner, "Are Bureaucracies Important? (Or Allison Wonderland)," *Foreign Policy* (Summer 1972).

Lyndon Johnson's number-two foreign crisis—next to Vietnam—occurred in 1965 in the Dominican Republic. Two books are essential reading on the subject: Jerome Slater, *Intervention and Negotiation: The United States and the Dominican Intervention* (1970) and John Barlow Martin, *Overtaken by Events: The Dominican Crisis from the Fall of Trujillo to Civil War* (1966). Slater is harsh in his judgment of Johnson's actions, while Martin, although not uncritical, is less strident. Also useful are Tad Szulc, *Dominican Diary* (1965); Theodore Draper, *The Dominican Revolt* (1968); and Abraham Lowenthal, *The Dominican Intervention* (1972).

Propelled by the war in Vietnam, American interest in foreign affairs swung from Europe to Asia during the sixties. Chinese-American relations are surveyed incisively by John K. Fairbanks, *China: The People's Middle Kingdom and the USA* (1967). Also see Frank Trager and William Henderson, eds., *Communist China 1949–1969: A Twenty Year Assessment* (1970). On the problems in Laos, consult Hugh Toye, *Laos* (1968) and Arthur J. Dommen, *Conflict in Laos* (1964).

Three works stand out on the Vietnam war: Frances Fitzgerald, *Fire in the Lake* (1972), which focuses on the impact of the conflict on Vietnam; David Halberstam, *The Best and the Brightest* (1972), which concentrates on American policy makers; and *The Pentagon Papers* (1971), based on the documents smuggled to the press by Daniel Ellsberg, one of the researchers commissioned by McNamara to chronicle the course of American involvement in the war. Ellsberg explains his own views of the conflict in *Papers on the War* (1972). For background, Joseph Buttinger, *The Smaller Dragon: A Political History of Vietnam* (1958), which carries the country's history up to 1900, and *Vietnam: A Dragon Embattled*, 2 vols. (1967), which traces events from 1900 to 1963, are excellent. Also good is Ellen Hammer, *The Struggle for Indochina, 1940–1955* (1956). Not to be missed are the works of the late Bernard Fall, a widely respected student of both the country and the war. See his *The Two Viet-Nams: A Political and Military History*, 5th rev. ed. (1965); *Street without Joy*, 4th rev. ed. (1964); *Hell in a Very Small Place* (1966); and *Viet-Nam Witness, 1953–66* (1966). Useful brief evaluations of the conflict are offered by Geoffrey Warner, "The United States and Vietnam," *International Affairs* (2 pts., July and Oct. 1972), and Leslie H. Gelb, "Vietnam: The System Worked," *Foreign Policy* (Summer 1971). See also George Kahin and John Lewis, *The United States in Vietnam* (1965);

Chester Cooper, *The Lost Crusade* (1970); Robert Shaplen, *The Lost Revolution* (1965); and John T. McAlister, Jr., *Vietnam: The Origins of Revolution* (1969). For a particularly incisive attack on American leadership based on the *Pentagon Papers*, read Ralph Stavin, *Washington Plans an Aggressive War* (1971). Two of the best radical critiques of the war are Noam Chomsky, *American Power and the New Mandarins* (1967) and Gabriel Kolko, *Roots of American Foreign Policy* (1969).

On specific incidents, see Eugene Windchy, *Tonkin Gulf* (1971); John Galloway, *The Gulf of Tonkin Resolution* (1970); Don Oberdorfer, *Tet* (1971); and Seymour M. Hersh, *My Lai* (1970). Important commentaries on the war by members of the Johnson administration include the President's memoirs; Rostow's *The Diffusion of Power*; Clark M. Clifford, "A Viet Nam Reappraisal," *Foreign Affairs* (July 1969); "Bill Moyers Talks about the War and LBJ: An Interview," *Atlantic Monthly* (July 1968); George W. Ball, "Top Secret: The Prophecy the President Rejected," *Atlantic Monthly* (July 1972); and Under Secretary of the Air Force Townshend Hoopes, *The Limits of Intervention* (1970). The last work is informative about the events of March 1968 leading to the decision not to escalate American involvement further. An enlightening book is *The Tuesday Cabinet: Deliberation and Decision on Peace and War under Lyndon B. Johnson* (1970) by Henry F. Graff, a professor of history at Columbia University. Graff periodically interviewed Johnson and other key foreign policy advisers about their views on the war. Interesting on the impact of the Vietnamese conflict on domestic America are Thomas Powers, *The War at Home: Vietnam and the American People, 1964–1968* (1973) and Albert H. Cantril, *The American People, Viet-Nam, and the Presidency* (1970).

# Index